KU-166-321

The Golden Girls of MGM

Books by Jane Ellen Wayne include:

Robert Taylor: The Man with the Perfect Face
Kings of Tragedy
Stanwyck
Cooper's Women
Ava's Men
The Life and Loves of Grace Kelly
Marilyn's Men
Clark Gable: Portrait of a Misfit

The Golden Girls of MGM

Glamour and Grief

Jane Ellen Wayne

ROBSON BOOKS

First published in Great Britain in 2002 by
Robson Books, 64 Brewery Road, London N7 9NT

A member of the Chrysalis Books plc

British Library Cataloguing in Publication Data
A catalogue record for this title is available from the British Library

ISBN 1 86105 407 6

All photographs courtesy of Chrysalis Images

Typeset in Weiss by SX Composing DTP, Rayleigh, Essex
Printed in Great Britain by MacKays of Chatham plc, Chatham, Kent

Contents

To Joan Crawford, who taught me
the ropes and drove me to drink . . .

Foreword

I am fortunate because my career as an author began in the late Sixties when so many of the great Golden Era movie stars and moguls were still alive. I had no idea that eight film-actor biographies would follow the one I was then writing on MGM's longest contract player, Robert Taylor. No-one refused an interview – he was so well liked in Hollywood. Taylor had lived a relatively clean life and consequently, my interviews often ended with lengthy discussions about other MGM personalities.

MGM press agent George Nichols and I often met at the Cock 'n' Bull restaurant on Sunset Boulevard. In the late afternoon, movie extras, stand-ins, technicians and stuntmen also gathered at our table. Word got round that I was doing a book about Robert Taylor so the old-timers had a good excuse to get together for some reminiscing and, I admit, inside gossip. Everybody knew everybody's business and the stories related to me were amusing, raunchy, revealing and very rewarding. John Wayne, Andy Devine and Jonn Huston, to name but a few, spotted George and sat down with us for a chat. As Nichols said, there were two prime interests in Hollywood: movies and gossip.

I was also privileged to spend a good deal of time with Howard Stickling, MGM's West Coast publicity chief. Howard protected his galaxy of stars and ultimately, took many of Hollywood's deepest secrets with him to his grave. He cooperated with me because he cared especially for Robert Taylor, not to mention the fact that I was engaged to a vice president of Loews (MGM's parent company). Howard arranged for me to meet writer Adela Rogers St. Johns, directors William Wellman, Tay Garnett and George Cuker, and a slew of others who worked at MGM during the twenties, thirties, forties and fifties.

Then there was Joan Crawford. I spent three exasperating afternoons with Joan, who talked about everyone in Hollywood other than Robert Taylor. It was frustrating at the time, but she actually gave me enough information for several other biographies. Her advice was invaluable: "The bigger they are, the less they tell," she said. "Talk to the writers, security guards, chauffeurs, cameramen, the 'little people', who are bigger than life. They knew more about me than I did." Through Crawford, I entered into the glittering world of MGM, a world she helped to mold. If the glamour of stars like her had endured longer, perhaps the same chiffon and tinsel might still exist today.

Director George Cukor told me that I would struggle with my conscience over whether or not to reveal unflattering stories in my biographies. But, "It takes the bad and the good for an honest portrayal," he stressed. "One cannot paint a true picture of a rose without the thorns."

Jane Ellen Wayne
April 2002

Introduction

Lana, Ava, Judy, Hedy and Liz. No need for surnames. They were exquisite properties of the most prestigious movie studio in the world. These silver-screen debutantes were pampered with furs, jewels, limos, designer gowns and handsome escorts. Each girl was unique because Metro-Goldwyn-Mayer was the Tiffany of Hollywood and their jewels of femininity were beyond compare. Like finely chiselled diamonds, every MGM girl had her exclusive aura.

There was no Marilyn on this roster of lovelies. Louis B. Mayer, head of MGM, considered Miss Monroe a cheap copy of her predecessor, Jean Harlow. 'There are two kinds of people in Hollywood,' Mayer remarked. 'The ones who eat at Romanoff's and the ones who wait on tables.' In his opinion Harlow dined and Marilyn served.

Mayer royally indulged his family of stars but they paid a price. Their seven-year contracts had a moral clause that read, in essence, '. . . the artist agrees to conduct himself with due regard to public convention . . . he will not do or commit any act or thing that will tend to degrade him in society or bring him into public hatred, contempt, scorn or ridicule, or that will tend to shock, insult or offend the community or ridicule public morals . . .'

Mayer's harem of beauties had to have his permission to marry. If they defied him, they were suspended without pay but if Mayer blessed the union he most likely gave the bride away at the wedding. Often he took the groom aside and whispered, 'We don't want babies, do we?'

Married or not, the MGM girls maintained their virginal image. They were above sex, an untouchable breed of womanhood. We pictured them in the bridal bed with every coiffed hair in place and their make-up impeccable. Were we that naive in the Golden Era? Of course! Our own lives were boring and drab but believing there was an Oz over the rainbow gave us hope.

Oz was Hollywood and the Wizard was Louis B. Mayer, born on 4 July 1885 in Minsk, Russia. The family emigrated to the United States and settled in Boston where Louis went into the scrap-metal business with his father. He married Margaret Shenberg in 1904 and had two daughters, Edith and Irene. Intrigued by movies, he bought several theatres for operas, stage shows and motion pictures and, in 1918, formed his own production company and headed west. Successful at his trade, Mayer hired Irving Thalberg and together they built the kingdom of Metro-Goldwyn-Mayer, the home of 'More Stars Than There are in Heaven'.

Every studio mogul had a casting couch and Mayer was no exception but he was more subtle with his favourites. He courted dancer Ann Miller and attempted suicide when she decided to marry another man. Miller thought enough of Mayer to marry him, but she did not want to give up her career. He worshipped Greer Garson who brought her mother along to chaperone their dates. Mayer respected her for that and fell in love with the stunning Mrs Miniver (the title role of the Oscar-winning film), whom he placed on a pedestal instead of the casting couch. He did, however, have his way with diva Jeanette MacDonald and was insanely jealous of her co-star and lover Nelson Eddy. Mayer might have destroyed Eddy's career if it hadn't been for the enormous popularity of the MacDonald–Eddy musicals that made millions for MGM. Mayer blessed Jeanette's marriage to the gay actor Gene Raymond, who preferred sleeping with Mary Pickford's husband, Buddy Rogers, on their honeymoon cruise.

Joan Crawford and Clark Gable might have tied the knot early in their careers had it not been for three obstacles – his wife, her husband and L.B. Mayer who threatened to fire them if they continued seeing each other. 'You'll never work in this town again,' he warned.

Crawford said, 'Clark and I were newcomers and scared to death. We continued seeing each other on the sly for a long time but looking back I think Mayer did us a big favour.'

If Mayer showed compassion there was usually a hitch. He agreed to walk the adorable June Allyson down the aisle but suspended her without pay for marrying a much older Dick Powell. 'Pops thought this marriage would hurt my little girl image,' June said.

Mayer was opposed to his family of stars marrying each other. When Mickey Rooney asked permission to wed the then unknown Ava Gardner, Mayer hissed, 'Your life is not your own, Mickey. Not as long as you're working for MGM. It's in your contract.' But Mickey was the number-one box-office attraction in the country, thanks to the *Andy Hardy* films, so Mayer relented, providing MGM made all the arrangements.

Ava recalled, 'Wherever we went on our honeymoon, Mickey and I were chaperoned by an MGM publicist. He was everywhere but in our bedroom. A year later I divorced Mickey and was entitled to half of everything but MGM convinced me to take a small settlement. In return they gave me better films.'

Ava said she liked Mayer. 'He called me a whore when I was seeing Sinatra, who had a wife and kids. Mayer could have fired me for violating the morals clause in my contract, but he didn't. I always knew where I stood with him.'

Lana Turner was dubbed the Sweater Girl because her breasts moved freely as she walked down Main Street in her first film. Still in her teens, she was also dubbed the Party Girl. Mayer was furious and called her to his office. Much to his distress she looked rested and radiant after only a few hours sleep. 'Dancing and drinking every night!' he barked. 'This has to stop. We can't airbrush cocktail glasses and cigarettes out of every picture taken at Ciro's and the Trocadero.' Lana pouted and shed a tear. Mayer sighed and shed a tear. 'Come sit on my lap,' he said. 'Think of me as the father you never had.'

Dear Lana knew how to tame the mean old Wizard. Sadly he wasn't around when her daughter killed gangster Johnny Stompanato in Lana's bedroom. The whole ugly mess could have been covered up. Mayer had managed that when Jean Harlow's impotent husband killed himself while she was asleep. A servant found the body and notified MGM. Jean was whisked to her mother's house where, Mayer insisted, she had spent the night.

Harlow was never a suspect, but Lana will always be one in the death of her mobster lover Johnny Stompanato . . .

Elizabeth Taylor was twelve years old when she joined the MGM family. Like Judy, Liz had a protective stage mother who was in charge. Following the success of *National Velvet*, Mrs Taylor confronted Mayer about a film she considered beneath her daughter. 'Don't tell me how to make pictures,' he fumed. 'Just remember, I took you and your daughter out of the gutter.' Liz fought back with, 'Don't you ever talk to my mother like that! You and your studio can go to hell!' She ran out of Mayer's office, but Sara Taylor stayed behind to discuss the matter with the Wizard with whom she was secretly in love. Why would she prefer the short and tubby Mayer over her handsome husband? Because Mr Taylor was a homosexual. This might explain Elizabeth's passion for gays such as Montgomery Clift, who rejected her marriage proposal but tried to bond their friendship in bed. Rock Hudson had no problem performing with Liz. . . .

Grace Kelly smouldered underneath her icy composure. Though Liz and Ava remained virgins until they married, Grace lost hers to a friend's husband before embarking on a film career. If she had seduction in mind, Grace surely succeeded by having affairs with her leading men, Gary Cooper, Ray Milland, Bing Crosby, Clark Gable and William Holden who said, 'Grace's romances are always serious. She puts her heart and soul into love affairs.' But occasional flings with charming suitors such as David Niven, Frank Sinatra, the Shah of Iran, Prince Aly Khan and Howard Hughes were rewarding for Grace, who preferred older men. She was engaged to couturier Oleg Cassini when she decided to marry Prince Rainier whom she barely knew. 'I will learn to love him,' she told Cassini. Grace thought she would make an occasional movie after her marriage but Rainier forbade it. As Her Serene Highness, Princess of Monaco, Grace embarked on a lonely life that ended in tragedy all too soon.

Mayer was reluctant to hire the Viennese actress Hedy Lamarr. 'I saw you in *Ecstasy*,' he told her with a scowl. 'I don't like what people would think about a girl who flits bare-assed across the screen. We make clean pictures and we want our stars to live clean lives. I don't like shenanigans but if you want to screw your leading man in the dressing room, that's your business.'

Was the Wizard actually telling Hedy that sex was allowed on the MGM premises? No, but he couldn't prevent it. Falling in love with one's leading man was inevitable and the romance usually ended when filming was over. If the affair continued, Mayer's spies were alerted. If one of the lovers was married, word was left at the main gate to announce the spouse's arrival. If the romantic scenes were overly passionate because the leading players were in heat, their spouses were banned from the movie set. Clark Gable's wife Carole Lombard was so jealous of Lana Turner, she glared at them during filming. Lana burst into tears and ran to her dressing room. Lombard was barred from then on.

Joan Crawford caught husband Franchot Tone in the throes of passion with a starlet. As she walked through the studio sound stages, the stagehands cringed, knowing what she would find in Tone's dressing room. The security guard tried to stall Joan with idle chatter and gossip, but not long enough.

Poor Judy Garland caught her husband Vincente Minnelli in bed with a man. As if she didn't have enough problems with addiction to pills, depression and broken love affairs with Artie Shaw, Tyrone Power, Joseph Mankiewicz, and many others. She chased them and they loved her for it. Her mother was to blame for Judy's destructive nature. Mayer has been wrongfully blamed and might not have been protective enough but he loved Judy and often paid her medical expenses in sanatoriums. When he was forced to let her go, Mayer sobbed, 'Why did little Judy have to grow up?'

Greta Garbo was not one of the girls. She allowed no one on the movie set when she was filming and her MGM colleagues were reminded not to approach her at any time. Everyone in Hollywood knew Garbo was bisexual but few knew where she lived or if she had a telephone. In the beginning, Mayer was interested in her Svengali, Maurice Stiller, who refused to leave Europe without his overweight and frizzy-haired Swedish protégée. To Mayer's great surprise Garbo was a screen sensation with the help of her famous leading man John Gilbert, whom she frequently jilted at the altar. He died a broken man as did Maurice Stiller a few years later when Garbo was in her prime. She was only in her thirties when she took a sabbatical from Hollywood in 1941. It was her intention to return after the war but it never happened. Spotting the elusive Garbo walking on Madison Avenue in New York City caused more excitement than an U.F.O. sighting. Her rare beauty and unique talent remain unsurpassed to this day.

The MGM girls got along well considering they asked for roles that went to someone else. They had little or no control over the films assigned to them, however. Joan Crawford complained about her rival actress Norma Shearer, who was married to Irving Thalberg, vice-president and production assistant to Mayer. Norma lacked the talent and beauty for major roles such as 'Marie Antoinette' but her authority on the screen drew the audience to her. This was star power and Norma had it, but Crawford maintained the only thing she had was Irving Thalberg. Joan begged

Mayer for a small role in *The Women* because her character steals Norma's husband in the movie. There were no major conflicts during filming, just little frustrating ones such as who arrived first at the photographer's studio for publicity stills.

It's too bad Joan didn't live long enough to read Mickey Rooney's memoirs in 1991. He describes how Norma seduced him after her husband's death. 'She was twice my age,' he wrote, 'but hotter than a half-fucked fox in a forest fire . . . She just wanted my body. We confined our lovemaking to her dressing room – lovemaking French-style with me sitting on her couch, my pants at my ankles and her on her knees.' Andy Hardy copulating with Marie Antoinette? Mayer didn't think this was amusing and put an end to it.

Mickey also had a brief affair with Lana Turner that consisted of lovemaking in the front seat of his convertible. Many years later she told Mickey about her pregnancy and abortion. Lana, the perpetual virgin, who hadn't been seen in public for years, appeared on television and denied it. Mickey retorted, 'Maybe it was a dream but I don't think so.'

Howard Strickling's job was to protect the MGM family from scandal or adverse publicity. The stars were told, 'If you get into trouble don't call the police, don't call the hospital, don't call your lawyer, call Howard.' And so it was when Clark Gable, at the wheel of his car in a drunken stupor, hit and killed a woman. Mayer covered up the incident and arranged for someone else to take the rap. Yes, the Wizard controlled the police department, too.

MGM had its own brothel but MGM publicist Jim Merrick said, 'Mayer used it primarily for business purposes, but actors frequented the place, too. The girls were duplicates of Greta Garbo, Jean Harlow, Clara Bow or whomever a customer wanted. It wasn't unusual to see the likes of Gable and Spencer Tracy sitting around having a drink but I doubt they used the facilities. No need. They had the real thing in the flesh.'

Abortions were commonplace, so Mayer was prepared to accommodate his beauties and often did so despite their reluctance. The studio came first and having babies had to be planned according to their filming schedules. This was one of the sacrifices the MGM girls had to make in return for their luxurious lifestyle.

During her marriage to Sinatra, Ava Gardner had an abortion without his knowledge. Filming *Mogambo* in Africa at the time she explained, 'MGM had all sorts of penalty clauses about their stars having babies. If I had one, my salary would be cut off. So how could I make a living? Frank was broke and my future movies were going to take me all over the world. I couldn't have a baby with that sort of thing going on. MGM made all the arrangements for me to fly to London. Someone from the studio was with me all the time. The abortion was hush hush . . . very discreet.'

Joan Crawford told this author, 'I would never leave home unless I looked every bit the movie star. The public has never seen me less than perfect. MGM taught us that. We were movie stars if we went shopping or picked up our kids at school. My God, leave the house without my false eyelashes? God forbid.'

A few years ago Lana Turner was forced to evacuate her apartment building when a fire broke out. Having only minutes to collect what she needed, Lana grabbed her lipstick, her eyebrow pencil and her hairdryer.

Class never goes out of style . . .

1

Jeanette

Jeanette MacDonald and Nelson Eddy have several fan clubs who meet faithfully every year. Only one of them recognises the love their idols had for each other despite a well-researched book entitled *Sweethearts* written by Sharon Rich and published in 1994. Other biographies about MacDonald and Eddy make no mention of their romance despite Miss Rich's extensive interviews with family and friends, who shared personal diaries and letters with her over a twenty-year period.

My thanks to Sharon Rich for allowing me to use portions of *Sweethearts*.

Eddy wrote these tender words to her:

> I felt your numb little fingers cling to mine, and you whispered my name . . . with joy in my heart I lifted my darling in my arms and carried you to my own bedroom and gathered you in heaven's own earthly bliss. And dearest, did you know you were a very intoxicated little girl? . . . The curve of your white little breast . . . that intimate glorious part of you . . . that magic evening . . . I remember telling you that you belonged to me – that I would never let you go . . .

She loved him dearly but he demanded too much of her. They were major players at Metro-Goldwyn-Mayer and had discussed marriage, but she would have to step aside, he said, and allow him to be the star in the family. He wanted a wife at home and a mother for his children.

She had worked too hard to get where she was as a movie star. Singing was her life and he should have been understanding of that since he had dedicated his life to singing as well. But for him, it was all or nothing.

She was intimate with MGM mogul Louis B. Mayer, who was in love with her. He promised to make her a star and he did. With her beauty and operatic talent, she was a natural. When she was paired with baritone Nelson Eddy, they became America's Sweethearts on and off the screen.

Mayer's intervention sent her to the altar with a man she discovered was a homosexual. Her lover, in a drunken stupor, eloped with another woman and sobered up to regret it.

Jeanette MacDonald was MGM's prima donna. With her bewitching smile, the twinkle in her eye and reddish-golden hair, she captivated America in the thirties. With Nelson Eddy, she stole the nation's heart with vocal renditions of 'Indian Love Call', 'Will You Remember?' and 'Maytime'.

Jeanette did not fare well without Eddy and faltered without the security of Metro-Goldwyn-Mayer. Her highs were the highest and her lows were the lowest.

Her story is bittersweet . . .

Jeanette MacDonald was born on 18 June 1903 in Philadelphia, Pennsylvania. Her tall red-headed father Daniel, of Irish-Scots descent, was a building contractor when he married Anna Wright in February 1893. In December of that year, a daughter Elsie was born, followed by Edith, nicknamed Blossom, in August 1895. Jeanette was 'the little mistake', according to her mother.

'I can't remember as far back as when I first began to sing,' Jeanette said, 'nor is it known where I picked up the word "opera". I sang in all languages – at least, what I fondly imagined were many languages. The operas did not exist any more than the words I invented. Yet wearing my mama's apron to help with the dishes or singing on the front porch banging away at a toy piano, I always sang at the top of my lungs.'

All three MacDonald girls were musically inclined. They went to dancing school and participated in school plays. When she was thirteen, Jeanette sang with a group called The Song Birds, three boys and three girls, who sang in local vaudeville houses. Blossom, whom Jeanette idolised, had the talent but not the good looks. She was determined, however, to make it as a dancer and moved to New York in 1919. While she was appearing as a chorus girl in *The Demi-Tasse Review*, Jeanette paid Blossom a visit and got a job with her sister in the chorus line. Daniel allowed his youngest daughter to stay in New York if she finished high school. She promised but lost interest in her education because she wanted to further herself in the theatre. Five-feet-five-inches tall, with green eyes, and golden-blonde hair, Jeanette was an appealing chorus girl.

> 'I attribute my own rise in the theatre largely to the fact that I was an excellent dancer long before my voice was recognised,' MacDonald said. "They"'discouraged me about singing. "They" said I was crazy. I became a featured dancer on Broadway; but I went ahead with dancing only because my singing was temporarily stalled. The only thing I ever

> wanted to do in my life was sing. But, as I look back over my career, I can see that it is the one thing on which I received no encouragement. I learned to dance, and worked hard and long and earnestly to become a good dancer, but it was only a means to an end.'

In 1922 Jeanette finally got a job, singing in a Greenwich Village show *The Fantastic Fricassee*, earning sixty dollars a week. Her solo number was 'I've Got the Blues'. The following year she appeared on Broadway in *The Magic Ring* for $250 a week. The *New York Times* said, 'Among the other merits of the evening must be listed the appearance and voice of Jeanette MacDonald.' The *Tribune* wrote, 'The blonde beauty of Jeanette MacDonald is one of the glowing things to be commemorated.'

On 1 August 1924, Daniel MacDonald died of a heart attack, at the age of fifty-five. 'My only regret,' Jeanette said, 'was that my father did not live to see my success.' In Daniel's wallet was a picture of only one of his children, Jeanette.

When her shows went on the road, Anna MacDonald accompanied her. But now, at twenty-one, Jeanette tried to break free of her mother and got her own apartment in New York. She took voice lessons from European conductor Ferdinand Torriani. After his death in 1926 Jeanette studied with his co-teacher Grace Newell for the rest of Newell's life.

Out of a job, Jeanette worked as an 'escort' in New York and reportedly had several abortions. Some sources say she worked as an escort when she arrived in Hollywood in 1929. Starlets were paid $100 a night to go out with influential men. Apparently Anna condoned it because Jeanette was supporting her. By now, Jeanette had had several boyfriends but no desire to get married because, as Anna put it, marriage and a career do not mix.

In 1927 she finally hit it big in *Yes, Yes, Yvette*. Jeanette recalled, 'The producer had decided to put my name in lights and star me, as a sort of Christmas present. I think I smiled and said, "Isn't that nice?" As soon as possible, though, I slipped out the stage entrance, hired a taxi and began circling the block. Each time I passed the theatre, I looked back to see my name in lights.'

Jeanette met stockbroker Bob Ritchie with whom she had a wild affair, but she would not consider marriage without Anna's consent, and that was not forthcoming. Ritchie became Jeanette's business manager and would commute between New York and Los Angeles to handle her financial affairs and negotiate her movie contracts. Jeanette and Bob were lovers on and off for years.

In 1927 Paramount Studios arranged a screen test for Jeanette, and wanted to sign her right away, but the Shuberts, with whom she was under contract, refused to let her go. Two years later, film director Ernst Lubitsch saw Jeanette in her last Broadway show *Boom Boom*. He was planning his first sound film, *The Love Parade*, an operetta with Maurice Chevalier. With an offer of $2500 a week, Jeanette, chaperoned by Anna, boarded the Super Chief for California on 5 June 1929.

Every newcomer to Hollywood relates the same anticipation and excitement over their arrival at the Pasadena depot. Joan Crawford and Ava Gardner were met by a studio representative and taken to a rundown hotel. Norma Shearer, dressed to the nines, stepped off the train like the movie star she wasn't to find no one there to meet her. Jeanette was so sick with indigestion and a puffy face from hay fever, she wasn't up to a big welcoming party as the train pulled into the station. As she tried to put herself together, a group of press agents from Paramount Studios hurriedly boarded the train to prepare her for a mob of reporters. Jeanette answered a few questions, posed for pictures and was then rushed to a limousine that took her and Anna to the Ambassador and a suite filled with flowers that set off her allergies again. Jeanette was invited to the typical Hollywood parties to meet the elite and the gossip columnists, who were miffed that she did not recognise them. Labelled as the prima donna from New York, she decided to act like one and moved into the elegant Beverly Wiltshire Hotel.

In *The Love Parade*, a musical sex farce, Jeanette is the queen of a mythical country, looking for a prince consort played by Maurice Chevalier. Jeanette was intimately involved briefly with him, as well as director Lubitsch. She did what was expedient to further her career. *The Love Parade* was a commercial success, garnering six Academy Award nominations, among them Best Picture, Best Actor and Best Director. However, *All Quiet on the Western Front* walked off with the Oscars. At Paramount Jeanette made six more films, the last two with Chevalier. She had acquired two titles during her three years in films. 'The Iron Butterfly' because she demanded (and usually got) what she wanted. And 'The Lingerie Queen' because she wore scanty negligées and nighties in bedroom farces. 'I don't think my career of risqué roles has really hurt,' she said. 'I just feel I have gone far enough in lingerie . . . I'm sure that people must say about me, on the screen, "Good gracious, is Jeanette MacDonald going to take off her clothes – *again?*"'

In 1930 Jeanette's name was mentioned in a European scandal. In Bruges,

Belgium, an unidentified man and woman were pulled from a sports-car accident. For some unknown reason the passengers were identified as Prince Umberto, heir to the Italian throne, and Jeanette MacDonald. Headlines across Europe announced her death. There were rumours that Prince Umberto's wife Princess Marie-Jose had murdered Jeanette. Though the victims were finally identified, the woman bore a striking resemblance to Jeanette. Many Europeans said it was a Hollywood publicity stunt.

Jeanette said her pictures were banned in parts of Europe as a result. 'The only thing I could do was appear in Europe and prove my identity with my voice,' Jeanette said. Bob Ritchie arranged a concert tour and accompanied her to France and England. It was so successful that she did another European concert in 1932, accompanied by Bob Ritchie and Anna. Besides France, Jeanette gave concerts in Holland, Spain, Switzerland and Belgium, earning $13,000 a week.

Bob Ritchie heard that Irving Thalberg, head of production at MGM, was vacationing with his wife, actress Norma Shearer, at the Hotel du Cap on the French Riviera. Thalberg and his boss, Louis B. Mayer, had been courting Jeanette for years and were still in touch with Bob Ritchie, who suggested she and Anna drive to the Riviera while he waited in London. Jeanette was very impressed with Thalberg and he with her. They discussed musicals such as *The Merry Widow*, but there were no commitments. When she joined Bob in London he suggested she ignore phone calls from Thalberg, who was involved in a power struggle at MGM. The man to deal with at the time was Louis B. Mayer, who offered Jeanette $4000 a week in July 1933.

Mayer had been obsessed with Jeanette for a long time. He had tried to get her under contract before Paramount and failed. He was not only interested in her professionally, but personally as well. It became common knowledge that she was Mayer's pet, who sat on his lap when she signed her contracts. He was in love with her and she used him. Though Jeanette would have preferred sitting on Thalberg's lap, this was not to be.

Mayer promised Jeanette the moon and the stars. He gave her the usual 'come to me with your problems' spiel and then proceeded to take control of her personal life. He got rid of Bob Ritchie by hiring him to scout European talent for $4000 a month. But Bob would remain an important figure in Jeanette's life for a long time.

Precisely when Jeanette and Mayer became intimate isn't known but she did not resist his first advances. He was the key to the MGM vault of lavish musicals made possible by the finest directors and technicians in the world.

Everything MGM did was first class, glamorous and elegant.

Jeanette's first film at MGM was *The Cat and the Fiddle* with Ramon Novarro, about a Broadway musical star who meets a European composer in Brussels. Though MacDonald and Novarro lacked chemistry, the film did very well.

Jeanette used her wiles on Mayer to do *The Merry Widow*, an Irving Thalberg production. The Boy Genius of Hollywood might have resented Jeanette for signing with Mayer after they had first met on the Riviera and discussed *The Merry Widow*, but Thalberg understood the needs and moods of artists. Though he and Mayer had their differences, they were responsible for the birth of Metro-Goldwyn-Mayer and were loyal to their high standards put forth in 1924. Thalberg was clever, however. To lure Jeanette he had got Ernst Lubitsch to direct and Maurice Chevalier, who demanded top billing. Irving said MGM's motto was 'Art for Art's Sake'. Jeanette was so completely charmed by Thalberg's style and soft-spoken manner, she gave in to second billing.

The Merry Widow was an enormous success. Regina Crewes of the *New York American* described Jeanette as 'the gorgeous, pulsing, palpitating butterfly, alive with love and life.' In December 1934, she put her hands, feet and signature in wet cement in the forefront of Grauman's Chinese Theater.

When Nelson Eddy met Jeanette MacDonald at a party he said, 'She was a vision or an angel, I don't know which. She was dressed in a flowing gown of pale lavender chiffon and walked toward me with grace and dignity in every step. I remember the first time I actually met her. I was tongue-tied and didn't know how to act.'

Jeanette remembered, 'He was a big awkward hunk of man, very shy. He made me feel uncomfortable because all he did was look at me. He stood there, trying to talk, but kept stuttering, and couldn't finish a sentence. Everyone was watching us. I wanted to walk away, but found I couldn't. There was something about him – his eyes. They haunted me, there was a sadness to them.'

His contract with MGM was about to expire. Jeanette told him to think it over, and then went to see L. B. Mayer. 'I want Nelson Eddy to co-star with me in *Naughty Marietta*,' she said.

'He's too pretty and he can't act,' Mayer said.

'Please . . .'

'Give me one good reason.'

'Because all my leading men are either too old or queer.'

Mayer gave in, as he usually did with Jeanette. Eddy had no idea that she was responsible for his getting the lead in *Naughty Marietta*. She didn't want him to know. He had proposed marriage not long after they met, but Jeanette said she didn't believe true love existed.

'Play your game with Louis B.,' Eddy barked. 'But when the chips are down and you want someone who really cares, just remember, I'm real.' He kissed her hand and stomped off.

Jeanette went to Mayer and asked to be taken off the film with Nelson. Mayer refused and it was then that the oft-told incident occurred. To reassure Jeanette that 'Marietta' was the part for her, he got down on one knee and sang, 'Eli, Eli,' to show her how to sing with real schmaltz. No amount of pleading with Mayer worked this time. She was stuck working with Nelson, facing weeks of togetherness in which her resolve to forget him would be sorely tested.

In June 1934 filming of *Naughty Marietta* began. Nelson was very nervous and it showed. Director Woody Van Dyke said, 'I've had 'em green, but never this green!' It didn't help matters when Jeanette paraded around like a prima donna and made a point of ignoring Nelson. Van Dyke was exasperated. He was a 'one-take' director and wanted to get the picture over with. For the 'love scene' he expected disaster but Nelson grabbed Jeanette and kissed her. She pushed him away so they did another take. The second kiss went better. Nelson glowed and loosened up. Jeannette went off into a huff. This display of emotions alerted other cast members to wonder what was going on between the klutz and the diva.

It was Nelson's attempt to jump on a horse and falling flat on his face that brought Jeanette around. When she laughed hysterically, Eddy said, 'I've had it!' and started to walk off the picture. She ran over to him and, with a hug, apologised.

Van Dyke was so relieved he put his arms around both of them and said he was turning the directing reins over to Jeanette. She began working with Nelson, going over his lines and showing him some camera tips. She also insisted that he have more songs, more film exposure and equal billing.

> Eddy said, 'I mean this professionally and personally. I was unknown to screen fame when *Naughty Marietta* was released, so it was to see Jeanette that people flocked to the theatre. And I might have still been unknown . . . but for her kindness to me during the jittery months of filming. There are the hundred and one things Jeanette taught me about acting – how to relax before stepping in front of the

camera, how to protect my eyes from the glaring lights, how to move and speak naturally with a hundred people staring at you from a dark void outside the circle of lamps. I'll never cease being grateful to her.'

MGM predicted *Naughty Marietta* would make 33-year-old Nelson Eddy a star. At this time, L. B. Mayer ended his intimacy with Jeanette because 'you're a superstar now.'

In *Naughty Marietta* Jeanette played a French princess who goes to America and falls in love with an Indian scout. Critic Judith Crist wrote, 'When these two profiles come together to sing "Ah Sweet Mystery of Life", it's beyond camp, it's in a realm of its own.' Other unforgettable songs were Eddy's 'Tramp, Tramp, Tramp', and 'I'm Falling in Love with Someone'. The picture was nominated for Best Picture but lost to Irving Thalberg's *Mutiny on the Bounty*.

Nelson Eddy was born on 29 June 1901 in Providence, Rhode Island. His father, Bill, was English and his mother, Isabel, of Dutch and Russian-Jewish ancestry. Bill, a heavy drinker and drifter, often abused his wife and son, but Isabel stayed in the bad marriage for Nelson's sake. If his parents had anything in common it was music. They sang in the church choir and in local Gilbert and Sullivan shows. At a young age, Nelson learned *The Mikado* from his mother. Because he was close to Isabel, Nelson was often labelled a 'mama's boy,' but he was not a sissy. He looked after his sickly mother until Bill deserted them in 1915. Isabel and Nelson went to live with her mother in Philadelphia, where he worked as a switchboard operator at an iron foundry and sold ads for the local newspapers. At the age of nineteen he was nowhere near his goal: to be a singer.

It was at an audition that wealthy widow Sybil Thomas took notice of Nelson whom she described as tall, blonde, blue-eyed, skinny, gorgeous and sad looking. She used her influence at the singing audition and he won first prize. Nelson had an affair with Thomas, an older woman, who most probably paid for his music lessons. There were other women who encouraged and financed his musical education. Nelson was very popular with women of all ages. If they chose to help him reach his operatic goals, he was not in the position to refuse. On 12 December 1924, Nelson starred in the Philadelphia Civic Opera Company's production of *I Pagliacci*. He stayed on with the Civic Opera and appeared in *Aida*, *Samson and Delilah* and *Cavalleria Rusticana*, to name a few.

In 1927, Nelson studied in Philadelphia with William W. Vilonat who, according to Eddy, taught him how to sing. Vilonat insisted his student give up girls, drinking and late nights. Nelson made three trips to Dresden, Germany, and learned to sing in seven languages. He turned down the chance to sing with the Dresden Opera because he wanted to make it big in America, where he took every opportunity open to him. 'The Depression enabled me to get good engagements,' he said. 'The giants of the old days were refusing to cut their fees. The public desired recitals but just couldn't pay the old prices. By being cheap, I became "the popular young baritone".'

By the end of 1932, Nelson was well on his way to becoming a millionaire as a result of sound investments. Knowing what it was like to be poor, he worked harder than ever. In 1933, Eddy made his concert debut in Los Angeles. One of those who gave him eighteen encores was Ida Koverman, L. B. Mayer's secretarial assistant. MGM offered him a contract for $1200 a week and were willing to work around his concert commitments. He had limited singing spots in *Broadway to Hollywood*, *Dancing Lady* and *Student Tour*. In *Dancing Lady* he became friendly with Clark Gable, who had married women for their money to get where he was. Nelson said they had much in common. He told Gable, 'For a while there it became too much. I was trying to study singing and getting laid every night, mostly by married women with their husbands gunning for me half the time. It seriously interfered with my goals. It got to the point where I had to stop and make a decision whether I was going to spend my time fooling around or singing.'

'So what did you decide?' Gable asked.

'I haven't made up my mind yet,' Nelson smiled. He was seeing several Hollywood starlets and his off-and-on girlfriend, Maybelle Marston, who would bear him a son.

Jeanette and Nelson had known each other for almost a year and, although they came very close to making love, he never went through with it. Though Eddy knew Jeanette was experienced he thought of her as a virginal angel, frail and untouchable – the one girl you saved for the wedding night. Jeanette had many encounters with men but few of them were gratifying except Bob Ritchie.

Nelson's mother had met Jeanette when he invited her to dinner at their home, but Isabel had inquired around about the red-headed diva and had reservations about her. She told Nelson, 'I hear she's been around and is Mr Mayer's mistress.' He responded, 'I don't care what she did before I came along, mother.'

Isabel decided to make friends with Jeanette and invited her for Sunday brunch. While they were eating Nelson scanned through the newspaper and came across an item about Jeanette's date with another man. He blew up. He accused her of cheating on him. Isabel excused herself and said she was going to visit a friend. She knew Jeanette would have to learn to dive with Nelson's mood swings if their relationship was to survive.

When he left the table and went into his bedroom, Jeanette followed. 'I thought you understood about us,' he growled, grabbing her by the shoulders. 'I won't play the Hollywood game. I won't have you running around! All this time I've kept my hands off you, trying to be a gentleman. Get this through your head once and for all. You're mine and don't you forget it!' He ripped off her blouse and told her in graphic detail what he would do to her if she ever forgot she belonged to him. Then he threw her down on the bed and raped her.

Jeanette was in shock. She had envisioned a romantic prelude to their lovemaking. Before she had got a chance to get off the bed, he was begging for her forgiveness. He was so upset she felt sorry for him. 'It's all right,' she said. 'All I want to know is what took you so long?'

Taking her in his arms, he suddenly realised her blouse was torn. Apologising, he gave her a sweater to wear. Struggling with the buttons, she looked like a little girl getting ready for school. Nelson put the sweater aside and made love to her. 'It was everything I ever dreamed of and more,' according to Jeanette.

When Isabel came home she found them asleep in front of the fireplace, his head on her breast, her arm around him, covered with a blanket. 'They looked so innocent and beautiful together,' was Isabel's reaction.

Jeanette told her sister Blossom, who was horrified that Nelson had taken her by force. Jeanette said it was worth it if that's what it took to bring them together – and afterwards, when Nelson made love to her, she admitted she had sexually 'lost control' for the first time in her life.

Nelson wrote to her about that Sunday afternoon: 'Last night your fear of yourself was just as great, and I hope that fear will pass. You can't be anything but you in my arms, and I am always going to force you beyond the limits you have set for yourself, for that's the vanity in me, darling.'

Jeanette soon found out that Eddy was frequently subject to mood swings, anxiety attacks and depression. He proved to be a passionate and overbearing lover. He was possessive to the extreme. When they were out together he watched her every minute. Some observers called it love, others called it a form of stalking to make sure she didn't flirt with another man. If she did, he grabbed her arm and marched her out of the room. They fought and made up. If they were estranged for any length of time, he played with other women and she knew it. Though they argued bitterly over her not giving up her career for him, one of the worst scenes took place at the famous Coconut Grove when Jeanette danced with another man. Nelson marched over to them, grabbed her and literally carried her out of the nightclub. Jeanette was so humiliated she told him they were through. He romanced actress Alice Faye and writer Frances Marion. She attended parties alone. At one such event, in mid-June 1935, she arrived at the home of Rozika Dolly (one of the Dolly sisters) alone. Someone whistled and she turned around. The man introduced himself as Gene Raymond. Miss Dolly opened her front door and assumed they were together. Jeanette and Gene met again under the same circumstances. 'Since everyone has us in love,' he said, 'don't you think we should at least have one date so everyone won't be wrong?'

Jeanette thought he resembled Nelson. 'Gene could have been his younger brother,' she said. They went out on a few dates but she was not in the mood for romance. She enjoyed Gene's company because he was a good dancer and made her laugh.

In August 1935 Jeanette and Nelson were back on the movie set. *Rose Marie* was the story of a diva (Jeanette) whose criminal brother (Jimmy Stewart) had escaped from prison. She tries to find him and meets Sergeant Bruce (Nelson) of the Mounted Police. He discovers her identity and accompanies her through the wilderness knowing he'll find her brother. The Mountie arrests her brother despite her pleas. When she suffers a nervous breakdown, the Mountie returns to be with her.

Being separated was good for Jeanette and Nelson. She knew she would never love anyone as she loved him, but was wary of his mood swings. He had time to think about his sudden rages and promised to control his temper. They became a steady couple during *Rose Marie*, but Nelson had marriage on his mind. Though he knew better than to propose again so soon, he did buy her a huge emerald ring surrounded by diamonds that Jeanette had admired. It cost $40,000 . . .

On 6 September, the cast and crew of *Rose Marie* set out for northern California to film on location at Lake Tahoe. It was a romantic site for Jeanette and Nelson, and their songs were just as romantic, 'Indian Love

Call' in particular. They enjoyed taking a canoe out on the lake where they made love. It was apparent to everyone that they were seriously involved. She sat on his lap and snuggled up to him on the set. No one was happier than director Woody Van Dye, who was having no problem with Nelson this time around. Jeanette, who was known to complain, was contented. There were no bathrooms in the mountains so she brought along a portable potty pulled along by a mule. Going in the bushes didn't appeal to her. Then the mule bucked and the potty went over a cliff. She laughed it off and went in the bushes like everyone else.

One of their favourite scenes in *Rose Marie* was cooking beans and bacon over a campfire. Jeanette, who usually nibbled, had to gobble up the beans and bacons through five days of filming. In later years, Nelson said their idea of a romantic meal by candlelight was bacon and beans. Jeanette often said those days in Tahoe were the happiest of her life. Away from the confines and pressure of Hollywood, Jeanette changed her mind about marriage. Perhaps she could make one film a year and do concert tours with Nelson. Long separations frequently meant infidelity on his part.

Jeanette said, in later years, if she could live any of her life with Nelson over again it would be when they were in the mountains at Lake Tahoe. He proposed and she wanted to accept but was afraid of being hurt because she loved him more than he loved her. She recalled, however, his telling her he could never love another woman and she believed him.

She finally accepted his marriage proposal, and against the setting of Tahoe's Emerald Bay, he slipped the emerald engagement ring on her finger. Then they exchanged their wedding vows, promising to love each other forever. He wanted to elope to nearby Reno, but she wanted a big church wedding. She reminded Nelson about their MGM contracts. 'We need Mayer's permission,' she said. 'So don't tell anyone we're engaged just yet.'

Then Jeanette discovered she was pregnant. Nelson was even more determined that they elope to Reno, but she insisted on calling Mayer, who was furious. Jeanette's mistake was calling Mayer in the first place. Her second mistake was telling Nelson she was having an abortion. As it turned out she began to haemorrhage during the night. Not able to find Nelson, she called Woody Van Dyke who stayed with her during the miscarriage.

Thinking she had had an abortion, Nelson refused to have anything to do with Jeanette. He accused her of getting rid of their baby so she could continue with her career. She called Blossom who rushed to Tahoe as did

Gene Raymond. Meanwhile Woody Van Dyke was trying to finish *Rose Marie* with his two stars not speaking to each other. He tried to convince Nelson that Jeanette did not have an abortion. 'I couldn't care less,' he told Van Dyke. Pointing to Gene Raymond, he said, 'She has what she wants. Somebody as phony as she is.'

L. B. Mayer, infuriated that Nelson had made his beautiful Jeanette pregnant, went on a campaign to sabotage him. It was Jeanette who realised this when the front office ordered more pancake make-up on Nelson, giving him a pasty feminine look. Mayer told Van Dyke to edit *Rose Marie* in Jeanette's favour, cutting out Nelson's good reels. Mayer told Eddy, in no uncertain terms, to abide to the rigid rules of MGM or suffer the consequences.

Rose Marie survived Mayer's wrath, thanks to Woody Van Dyke and the team of MacDonald and Eddy whose 'Indian Love Call' was unsurpassed. The film opened in January 1936 to rave reviews. Nelson was more popular than ever, but Mayer had no plans to team him with Jeanette again. The public would convince him otherwise, however.

During the last few weeks of filming *Rose Marie* in Hollywood, Jeanette finally got through to Nelson. They spent twenty-four hours discussing their problems, making love and trying to resolve their differences to no avail. They decided it was better to part as friends now, rather than continue as enemies.

Jeanette began to see a lot of Gene Raymond. Possibly it was his resemblance to Eddy that attracted her at first. If so, she found in Gene a tender lover unlike Nelson who, too often, ravished her with overwhelming passion that was more frightening than it was satisfying.

Jeanette buckled down to do *San Francisco* with Clark Gable who 'didn't give a damn' for her. He felt she had treated Nelson badly and considered her flighty, conceited and overrated. He was disgusted at the thought of sitting around like a lump while she sang in a close-up with the camera picking up the back of his neck. But he gave in ultimately because he liked his character Blackie Norton, who owns a saloon on the Barbary Coast, and falls in love with a minister's daughter, played by Jeanette. Spencer Tracy was the priest who tries to prevent her from marrying his roguish friend.

Jeanette was disappointed in Gable. She complained that he had garlic breath and drank too much. They had one blow up that ended in Mayer's office.

The theme song was the spirited 'San Francisco' that Jeanette did so well.

And can anyone forget the devastating earthquake of 1906 that felled the city on the bay at the end of the film?

Nelson returned from his concert tour in time to visit Jeanette on the set of *San Francisco*. They were so happy to see each other that they shamelessly embraced and kissed in front of the cast and crew. Spencer Tracy said, 'They get more out of a look than I get out of the whole sex act.'

San Francisco was a huge success. The *Hollywood Reporter* said Jeanette's performance 'established her unchallenged right to the title of first lady in the ranks of singing actresses . . . You have never seen anything that approaches the power of the scenes of buildings toppling and catching fire. The MGM technical effects department eclipses by a wide margin all previous efforts of the sort.' The *World Telegram* claimed, 'Jeanette MacDonald is superb. Looking more attractive and appearing in better voice than ever before, she plays the part with uncommon charm, forbearance and emotional depth. Not only does she give the finest performance of her screen career, but she has never sung more thrillingly than she does here.'

San Francisco was nominated for Best Picture, Best Supporting Actor (Spencer Tracy), Best Writing, Best Original Story, Best Assistant Director and Best Sound Recording (the only Academy Award it won).

In the summer of 1936 Jeanette signed a new contract with MGM calling for $125,000 per picture.

Gene Raymond was Jeanette's date at her thirty-third birthday party on 18 June 1936. Nelson came with actress Anita Louise, but he appeared adrift and drained. Jeanette couldn't bear to see him this way and she agreed to see him. Knowing Mayer had spies everywhere, Nelson rented a house in Lake Arrowhead, a mountain resort two hours away from Los Angeles. Here they could be together without fear of being discovered. Their talks about marriage were endless but the result was always the same – she must give up her career. For Jeanette there was only one solution. On 20 August 1936 Anna MacDonald announced that her daughter Jeanette was engaged to be married to Gene Raymond.

Though L. B. Mayer detested Nelson, the public clamoured for more MacDonald-Eddy films, and Irving Thalberg obliged with Sigmund Romberg's *Maytime*. The film begins with Jeanette, as an old woman, reminiscing about marrying her music teacher (John Barrymore) rather than her lover (Nelson) who is killed by her husband. Jeanette dies at the end, emerges young again and is reunited with the man she loves. With orange blossoms falling from an orchard they sing to a romantically beautiful crescendo of 'Maytime'. Thalberg planned to do the picture in Technicolor, but when he died suddenly in September 1936, Mayer stopped production, revised the script and ordered the film to be shot in black-and-white.

Jeanette and Nelson were barely civil when they recorded their songs for the film. Standing for many hours in front of the microphone, he put a wicker rocking chair behind Jeanette who tired easily and was prone to fainting. He was so accustomed to looking after her that he instinctually held her up if she showed signs of passing out.

One night Nelson was restless and came back to the studio to see if he could find Gable or someone else to have a few drinks with him. He walked through the *Maytime* set and heard a voice. It was Jeanette, sitting under the tree where they filmed a love scene and sang 'Will You Remember?' She asked him, 'Why can't we be friends?' Nelson said he wanted more than that and started to walk away. She threw herself in his arms and they made love under the tree. Nelson told his mother, 'This time she seduced me!'

They began spending time together in their trailers and alerting trustworthy friends to be on the lookout for Mayer and Gene. Jeanette should have known better. Mayer always knew what mischief his stars were up to, Jeanette and Nelson in particular. He posted guards near their trailers and told Anna MacDonald to keep an eye on her daughter and report back to him. Since Anna disliked Nelson, she was happy to comply. Mayer told Jeanette to remain faithful to her engagement to Gene Raymond, and he told Nelson, 'Stay away from her or else.'

Mayer was frantic, seeing that his singing stars were making millions for MGM. But he was afraid marriage would destroy their chemistry on the screen. And if they divorced, they were through as the operatic lovebirds.

Nelson began drinking heavily, often disappearing for days, sometimes with Clark Gable. The two men came up with the idea of offering Gene Raymond $250,000 to cancel his marriage plans. Nelson got hold of as much money as he could and made the proposition to Gene, who accepted, but Mayer refused to cancel the wedding, and Gene returned the money.

Those who were close to Jeanette thought she should have married Nelson. Those close to him thought that he should stop pushing Jeanette to give up her career. Their love for each other became very apparent when they were doing the 'Will You Remember?' number under their 'passion' tree. They were saying goodbye in the story and for real. In tears, they did the scene over and over again until Nelson focused on the tree instead of Jeanette.

It's no surprise that *Maytime* was a box-office success. The *New York Times* hailed the film as 'the most entrancing operetta the screen has given us.'

While Nelson was on another concert tour, Jeanette made *The Firefly* with Allan Jones. She plays a Spanish spy in Madrid, in 1808, seeking Napoleon's plan of invasion, but is found out by a French spy. They fall in love, argue over politics and find each other in the end. The hit song, 'Donkey Serenade', became identified with Jones for the rest of his life. In *The Firefly* Jeanette dances as much as she sings. Her Spanish outfits were elaborate and expensive, and her dancing very seductive. Though the picture did well, it got mixed reviews. There is no doubt *The Firefly* introduced a different Jeanette and a very good one, but it is her least-remembered film.

Allan Jones was determined to seduce Jeanette during production. She fought him off until he finally gave up but Nelson, back from his tour, heard about Allan's chasing Jeanette, went berserk and beat Jones to a pulp. There were rumours Eddy went to Mayer and threatened to leave if MGM didn't get rid of Jones. Mayer, who had received an invitation to Jeanette's wedding, knew Nelson was out of her life so he got rid of Jones.

Two days before Jeanette got married she wrote to Bob Ritchie about her fears and qualms, but she was going to make a go of her marriage. And to Isabel Eddy she wrote that 'I must go to Gene not with my heart's love, for that is impossible, but with purity of spirit – and a calm mind – a prayer in my heart. These two men are so strangely alike – I must try to find enough of Nelson in Gene to make me contented. Gene understands and thinks he can help me.'

The night before the wedding Jeanette was at home with Blossom and Anna when Nelson barged into the house. Jeanette ran for the bedroom but he caught her, pushed Anna aside and tried to get Jeanette in his car, but she fought him off. He wanted her to look him in the eye and say she didn't love him. She turned away. 'Jenny,' he said, 'people search all their lives for what we have and you throw it away with your wanton greediness.' Then he sped away leaving her alone in the middle of the street.

On 15 June 1937, thousands gathered outside the Wilshire Methodist Church for the 9.00 p.m. wedding of Jeanette MacDonald and Gene Raymond. Gossip columnist Sidney Skolsky wrote, 'It was the usual Metro production – lavish, with red lanterns hanging outside, while inside the church was decorated with pink ribbons and pink roses . . . The Metro publicity men stood at the door to see that the right guests entered and distributed the credit sheets, which told about principals and supporting cast.'

Mayer had asked Nelson to sing at the wedding which seems almost barbaric. He sang 'I Love You Truly', and 'O Perfect Love' with a trembling voice. Mayer gloated, 'Just the look on the face of the baritone is worth the expense of this wedding.'

Jeanette, wearing a gown of flesh-pink organza over matching taffeta with leg-of-mutton sleeves and a high-neck collar trimmed with lace and a tiny spray of roses, walked down the candlelit aisle alone. She carried a single rose and a pink satin prayer book.

The reception for 250 people was held at Jeanette's house. She changed into a white dress and showed everyone her diamond necklace that Gene had given her. On her left hand was her nine-carat diamond engagement ring and plain platinum wedding band. Isabel attended the reception. Nelson did not, but he received a phone call from Jeanette saying she could not leave without seeing him. He and Isabel went to the MacDonald house where Jeanette and Nelson went into seclusion for ten minutes. According to Isabel, Jeanette put her arms around his neck and kissed him. Then she told everyone, including Gene, they wanted to be alone. No one ever found out what the lovers said to each other . . .

Jeanette thought she was spending her wedding night at a rented seaside bungalow but Gene drove her to an enormous Tudor-style mansion on Bel Air Road. Secretly, he had bought and furnished the house they called Twin Gables.

On 26 June, the Raymonds sailed on the *Lurline* for a Hawaiian honeymoon. Also on board were newlyweds Mary Pickford and Buddy Rogers. The couples soon split up into another honeymoon couple – Gene Raymond and Buddy Rogers.

A hysterical Jeanette called Nelson, who wasn't in the mood to talk to her. When Isabel asked what she wanted, he said, 'I don't know. Something about Gene . . .'

Gene Raymond was born Raymond Guion on 13 August 1908, in New

York City. He had been a professional actor since the age of five, and appeared on Broadway in *The Potters* when he was fourteen. With an ambitious and domineering mother behind him, Gene was cast in the Broadway hit *Cradle Snatchers* with Humphrey Bogart, and *The Sinners*. His success on Broadway led to a contract with Paramount Studios in 1931. Two years later he signed with RKO and did *Red Dust* with Clark Gable and Jean Harlow, *Flying Down to Rio* with Dolores del Rio and *Zoo in Budapest* with Loretta Young. His contract at RKO was cancelled when he became involved with a teenaged boy whose parents pressed charges. RKO paid them off and quietly let Gene go. After that he made mostly B-pictures.

Gene's mother, Mary Kipling, had a strong and strange hold on him. She was the typical stage mother who enjoyed fame through her son. She divorced Gene's father and remarried, but frowned on anyone who might come between her and Gene. She wanted Jeanette to promise she would not marry her son. Did Kipling go to this extent to conceal Gene's homosexuality? Or was she abnormally possessive of him? They had lived together throughout his lifetime and he supported her in grand style. To placate her, Gene promised to continue this support after he married. But Kipling never did accept her son's marriage. She refused to attend the wedding and referred to Jeanette as 'that woman' and 'cradle robber' because Gene was six years younger than MacDonald. As Hollywood insiders said, 'Gene had to break up with his mother to get married.'

Gene said he loved Jeanette, and friends truly believe he did. He married her knowing she loved him but was 'in love' with Nelson. Jeanette found out about his bisexuality on her honeymoon and confronted Gene who reminded her, 'You're no angel, either.' She had no choice but to stay married or risk her good name. To Blossom she said about marrying Gene, 'I must have had rocks in my head.' The Raymonds would stay married until the appropriate time when they could end it gracefully.

The sad part of this is that Anna MacDonald knew that Gene was bisexual. She heard it from her Hollywood mothers' group, but kept it to herself because she disliked Nelson.

Sharon Rich in her book *Sweethearts* suggests that Jeanette returned to Los Angeles in July, leaving Gene in Hawaii. Sources claim they saw her at a picnic with Nelson. If she was in California, she remained well hidden and then rejoined her husband in Hawaii so they could sail home together. On 5 August, reporters were at the pier in Pasadena to greet them.

Nelson made *Rosalie* with dancer Eleanor Powell. It received rave reviews and Eddy was more popular than ever. This came as a relief to him since he had so long been identified with Jeanette. Songs featured in the movie were the title song 'Rosalie' that was a big hit in 1937, and 'In the Still of the Night'.

Nelson was not happy to learn that his next movie *The Girl of the Golden West* would co-star Jeanette. He had accepted the fact that he would always love her and was able to control his feelings if he kept away from her. Now he would have to endure the scent of her perfume, kissing her for the camera, and watch Gene Raymond come for his wife at the end of the day. Thinking about it, he turned to the bottle and kept it nearby during production. *The Girl of the Golden West* revolved around a virginal saloon owner (MacDonald), a 'Robin Hood' bandit (Eddy) and a sheriff (Walter Pidgeon). At the end of the film, Jeanette plays poker with the sheriff for the life of a wounded Nelson, who got an erection when Jeanette leaned over to comfort him as he lay prone on the floor. Maybe he got aroused by her, but they were so cold to each other on the set that word got out they were feuding. He was making $4000 a week and wanted $6000, they said. He was jealous of Jeanette, they said. He was turning into a prima donna like her, they said. News of Nelson's heavy drinking did not reach the press, of course. Mayer tried to talk to him and was told to 'butt out'. Jeanette tried, and was told the same thing. When he fell off a horse, she did not laugh this time. Fortunately, he was pulled away from the trampling hooves of a herd of horses just in time.

Their love scene was 'Obey Your Heart', serenading each other under a tree. Jeanette broke down during every take. Finally, director Robert Leonard spoke to Mayer who told him to forget the duet because he feared Jeanette was heading for a nervous breakdown. He was told she was suffering from insomnia and often spent the night in her dressing room. Mayer asked the studio doctor to supply her with pills to remedy the situation.

In January 1938, near the end of filming *The Girl of the Golden West*, Jeanette drove to Nelson's house late at night. In a faint she lingered in her car until Isabel spotted her and called for Nelson, who carried Jeanette into the house where she passed out. When she came to, she started to say something, got up to leave and then stopped at the door. 'I can't go back there. I just can't . . .'

Nelson insisted she sit down and tell them about it. Jeanette looked at Isabel who said, 'I've been around, my dear, so don't worry about me.'

Jeanette explained that earlier in the evening Gene had been arrested 'on a morals charge'. He was at a homosexual club when police raided the place. Not thinking clearly, Jeanette bailed him out and paid $1000 in hush money.

'Why didn't you call Howard Strickling?' Nelson asked.

'I was upset . . .'

'That's what Howard's there for, Jenny. Don't you know the bastard Mayer has the chief of police in his back pocket?'

'I was too ashamed to call Howard.'

'Honey, he saw Harlow's husband Paul Bern with a bullet through his head. He got someone else to take the rap for Gable when he was driving drunk and ran over a woman. And God knows how many times he's saved every Goddamn homosexual on MGM's payroll. I'd love to see your pansy-husband's mug shot.'

'I paid them off so there should be no record of it,' she sobbed, ignoring Nelson's sense of humour.

'Listen to me, Jen. Tell Mayer or Howard to make sure the whole damn thing has been erased from the books. As for now, you're spending the night here.'

Within a few days Jeanette quietly filed for a divorce that would be final in a year. Gene, whose latest movie *Stolen Heaven* had just opened, set off around the country to promote the film. For appearances' sake, Jeanette met him in New York for a press luncheon and then joined Nelson who was on a concert tour. Sometimes she waited for him backstage and often she sat in the audience. Nelson might introduce her or ask her to join him in a duet on stage. His fans didn't like that because he 'bowed' to her presence, giving her the spotlight and gazing down at her as they harmonised one of their classic songs.

This relaxing time in between films was a joy for the couple who had plans to marry when Jeanette's divorce was final. Nelson had three residences, one a small house in Burbank, on a dirt road overlooking the Los Angeles River. Jeanette had the key to this place. Another was a hunting lodge in the Angeles Forest, and the third was in Beverly Hills off Benedict Canyon where he and Isabel lived.

Sweethearts was their first Technicolor film. It is the story of a happily married couple who have appeared in a Broadway operetta, *Sweethearts*, for several years. When they decide to try Hollywood, the play's producers try to break up the marriage and almost succeed.

If anyone believed Jeanette and Nelson were feuding, there was not a hint of it during production of *Sweethearts* that began in May 1938. But when all seemed rosy, Jeanette found out she was pregnant. By the time she went before the camera, she was three months along. Nelson found out when he heard her retching during the night at the little Burbank house. His first reaction was suspicion, but she assured him she wanted his baby. The problem was how to do it without Mayer's permission. Nelson explained they would finish *Sweethearts* and go to Arizona where he knew a doctor who would falsify the birth certificate. By that time the divorce would be final and they would marry. They confided in director Woody Van Dyke who said he would film Jeanette's sequences first. Within a month she was busty and plump and radiant. Isabel was on the set of *Sweetheart* and was relieved to see Nelson so cheerful and Jeanette so flushed with happiness.

When Gene returned to Twin Gables, he and Jeanette had an argument and he hit her. Nelson swore he'd kill him if he ever touched him again. Gene did not take the threat seriously, because he abused Jeanette again. Nelson called to tell her he was picking her up for a party at Woody Van Dyke's house. When she didn't answer he called Woody and was told she was there. Nelson found her, wearing a head scarf, talking to Woody in the corner. He walked over to them and pulled the scarf off Jeanette's head, exposing the black and blue bruises on her face. Nelson tore out of the house in a rage. Woody followed and found Nelson beating Gene unmercifully. He was taken to the hospital, reportedly after falling down a flight of stairs.

Because her face was so badly bruised, Jeanette was unable to go before the camera for a week.

Gene Raymond was sharing a house with a nineteen-year-old actor under contract to Universal while rumours turned into truth about the MacDonald–Eddy affair. How long would it take for MGM's 'father' to find out what his precious million-dollar darlings were up to? It took only a few pictures taken at Jeanette's birthday party on the set. She and Nelson were closer than ever and, in one photo, their passionate kiss said it all. This picture, among others, landed on Mayer's desk. He called Jeanette, Nelson and Gene to his office. She was to have an abortion immediately, and there would be no divorce. Nelson told Mayer he would marry Jeanette and their fans would be delighted. Then he took her by the hand and led her back to the set. Mayer realised Jeanette was going to have Nelson's baby and he could do nothing about it.

He didn't have to. While shooting a scene in *Sweethearts*, Jeanette tripped on her long dress while running upstairs, fell, and slid down the steps on her stomach. On 26 July she collapsed in Nelson's arms on the set and was rushed to the Good Samaritan Hospital for 'an abscess in her right ear'. Nelson arrived with Jeanette and refused to let her go. He was so upset that doctors had to give him a sedative. When he woke up, he was told Jeanette had lost the baby. Doctors said she was not strong enough to have children so there would be no more pregnancies. When Jeanette was well enough she and Nelson went back to Lake Tahoe to sort things out.

When they returned to Los Angeles in mid-September, Mayer had a long talk with the lovers. This time he took a different approach and praised their talent. He was planning to obtain two new projects for them, *Rio Rita*, and *Desert Song*. In the meantime they would work separately, Jeanette in *Broadway Serenade* and Nelson in *Let Freedom Ring*.

Mayer's plan was to pretend he was reconciled to their romance but, like the warrior he was, he was waiting for them to let their guard down again. Word got back to him that Jeanette was planning to get a quickie divorce in Mexico and marry Nelson. Mayer knew he could get an annulment and destroy all records of the marriage but, as always, he feared the press would find out. He spoke to Jeanette privately and threatened to do whatever it took to get rid of Eddy. She was terrified that he would have Nelson beaten up or worse. Seeing her cave in, Mayer said, 'I'll make sure Gene comes home to stay. I want you both to go out and be seen around town as a happily married couple. Is that understood?'

Jeanette said nothing to Nelson about this. Instead she continually ignored his urging her to go to Reno or Mexico. She was busy making *Broadway Serenade*, she said. Nelson should have noticed Jeanette wasn't looking well, but he was feeling sorry for himself and stormed out of her dressing room one day and eloped with another woman.

Ann Franklin, who was seven years older than Nelson, was divorced from director Sydney Franklin. She was a member of Nelson's opera crowd and became close to Isabel who confided in Ann about her son and Jeanette. The patient Mrs Franklin waited for the right opportunity and seized it when Nelson got so drunk he eloped to Las Vegas with her on the night of 19 January 1939. Isabel said he woke up on the train back to Los Angeles and remembered nothing.

The following morning Jeanette reported for work, heard the news and locked herself in her dressing room. Woody Van Dyke broke down the door and found her unconscious on the floor. When he noticed an empty bottle of sleeping pills, he called the studio doctor. Mayer was notified immediately and rushed to Jeanette. 'The baritone did this to my beautiful star,' he told Van Dyke. Mayer picked up Jeanette in his arms, carried her to his car and rushed her to the hospital where her stomach was pumped. After she returned home Isabel paid her a visit to explain the circumstances of Nelson's wedding. For Jeanette the hurt was too deep to forgive and she made it a point not to attend parties if Nelson was invited. Almost as depressing was the lack of interest in *Broadway Serenade* that the *New York Times* said was 'the biggest bad show of the year'.

Now that Eddy was married, Mayer thought it was safe to co-star Jeanette and Nelson in *New Moon*, a rehash of *Naughty Marietta*. The lovers managed a few nights of intimacy together in late 1939. They did not discuss a future together. This was too complicated for now. They were in love and would see each other whenever possible. During a concert tour, Nelson became so ill in Milwaukee that he sent for Isabel, who accompanied him home. Doctors said he was suffering from a complete nervous breakdown. Jeanette once again took stock of their lives. How long could they suffer the agonies of being apart? She and Gene discussed divorce and she may have talked it over with her lawyer. Nelson, who had asked Ann for a divorce many times, did not give up. She threatened to expose his affair with Jeanette and the matter was dropped. This would be her hold over him. A close friend said, 'Jeanette and Nelson did not have a chance. Even if Mayer were out of the picture, Ann Eddy was determined to destroy Jeanette if Nelson filed for divorce. Adultery was not accepted in the forties, especially if the ones involved were the most famous singing stars in the world. Unfortunately, Ann knew about Jeanette's pregnancies, too, and she was willing to tell the whole sordid story.'

The popularity of MacDonald/Eddy films was waning. *New Moon* was not well received. The *New York Times* said, '. . . this sort of sugar-coated musical fiction has seen its better days.'

Mayer went ahead with his plans for *Bittersweet* anyway. Filmed in Technicolor, the film was too reminiscent of *Maytime* without the charm. It was the first MacDonald/Eddy picture to lose money. Nelson's fans complained he had little exposure in *Bittersweet*. Jeanette came across with 'self-conscious high spirits,' according to the *New York Times*. Their films did not interest the public, but their concert tours were very successful. Being separated was always good therapy for both of them, especially for Nelson who could not be around Jeanette for very long without seducing her. If his marriage to Ann was not satisfying sexually, Nelson found satisfaction with other women.

Jeanette was to co-star with Jimmy Stewart in *Smilin' Through*, but he joined the Air Force. In May 1941 filming began without a leading man so

Gene Raymond stepped in. The sentimental story is about a woman (Jeanette) who is forbidden to marry her lover (Gene Raymond) because her guardian had a grudge against the lover's family. Jeanette and Gene did not have chemistry on the screen, however, and *Smilin' Through* received bad reviews. Jeanette, of course, was always applauded for her singing and for her great beauty in Technicolor even at the age of thirty-nine.

In *I Married an Angel*, Jeanette plays a dual role, that of a shy secretary whom playboy Nelson finally marries, and the angel in his dream. 'In our films together,' Nelson said, 'we always depicted pure love and we had a lot of trouble with this script because religious groups disapproved of an angel going to bed with a man. Everyone on the lot told us it was either going to be the best picture we ever did or the worst. It was the worst. It took the studio years to figure out how to present it without offending anybody and then they slashed it to pieces. When we finally finished it, it was a horrible mess.'

It was during the filming of *Angel* that Jeanette went to Mayer's office and returned to the set obviously very upset. She refused to tell Nelson what had happened. He figured it out by himself. Mayer tried to seduce her during *Sweethearts* and he had tried again. Nelson went to the mogul's office, took Mayer by the throat and dragged him over to an open window. It was actor Frank Morgan who came into the office and saved Mayer's life.

In January 1942 Gene Raymond joined the U.S. Air Force and was sent to England.

After playing a movie star to Robert Young's war correspondent in *Cairo*, Jeanette left Metro-Goldwyn-Mayer, as did Nelson, who bought out his contract. They departed with no fanfare or farewell parties. Many Hollywood insiders thought they lingered too long at MGM, but the truth is that their type of films were outdated. *Sweethearts* had a touch of the modern and they were very good without period costumes and old ballads. Maybe it was Mayer's lack of interest or his disgust. Most probably the former because he did what was best for MGM.

At this time the lovers discussed divorce realistically. Jeanette was shocked, however, when Ann told the press she was pregnant. At forty-seven, it was unlikely. She threatened to have Nelson followed to catch him with Jeanette so it makes sense that she would spread the pregnancy rumours to upset her husband's mistress. Also, around this time Ann attempted suicide with pills and alcohol. Nelson found her in time to call a doctor.

Jeanette went on tour to raise money for the Army Emergency Relief

Fund. While she was away, Nelson made *The Phantom of the Opera* for Universal. In December 1942 they took a short vacation that he described in a note to his mother: 'Perhaps some day we shall see and understand why we had to go through years of cruel agony – and in the end obey the law of God while we break the law of man. But I know that we break no law. Jeanette has never been a wife and I have never had one – we owe no affection or vows to anyone. But we do owe them to each other, we took them long ago and have never broken them. Now they are made secure and forever.'

In May 1943 Jeanette set out to attain her dream: opera. She had hoped for the Metropolitan, but was not invited to audition. She did, however, do *Roméo et Juliette* in Canada to standing ovations and rave reviews. Captain Gene Raymond joined her in Montreal while on leave from the Air Force.

Nelson embarked on an overseas concert tour to Brazil, Central Africa, Arabia and Egypt. He had been recruited by the Counter-Intelligence Corps to do undercover work. His asset was knowledge of the German language but little is known about his assignment. Jeanette knew about his undercover work and how to keep in touch with him by mail, but in early January 1944, her concern for his welfare caused her to have a complete nervous collapse. Later that month she met Nelson in Florida and they disappeared. She was so pathetically thin and pale that his only concern was getting her well. With Gene stationed in Arizona and Nelson caring less what Ann thought, he and Jeanette could do as they pleased for several months. With Isabel and Anna, they spent a cherished Christmas together, lavishing each other with gifts.

In 1945 they were busy doing radio shows and concerts, but if Jeanette was alone for any length of time, she neglected her health. Nelson literally spoon-fed her. He piled food on her plate, cut the meat into little pieces and fed her like a baby. Gene was present at a gathering where Nelson tended to her eating. When someone asked him about it, Gene responded, 'Oh, that's nothing. It's been going on for years.'

Gene was so gracious about his wife living with Nelson off and on, it would have been no problem if Jeanette had wanted a divorce. There was nothing between them now except friendship. But Ann Eddy was mentally unbalanced, according to her doctor. A divorce could easily send her over the edge. She was content to see Nelson whenever he chose to come home or take her to an occasional party. She was even civil to Jeanette socially. Nelson, for the most part, did not tell her where he was going other than a concert tour. One time she barged into Isabel's home and Nelson threw her out with orders never to come to his mother's house again. In early 1946 Nelson nearly died from pneumonia but stayed with Isabel and Jeanette after he was well enough to leave the hospital. Ann phoned to see how he was but was reminded she was not welcome at Isabel's.

Jeanette ran into gossip columnist Hedda Hopper on the street minutes after she had dropped Nelson off to do a radio show. 'When are you going to give me a scoop on yourself, young lady?' Hedda asked.

'We're so grateful to all of you for being so kind to us.'

'Well, Jeanette, I've been tempted to talk plenty of times, but you two are too well loved, and if I did, every other reporter in Hollywood would murder me.'

Nelson was thrilled when Jeanette agreed to do a movie with him but she suddenly withdrew without giving him a reason. Suspecting him of having an affair with Ilona Massey, who replaced her in *Northwest Outpost*, Jeanette did not tell Nelson she was pregnant again, and accepted a concert tour in England. In May, she had a miscarriage in London.

Jeanette returned home and signed with MGM to do *Three Daring Daughters* with Jane Powell, about a divorcée whose love affair incites her children. L.B. Mayer welcomed her home with tears in his eyes. In an interview she said, 'It's a wonderful feeling to be back. I hadn't realised how much I missed picture-making until I came back to it. And to add to the sense of being home again, the studio gave me the crew that worked with me in former pictures.' Her love interest in *Three Daring Daughters* was pianist José Iturbi who was too short and plump for Jeanette. She told Hedda Hopper, 'Just between you and me I always felt confident that if Nelson had played in the movie, instead of Iturbi, it would have rekindled another hot box-office set-up.'

Three Darling Daughters fared well at the box office. Jeanette had no illusions about it and accepted mild reviews. She was welcomed back by critics who thought she was as beautiful as ever with a voice to match.

Jeanette was satisfied to give concerts and do an occasional opera. Meanwhile, Nelson was trying to make a home with Ann. He had turned to religion for comfort and told Jeanette he was pledged to celibacy. He reasoned if they could not be married in this lifetime they would be in the afterlife if they made amends now. Jeanette went along with his religious beliefs to be part of his life, but when Anna MacDonald had a fatal heart attack in May 1947, Jeanette collapsed after the funeral. Nelson lost his spirituality soon enough and took her to Lake Tahoe for a rest and to renew their wedding vows that they made over ten years ago. He wrote, 'My darling, how can I explain the pure and holy spirit that possesses me when I hold your body . . . that is why it is oh so deeply spiritual and why only you and I can give to each other this love, this religion.'

Jeanette became pregnant again at the age of forty-five. Three months later she miscarried. The doctor said one more pregnancy would kill Jeanette, who was obsessed with having Nelson's baby. Isabel feared their relationship was unnatural, and destroying both of them. She was right. When Ann Eddy found a love letter from Jeanette, she and Nelson had a bitter fight. He accidentally, or deliberately, took an overdose of sleeping pills. Ann called Isabel, who found a doctor and Nelson survived. He insisted on going home with Isabel, leaving Ann behind.

Jeanette was back at MGM for *The Sun Comes Up*, which is about a concert singer who seeks solitude after her teenage son is killed. Her co-stars were Claude Jarmon Jr from *The Yearling* fame, and the famous collie, Lassie. This would be Jeanette's final film and though it was a pleasant one, she realised her beauty was fading, and wore wigs with elastic that pulled back her skin and gave her an instant face lift. During production, Jeanette suffered a minor heart attack and swore her doctor to secrecy. But it wasn't her frail health that kept her away from Nelson. It was her fading beauty that was all too apparent. Gene admitted her to a sanatorium after she attempted suicide twice. Reliable sources think she had shock treatments, and somehow she got through Gene's being arrested for soliciting young men.

In 1952 Jeanette was surprised by Ralph Edwards on *This is Your Life*. When Nelson sang to her from offstage, she wept, and greeted him by practically falling into his arms.

Louis B. Mayer died of leukaemia on 29 October 1957. At his memorial service Jeanette sang 'Ah, Sweet Mystery of Life' because 'I think he would have been pleased. It reflected the favourable times he represented.' Of Mayer she said, 'One of the greatest sadnesses of life is to realise how much you owe someone when it's too late to express any gratitude.'

In the same year Isabel died, and Nelson was inconsolable. He turned to Jeanette and begged her to marry him. This time they got as far as his attorney's office to discuss the details, but when he found out how much it would cost him to get rid of Ann, he walked away. Jeanette suffered another heart attack. She was hospitalised for heart surgery but when doctors opened her up there was nothing they could do so they sewed her up again. She recuperated with Gene in Europe.

Over the next few years Jeanette and Nelson saw each other at social events. When he was out of town he called her often, but she never mentioned her heart condition.

At Houston's Methodist Hospital, on 5 November 1963, Dr Michael DeBakey performed 'a right carotid endarterectomy to relieve the obstructive blood flow to the brain on that side'. But a year later she was back in the Houston hospital for open-heart surgery. Unfortunately, Jeanette was too weak to undergo the operation. She died at 4.32 p.m. on 14 January 1965.

Nelson was having breakfast in a coffee shop in Anaheim, California, when reporters told him about Jeanette's death. He broke down in tears.

When Jeanette's body arrived back in Los Angeles, Nelson went to the mortuary to be alone with her. The funeral was held at Forest Lawn Memorial Park in Glendale on 18 January. Jeanette was laid out in a dress of silver brocade with flowers. Covering her from the waist down was a blanket of pink roses in an open bronze casket lined with tufted pink satin. After the minister said, 'Thank you, Jeanette, for putting something beautiful into our lives that we shall always cherish,' her voice could be heard singing 'Ave Maria'. Lloyd Nolan, her co-star in *The Sun Comes Up* gave the brief eulogy: '. . . There was warmth in her heart and in her song – magic in her voice – tenderness and affection for all mankind. She sang to you – and to you alone – and to you she sent her message of love.' Jeanette's voice then filled the church with 'Ah, Sweet Mystery of Life'.

On 6 March 1967, Nelson Eddy was performing at the Hotel San Souci in Miami Beach. In the middle of his act he became disorientated and he collapsed. He was rushed to hospital and died the following day at 7.30 a.m., from an apparent stroke. He was buried next to Isabel at Hollywood Memorial Park. At the private funeral Ann Eddy leaned over to Gene Raymond and whispered, 'Now they can sing together forever.'

The Films of Jeanette MacDonald

The Love Parade (Paramount, 1929)
The Vagabond King (Paramount, 1930)
Monte Carlo (Paramount, 1930)
Let's Go Native (Paramount, 1930)
The Lottery Bridge (United Artists, 1930)
Oh, For a Man (20th Century-Fox, 1930)
Don't Bet on Women (20th Century-Fox, 1931)
Annabelle's Affairs (20th Century-Fox, 1931)
One Hour With You (Paramount, 1932)
Love Me Tonight (Paramount, 1932)
The Cat and the Fiddle (MGM, 1934)
The Merry Widow (MGM, 1934)
Naughty Marietta (MGM, 1935)
Rose Marie (MGM, 1936)
San Francisco (MGM, 1936)
Maytime (MGM, 1937)
The Firefly (MGM, 1937)
Girl of the Golden West (MGM, 1938)
Sweethearts (MGM, 1938)
Broadway Serenade (MGM, 1939)
New Moon (MGM, 1940)
Bittersweet (MGM, 1940)
Smilin' Through (MGM, 1941)
I Married an Angel (MGM, 1942)
Cairo (MGM, 1942)
Follow the Boys (Universal, 1944)
Three Daring Daughters (MGM, 1948)
The Sun Comes Up (MGM, 1948)

2

Norma

She was MGM's 'Queen of the Lot' and was frequently referred to as the 'boss's wife'. Married to Metro's boy genius Irving Thalberg, she got the plum roles and performed them artfully. In spite of a cast in one eye, lack of facial bone structure and a stubby figure, she personified glamour through sheer determination. She was not a great actress but she learned the tricks of the trade and used them to her advantage. She had an aristocratic air, sense of style and gracious manner that was outstanding in the lavish production of *Marie Antoinette*.

Before marrying Thalberg, who had a weak heart, she had many lovers including every woman's dream, director Victor Fleming, the very popular Billy Haines, and heart-throb John Gilbert. She remained faithful to Thalberg, but her leading men claimed she was overly flirtatious and seductive. Clark Gable said she did not wear panties underneath form-fitting gowns. 'She's flaunting it,' he told a friend. 'She must be one hot lay if she can behave like that with the camera turning.'

After the untimely death of Thalberg, she made up for lost time. She seduced Mickey Rooney, half her age, who joked, 'Can you picture Marie Antoinette with Andy Hardy?' L.B. Mayer put an end to the affair before the gossip columnists got wind of it. She pursued Jimmy Stewart, who tried to get away from her and she managed a serious affair with George Raft, known for his gangster roles on and off the screen.

Now referred to as 'the widow Thalberg', who had inherited her late husband's shares of MGM profits, it was difficult for these men to turn her down. Tyrone Power, who was not under contract to MGM, ignored her efforts to seduce him.

Norma Shearer's dreaded secret was a streak of manic depression that ran through the family . . .

To review Norma Shearer's life is a lesson in how to overcome setbacks, remain patient and forge ahead regardless of obstacles that most people would have considered insurmountable. She once said, 'It is impossible to get anything major accomplished without stepping on some toes; enemies are inevitable when one is a *doer*.' Though Shearer's demeanour was ladylike and pliable, make no mistake about it, she wanted power. With a taste of it, she had a feast and fought anyone who stood in her way. She ignored her catty enemies and was fiercely loyal to her friends.

Shearer said her attitude was largely due to her childhood of privilege that took a sudden plunge into poverty. 'At an early age,' she said, 'I formed a philosophy about failure. Perhaps an endeavour, like my father's business, could fail, but that didn't mean Father had failed.'

She also had no illusions about her image in the mirror. She had small eyes that appeared crossed due to a cast in her right eye. Cleverly, Norma made up her face to camouflage this handicap at a young age. She had a keen sense of how to detract from her dumpy figure by wearing clothes that made her appear thinner and taller. 'I had no illusions about myself,' she said.

Norma had a very special type of beauty that lent itself to the camera. She was known as a scene stealer, but before she learned this technique all eyes focused on her when she was on the screen. This was and is star quality.

Norma Shearer was born on 10 August 1902 in Westmount, a suburb of Montreal, Canada. Her Scottish father, Andrew, was president of Shearer, Brown and Wills Constructing Company. Her mother, Edith, was of English descent, anD though very little is known about how Andrew and Edith met, we do know their first child, Douglas, was born in 1899, then a daughter, Athole, in 1900 and Norma in 1902.

Andrew was laid back while Edith was flamboyant and stylish. Friends in Montreal claim the Shearers' marriage was not a happy one when the children were growing up. There was gossip that Edith was a heroin addict and unfaithful to her husband, but there is no evidence to prove these rumours to be true. She was a social climber as opposed to Andrew who stayed in the background. He was prone to manic depression as was Athole, a fact that frightened Norma throughout her lifetime. Edith saw in Norma a very talented and outgoing child who did everything well. She had an ear for music and began to take piano lessons when she was seven years old. Edith hoped Norma would be a concert pianist. Edith was so intent on on seeing her youngest daughter succeed, she tutored her at home. Norma said, 'I was afraid of school. I don't know why.'

When Norma's piano teacher Blossom Connelly died, Norma closed the piano and never took another lesson. 'My future and Miss Connelly were so intertwined,' she said, 'that it seemed impossible to imagine continuing alone.'

Edith decided it was best for her to attend school and make friends. Norma and her classmates went to the cinema and never missed an episode of *The Perils of Pauline*. Edith was thrilled when Norma said, 'I'd like to try acting. What do you think?'

'I think you can do anything,' Edith said. 'Do you remember the beauty contest you thought was hopeless? But you put your best foot forward and won it.'

'After I learned how to use eye shadow and liner effectively.'

'Every woman, no matter how beautiful, has to rely on make-up,' Edith replied.

Norma described her early-teen years as a 'pleasant dream', but in 1919 her father Andrew lost his business. They had to sell the family home and move into a small dreary house in an inferior suburb. Douglas went to work to help the family out and Athole, fighting bouts of depression, did the same. But Norma had made up her mind to be an actress. Edith took stock of her life. Her son Douglas had a good job at the Northern Electric Company and would make it on his own if he did not have to support his family. She had no feelings for her husband Andrew who had, in essence, given up all hope of recovering his losses and his pride.

'I've decided to go for it,' Edith told her daughters. 'My brother is married to an actress and living in New York. He manages a touring company and has connections. I sold the old upright piano for four hundred dollars. That will get us to New York. We'll make an adventure of it!'

In January 1920 the Shearer girls arrived in New York City, dressed to the nines. They didn't feel so elegant when they saw their rented room in an apartment building at 8th Avenue and 57th Street. Norma recalled, 'There was one double bed, a cot with no mattress, and a stove with one gas jet.The bathroom was at the end of a long dimly lit hallway. Athole and I took turns sleeping with mother in the bed but sleep was impossible, anyway, because the elevated trains rattled past our window every few minutes. The rent was seven dollars fifty a week.'

Edith got a job in a department store while Norma and Athole made the rounds, looking for work as extras in the movies. It's no surprise that Ziegfeld, who was casting his *Follies*, turned down Norma – flat. At five-feet three, she wasn't tall enough to be a Ziegfeld Girl. If she had been taller, her very stubby unattractive legs would have been a major drawback. Ziegfeld called her a 'dog', referring mainly to her crossed eyes and bad teeth that were eventually capped. While most girls might have wept over Ziegfeld's crude comments, Norma kept her feelings to herself and continued making the rounds, talking to other film extras and following up on their tips.

Norma and Athole were finally hired as extras for $5.00 a day by the Famous Lasky Players. The silent film was *The Flapper* with Olive Thomas, who married Mary Pickford's brother Jack and died mysteriously from barbiturate poisoning several months later. Norma managed a bit part and close-up in *The Flapper*, but the film no longer exists.

In need of money, Norma did some modelling. With little else to cheer her, she was proud to be called 'Miss Lotta Miles' by Kelly-Springfield tyre executives who liked the poster of her peeking out from one of their tyres. She modelled everything from rouge to housecoats, but the truth was Norma was not a successful model.

She was an extra in *The Restless Sex*, a film with Marion Davies, the mistress of newspaper mogul, William Randolph Hearst. In later years, Norma and Marion would become close friends. In *Way Down East* with Lillian Gish, Norma got up the nerve to talk to director D.W. Griffith about a screen test. He told her to forget about it and go back home. Norma almost took his advice, but to the rescue came talent agent Eddie Small, who got her work in *The Sign on the Door* with Norma Talmadge. However, *The Stealers* was the ultimate breakthrough though she didn't know it at the time. Norma played the sweet daughter of a corrupt minister, who finds a way to reform him. She got fourth billing in a case of unknowns. The *Los Angeles Times* said, 'The daughter is aptly interpreted by Norma Shearer.'

A good review did not pay the rent, however, and, with little money left, the Shearer women went back to Montreal. 'We spent a week mending our clothes,' Norma said. 'That was our excuse for leaving New York. Then Eddie Small sent me a telegram about an offer from Universal Studios in Hollywood so we borrowed money and rushed back to New York.' Edith, however, demanded the train fare for herself and Universal refused. Eddie Small managed to get Norma in a series of forgettable films that she said were good experience and earned her enough money to remain in New York. Her first leading role was in *The Man Who Paid* as the long-suffering wife of a Canadian trapper. Norma received glowing words from *Exhibitor's Herald* in New York; 'Miss Shearer's good looks are shown to advantage, and she not only photographs extremely well but shows no small amount of talent in the portrayal of her part.'

Now twenty years old, Norma was learning how to handle men by keeping her distance. 'I saw what happened to other young actresses when they let men get too familiar with them . . . they got dumped in short order.' Though Edith allowed Norma her freedom she had warned her repeatedly about social diseases. 'Never let a man know you like him,' was another piece of advice. More than likely, Norma was still a virgin.

Early in 1923 producer Hal Roach offered Norma a contract. Eddie Small was working on the terms when he received word that the Mayer Company in Hollywood wanted to sign Norma to a six-month contract, with options, for $150 a week. Louis B. Mayer was willing to pay Edith's train fare, as well.

Athole, who had been dating a writer, decided to get married rather than go to California. Edith disapproved, but attended the wedding shortly before leaving for Hollywood with Norma in the spring of 1923.

In newsreels she had seen famous actresses and soon-to-be-famous actresses arriving at the Pasadena Station in Los Angeles, greeted with an armful of roses. They always smiled, posed for pictures and then took the arm of a pudgy movie mogul who led them to a waiting limousine. 'Mother and I spent hours getting me ready for the greeting that I was sure would be waiting for me,' Norma said.

She chose her wardrobe very, very carefully, making sure her skirt was long enough to cover her unattractive legs. With the aura of a star she disembarked, smiled and waited. And waited. And waited. Edith spoke up, 'This is ridiculous. We'll take a taxi to the Hollywood Hotel. I understand it's not too expensive'.

Edith had done her homework. Though she expected a representative from the Mayer Company to greet them, she was prepared for anything. Norma was disappointed but she was captivated by this city of palm trees and orange groves. Another thrill was the Hollywood Hotel where Valentino tangoed at Thursday's tea dances and where he had spent his wedding night.

The next morning Norma put on her 'arrival' outfit and went to the Mayer Company on Mission Road. Still annoyed that no one had bothered to meet her at the station, she introduced herself to the receptionist in haughty fashion. Within minutes a young man appeared. 'Miss Shearer, we've been expecting you,' he said, motioning for her to follow him. Assuming he was an office boy she went into a small office with an unoccupied desk, looked around and waited. The young man took his place behind the desk, put his feet up and said, 'I'm Irving Thalberg.'

She was stunned that he was so young. Twenty-three, to be exact. Norma wanted him to know how important she was. 'I've had many offers from Hollywood,' she lied. 'In fact Universal offered me a lot of money before you did.'

Thalberg smiled. 'They didn't offer you *that* much, Miss Shearer.'

'How do you know that?' she asked sarcastically.

'Because I was at Universal and made the offer,' he said.

'Hal Roach was very generous, too.'

'Not *that* generous, Miss Shearer. You see, I was with Roach just before I joined Mayer. I've been following your career since I saw *The Stealers* and thought you deserved a chance.' He went on to explain she would have to make a screen test for *The Wanters*, her first proposed film. They would take it from there. In the meantime, the studio would help her find a house or apartment to rent.

Thalberg was gracious but he had a quiet authority that meant business. It's not known if Norma knew that Thalberg was the boy wonder of Hollywood and it's most eligible bachelor, but he impressed her as someone likely to be a sincere ally if she proved herself worthy. Unfortunately, Norma's first attempt at achieving this goal failed miserably. Her screen test was a disaster. A cameraman, who saw Norma crying in the hallway, had a talk with her, viewed the test and decided she had not been handled properly. With the studio's permission, he did another test, reminding Norma about the cast in her eye that she was able to correct on cue. With proper lighting, the new test met with Thalberg's approval. After the lead role in *The Wanters* was taken away from her, Norma knew she would have to succeed as a flapper in *Pleasure Mad* or

Mayer would not pick up her six-month option. Reginald Barker, the director, lost patience with her and complained to Mayer who called Norma to his office.

'He shouted at me,' she said of Barker. 'He frightened me.'

L.B. Mayer proceeded to show Norma what shouting was all about. Was she going to fight with a director and destroy her career? He called her a fool and a coward. She reacted as he hoped she would by insisting she was no coward. 'I'll show you!' she exclaimed.

Norma went back to the set and tore into her role of flapper. 'I took that scene, lock, stock and barrel, fur, fins and feather,' she said. *Pleasure Mad* got bad reviews, but *Variety* said, 'Little Norma Shearer manages to put over another wallop for herself in this picture that shows she can troupe.'

If Mayer and Thalberg had not been so busy forming Metro-Goldwyn-Mayer at the time, Norma might have been on the train back to New York. Her appearance on camera left much to be desired, as did her attitude. She came to Hollywood with her nose in the air, wanting to succeed but not knowing how to go about it. Highly strung and sensitive, Norma did not take criticism well. And criticism was something directors spouted freely and often. It would take six or seven quickie films before Norma would find her way as an actress. And as a woman.

As a maidservant in *Broadway After Dark*, Norma was directed by Monta Bell, who took an interest in her professionally and personally. He would direct her in several pictures, and propose marriage eventually. Norma was flattered by his regard for her and regained her confidence as an actress.

In *Empty Hands*, Norma played the part of a spoiled rich girl. It was filmed in Oregon and directed by Victor Fleming, a handsome bachelor and womaniser. Norma fell head-over-heels in love with forty-year-old Fleming, who took their affair in his stride. Most likely this was Norma's first intimate relationship and she took it seriously. Director George Cukor said, 'If she were going to go all the way' with anyone at the time, it would probably have been with Victor. He was positively irrestible to women. He had an overwhelming male charisma, projecting what would be more vulgarly known as 'penis impact'. Director Henry Hathaway recalled, 'I lived through that love affair she had with Victor Fleming. Every dame he worked with fell on her ass over him.'

The romance continued in Hollywood until Fleming became interested in the 'It' girl, Clara Bow, who was more experienced in the boudoir and far more attractive than Norma at the time.

By early 1924, the Shearers had moved into a rented bungalow at 2004

Vine located below the HOLLYWOODLAND sign. This famous landmark was Mack Sennett's idea to sell real estate in this growing community. Eventually the 'land' would be deleted.

Athole, whose marriage had ended, arrived with her infant son and joined the family in the three-bedroom house on Vine. Norma found herself with another family that spring – Metro-Goldwyn-Mayer.

Marcus Loew, who owned one of the largest theatre chains in the country, had purchased Metro Pictures to supply his theatres with movies. After Rudolph Valentino refused to renew his contract with Metro, Loew was advised to buy Goldwyn Studios in Culver City. Loew then bought out Mayer Pictures and hired Mayer and Irving Thalberg to be in charge. During these negotiations, movies were released with the trademark Metro-Goldwyn or Metro-Goldwyn-Mayer until the latter was established in 1924. Thalberg, as second vice-president and supervisor of production, reported to Mayer, first vice-president. He, in turn, reported to Marcus Loew and second-in-command Nicholas Schenck, both in New York.

On 26 April 1924, the stars gathered on the front lawn in Culver City, the site of Metro-Goldwyn-Mayer. From Goldwyn came Billy Haines, Eleanor Boardman, Conrad Nagel, Aileen Pringle, Mae Murray, Blanche Sweet and John Gilbert. From Metro came Ramon Novarro, Alice Terry, Buster Keaton and Viola Dana. From Mayer came Lon Chaney, Norma Shearer, Renee Adoree and Barbara La Marr.

Army and Navy airplanes flew in formation over the celebration, dropping rose petals. Three hundred naval personnel in white dress uniforms, were led by the Pacific Fleet. L.B. Mayer, in tears, told the assemblage,

> 'I hope that I can live up to this great trust. It has been my argument and practice that each picture should teach a lesson, should have a reason for existence. With seventeen of the best directors in the industry calling this great institution their home, I feel that this aim will be carried out . . . This is a great moment for me. I accept this solemn trust and pledge the best that I have to give.'

Mayer went on to say that Metro-Goldwyn-Mayer would reach the point of perfection never approached by any other studio. The company motto was *Ars Gratia Artis* – 'Art for Art's Sake'. Art Lahr, former head of

Goldwyn Pictures, then handed L.B. Mayer a giant key engraved in gold with one word – SUCCESS.

Actor Billy Haines recalled this event and said, 'While Mayer was speaking the gospel, all the stars were trying to make up their minds who they wanted to take to bed.'

Norma knew she had gained Thalberg's favour when he cast her as a circus bare-back rider in love with a lion tamer in Leonid Andreyev's *He Who Gets Slapped* with John Gilbert and Lon Chaney. Norma considered it an honour to be part of MGM's first official production. The film was a success, as was Norma in a film dominated by the great Lon Chaney. She was concerned about wearing a tutu but director Victor Seastrom used long shots when she rode horseback and focused on her from the waist up in other scenes.

Norma and John Gilbert had co-starred earlier that year in *The Wolf Man* and spent a great deal of time together. Observers said they enjoyed a brief romance, and who better to be involved with than John Gilbert after losing Victor Fleming. The fact that Gilbert was married to actress Leatrice Joy might have held Norma in check, but she admitted being enormously attracted to him. Her many biographers hint that she was in love with Irving Thalberg and biding her time until he gave her a nod. This may be true, but it surely didn't stop her from enjoying highly charged romances with other men. She was sure Thalberg had heard rumours about her lovers and that's what she wanted. She was testing him and he might have been testing Norma when he put her in *The Snob* with John Gilbert and directed by Monta Bell, who did not care if everyone knew he wanted to marry her.

In 1925 Norma signed a new contract with MGM for $1000 a week escalating to $5000 during the next five years. She was voted fourth on the list of the top box-office stars. Yet she felt she deserved better films. After Thalberg recuperated from a heart attack in January 1925, Norma approached him about her frustrations. He was surprised that she was dissatisfied because he had given her many good properties. She emphasised the fact that she had changed her image over the past year and was currently being miscast. Thalberg listened as he always did, saying very little if anything other than, 'MGM knows best.'

In July, as she was getting ready to leave for the day, Norma got a call. 'Miss Shearer, this is Mr Thalberg's secretary. He would like to know if you could attend the premiere of *The Gold Rush* with him this evening.'

'I'd be delighted,' Norma replied. She told a friend, 'I think he was listening in on the extension.' Thalberg picked her up in his black Cadillac limousine and she emerged with him to crowds of cheering people outside the Egyptian Theater. After the premiere Thalberg took her for dinner and dancing at the famous Coconut Grove. He dropped her off at 2004 Vine around midnight and did not ask for another date.

Thalberg's life was no secret. He had a weak heart, lived with his parents and was in love with actress Constance Talmadge, who preferred playing the field. Thalberg was so smitten with her he parked near her house at night to see who brought her home. When she married, he began seeing his old flame Rosabelle Laemmle, who let him know she'd marry him in a heartbeat. When Constance divorced and returned to Hollywood, Thalberg pursued her again. It isn't known if they engaged in sex or if he tried to avoid it, knowing that his limitations included premature ejaculation. Keeping up with Constance would have killed him according to his mother Henrietta, who reminded him doctors predicted he might not live to see his thirtieth birthday.

Thalberg had dated Rosabelle Laemmle off and on for a long time, but she was more impressed with who he was than what he wanted. His life was the motion-picture business and she had no interest in movies. If he was looking for an out with Rosabelle, he found it when they were in New York. Working late, he called to tell her he would send his car to pick her up. He'd meet her later. She refused to attend a public affair alone, forcing Thalberg to hurry home, get dressed and pick her up. He never saw her again.

Norma knew about Thalberg's women but she was willing to wait for him to call her again. It happened a year after their first date. Would she like to attend the premiere of King Vidor's film *Bardelys the Magnificent*? This time they were joined by Greta Garbo and John Gilbert, and King Vidor and Eleanor Boardman. Norma was thrilled to be part of this elite group.

Irving Thalberg was born on 30 May 1899 in Brooklyn, New York. Doctors said he had a congenitally defective heart and doubted he would live much beyond the age of thirty. His parents were German-Jewish immigrants who owned a department store. His mother, Henrietta, was Irving's faithful nurse through his health setbacks. A bright student and avid reader, he wanted to be a lawyer until he contracted rheumatic fever when he was sixteen. After his recovery, he took a business course at New York University. It was Rosabelle Laemmle's father, Carl, who offered Irving a job as his secretary at Universal Film Company in New York. In the summer of 1920, Carl asked Irving to join him at Universal City in California. Thalberg spent long hours learning the business and screening movies on his own. He became so valuable that Laemmle promoted him to general manager.

At the age-of twenty-two Thalberg became a producer but Laemmle refused to pay him accordingly so Irving accepted an offer from Hal Roach. When that job did not materialise, he went to see Louis B. Mayer, who took a liking to him right away. On 15 February 1923, Thalberg joined the Mayer Company at a salary of $600 a week. L.B. Mayer took a fatherly interest in the frail young man who padded the shoulders of his jacket to appear more robust. When Metro-Goldwyn-Mayer was formed, Thalberg got a percentage of the annual profits. He worked long hours seven days a week on such lavish productions as *The Merry Widow*, *Ben Hur* and *The Big Parade*. Despite his low profile, Hollywood labelled Irving Thalberg 'The Boy Wonder'.

Any girl who hoped to marry him would have to meet the approval of his protective mother, Henrietta, who moved west with her husband and daughter Sylvia to take care of Irving and run his household.

Henrietta did not approve of either the flighty Constance or the demanding Rosabelle. Nor did Norma, who felt she was a 'spare tyre' when Irving called her for a date. 'I guess Constance and Rosabelle are busy,' she told Edith. There is no doubt whatsoever that Thalberg carried a heavy torch for Constance. But Norma was so much in love with Irving, she didn't mind that she was third choice. He had his life and affairs and she had hers.

If she went out with Irving and his mother, Norma insisted he drop her off first while Henrietta waited in the car. When she went out with him alone, she made sure he was home by midnight.

Norma was serene and proper with Thalberg even though she had become a very flirtatious and sexy young lady. During production of *A Slave of Fashion* in which she played a small-town girl who makes it big in New York, Norma was overly playful with co-star Lew Cody, who was determined to chase her all the way to the bedroom. Norma knew he was a scallywag, but enjoyed his company and dated him often. Also in *A Slave of Fashion* was known homosexual Billy Haines who became one of MGM's biggest stars in the twenties. It was Billy who helped Clark Gable get a job as an extra in 1925 in exchange for sex. It was a one-time-only homosexual experience for Gable who was desperate for work at the time. And it was Billy who said of Norma, '. . . she was the one woman who really got a rise out of me, and for me, that's saying a mouthful!' Norma dated Billy, also, because he had a delightful sense of humour. Director George Cukor said, 'There was no romance here. Only sex.'

Lew Cody, who was accustomed to bedding his women, was perturbed by this. Billy called him a vain stuffed shirt. Lew said, 'As if I care what that queer says.' But Cody did care and reported to Mayer about Billy's activities with actor Ramon Novarro at a gay bordello on Wilshire Boulevard. Mayer was well aware that Haines was a homosexual, but he did not want the public to get wind of it. He closed down the bordello and was prepared to get rid of Haines if Thalberg hadn't stepped in to prevent it. Billy often served as escort for Irving's sister Sylvia and frequently joined the Thalberg family on vacations.

Norma continued to complain about her mediocre films to Thalberg. Often in tears, she sat in his office hoping for some encouragement. He reminded her it was the movies she disliked that made her popular at the box office, so apparently MGM was doing right by her. She had been rewarded with a substantial raise in pay, a $10,000 bonus, and L.B. Mayer had presented her with a diamond bracelet to show the studio's appreciation. He intimated she was ungrateful and should reconsider her objections. If he was busy, Thalberg reminded her about her contract, which stated she was obligated to make the films assigned to her. Norma said she received no satisfaction from Irving regardless of how often she complained.

Thalberg never gave her a hint that he, too, was frustrated. He was usually persuasive in his endeavours to placate his stars. He had gained Garbo's confidence and that was not an easy task. He got his way with L.B. Mayer more often than not. Even if they disagreed with Irving, they were satisfied. All but Norma, and this puzzled him. Intrigued him, too. He took pleasure in listening intently and then dismissing her without further discussion. When Norma's name was brought up for the role of an abused girl, Thalberg rejected the idea because 'she seems the type who can take care of herself'.

What went on in Irving's mind was a mystery. He lived for his work and was only seen socially if there was a business connection. At parties he talked about film making, at dinner he discussed movies, and he surrounded himself with actors, directors and production people. He was good company, however, because he was a born listener. His advice, if he chose to express it, was sound advice. He was a quiet man but not a dull one. Because of his reputation as a genius, his modesty was mistaken for aloofness. He accepted homosexuals without discrimination, as opposed to Mayer who was disgusted by anyone who was not heterosexual. Mayer revered motherhood and cursed those who spoke harshly of their mothers. Without knowing this, Thalberg mentioned his mother to Mayer at their first meeting – how Henrietta had nursed him day and night for eighteen years and how he was indebted to her. Mayer was touched. If he had any doubts about Thalberg, they were erased by his deep devotion to his mother. Irving was not a mother's boy, by any means. Henrietta did not control his life. Proof of this was her inability to get rid of Constance and Rosabelle. There were other women before and after Henrietta moved to California; the beautiful Bessie Love, Ziegfeld girl Peggy Hopkins Joyce and comedienne Marie Provost. There might have been more if it hadn't been for Constance Talmadge whom he met on a yacht and fell in love with at first sight.

Producer-writer Sam Marx said Thalberg was a different man with Constance. He laughed, his eyes sparkled, he was alive with happiness and never took his eyes off her. But Marx doubted they were sexually involved because he was afraid of letting her down. 'Constance would have laughed in his face,' Marx said. 'That would have destroyed him. But he and Rosabelle made love. I think she might have been his first because he knew her in New York. Her mother tried to arrange a marriage with Henrietta, who was against the idea because Irving was just getting started in Hollywood. He didn't want it anyway. Mayer might have tried to fix Irving up with one of his daughters but he dreaded the thought of either being a young widow.'

Marx went on to say that Thalberg hung out with John Gilbert, Victor Fleming, director Jack Conway and Howard Hawks.

> 'They played poker with high stakes and Thalberg was usually lucky. These guys were crazy about women and they loved to compare notes. They were hearty drinkers, too. Thalberg fitted in very well even though he couldn't keep up with them because of his health. MGM had a brothel for their actors and these guys went there. I know because I met Thalberg in the lobby. He was reading the newspaper waiting for the others to get dressed. Irving got a vicarious thrill talking to his buddies and, I'm sure, he found out who was sleeping with whom. I'm sure he knew about Norma's affairs. That's when he began taking her out. He might have been shocked at times but it also intrigued him. I don't think he knew what made Norma tick, but she sure as hell knew what made him tick.

Actress Louise Brooks had a dinner party in 1926. She said,

> All the place cards at dinner were books. In front of Thalberg's place was Dreiser's *Genius*. In front of Norma's place I put *The Difficulty of Getting Married* – she'd been trying and trying, and Irving's mother wanted him to marry a nice Jewish girl. It was so funny because Irving walked right in and saw *Genius* and sat down. But Norma kept on walking around. She wouldn't sit down in front of *The Difficulty of Getting Married*. Not at all!

Norma was still seeing director Monta Bell who told anyone who would listen how much he wanted to marry her. Hollywood insiders knew she was waiting for Thalberg to propose. Did he know she felt that way? Apparently so. According to Sam Marx, 'Norma told several people she was going to marry Irving. She came right out with it to Monta Bell, but Thalberg heard it from Jack Gilbert who said Irving was still very much in love with Constance and would love her always.'

In early 1927 Norma played the part of the barmaid in *The Student Prince* with Ramon Novarro. In the past she had filmed at an easy pace doing as many retakes as she needed. But director Ernst Lubitsch didn't see it her way and they clashed. Thalberg was summoned to the movie set. He listened to both sides, turned to Norma and said, 'Everyone has a lot to learn from Mr Lubitsch.' Thalberg should have taken his own advice. Lubitsch told him that Norma and Ramon Novarro were miscast in *The Student Prince* and the critics agreed. *The New York Times* said, '. . . Miss Shearer does not put her soul into the part.' *Life* thought Norma was 'laborious', and *Photoplay* wrote, 'Norma Shearer is miscast and Lubitsch isn't completely in his element.'

The Student Prince was supposed to be Norma's masterpiece but Thalberg wasn't thinking clearly. He had come to the conclusion that he wanted to get married and have children. Doctors predicted he might not make it to his thirtieth birthday, which was two years away. How much time did he have left? Constance wasn't interested in him and Rosabelle was out of his life.

Norma was finishing *The Student Prince* late in the day when she got a call from Thalberg to come to his office. When she got there he was sitting at his desk looking at a tray of diamonds. He looked up at her with a weak smile and told her to choose the ring she wanted. Norma said she held back tears that were inappropriate somehow, and picked out a ring.

L.B. Mayer went home that night and excitedly told his family, 'Irving's decided to marry her! There's no risk – everything will go on as it is. Henrietta's accepted the situation.'

It would be a September wedding and to make things more convenient for Irving, Henrietta agreed he and Norma should spend the summer at their beach house in Santa Monica. For the bride-to-be there would be no more passionate lovemaking. She would have to be as subdued in bed as she was in the parlour. To get what she wanted, Norma had to make sacrifices and satisfying sex was one of them. Living with Henrietta was another. The least of her worries was converting to Judaism.

Joan Crawford, who joined MGM in January 1925, was anxious for her first assignment. While she waited, Joan observed and made friends with the technicians who identified Thalberg as the young man tossing a silver dollar on the set talking to Norma. She knew right away that Shearer was playing up to the boss. Joan commented, 'I don't get it. She's cross-eyed, knock-kneed and she can't act worth a damn.' Needless to say, Joan was not happy to double for Norma in *Lady of the Night* in 1925. 'I don't look like her,' Joan told director Monta Bell.

'No problem,' he replied. 'Norma's playing a dual role so they'll only see the back of your head.'

From then on Crawford resented Shearer and decided to play the same game by making friends with Thalberg's production assistant, Paul Bern. But Joan worked harder than Norma without reward and that's what she said to Thalberg, who punished her with a B-western. When MGM announced his engagement to Shearer, Joan lamented, 'What chance do I have? She's sleeping with the boss.' But Crawford became a big star on her own. The consensus was that Shearer got the big productions, Garbo supplied the art and Crawford made the money to pay for them both, a frustrating truism for Joan.

Writer Anita Loos commented, 'Norma was bent on marrying her boss, and Irving, preoccupied with his work, was relieved to let her make up his mind . . .'

Norma told a friend in later years that Irving never said he loved her, but that he proved it in many other ways.

On 29 September 1927, Norma married Irving at his home at 9401 Sunset Boulevard. She wore a gown of soft ivory velvet studded with pearls and a yoke of handmade rose lace. The diamond pin on her bodice was a gift from Irving. The bridesmaids, wearing organdy gowns and hats, were

Marion Davies, Bessie Love, Sylvia Thalberg and L.B. Mayer's daughters, Irene and Edie. L.B. Mayer was best man and Douglas Shearer, who was now working in MGM's special effects department, gave the bride away.

The ceremony was conducted by Rabbi Edgar Magnin, who helped Norma with her vows in Hebrew when she stumbled over them. After a supper with bootleg champagne, the newlyweds took a train to the Del Monte Lodge on the Monterey Peninsula.

Norma did not have the pleasure of setting up her own household. She returned to a house that was not a home. Henrietta ruled the roost. She decided the newlyweds should have separate rooms, which was common in those days in Hollywood, but not at opposite sides of the house. Henrietta was, however, not the wicked old witch as portrayed. She knew that Norma intended to work and that her hours would differ from Irving's. If there was tension between the two women it had to do with Norma's plans to entertain. Often she prepared for the evening's dinner party before leaving for the studio and returned to a different setting. Norma accepted this because she was prepared for it. Her saving grace was that Henrietta was not invited to the elaborate dinner parties at Pickfair given by Mary Pickford and her husband Douglas Fairbanks Sr. Nor was she a guest at San Simeon, home of William Randolph Hearst and his mistress Marion Davis, who enjoyed giving costume-parties.

After a three-month vacation in Europe, Norma appeared in *The Actress* and *A Lady of Chance*, her last silent film. Following *The Jazz Singer* at Warner Brothers, Thalberg and Mayer admitted they had been sceptical about sound. It took an order from Nicholas Schenck to gear up for 'talkies'. Douglas Shearer was sent to Bell Laboratories in New Jersey where the latest sound equipment was being made. He managed to put a qualified staff together at MGM and, in August 1928, Leo the Lion roared for the first time. How many roars? One, two, or three? Mayer finally decided two fast roars, a pause and then a third.

Broadway Melody, MGM's first sound film, won the Academy Award for Best Picture of 1929. Thalberg's former girlfriend Bessie Love was in the film and received flowers from him on her first day on the set. When Norma found out she walked out on Irving, staying with Edith for several days until he made peace with her.

In her first talkie, *The Trial of Mary Dugan*, Norma played a brassy showgirl on trial for the murder of her boyfriend. The *New York Times* said, 'She reveals herself quite able to meet the requirements of that temperamental device – the microphone.' The *Los Angeles Times* wrote, 'She emerges as a definitely compelling actress of greater individuality than she has ever revealed in silent pictures.'

Norma was making $5000 a week to Irving's $4000, but he received thirty per cent of MGM's yearly profits. He had suffered heavy losses when the stock market crashed in 1929 and needed money desperately. Mayer knew that Nicholas Schenck would not approve a raise in pay so he reduced his own percentage of the profits by ten per cent and gave it to Thalberg.

Joan Crawford was being considered for *The Divorcee*, the screen adaptation of the banned book *Ex-Wife* about a divorced woman who gets even with her ex-husband by enjoying many affairs without commitments. Norma read the book and wanted the part. Irving didn't think she was the type. To prove she could do it, Norma went to photographer George Hurrell who was amazed at the preparation she put forth to change her image in his stills. 'Norma came to my studio in her yellow Rolls Royce,' Hurrell said. 'I found out later her husband didn't think she was glamorous enough for a particular role. Her hair was styled over one eye that was very becoming because she had a high forehead, She put on a silver lamé dressing gown that was low cut and slit up the front to show her legs that she crossed most effectively. She was beautiful and very, very sexy pose. she was not the old-Norma-Shearer any longer.'

Thalberg was astonished when he saw the still of his wife lounging seductively in an armchair. He was both amused and excited, and was convinced that his wife could handle *The Divorcee*. Not long into production, Norma discovered she was pregnant. Though she wanted to have children to please Irving, Norma's temperament was not suited to motherhood. Having babies interfered with her career and would ruin her figure. She was also afraid her fans would forget about her if she was absent from the screen for very long. She had morning sickness and fought with Henrietta about the corsets she wore to get into the slinky dresses for *The Divorcee*. Norma got through it with one thought in mind. Now that she and Irving had a child it was time to move into a home of their own. Somehow she managed to make *Let Us Be Gay* before giving birth to Thalberg Jr on 25 August 1930, at the Good Samaritan Hospital. When Norma returned home, it was to a rented house while a new beach house was being built. Like most movie stars, Norma would hug and hold her child for fan magazine photos and then hand the baby over to a nurse. She had done her duty as a wife and now it was time to get back to the movie set where she belonged.

Norma won an Oscar for Best Actress in *The Divorcee*. She was now on her way to being crowned MGM's Queen of the Lot. But she would have to fight for the roles she wanted. Irving did not always agree with her choices. If there was a good part in a film that other actresses were being considered for, the contest was over when Irving said, 'Norma would like to do that one.'

After *Strangers May Kiss*, Norma made *A Free Soul* with Clark Gable, a new contract player at MGM. He played a rough racketeer to Shearer's spoiled rich girl who likes rough sex and gets it from Gable. When she jabs that he's not good enough for her, he throws her on the couch. Shearer stands up to protest but is pushed back down – 'where you belong!' he tells her.

Audiences loved it. Here was a poor guy trying to make a crooked buck (who cared during the depression?), and here was a rich dame who changed her furs as often as she changed her stockings. Men cheered and women swooned. Thousands of letters were addressed to MGM about 'the guy who slapped Norma Shearer.' People often exaggerate when they're excited. Gable does not slap Norma in *A Free Soul*, but the nonexistent blow remains a legend.

The lovemaking between Gable and Shearer was so passionate that rumours spread about a romance off the set. Thalberg did not appreciate the talk about his wife but he had never seen her react to any of her leading men as she had to Gable. During production, Gable remarked to director Clarence Brown that Shearer wasn't wearing any underwear during the shoot. Was she trying to tell him something? 'She must be one hot lay if she can behave like that with the cameras rolling,' he exclaimed.

'That's a woman with limited sex,' Brown said.

'Apparently so,' Gable sighed. 'She kisses like a whore in heat.'

A Free Soul was nominated for Best Picture, Shearer for Best Actress. Neither won, but Lionel Barrymore walked off with his only Oscar for his portrayal of Norma's father.

The Thalbergs, at long last, moved into their ten-room French-provincial beach house at 707 Ocean Front in Santa Monica. Irving wanted a bigger house but Norma opted for cosier surroundings. It's also possible she was avoiding Henrietta's intrusion. There were two bedroom suites on opposite ends of the house, two guest suites, a large living and dining room, a library with a concealed movie screen, nursery and card room for Irving and his poker-playing buddies, a pool and *lanai* (veranda). Because the damp salt air was bad for Irving, the beach house was one of the first with air conditioning. The Thalberg's personal staff consisted of Norma's maid, a butler, chef, nurse for the baby, a cleaning woman, gardener and pool man. Their neighbours along the Pacific Coast Highway, as it was called in those days, were L.B. Mayer, Marion Davies and Douglas Fairbanks Sr with wife, Mary Pickford.

Approaching her thirtieth birthday, Norma was very concerned about appearance. After the birth of her baby, she swam with vigour every day in the pool, had massages to firm her body, and maintained a strict diet. She tried various kinds of make-up, spending hours in front of the mirror to improve her attractiveness, always concentrating on her beady eyes that were too close together. She admired Garbo's Silver Stone make-up with its translucent effect and went one tone lighter. On the screen Norma literally put her co-stars 'in the shade' since their make-up was darker. In later years, she wore this ghostly foundation in public, giving her, as described by author Gavin Lambert, the Kabuki-look. Joan Crawford referred to it as 'Norma Shearer's Ethiopian cast'. Her obsession to be as closely identified with the likes of Garbo, who was both stunning and exciting, did not go unnoticed by Thalberg who understood the quirks of actresses. He was miffed, however, that she lingered too long in her dressing room fussing over her make-up. When her directors complained about it, he had a talk with Norma who made it a point to be on time.

Now that his wife was 'Queen of the MGM Lot', Irving wanted her identified with the theatre by casting her in such famous plays as Noel Coward's *Private Lives* and Eugene O'Neill's *Strange Interlude*. These film productions, however, lacked the sophistication and amusement that came across in live theatre. *Private Lives*, the story of a divorced couple who stay at the same hotel with their new spouses, was not right for Norma, who overacted in the comedy sequences – almost forcing herself to be comical. Co-star Robert Montgomery worked at an easier pace and lent the style lacking in Norma's performance.

Strange Interlude revolves around a married woman with an impotent husband. She has an affair with her doctor (Gable), gets pregnant, and tells her husband the child is his. Clark Gable, who sported a moustache for the first time, did his best to get out of doing the movie and he was right. His role of the glum doctor was very unlike his screen image, but Mayer told him, 'Hell, you're *knocking up* Norma in this one. You only knocked her in a chair your last time out.'

Because of the daring theme, reviews were mixed. Those critics who liked *Strange Interlude* loved it. Those who did not, hated it, as expressed by

Alexander Bashky in the *Nation*:

> For once Hollywood has dared to produce a picture that deals with life in terms of adult intelligence. But though the courage thus shown deserves every credit, the outgrowth of this courage, the film itself, is hardly a feather in the producer's cap. It conforms faithfully to its Hollywood type of uninspired crossbreed of the stage and screen, and it is badly miscast in its two principal parts. Neither the beautiful but cold Norma Shearer, nor the uncouth Clark Gable are the actors for the parts . . .

Nonetheless, the Thalbergs considered *Strange Interlude* a rewarding accomplishment. Irving agreed that George Cukor would have done a better job of directing but he was not available.

The year 1932 was not a happy one for the Thalbergs. Irving's good friend and business associate Paul Bern married 'The Blonde Bombshell' Jean Harlow on 2 July. It was an odd union, but the Thalbergs attended the wedding reception and hoped for the best. On 5 September, Bern was found at home with a bullet in his head and a gun clutched in his hand. MGM cleverly covered up many of the details to protect Jean Harlow, but over the years more information has emerged. Under no circumstances did Mayer want Jean anywhere near the scene of Bern's suicide, but she was the one who found his body. As instructed by the studio, she did not notify the police. She called MGM publicity chief, Howard Strickling. He got in touch with L.B. Mayer who rushed Jean to her mother's house.

Norma and Irving were having a luncheon for the Goldwyns at their beach house when they heard the news. Thalberg was in a daze watching Bern's body being removed but he pulled himself together for the sad task of telling Jean who pretended to be shocked by collapsing on the balcony of her mother's house.

Irving was shattered by Paul's death. Though he understood Mayer's protecting Harlow at all costs, he was appalled to what lengths he would go. Bern had an 'undersized' penis and was supposedly impotent even though he was linked with many beautiful women. Mayer's theory was to make Harlow the innocent victim and Bern the depressed husband who could not perform his duties as a husband so he shot himself. Sadly, this was partly true, but Thalberg was furious that Mayer would make such intimate details public. He attended Bern's funeral and wept. When he got home he went into seclusion for several days. Quietly he went on with his work, but Irving's suffering was apparent. *Fortune* said that Thalberg 'weighed 122 lbs after a good night's sleep', but 'in frantic moments he appears as a pale and flimsy bag of bones held together by concealed bits of string'.

Deeply affected by the loss of his friend, Thalberg was tired and depressed, and fed up with Mayer's insensitivity. He told Norma that he was going to terminate his contract. She saw her glamorous life at MGM pass before her like a shining comet falling from the sky filled with 'more stars than there are in the heaven'. But she told Irving, 'I'll go with you, of course.'

Thalberg met with Nicholas Schenck and Mayer, who stormed out in a rage. Schenck, however, was concerned that Irving would be hired by another studio, and he didn't want that to happen. He offered Thalberg 100,000 shares of Loew's stock at twenty per cent of the market value. The boy genius was taken aback. How many times had he fought over money? How often did he have to prove his worth before getting satisfaction? Now that he sincerely wanted to leave MGM because he was worn out and fed up, he was handed a plum he couldn't refuse.

Norma was relieved. Though she was married and financially secure, MGM had been her home for nearly ten years. Like Irving, she could make pictures at another studio, but none as glamorous and prestigious as MGM. She and Irving discussed what films she would like to do. Both agreed on *Marie Antoinette* but this would be a big production and would take a year or so to get organised. Irving suggested *The Barretts of Wimpole Street*, but Norma did not want to play an invalid. Joan Crawford said, 'Norma liked to make love in her movies. She got her thrills that way.'

On 24 December 1932, MGM shut down early for the annual Christmas party or, as Anita Loos referred to it, 'the MGM orgy'. Secretaries, hairdressers and receptionists sat on the executives' laps. There was plenty of drinking, kissing and disrobing. Music was blasting while ladies of the night were snuck in the back door. It was a night that many wanted to forget and often did with a hangover that dulled the memory.

Norma went home early but Irving stayed at the party to celebrate his victory and have some fun that was not hard to find. The office girls rushed into his office, covering his face with lipstick. He had more to drink than usual and left around eleven o'clock. On Christmas morning he had his second heart attack. Norma called the doctor who examined him and diagnosed a 'mild coronary'. Irving did not have to be hospitalised, however. The doctor recommended plenty of bed rest without visitors or phone calls. Norma turned away Mayer and Henrietta with a pleasant but firm smile. In February Thalberg was recuperating nicely and told Norma he'd like to take their annual European vacation before going back to work. Mayer took it upon himself to hire his son-in-law David Selznick to produce films at MGM. Irving felt he should have been consulted first and, once again, the two men had a disagreement.

Thalberg was given the impression he had been replaced, but eventually he would have his own production unit at MGM with a lighter workload and time to concentrate on Norma's films. On his way back from Europe he met with Nicholas Schenck who told Irving, 'You'll report directly to me from now on, not Mayer.'

'He won't like that,' Irving said with a crooked smile.

'That doesn't concern me so it shouldn't bother you,' Schenck replied.

Norma had been off the screen for over a year and, though she did not like Irving's choice of *Riptide*, she did it for him. It was a flop despite Irving's rewrites and retakes. Perhaps it was the worn-out story of an unfaithful wife or perhaps it was Norma's lack of enthusiasm or perhaps it was Thalberg's trying to get back into the swing after so much bitterness between him and Mayer. The truth was *Riptide* had failed, so Norma cheered up her husband by agreeing to play Elizabeth Barrett Browning in *The Barretts of Wimpole Street*. Though Norma was splendid in the film, she felt the part of an invalid was too close to home. Athole, who had two children by her second husband, director Howard Hawks, had a nervous breakdown and would eventually be institutionalised. Norma was suffering from anxiety attacks and had a dreaded fear that she would have to endure shock treatments like her sister who was diagnosed as schizophrenic.

Irving, who had read and absorbed Freud, told his wife to accept Athole's condition and get on with her life. Norma blamed Howard Hawks rather than admit heredity had anything to do with it but she, too, was showing signs of instability. Irving decided it was time for Norma to sink her teeth into the role of the sickly Elizabeth Barrett pampered into weakness by her father (Charles Laughton) and brought back to life by Robert Browning (Fredric March). Laughton's portrayal of Elizabeth's father was a touchy one since there was an incestuous overtone. He conveyed it with a gleam in his eyes that said it all without dialogue. Irving and Norma became very friendly with Laughton, who hesitated to do more films at MGM because he was a homosexual. It was no secret in Hollywood that, during Irving's absence, Mayer gave Billy Haines an ultimatum when he was arrested for picking up a sailor – give up your gay lifestyle or else. Billy refused and his career in movies was finished. Mayer kept the scandal out of the newspapers to protect MGM's image and allowed Billy's contract to expire. Haines went on to become a very successful interior decorator.

Thalberg was grateful to get Laughton for *The Hunchback of Notre Dame* and *Mutiny on the Bounty* as Captain Bligh.

The Barretts of Wimpole Street was nominated for Best Picture and Norma for Best Actress. However, *It Happened One Night* with Claudette Colbert and Clark Gable swept the Academy Awards that year.

In late October 1934 Norma found out that she was pregnant again. As with the first baby, she accepted the news with mixed emotions. At thirty-three, she worried about how long her movie career as a glamorous leading lady would last. She had set a high goal for herself and achieved it with clever make-up, expert lighting and direction. But was time running out? Having a baby took a toll on her figure as well as her mental stability. She did not like to be seen in public when she was pregnant though she could hardly avoid it since Irving made a point of attending premieres and other Hollywood functions to keep in touch with his peers in the industry. He was, however, thrilled to find out he would be a father again and was sure it would be a daughter this time. He also felt it was a boost to his virility. It was all right, he told Norma, that her film projects were shelved for a while. They would do *Romeo and Juliet* and then the ultimate, *Marie Antoinette*, before she retired.

Meanwhile, Irving kept busy with *Mutiny on the Bounty* as well as the Marx brothers in *A Night at the Opera*. Groucho Marx said he was often frustrated with Irving who always kept them waiting for hours. On one occasion, the brothers stripped naked and were roasting hot dogs in Thalberg's office fireplace when he returned.

Though Thalberg was not overseeing as many films, he was making bigger and better ones that demanded more attention and more responsibility. Norma feared he was overdoing it, but he was more determined than ever to extend himself professionally and socially. No longer having to report to Mayer, Irving had the freedom to use his talent freely, and the results of such classics as *Grand Hotel* proved how extremely creative he was. If Norma was concerned about his health, she knew he could not live without his work. She could only do what Henrietta had done, be supportive, make him a mild scotch and soda when he got home, make sure he had a hot meal, and a good night's sleep.

Norma was most supportive and, despite her pregnancy, attended dinner parties and other social affairs, making her usual grand entrance, arriving late and standing in the doorway with a glamorous pose that commanded attention. Irving gave her the spotlight and slipped off to discuss business with one of the guests. There were rumours that the marriage was over, but nothing could have been further from the truth. Norma was very much in love with her husband. She was not satisfied sexually but she did not take a lover. She was a devilish flirt and kissed her leading men with fervour, but there was never a hint of disloyalty on her part. Carrying her second baby, Norma worried about being left alone with two children. She was not and never would be a devoted mother. Irving, on the other hand, found the time to play with his son and doted over him on their European vacation. A close friend said, 'Norma loved her children, but she wasn't close to them.'

On 13 June 1935, Katharine Thalberg was born at the Good Samaritan Hospital. Sam Marx joked, 'Norma said father and child are doing very well.'

Norma did not waste time getting herself in shape for *Romeo and Juliet*. Though many doubted she could do Shakespeare, Norma studied with British stage veteran Constance Collier and conferred with director George Cukor. Thalberg brought in John Tucker Murray, an authority on Elizabethan theatre, and Professor William Strunk, who had been the Shakespearean advisor on Katharine Cornell's stage production of *Romeo and Juliet*. Thalberg was given a million-dollar budget though he would double that figure.

British actor Leslie Howard was cast as Romeo, Basil Rathbone as Tybalt and John Barrymore as Mercutio. Norma was highly amused by Barrymore, who was losing his fight with the bottle, but he struggled through, occasionally forgetting his lines and showing up late. Through it all, Norma could be heard giggling when he 'rewrote' Shakespeare. 'He heareth not, he stirreth not, he moveth not.' Then a pause, 'He pisseth not.'

Thalberg tried to get him to say his lines correctly. Barrymore said, with a wicked grin, 'Just once I will say it and thou mayst see how it stinketh.'

Romeo and Juliet was not a success. Critics were favorable without a hint of enthusiasm. They were kind to Norma whose efforts were admirable. She had tackled Shakespeare and got through it even though she was an unlikely Juliet at thirty-three. Observers said she took on the role off the set as well, acting and looking younger than her years.

Thalberg had no time for regrets. He was involved in future productions of *Maria Antoinette*, *Camille*, and *The Good Earth*.

On Labor Day, Irving and Norma went to Del Monte Lodge where they had spent their honeymoon. Their guests for the weekend were his bridge friends Jack Conway and his wife, director Sam Wood and Chico Marx. Despite a chilly breeze coming in from the ocean and despite Norma's pleas that he wear a sweater, Irving did not want to be pampered in front of his buddies and lingered on the veranda in the cool night air. When they returned to Los Angeles, he came down with a head cold. On Tuesday 8 November, he worked all day and went to the Hollywood Bowl for the dress rehearsal of Max Reinhardt's production of *Everyman*. Two nights later he and Norma attended the premiere, but the next morning he woke up with chills and a fever. Irving was diagnosed with a throat infection but did not respond to medication. When he had difficulty breathing, a specialist diagnosed lobar pneumonia, but said Irving's heart was not affected.

On Sunday 13 September, he missed MGM's picnic. At this annual outing, the tug-of-war was the highlight – Mayer leading one team and Thalberg the other. Norma sent a telegram in Irving's name: ONLY ILLNESS KEEPS ME FROM BEING WITH YOU.

The following morning Irving Thalberg died at the age of thirty-seven.

Norma called L.B. Mayer who rushed to the beach house and broke down in tears. She told him that Irving regretted their broken friendship and how often they discussed those glorious days when Metro-Goldwyn-Mayer was born. Though Mayer might have been pleased to regain whatever power he lost to Thalberg, he was deeply saddened by the death of the genius he once embraced as his son.

On 17 September, the day of Irving Thalberg's funeral, MGM closed down. At 10:00 a.m., when the service was scheduled, the other Hollywood studios observed five minutes of silence. A crowd of over 5,000 gathered outside the B'nai B'rith Temple on Wilshire Boulevard to watch the great stars arrive. Wearing a black veil, Norma arrived with Howard Hawks and Irving's parents. Rabbi Magnin praised Thalberg's creative mind and called him 'sweet and kind and charming'. He spoke about Irving and Norma – 'a love greater than in the greatest motion picture I have ever seen, *Romeo and Juliet*.' Norma sobbed uncontrollably when Grace Moore sang the Twenty-third Psalm, but pulled herself together to leave the temple, walking behind Irving's coffin of burnished copper. He was interred at Forest Lawn Memorial Park in the Sanctuary of the Benediction. The most opulent floral tribute came from Mayer in the form of a huge throne of white gardenias with a caged dove suspended above it.

Five months after Irving's death, *The Good Earth* was released with a tribute – 'To the memory of Irving Grant Thalberg, we dedicate this picture – his last great achievement.' The new MGM administration building was also named after him.

The Motion Picture Academy inaugurated the Irving G. Thalberg Award to be presented each year to a deserving member of the Academy.

Though Irving had been frail for some time, his death came suddenly, brought on by a simple head cold. In shock and grieving, Norma faced an uncertain future in films without her husband. She was still under contract to MGM, but was not bound to it without Irving. Her agent, Charles Feldman, told her MGM wanted to proceed with *Marie Antoinette* after spending half a million dollars on movie sets and costumes. Norma asked and was given sixty days to think it over. During this time she paid regular visits to Forest Lawn Cemetery, placing flowers at Irving's marble tomb.

The pressure of the past few weeks caught up with Norma. She came down with a serious case of pneumonia and was confined to bed for several weeks. Henrietta and Edith took over the household and care of the children during Norma's illness. When she recovered there were legal issues to be considered. Irving's estate, estimated to be $10 million, turned out to be only $4.5 million that eventually dwindled to only $1 million after back taxes were paid. Still to be taken into account were shares of stock that Mayer refused to acknowledge now that Irving was no longer living. Norma fought back with a vengeance and won. She used Mayer's tactics by leaking out the news that MGM refused to live up to their obligations. She went as far as to plead poverty, which got a few chuckles in Hollywood. Norma told columnist Louella Parsons that she would not go back to work for a studio that did not live up to its obligations. Norma also encouraged rumours that she was being considered for the part of Scarlett in *Gone With the Wind*. This infuriated Mayer because Thalberg had convinced him not to buy Margaret Mitchell's best-selling novel. The pressure was on Mayer who remained stubborn until Nicholas Schenck intervened and gave Norma the shares of stock that had influenced Irving not to leave Metro. With the legalities out of the way, MGM agreed to pay Shearer $150,000 a picture and gave her a $900,000 bonus in July 1937.

Columnist Hedda Hopper said, 'Norma gave you the impression she was a poor widow about to be put out in the street with her two starving children. She was entitled to Irving's share, yes, but what she didn't say was that her and Irving's money were separate so her earnings were stashed away. The widow Thalberg was rich, rich, rich and getting richer.'

Ten months after Irving's death, Norma began accepting invitations to parties and nightclubs. Usually with another couple, she was seen in the company of David Niven and Douglas Fairbanks Jr. But when she began *Marie Antoinette*, Norma limited her social life, as was her habit. She had endless fittings for over thirty magnificent Renaissance gowns made of imported brocade, silver and gold laces, and silks. She had to practise walking gracefully in wide skirts lined with thick crinolines, which was no easy feat.

There was casting to be considered as well. Robert Morley played her husband, Louis XVI, and Tyrone Power her lover Count von Fersen. Norma met Power at a dinner party and was immediately attracted to the handsome 24-year-old actor. Though he was under contract to 20th Century-Fox, she managed to convince Mayer to loan out one of his stars in exchange for Power. Mayer might not have been so agreeable if he did not have revenge in mind. *Marie Antoinette* was an expensive film to produce and Norma demanded many retakes until she was perfect. She and Irving had chosen Sidney Franklin to direct the picture because he was patient and understanding to her whims. Mayer wanted to speed up production and told Norma he was replacing Franklin with 'One-Take' Woody Van Dyke, who was known for getting his films finished quickly.

Norma was crushed. She knew Mayer was deliberately trying to upset her and she was determined he would not have his way. She rehearsed with the cast before an important scene so they would get it right the first time and it worked. When Norma tripped on her skirt and fell, there was a moment of silence until Norma kicked up her heels and laughed. Van Dyke, who expected her to be ruffled, was impressed by her sense of humour. As for Woody's directing, she said there was something to be said for spontaneity.

It was obvious that Norma was seducing Tyrone Power in their love scenes. He felt it, too, and did not want to be involved with any woman (or man) who was overly anxious. Power, who enjoyed affairs, might have been Norma's lover for a night or a week, but he sensed she wanted a more rewarding and lasting relationship. This turned him off.

On the prowl, Norma met thirty-year-old Jimmy Stewart, a newcomer at MGM, at a party. A bit tipsy, he told her she was the most beautiful creature he had ever seen. Norma was overwhelmed by the young man who couldn't get away from her for six weeks. He crouched down in the back seat of her yellow Rolls-Royce, embarrassed by the attention he was getting on his dates with 'The Queen of the Lot.' Norma gave him a gold cigarette case studded with diamonds, but when she asked for a cigarette in public, Jimmy fumbled around in his pocket for a pack of Lucky Strikes.

With Stewart out of her life, Norma asked Tyrone Power to escort her to the gala premiere of *Marie Antoinette*, and he obliged. Mayer threw a party at the Trocadero where Power left her to be with Annabella, a French actress, whom he would marry. Norma enjoyed the evening in the company of Mayer and Woody Van Dyke.

Marie Antoinette received mixed reviews. *Variety* said of the film, 'Produced on a scale of incomparable splendour and extravagance, it approaches real greatness as cinematic historical literature.'

New Yorker thought the picture was 'a resplendent bore.'

The Great Romantic Films said, 'Norma Shearer dominates the film throughout, not only because scriptwriters, director and all concerned have focused on her but because her beauty and talent magnetise the attention. It takes a true star to shine amidst so much glittering splendour and mammoth production opulence; there is pageantry; there are revolutionary onslaughts, palace stormings, court balls, crowded theatre scenes – in all of them the star is the centrepiece.'

There were items in the gossip columns that Norma was going to play Scarlett O'Hara in *Gone With the Wind*, but her fans reacted with hundreds of letters saying she was too dignified to play the bitchy southern belle. The author, Margaret Mitchell, thought Norma was a great actress but she would have been miscast as Scarlett. So Norma told Mayer she'd like to do Robert Sherwood's *Idiot's Delight* with Clark Gable. In this delightful film, Gable first meets Shearer in an Omaha burlesque house. They have a brief affair and go their separate ways until years later when they meet again in Europe, but Shearer is posing as a Russian countess and denies they ever met. *Time* considered the movie 'first rate.' The *New York Times* raved, 'If you don't see it, you'll be missing one of the year's events.'

Though Gable was engaged to Carole Lombard, he might have considered giving Norma a tumble. His restraint may have been inspired by ongoing loyalty to Thalberg. Gable was usually happy to accommodate a lady, but turned one down when he found out her father was a Mason.

In late 1939, Norma ran into nineteen-year-old Mickey Rooney in New York. They had dinner and she invited him to her suite at the Waldorf Astoria for a nightcap. In his comical and revealing book, *Life is Too Short*, Mickey wrote, 'We had a drink, sitting on the couch together. She edged over to me, getting very kittenish, very languid. When she turned her face toward mine and closed her eyes, I finally realised what was up.' Reluctant to make a move, he kissed her hand and said good night. Back in Hollywood, however, Norma let him know she wanted him. They confined their lovemaking to her elaborate trailer that had been built for her during *Marie Antoinette*. 'Her French boudoir,' Mickey said, 'was entirely appropriate for our liaison – lovemaking French style, with me sitting on her couch, my pants at my ankles and her on her knees. Here was the grand lady herself copulating with Andy Hardy.'

Mayer found out and put an end to the affair before the Hollywood gossip columnists got wind of it. There is no doubt that Mayer had his hands full with *Photoplay*'s scandalous article about 'Hollywood's Unmarried Husbands and Wives', citing Robert Taylor and Barbara Stanwyck, and Clark Gable and Carole Lombard as living together without benefit of marriage. Mayer got both couples to the altar in a hurry. He did not need further scandal revolving around America's favourite son, Andy Hardy, in bed with Irving Thalberg's widow!

It's not known what Mayer said to Norma but it had to be a very embarrassing experience for her. She had worked hard to gain the power to stand up to him and then lost it by having sex with a nineteen-year-old boy, who just happened to be the most popular star in the world.

Norma was looking for the part of a sophisticated but naughty woman of the world but she did not want to antagonise Mayer at this time. If she thought he might leak her seduction of Mickey Rooney to the press, she was mistaken. Of all his stars, it was Rooney whom Mayer would protect at any cost.

The part of Mary Haines in *The Women* dominated the picture but she is a married woman very much in love with her husband who, she finds out from her catty girl friends, is unfaithful. Norma did not want to be goody-goody again, but she agreed to do the picture that had an all-woman cast of rich busybodies who gossip behind each other's back. A successful play by Clare Boothe Luce, *The Women* had to be toned down for the screen but maintained its spicy flavour.

George Cukor, who was referred to as 'the woman's director' had been fired from *Gone With the Wind* after clashing with Clark Gable, who resented being referred to as 'dear' by the gay director. Gable was uncomfortable knowing Cukor must have heard about his 'sexual encounter' with Billy Haines, who was a good friend of Cukor. Victor Fleming took over and won an Oscar for directing *Gone With the Wind*, and Cukor was assigned to *The Women*.

Joan Crawford asked Mayer for the part of Crystal, who is having an affair with Shearer's husband in the film. He thought the role was too insignificant for her, but Joan insisted. And so, at long last, Crawford and Shearer would come face to face on the movie set. Joan demanded equal billing and, though Norma's contract denied this, Mayer convinced her to make an exception. Not to be outdone, Rosalind Russell asked for the same courtesy and was turned down by Norma. Russell called in sick to get her point across and was afforded third billing on the screen under the names of Shearer and Crawford.

The rivals had only one scene together. This occurred in the fitting room where Norma tells Joan the outfit she's wearing would not please her husband. Joan replies, nose to nose with Norma, 'When Stephen doesn't like what I wear I take it off!' And Joan said it with gusto and pleasure. But when she had to read lines to Norma off-camera, Crawford knitted an afghan with large knitting needles that distracted Norma, who complained. 'Mr Cukor, would you kindly tell Miss Crawford her knitting needles are distracting.' Joan pretended not to hear and continued knitting. Norma then asked Cukor to read the lines himself and send Joan home. Crawford got up to leave and Cukor took her aside. 'I want you to apologise,' he said.

'I will not. I'll send her a telegram,' Joan replied, and she did just that. What was in that wire isn't known. Publicity chief Howard Strickling claimed Joan said she had no idea her knitting needles were distracting since no one else complained about it. Apologise? Never.

During production, the leading ladies took time off for stills. An hour late, photographer Laszio Willinger called Crawford, whose dressing room was across the street from his studio.

'You're late,' he said. 'What's the problem?'

'I'm waiting for my limousine,' Joan said.

'But, Joan, I'm just across the street.'

'It's in my contract that I take a limousine.'

Willinger saw Crawford get into the car and noticed Norma going by in her limousine. Round and round they went. The photographer called Strickling who said, 'Shearer is not going to come in until Crawford does, and Crawford is not going to come in until Shearer does. I'll have to stand in the middle of the street and stop them.' Strickling waved down both cars and delivered the ladies. Norma walked in the door first while Strickling held Joan from trying to squeeze in too.

Rosalind Russell was already at the photo studio and emerged with spike heels and a hat with big feathers. Norma accused her of overdressing.

Russell, who didn't give a damn, said, 'Maybe so, but I sure as hell am going to wear it!'

Willinger posed the three women on stairs, turned his back for a few seconds, looked through the camera lens and saw only legs. As one moved up, the others followed. He took as many shots as possible, but with the ladies shifting for the number-one position, he got only three shots.

Norma became impatient and asked Willinger, 'Don't you think it's about time you started working with the stars and send Miss Russell home?'

Joan was in heaven . . .

The Women was a huge success. Shearer and Crawford were both applauded for their performances. The *New York Times* raved about the cast of women, 'They're really appallingly good and so is their picture.'

In the spring of 1940 Norma went to New York at the invitation of the Charles Boyers. At a party given for her, she met actor George Raft, forty-four. There was an immediate mutual attraction that led to the bedroom only hours after they were introduced. In August they sailed on the *Normandie* to Europe with the Boyers.

George Raft was born in the Hell's Kitchen area of New York where he worked as a hoofer-gigolo in local dance-halls. In 1929 he made his film debut in *Queen of the Nightclubs* and went on to appear in gangster roles. His most famous was the coin-tossing hood in *Scarface*. His private life made the news while he was dancing in New York, connecting him to mobsters like Bugsy Siegel and Lucky Luciano. When asked about his gangland connections he replied, 'Friends are friends. It's a cold world out there.' One of his better films was *Bolero* with Carole Lombard. When she was asked who was Hollywood's greatest lover, she replied, 'George Raft . . . or did you mean on the screen?'

After her divorce from William Powell, Lombard had many flings and one of them was with George Raft whom she considered more agreeable because 'when George givs me a smile or a present I don't hear wedding bells behind the thought.' George, who admitted being in love with Carole, kept a blown-up picture of her over his bed for many years. Since Norma was spending as much time at George's house as her own, he obviously took down the revealing picture of Lombard.

What Raft lacked in height he made up for in bed, according to Pin-Up Girl, Betty Grable. In 1932, George married actress, Grayce Mulrooney, but left her a few months later for wealthy Virginia Pine whom he was seeing when he met Norma. Romantic and shrewd, Raft preferred the company of the upper crust and, in his opinion, Norma was the epitome of class. They toured Europe and continued their affair in Hollywood. He took an interest in her children, who got along with him famously. When George proposed marriage, Norma accepted. The only problem was convincing his wife to give him a divorce. Meanwhile, Norma and George were seen everywhere in Hollywood much to the amusement of L.B. Mayer, who got a chuckle when the couple made a grand appearance at the Academy Awards. Edith, who considered Raft a common hoodlum, was shocked by Norma's flaunting of the affair.

George met with his wife Grayce and their attorneys. She demanded $500,000 and 20 per cent of his earnings, knowing he could not afford it. Hollywood insiders wondered why Norma didn't come up with the needed money if she loved George. The answer was simple. Norma had her pride and she was very close with a buck so she faced the fact that George would never be free to marry her and she bowed out. In October 1941, Raft told the press, 'We had a wonderful romance . . . She is the swellest person I have ever known, and I wish I could tell you that we are going to be married soon.'

Norma said it was very sad but necessary, and turned her thoughts to making movies. *Escape* had to do with an American (Robert Taylor) who is trying to rescue his mother (Nazimova) from the hands of the Nazis. He enlists the help of a widowed American-born German countess (Shearer) who is under the protection of a German general (Conrad Veidt). Taylor wants Shearer to return to America with him and his mother, but she chooses to remain with the ill Veidt. Audiences are kept in suspense until the surprise ending. *Modern Screen* wrote: 'One of the most poignantly dramatic films of the year is *Escape*, a gripping and spine-tingling melodrama. Norma Shearer and Robert Taylor are excellent, and the subject matter is very provocative.'

Mayer offered Norma *Mrs Miniver* and *Madame Curie*, but she did not want to make heavy films. Though Greer Garson won an Oscar for *Mrs Miniver*, Norma had no regrets because she did not want to play a middle-aged wife and mother with grown children. This is sad because she would have been a believable Mrs. Miniver, a role that might have turned her career around and kept her on the screen a little longer. Turning forty frightened Norma, who clung ferociously to youth. She had spurned the role of Mrs Miniver for the same reason she chose to keep her own children in the background.

In December 1941, Shearer began *We Were Dancing* with Melvyn Douglas. They played two penniless aristocrats who sponge off the rich.

Photoplay said about the film, 'Too utterly utter and all that sort of rot, my deah . . .' *Time* thought *We Were Dancing* was 'embarrassing'. Norma's peers suggested she was living in the past, wearing her stark white make-up, checking and double-checking the lighting, admiring herself in the mirror longer than her co-stars could abide, and asking repeatedly how everyone liked her lightened hair styled in a feather cut. Melvyn Douglas did not know at the time that Norma's ultra-white make-up put everyone else in the 'shade.' He told author Lawrence Quirk, 'Norma was delightful to work with but she did want everything her own way, and we had to wait around for what seemed forever while she got the lighting and angles she felt were necessary for herself . . . I was photographed more lousily in that picture than in anything I did in that period. I was kept in the shadow and half shadows . . .'

Mayer told an associate he thought Norma was uneasy, flighty and restless. 'She's not getting enough sex,' he said. 'She's having one-night stands with guys like Howard Hughes. I wonder who's richer, Shearer or Hughes?'

For her next and last film under her current MGM contract, Norma chose *Her Cardboard Lover* about a woman who hires a handsome young man (Robert Taylor) to keep her away from a former lover (George Sanders). The film was another frothy comedy with a silly theme and, as Robert Taylor put it, 'There was a war going on so I had more important things on my mind.' Gearing themselves for war, Americans ignored *Her Cardboard Lover*.

Mayer wanted to sign Norma to another contract but she wanted time to think it over. She turned down *Old Acquaintance* with Bette Davis because, here again, she did not want to play a middle-aged woman with grown children. MGM press agent George Nichols said, 'Norma was living in the past and was not about to change. She made an attempt by changing her hair colour to an off-blonde shade and wore it all fluffed up. She was very attractive at forty. But she lived in her own little dream world of the thirties. She refused to accept the fact she would have to play middle-aged women on the screen and that's sad because she could have done it with style. Rather than leave her fans with that image in mind, she retired.'

Joan Crawford left in 1942 after eighteen years at MGM because they had nothing for her. She was box-office poison, they said, but Joan went to Warner Brothers and won an Oscar for *Mildred Pierce*.

And so the two grand ladies in L.B. Mayer's family were suddenly gone. No farewell parties or formal announcements.

'You have to pick yourself up and keep going,' she said.

Unlike Garbo, who remained single, it was Norma's intention to marry again. She was financially secure but needed a man in her life. In June 1942 she took Irving and Katharine on a skiing vacation to Sun Valley, Idaho, where she met Martin Arrougé, a ski instructor, who was twelve years younger than Norma. She said he reminded her of Irving. Though taller, he had the same black hair and and dark eyes.

Arrougé gave the Thalberg children skiing lessons and helped Norma improve her skills on the slope. Though he found her attractive, he did not do the chasing. She did because Marti, as she referred to him, was what she wanted. According to Anita Loos he had a beautiful body and knew how to handle it. 'Marti was romantic and sexy,' she said. What Loos didn't say was Arrougé had no money and was earning $150 a week.

On 22 August, Norma told the press that she and Marti had signed a prenuptial property settlement. She said she was not as rich as most people thought and that she had been living off the interest from $1,500,000. As always, Norma did not mention her own earnings from MGM that came to well over a million. Marti said he was not marrying Norma for her money and that he was perfectly able to make a living on his own.

The following day they were married at the Church of the Good Shepherd in Beverly Hills. Her wedding ring, with bands of gold welded on either side, was the one Irving put on her finger fifteen years previously.

Before meeting his wife, Arrougé had volunteered for the service, so Norma became a 'navy wife'. While he was in San Franciso training naval pilots, Norma had an active social life. To her children's dismay, Norma closed up the beach house and moved into a bungalow at the Beverly Hills Hotel. Irving Jr disliked being the son of a movie star who never allowed herself to be anything less than glamorous and standoffish. Katharine felt the same aloofness and neglect from her mother. There would not be a definitive breakup between Norma and her children, merely a continuance of indifference.

When Marti was discharged from the service in early 1946, he and Norma continued living at the Beverly Hills Hotel and opened the beach house only for dinner parties. For once, Norma seemed uninterested in budgets. She bought Marti a Ferrari, hired tutors for the children and employed a personal maid.

With Marti home again, they vacationed in Sun Valley. Norma noticed the photo of a very attractive girl in the hotel's souvenir album. She had the picture blown up and sent it to L.B. Mayer, who agreed the girl should be given a screen test. The young lady was Janet Leigh who met Norma when she signed a contract with MGM. Janet was invited to a party at the beach house and remembers Norma rushing through the front door two hours late. Laden down with packages, she excused herself and emerged two hours later looking as if she were headed for the movie set. Maybe Janet was starved for a bite to eat by that time, but she was in awe of Norma who, she said, was everything a movie star should be.

On a European vacation, Norma purchased a chalet in Switzerland where they lived for a year until she realised she was overextending herself financially. She asked the court for a monthly allowance drawn from the children's trust funds and got it. This did not sit well with Irving and Katharine who wondered why Marti didn't go to work.

In 1951 L.B. Mayer was forced to resign from MGM. Norma was shocked that Nicholas Schenck was responsible for Mayer's ousting. But her feelings went deeper. It was the end of an era in Hollywood that Irving Thalberg helped turn into the Golden Era. With his genius and Mayer's guiding hand, they built the greatest movie studio in the world. The following year Norma was asked to speak when the Screen Producers Guild paid tribute to L.B. Mayer. With tears in her eyes Norma Shearer thanked Mayer for bringing her 'the happiest days of my life'. Mayer's death in 1957 was a blow to Norma. With so many memories haunting her at the beach house where Irving had died, where Mayer had talked to her about the early days, and where she had enjoyed romantic evenings with George Raft, there was no need to hang on to the house that Irving had built. She sold it in 1961 and decided it was time she and Marti found a place of their own. Now that Irving and Katharine were both married, Norma found a smaller and less pretentious house at 1207 North Sierra Alta Way. The only servant was a maid who came several times a week.

Norma had tried for years to keep Irving Thalberg alive in print by writing her autobiography, which, like her conception of life, was a fairy tale. After futile attempts to get it published, she put it aside. Another chance to honour Thalberg came when Universal planned to film the life of Lon Chaney with James Cagney, and contacted Norma about Thalberg's character in the movie. Norma agreed to help but wanted the authority to approve the actor who would portray her late husband. By coincidence she had seen a young man at the Beverly Hills Hotel pool who resembled Irving. His name was Robert Evans. After a successful screen test at Universal, he played Thalberg in *A Man of a Thousand Faces* in 1957.

Having the rights to F. Scott Fitzgerald's unfinished novel *The Last*

Tycoon, based on Thalberg's life, Norma approached MGM about the screen version. She would be in charge of the production, Marti would be her production assistant and George Cukor would direct the film. But Evans was now tied up with another movie and Cukor wasn't available so Norma gave up on the idea. *The Last Tycoon* would be filmed in 1976 with Robert de Niro playing the part of Thalberg.

Robert Evans went on to become head of production at Paramount, much to Norma's delight and satisfaction.

Always the star, Norma was faithful in her effort to keep herself attractive and fit. She continued her routine of exercising regularly and maintained a youthful body. There was no way, however, that she could prevent the penetrating wrinkles in her face, emphasised by her favourite deathlike white make-up.

In 1970, Norma's anxiety attacks returned and she went into deep depressions. Shock treatments helped, but caused memory lapses. She referred to Marti as 'Irving' and would continue to do so until her death, but he never corrected her. She tried suicide by attempting to jump from the top floor of a high-rise building. More shock treatments followed. She became a recluse and insisted Marti stay at home with her. When her eyesight failed, he read to her, but Norma had lost her concentration. Not feeling well himself, Marti was forced to hire a nurse. When Norma's weight dropped to eighty pounds, he called The Motion Picture country house, a retirement home for actors. With its adjoining hospital, even the elite in Hollywood opted to spend their golden years in this landscaped Country House in Woodland Hills. Movies were shown in the Louis B. Mayer Memorial Theater, meals were served in the Mrs L.B. Mayer Dining Room, and a Samuel Goldwyn Plaza offered shuffleboard and croquet. This would be Norma's home until the end. Like her sister Athole and her father, Norma was a manic depressive and lived out her days talking to Irving when Marti visited. Her long hair was white and stringy but she turned away anyone who tried to fuss over her. One visitor to the Home recalled that she resembled the imprisoned Marie Antoinette.

On 12 June 1983, Norma Shearer died of bronchial pneumonia. She was interred next to Irving . . .

Norma Shearer's life mirrored that of Marie Antoinette. They were not beautiful women, but with power and wealth, they gained the poise and elegance that gave the illusion of beauty. They married men who did not arouse their passion but they ascended the throne and made history. Marie lost her head and poor Norma lost her mind . . .

Norma's father died in 1944, Edith in 1968, and Irving Thalberg Jr in 1987.

The Films of Norma Shearer

The Flapper (Selznick, 1920)
The Restless Sex (Paramount, 1920)
Way Down East (United Artists, 1920)
The Stealers (Robertson-Cole, 1920)
The Sign on the Door (FN, 1921)
The Devil's Partner (Iroquois, 1922)
Changing of the Northwest (Selznick, 1922)
The Bootleggers (FBO, 1922)
The Man Who Paid (Producers Security, 1922)
A Clouded Name (Play Company, 1923)
The Wanters (FN, 1923)
Pleasure Mad (Mayer Company, 1923)
Lucretia Lombard (Warner Brothers, 1923)
Man and Wife (Arrow, 1923)
Broadway After Dark (Warner Brothers, 1924)
Trail of the Law (Oscar Apfel, 1924)
Blue Waters (New Brunswick, 1924)
The Wolf Man (Fox, 1924)
Empty Hands (Paramount, 1924)
Broken Barriers (Metro-Goldwyn, 1924)
He Who Gets Slapped (Metro-Goldwyn, 1924)
The Snob (Metro-Goldwyn, 1924)
Married Flirts (Metro-Goldwyn, 1924)
Lady of the Night (Metro-Goldwyn, 1925)
Waking up the Town (United Artists, 1925)
Pretty Ladies (Metro-Goldwyn, 1925)
A Slave of Fashion (Metro-Goldwyn, 1925)

Excuse Me (Metro-Goldwyn, 1925)
The Tower of Lies (Metro-Goldwyn, 1925)
His Secretary (Metro-Goldwyn, 1925)
The Devil's Circus (Metro-Goldwyn, 1926)
The Waning Sex (Metro-Goldwyn, 1926)
Upstage (Metro-Goldwyn, 1926)
The Demi Bride (MGM, 1927)
After Midnight (MGM, 1927)
The Student Prince (MGM, 1927)
The Latest from Paris (MGM, 1928)
The Actress (MGM, 1928)
Lady of Chance (MGM, 1928)
The Trial of Mary Dugan (MGM, 1929)
The Last of Mrs Cheyney (MGM, 1929)
The Hollywood Revue of 1929 (MGM, 1929)
Their Own Desire (MGM, 1930)
The Divorcée (MGM, 1930)
Let Us Be Gay (MGM, 1930)
Strangers May Kiss (MGM, 1931)
A Free Soul (MGM, 1931)
Private Lives (MGM, 1931)
Strange Interlude (MGM, 1932)
Smilin' Through (MGM, 1932)
Riptide (MGM, 1934)
The Barretts of Wimpole Street (MGM, 1934)
Romeo and Juliet (MGM, 1936)
Marie Antoinette (MGM, 1938)
Idiot's Delight (MGM, 1939)
The Women (MGM, 1939)
Escape (MGM, 1940)
We Were Dancing (MGM, 1942)
Her Cardboard Lover (MGM, 1942)

3

Garbo

She was the ultimate standard against whom all other screen actresses were measured. Was it art or instinct? Was she a remarkable actress or a woman so extraordinary that she made everything she did on screen remarkable? She was an enigma and no one has yet solved the mystery of her. 'Being a movie star,' she said, 'and this applies to all of them, means being looked at from every possible direction. You are never left at peace, you're just fair game.'

She retired from film-making when she was thirty-six. She never won an Oscar and you can't find her footprints in front of Grauman's Chinese Theater in Hollywood. Yet she remains the screen's greatest actress.

Greta Garbo once said, 'If only those who dream about Hollywood knew how difficult it all is.'

She was born Greta Lovisa Gustafsson on 18 September 1905 in Stockholm, Sweden. She resembled her father Karl, who had married Anna Karlsson in May 1898. A son Sven was born in July of that year, which may explain why the couple moved from farming country to Stockholm where Karl made a meagre living as a gardener. A daughter Alva was born in 1903, followed by Greta two years later. All three children had their father's well-chiselled features and tall lanky frame. In direct contrast Anna was short and stocky with a plump cheerful face. The family lived in a four-room cold-water flat with no bathroom. The toilet was in the backyard.

Greta yearned to be on stage at the age of seven or eight when she watched the actors and actresses going into the Southside Theatre in Söder, a long walk from Stockholm. She was attracted to the costumes, make-up and the laughter, all the colourful elements missing from her life.

Karl died in 1920 at the age of forty-eight from kidney failure. Greta, who attended school and worked part-time at a fruit store, was fourteen when her father became sick. It was she who took him to the free clinic and waited in line. She was very close to her father, who was the only one willing to listen to her dreams about the stage even though she was overweight and too tall at five-feet seven-inches.

After Karl's death Greta dropped out of school and got a job as a soap-lather girl in a barber shop for a dollar a week. She mixed the lather, set up the razors and cleaned up. Needing more money, Greta worked in the millinery department at the Paul Bergstrom department store for twenty-five dollars a month. Most probably she had her first sexual encounter with a wealthy customer who invited her for dinner. They dated for about a year until he got married, but they remained good friends.

When Greta began modelling hats she was asked to appear in a commercial film to promote millinery, *How Not to Dress*. This led to another commercial film for a bakery, *Our Daily Bread*.

Greta recognised the actresses who shopped in the department store and she went out of her way to wait on them. She also knew who Erik Petchler was and approached the producer-director for a job. She read for him and he put her in his film *Peter the Tramp* in 1922. It was an insignificant picture, but Petchler was impressed by her and suggested he audition for the Royal Dramatic Theatre Academy that was state-sponsored and tuition-free. Greta was accepted in 1922 at the age of seventeen.

The following year she auditioned for director Mauritz Stiller and was cast as Countess Elisabeth Dohna in *The Saga of Gösta Berling*, about a defrocked minister who falls in love with a virginal countess. Forty-year-old Stiller told his protégée to lose twenty pounds, and then set about making her over, changing her name to Mona Gabor, but finally settling for Greta Garbo. It was Stiller who thought she was beautiful. He commented on her brown-black hair, her grey-blue eyes and long lashes. But he was tough on her during production of *The Saga of Gösta Berling*, often humiliating her to tears. But Greta was determined to be a good actress and listened to his every word. At his suggestion she left the Royal Dramatic Theatre Academy and became his exclusively, but not sexually because Stiller was a homosexual. They would share a very special bond, however. 'She belongs to me,' he said. In Greta he had found the perfect actress to mould. She was enthralled by his wisdom even when he criticised her unmercifully during rehearsals.

The Saga of Gösta Berling was well received in Sweden. Though there was no mention of his protégée in the reviews, Stiller insisted Garbo attend the Berlin premiere with him. This was exciting for Greta since she had never been out of Sweden. The film was more popular in Germany than Sweden, bringing Garbo to the attention of director G.W. Pabst, who cast her as a prostitute in *The Joyless Street* in 1925. Stiller was with Garbo on the set at all times until Pabst, annoyed by his interference, banned him from the set. Just as well, perhaps, because *The Joyless Street* was a bigger success than *The Saga of Gösta Berling* though it was the latter that caught the attention of Louis B. Mayer, vice-president of Metro-Goldwyn-Mayer Studios in Hollywood. Mayer was in Europe to oversee *Ben Hur* in Rome and ventured to Berlin to find someone to represent MGM in Germany. He also wanted to meet Stiller and his plump leading lady.

Mauritz Stiller, a Slavic Jew, was born in 1883 in Helsingfors, Finland. He was pursuing a stage career when he failed to report for military duty and almost landed in jail for twenty-five years. In 1904 he forged a passport and settled in Stockholm where he became interested in movies. But Stiller hated what he looked like on film and it's no wonder since he was tall, ungainly and very unattractive. As a result he worked on the other side of the camera and had directed over 45 films by the time he met Garbo.

Louis B. Mayer was under a great deal of pressure when he was in Berlin. *Ben Hur*, a film MGM inherited during the merger with Goldwyn Pictures, was having production problems in Rome and would eventually be done in Hollywood. At considerable expense everything had to be shipped to Los Angeles. By the time Mayer arrived in Berlin he was exhausted but arranged a meeting with Stiller and his star of *The Saga of Gösta Berling*. Though Mayer was sincerely interested in Stiller, his primary target was now the beautiful Greta, but he was shrewd enough not to reveal his true feelings.

Greta was wearing an unattractive black taffeta hat and a drab outfit. With no make-up, she did not resemble an actress but Mayer was unperturbed because he had seen her on film. He concentrated on Stiller, and took Garbo as part of the team. Mayer admitted later he would have taken her without her mentor, who accepted an MGM contract for $1000 a week. Stiller told Greta to sign a contract for £100 a week. She was not happy about leaving her family, but did what Stiller wanted. She said goodbye to her mother on 30 June 1925 and sailed on the *Drottningholm*, which arrived in New York on 6 July.

For two months Stiller and Garbo stayed at the Commodore Hotel, waiting for word from Mayer who stalled on purpose when he realised Greta was underage when she signed the contract in Berlin. Though MGM reps showed her New York, wined and dined her and Stiller, as a strict chaperone, Garbo indicated she wanted to go home. That's when Mayer offered her a $400 a week contract with a clause that mentioned she had her mother's permission. In September Stiller and Garbo boarded the *Twentieth Century* for California. They arrived in Hollywood on 10 September 1925, and were met by MGM publicity man Pete Smith, reporters and photographers. Garbo, smothered with flowers, was enchanted by a group of Swedish people in the appropriate garb. Photos of her that day show a frizzy-haired frightened young girl shrouded in flowers and flanked by little Swedish girls in delicate costume bonnets. Unable to speak English, she tried to answer questions fired at her from all directions. She knew what to say when asked, 'What are your plans?'

'I wait for what the studio decides for me to do,' she answered.

But Pete Smith cringed when a reporter asked her where she was staying in Hollywood and she replied, 'I will look for something not too expensive, a room with a private family.' One reporter wrote that Garbo had a run in her stocking and her shoes needed new heels. She did not make a good impression.

MGM had rented a small house for Stiller in Santa Monica and an apartment for Greta in the Hotel Miramar nearby. She spent most of her time with Stiller, swimming in the pool and sunbathing in the garden. In a letter to a friend in Stockholm, Greta wrote, 'Oh, you lovely little Sweden, I promise when I return to you my sad face will smile as never before.' She complained of doing nothing all day and going to bed as early as possible. 'I don't care if I act like a little old woman,' she added.

When depression set in, Stiller approached Irving Thalberg, who was in charge of production at MGM. Having an appointment with the Boy Genius meant waiting hours before being admitted to his office. So Stiller went every day and took Garbo with him. Thalberg told her to lose weight, have her teeth straightened and see one of their hairdressers. Then he would arrange for some photos of her and a screen test. This was viewed by director Monta Bell who thought she'd be perfect for his next film, *Torrent*, opposite the very popular actor Ricardo Cortez. Greta portrays a budding diva in love with a mother-dominated politician. Garbo was thrilled to be working at last but devastated that Stiller would not be her director. She wanted to return to Sweden but he convinced her to stay on and do the film. He would coach her at night.

Torrent opened in New York on 21 February 1926 and was a box office sensation. The Brooklyn *Eagle* wrote, 'Miss Garbo is not beautiful, but she's a brilliant actress.' *Motion Picture* said Garbo was endowed with individuality and magnetism. *Variety* thought she had everything – looks, acting ability and personality.

If she was thrilled with the reviews, Garbo didn't indicate it in her letters to friends in Sweden, the country she referred to as the only paradise in the world. She said Americans had spoiled their beautiful country with tall buildings, too many cars and too much noise. She referred to the studio as 'hideous'.

Thalberg and Mayer were so delighted with *Torrent* that they rushed Garbo into *The Temptress* with Antonio Moreno, and directed by Stiller. Though she would complain later about playing vamps she was relieved that she was working. In her role as a married woman who follows her lover to Argentina and disaster, Garbo is stunning. But Stiller's slow methods of directing and his bitter disputes with Antonio Moreno were holding up production. Moreno complained to Thalberg, who had no choice but to take Stiller off the picture and replace him with Fred Niblo.

Losing Stiller was a blow to Greta, who also learned that her sister Alva had died from cancer at the age of twenty-three. Garbo said she didn't know how she got through *The Temptress*. Critics said little about the film. Instead they raved about Garbo's beauty, poise and acting skills. She said it was terrible and so was she. 'Everything went wrong,' she said. 'I am not a good actress.'

But MGM considered her, after only two films, a rare commodity, so why not co-star her with their male counterpart – John Gilbert, America's heart-throb? Earning $10,000 a week, he might have been in control at MGM were it not for his constant disagreements with L.B. Mayer. Thalberg had to step in often to ease the strain between the two men.

Garbo was not pleased with *Flesh and the Devil*. She told Mayer, 'I don't want to be a silly temptress. I cannot see any sense in getting all dressed up and doing nothing but tempting men in pictures.' She said she was tired and ill and after *The Temptress* and her sister's death. Mayer gave her a few days to think it over and then summoned her to work and she obliged.

Gilbert (known as Jack) wasn't keen on doing *Flesh and the Devil* either, but Thalberg asked him to do it. Jack was curious about Garbo, however, but changed his mind when he met her on the MGM lot and said, 'Hello, Greta.' She muttered, 'It's Miss Garbo.'

On the first day of filming, director Clarence Brown suggested to Jack that they go to Garbo's dressing room and welcome her.

Gilbert said, 'Let her come to me.' So Brown brought Garbo to Jack's dressing room and, in no time, he had her laughing. 'I think it was love at first sight,' Brown said. 'Then they did the love scene . . . it was the damnedest thing you ever saw. No one else was even there. They were in a world of their own. It seemed like an intrusion to say "cut". So I just motioned to the crew to move over to another part of the movie set and let them finish what they were doing. It was embarrassing.'

In *Flesh and the Devil* Greta plays another adulteress, who causes the death of her husband and comes to a violent end, this time falling through the ice and drowning. She was also drowning in love that first day on the movie set and that night at Gilbert's house near the top of Tower Road. Garbo said he had come into her life just in time. She was depressed and lonely, and ready to run back to Sweden. She had no faith in herself or anyone else but Gilbert changed all that. He gave her confidence on the movie set and taught her techniques in front of the camera, explaining how and what to do in simple terms. Despite the language barrier, he somehow managed to get through to her.

Filming ended in September 1926. A month later Garbo had moved in with Gilbert.

L.B. Mayer was usually opposed to his stars having love affairs, but he allowed the studio to publicise the highly charged romance between Garbo and Gilbert. As a result, *Flesh and the Devil* was a box-office bonanza. Men were expected to wait in long lines to see Garbo but women were entranced by her as well. *Flesh and the Devil* opened on 9 January 1927. The New York *Herald Tribune* raved, 'Never before has a woman so alluring with a seductive grace that is far more potent than mere beauty, appeared on the screen . . . Never in our screen career have we seen seduction so perfectly done.'

Garbo was a different person with Gilbert. She enjoyed entertaining his friends on Sundays, playing tennis and swimming nude in the pool. The guests wore bathing suits and tried not to gawk. Garbo attended the premiere of *Bardelys the Magnificent* with Gilbert, Thalberg and his date, actress Norma Shearer. She did not join the others at the Coconut Grove for dinner, however. This was the only premiere Garbo ever attended.

Jack was more in love with Greta than she was with him. He wanted to marry her during *Flesh and the Devil* and she accepted for some unknown reason, although she had no intention of going through with it. Gilbert held out hope, however. It was to be a double wedding with director King Vidor and actress Eleanor Boardman. L.B. Mayer approached Gilbert who was waiting patiently for Garbo. 'What's the matter with you?' Mayer laughed, patting Gilbert on the back. 'What do you have to marry her for? Why don't you just fuck her and forget about it?'

Gilbert spun on Mayer and pushed him through the door of the guest bathroom, got on top of him and proceeded to choke him almost to death. MGM executive Eddie Mannix pulled them apart and tried to soothe Mayer who hissed, 'You're finished, Gilbert! I'll destroy you if it costs me a million dollars!'

Garbo, who was spending time with Mauritz Stiller, eventually returned to Gilbert's house. He left her a note suggesting she pay rent but she never did and, before too long, they were back in the same bed. Garbo once said, 'There are some who want to get married and others who don't. I have never had an impulse to go to the altar. I am a difficult person to lead.'

Over the years Garbo's comments about her feelings for Gilbert varied considerably. He was either the love of her life or just a dear friend. Or she had no idea what she saw in him. Writer Anita Loos said Garbo used Gilbert. 'She spread her legs like most actresses who wanted to get ahead.'

Garbo turned to Gilbert for advice about her career. She wanted more money but had no one to negotiate for her. Gilbert suggested his friend and business manager Harry Edington. She was making $750 a week and wanted $5000. Mayer was outraged and blamed Gilbert. Nonetheless, Garbo refused to report for work and Mayer suspended her without pay.

John Gilbert was born John Cecil Pringle on 10 July 1899 in Logan, Utah. His mother Ida wanted to be an actress and married stock company producer John Pringle. To her great dismay she became pregnant. Not wanting to live with her husband, she travelled with her baby all over the country, leaving Jack with anybody who was willing to take care of him. He lived with a prostitute for a while and said he was only seven but he knew more about the world than most people did in a lifetime. Ida divorced Pringle and married a comedian, Walter Gilbert, but they soon went their own way as performers. Ida died of tuberculosis in 1913. She was in her late thirties.

Having been around performers all his life, Jack wanted to be an actor. Walter Gilbert, who was working as a director in a playhouse in Portland, wrote to director Thomas Ince in Hollywood about Jack, who was fifteen when he began his career in films doing whatever work was available. He was married briefly in 1918, divorced, and eventually married actress Leatrice Joy. They had a daughter in 1924, the year they were divorced and the year that Gilbert signed a contract with MGM. His career soared in *The Merry Widow* and *The Big Parade*.

Mayer never liked Gilbert. Some said it was because Jack divorced Leatrice Joy when she was pregnant and he was having an affair with actress Laurette Taylor. Or was Mayer outraged by their discussion about prostitutes? Jack said his mother was a whore and to Mayer all mothers were saints. Or was it Jack's heavy drinking that would eventually take its toll? Whatever it was, the incident when Gilbert tried to choke Mayer sealed their hatred for one another. Mayer obviously resented him even more when he became Garbo's adviser, which led to her suspension. But Mayer was a businessman and he knew all too well that Garbo was worth far more than $750 a week.

Meanwhile, she lived with Gilbert and continued to visit Stiller, who was directing pictures at Paramount Studios, but not faring well. Gilbert resented these visits but he would never tame Garbo. Neither would anyone else, for very long.

Mayer finally came up with an offer of $3000 a week, escalating to $5000 over a period of five years. Almost immediately MGM announced that Garbo and Gilbert would co-star in *Love*, a story about a woman who leaves her husband and child for her lover, then realises she is losing him as well. Garbo was twenty-two when she played the mother of a ten-year-old boy in this film. *Love* was the most profitable picture that teamed Garbo and Gilbert. *Time* magazine said, 'They are in a fair way of becoming the biggest box-office team this country has yet known.'

The lovers made another attempt at getting married. Driving to an unknown destination, Gilbert stopped for gas and Garbo went to the rest room, climbed out of the window and managed to get back to Los Angeles. Gilbert got drunk and went to the Miramar Hotel. When she refused to let him in, he tried to climb up to her balcony and Stiller knocked him to the ground. Jack got a gun and went to the police station to demand Stiller's arrest. Instead, Jack went to jail overnight. The incident made headlines to Mayers' distress.

Greta had challenged Jack at one point in their relationship. She wanted to move to Montana or Utah and live a quiet married life. He refused. 'You're in love with Garbo the movie actress!' she said.

'You're damn right I am,' he replied.

Her next film, *The Divine Woman*, based loosely on the life of Sarah Bernhardt, co-starred Lars Hanson with whom she had worked in *Gösta Berling* and *Flesh and the Devil*. But *The Divine Woman* was panned by critics as was Garbo's next effort, *The Mysterious Lady*, with Conrad Nagel.

In 1928 she was advised by Harry Edington to give an interview to *Photoplay* magazine. Garbo spoke of how much she missed Sweden. In Hollywood she got up early, went to work, came home and went to bed. She did not think an actress could portray a woman in love unless she had experienced it for herself. In summation, she said she was born, she grew up, she worked and when she quit she would travel the world. The end.

In November 1927 Mauritz Stiller returned to Sweden, a broken man. He had pleaded with Mayer for a job and had been rejected. Garbo said her goodbyes to her mentor in Los Angeles. She would never see him again.

Garbo and Gilbert played doomed lovers in *Woman of Affairs*. The *New York Times* critic said Gilbert was overshadowed by the 'particular cleverness of Garbo'. Clarence Brown, who directed the film, wanted to build up Gilbert's part but he refused. It was during her next film, *Wild Orchids*, that Greta received the news that Mauritz Stiller had died on 8

November 1928 at the age of forty-five. She left the movie set in a trance and stayed at home for two days. She pleaded with Mayer to let her go to Sweden, but he insisted she finish *Wild Orchids*, which would turn out to be a disaster because Garbo was not herself. Mayer did, however, give her permission to go home for the holidays. In late December 1928 Garbo returned to Sweden. 'I am happy now,' she said. Greta called Jack to wish him a Happy New Year and kept in touch with him by mail during the three months she was away.

In March 1929 Garbo arrived back in New York and was greeted majestically by MGM and their boss Nicholas Schenck, who presented her with flowers. Gilbert, with a huge bouquet of roses, met Greta at the San Bernardino station to avoid the press. His loneliness over the past three months prompted him to propose to her again and she turned him down once again. 'We are both insomniacs,' he said in desperation. 'Together we get through the long nights. Without you it's unbearable.' But Garbo was detached at this stage and had lost interest.

Gilbert had confided in MGM publicist Howard Dietz that Garbo didn't care if he went out with other women. 'She tells me she'll leave the door open,' he said. 'Then I tell her I'm going out to sleep with Anna May Wong and she says she'll still leave the door open. What in hell do I do?'

'That's obvious,' Dietz replied. 'You go out and sleep with Anna May Wong.'

But Jack wanted to sleep with Garbo. He wanted to marry her.

'You are a very foolish boy,' she said. 'You quarrel with me for nothing. I must do it my way, but we need not part.'

'Not this time,' he said. 'It's going to be all or nothing.'

Garbo was rushed into her next film, *The Single Standard*, about a married woman who has a shipboard romance but decides her husband is more important to her. Filming took place on Catalina Island so Garbo did not hear the news about Gilbert's engagement to actress Ina Claire. She called Harry Edington only hours before the wedding, begging him to stop it because Gilbert belonged to her. Edington was Jack's best man and in a sweat. He told Greta she was the only one who could stop the wedding, knowing she was not about to expose herself to that sort of publicity. And so on 9 May 1929, Gilbert married Ina Claire whom he had known for only six weeks. The marriage lasted until September 1930.

Greta moved out of Jack's house into the Santa Monica Beach Hotel.

The Kiss was Garbo's last silent movie. She plays a married woman who resists the advances of a young man (Lew Ayres). When he suddenly embraces her, they are discovered by her jealous husband who accidentally kills himself with his gun in the struggle. *The Kiss* did well at the box office despite the stock-market crash. MGM was concerned that without Gilbert, Garbo's films would not do well, but she was now enormously popular on her own. The question was, could she survive sound? Would the public accept her Swedish accent? How would she react to that awful contraption, the microphone?

Film historians claim that almost ninety per cent of the silent stars faded at sound's outset – because their voices were ill-placed and embarrassing. The most famous casualty was John Gilbert. In *His Glorious Night* with Catherine Dale Owen, his 'I love you, I love you, I love you,' drew snickers from audiences in 1929. There was nothing wrong with his voice. It was the fact that the bass on the sound equipment was not turned up that distorted the tone of his voice. Whether it was done on orders from Mayer will never be known. It's true his voice did not match his tall, dark, handsome and virile image, but the correct handling of the sound equipment might have given his voice quality a deeper resonance. After the initial shock, there was little anyone could do to repair the damage done to Jack's image.

Before his disastrous sound debut, Gilbert had gone over Mayer's head to Nicholas Schenck who signed Jack to a million-dollar contract. Did Mayer conspire with director Lionel Barrymore and sound engineer Douglas Shearer to get out of paying this kind of money to a man he hated? Many Hollywood insiders think he did.

Not only was Garbo upset over what happened to her former lover, she was terrified that it might happen to her. No star has made more money for MGM than John Gilbert. Was his career in films ruined by 'I love you, I love you, I love you?' Sadly it was downhill all the way for Jack from then on. Not even Garbo would be able to save him . . .

In her first talkie, *Anna Christie*, Garbo plays a prostitute who saves a seaman (Charles Bickford) from drowning. He then saves her from an otherwise doomed life. Audiences held their breath when she appeared on the screen, entering a bar. Slouched over and tired, she sits down at a table and tells the bartender, 'Gimme me a viskey, ginger ale on the side – and don' be stingy, baby!'

The New York *Herald Tribune* described Garbo's voice as 'a deep, husky, throaty contralto'. *Picture Play* said it was the voice that shook the world.

In her second talkie, *Romance*, Garbo is an opera-singer mistress of an industrialist who falls in love with a clergyman. In 1930 she was nominated for an Academy Award for Best Actress in both *Anna Christie* and *Romance*, but Norma Shearer won the Oscar for *The Divorcee*.

Inspiration, with a very young Robert Montgomery, was too much like *Romance* to suit the critics. Garbo was bored with it and, though she was praised for her performance, there were too many script changes every day to suit other cast members who were unable to memorise their lines the day before. It was rumoured that Garbo was fed up with making films. Her restlessness was showing on the movie set but fortunately her moods did not affect her performance.

Thalberg, in his attempt to revise Gilbert's career, hoped to star him with Garbo in *Susan Lennex: Her Fall and Rise*, and with Jean Harlow in *Red Dust*. But it was newcomer Clark Gable who was the chosen one. Garbo would be energised by a new crop of young actors like Gable.

In *Susan Lennex: Her Fall and Rise*, Garbo is a farmer's daughter who runs away from her father to avoid an arranged marriage. She comes upon a mountain cabin owned by an engineer (Clark Gable). On screen there is no chemistry between Garbo and Gable but they make it work. Though there was no off-screen romance, they got along very well. Maybe Garbo's clinches were not as torrid as the ones with Gilbert, but Gable's masculinity made up for that.

One had to give Gable credit for holding his own with Garbo. He had a bit of an ego as early as 1931 and was concerned that she would completely take over the film, leaving him in the background. That didn't happen, though Garbo walked out several times because she didn't like the script. 'Every actor should work with her,' Gable said. 'She gets what she wants and goes home every day at five, regardless of what is going on. It's in her contract.' He would be able to demand the same very soon.

When Garbo was irritating she could also be amusing. A knock on her dressing-room door would get the response, 'Not in!' Asking her for dinner on Wednesday would prompt the response, 'How do I know I'll be hungry on Wednesday?' If she did not speak to you o the street, that was okay. If you did not speak to her, she'd react with a 'Hull-lo'.

In *Mata Hari* Garbo plays the famous Dutch spy who faces the firing squad at the end. Her costumes are magnificent, especially the many hats she wears. Helping Garbo with this elaborate wardrobe was her lesbian lover, screenwriter Mercedes de Acosta. It was no secret that Greta was bisexual, but she had been partial to girls for most of her life. Was this the real reason she did not marry Gilbert? No, it was more probably because Garbo did not want to belong to anyone, man or woman, and that included

Mercedes who was very much in love with her, but Greta would eventually dismiss her abruptly.

Barry Paris, in his superb book *Garbo*, relates that Greta, in pre-adolescence, had physical encounters with certain girlfriends and possibly with her sister, Alva. She was involved with Mona Martenson during *The Saga of Gösta Berling*.

Diana McLellan, author of *The Girls*, discovered that Marlene Dietrich, using a different name, appeared in *The Joyless Street* with Garbo. Dietrich related revealing details of their intimacy to a group of friends, including writer-producer Sam Taylor. She said that Garbo was 'awfully big down there' and that she wore 'dirty underclothes'. According to McLellan, Dietrich referred to Garbo as 'narrow-minded, ignorant and provincial'. Both women denied knowing each other, Dietrich because she was hiding the existence of an ex-husband, and Greta because of their intimacy. They were formally 'introduced' in 1945 at a cocktail party in Hollywood. Marlene flooded her former lover with compliments that were not returned. Garbo was so icy cold, Marlene left the party. If Dietrich was smug over her affair with Mercedes de Acosta, it should be noted that Garbo didn't care any more than she did when John bedded another woman.

Actress Louise Brooks claimed she spent one night with Garbo whom she described as a 'completely masculine dyke' but she was also a 'charming and tender' lover. Brooks also insisted Garbo's romance with Gilbert was publicised to cover up her lesbian proclivities.

But if Mayer was worried about Garbo's reputation as a bisexual, he would have suggested marriage as he had done with many of his gay stars. Forcing her to find a husband, however, was out of the question since Garbo was waiting for an excuse to return to Sweden. Mayer was also aware of her obsession for privacy to safeguard her most intimate secrets.

After her affair with Gilbert and Stiller's death, Garbo was free to enjoy the company of women 'almost' exclusively.

Author Barry Paris mentioned that Marie Dressler, Garbo's co-star in *Anna Christie*, might have been a lover, also. But as Paris commented, 'A full inventory of Garbo's alleged affairs with women would be long and pointless.'

Garbo took a long and seemly romantic vacation with Mercedes de Acosta, who related it in her memoirs, *Here Lies the Heart*. Garbo got the key to Wallace Berry's cabin on Silver Lake in the Sierra Nevadas. Mercedes described their time together as 'six perfect weeks out of a lifetime'. No one, she said, could possibly know Garbo as she had seen her on that island. 'I could see her above me, her face and body outlined against the sky, looking like some radiant, elemental, glorious god and goddess melted into one.'

Perhaps the most telling aspect of Garbo's masculinity was her passion for men's clothes. She was one of the first women to wear slacks in public. Greta and Mercedes caused quite a sensation when they went shopping in trousers. We know now that Garbo was well ahead of her time and, like most women today, she felt more comfortable in slacks.

Greta was living in a house on North Rockingham Road in Brentwood. Garbo moved eleven times during her Hollywood days. She took little interest in decorating or furnishing. A house was merely a place to get away from the world and retire early. Seven, when she was working. Around ten, otherwise. When air conditioning became available, she shunned it no matter how hot the weather was. She had a very simple wardrobe, often travelling with only one change of clothing.

Grand Hotel remains a classic to this day. The Academy Award-winning picture had a cast of players unsurpassed – Garbo as the lonely ballerina in love with the baron, John Barrymore, and Joan Crawford as a prostitute-stenographer who cheers up sickly and old Lionel Barrymore. Garbo and John Barrymore were convincing lovers in the film. She was honoured to work with him and told him so with a kiss on the lips. It was in *Grand Hotel* that she spoke those famous words, 'I want to be alone . . .' Barrymore said acting with her was 'a kind of magic'.

Joan Crawford, who had no scenes with Garbo, was determined to get a look at her. No visitors were allowed on a Garbo set when she was filming and her fellow MGM contract players were not supposed to take the same route as Garbo did from her dressing room to the movie set. Crawford dared to use the same stairs as Garbo and came face to face with her idol. According to Crawford, 'She stopped and cupped my face in her hands and said, "What a pity. Our first picture together, and we don't work with each other. I am so sorry. You have a marvellous face." If there was ever a time in my life I might have become a lesbian that was it.'

As You Desire Me with Melvyn Douglas and Erich von Stroheim featured a blonde-haired Garbo as a woman with amnesia who is torn between her lover and the man who claims to be her husband. There were serious and comical scenes in the picture, but perhaps the best is one in which Garbo gets drunk, because she does it with a sense of confusion rather than vulgarity. She and Melvyn Douglas would co-star in two more films, including her disastrous swan song.

Garbo's MGM contract expired in 1932. She told Mayer she did not want to continue making movies. He convinced her otherwise and offered her $250,000 per picture, $100,000 on signing. She told him how very unhappy she was in Hollywood. Mayer sat down and wrote out a cheque for half her salary for her next picture. She tucked it in her blouse and booked a passage on the *Gripsholm* for a vacation in Sweden in July 1932. She visited places with her mother and brother, but otherwise stayed in seclusion. In Paris she complained there was no peace for her though she wore a black wig. On her return trip in April 1933, she chose the privacy of the freighter *Annie Johnson*. Garbo signed on as 'Harriet Brown' and had her meals in the lifeboats as the *Annie Johnson* cruised the Atlantic and then through the Panama Canal to California.

Before she left on vacation Garbo had discussed her next film, *Queen Christina*, in which the title character abdicates her throne for the man she loves. Garbo wanted very much to play the bisexual monarch raised as a boy. She wears men's clothes, hunts and fishes and kisses her lady-in-waiting on the lips. When her chancellor tells Christina she must marry and have children, she replies, 'I will die a bachelor.' Disguised as a man she meets Antonio and is forced to share a room with him. When she reveals herself as a woman he says, 'Life is so gloriously improbable.'

Many actors were considered for the part of Christina's lover, Antonio. John Barrymore was one candidate. Garbo thought Laurence Olivier would be perfect, but he was so nervous Garbo dismissed him. Perhaps she had John Gilbert in mind all the time. He made a test and got the part. Jack was married to actress Virginia Bruce, who had just given birth to a daughter. But this marriage was not any better than his union with Ina Claire. It's not known if he hoped for a reconciliation with Garbo, but it would be ridiculous to think it wasn't somewhere in the deep recesses of his mind. He did not, however, make an attempt. He was more concerned about his performance. Garbo went out of her way to make him feel at ease, he said.

Queen Christina opened in December 1933. It was popular with the critics but a financial failure. Moviegoers preferred musicals and comedies to cheer them up during the depression years. Who cared about a queen's abdication when folks wondered where their next meal was coming from?

John Gilbert received good reviews, but working with Garbo broke up his marriage to Virginia Bruce who suspected he was still in love with her.

Actually he was too absorbed in not letting Greta down after she had gone to bat for him. Gilbert did one more film after *Queen Christina*, but his heavy drinking was taking a toll on his career and his health. When Marlene Dietrich found out he was drinking himself to death, she decided to take charge and moved in with Jack in 1934. She worked miracles and planned for him to co-star with her in *Desire*. These plans had to be shelved when Jack suffered a mild heart attack in the swimming pool with Marlene, who nursed him, fed him and stayed by his side to make sure he didn't drink.

Then one day Marlene saw Garbo's old Packard pull up in front of the house. Jack went out to talk to her and Marlene watched them intently from an upstairs window. No one knows what she saw – or didn't see – but it was enough for her to leave Gilbert. In December 1935 he had a series of heart attacks and Marlene returned.

On the night of 9 January 1936 Jack had a problem sleeping and a nurse gave him an injection. The next morning he was dead. Though the official cause of death was heart failure, apparently the nurse hadn't bothered to stay with Jack while the drug was taking effect and he choked to death on his own tongue. John Gilbert was thirty-six years old.

Garbo heard the news in the lobby of a Stockholm theatre. She returned to her seat but left after the curtain went up. She was quoted as saying 'What is that to me?' when she heard about Gilbert. Usually Garbo ignored news items if she was misquoted but she came forth and said it was a 'vicious misquoting' about a man for whom she felt deeply.

In 1933 Garbo made *The Painted Veil* as the discontented wife of Herbert Marshall in faraway China. Her love affair with George Brent falls apart and she atones for her sins by working with her husband and his cholera patients. For quite a while Garbo was linked with George Brent, who is rarely mentioned as one of Hollywood's most tempting leading men. Torrid affairs with his leading ladies such as Bette Davis and his marriage to the 'Oomph Girl' Ann Sheridan have been overlooked. Garbo was seen with Brent in cosy restaurants and small movie houses, spending most of her spare time at his home. So much so, in fact, that he built a high wall so she could have privacy. Brent hinted to friends they would be married.

With Fredric March, Garbo did the tragic *Anna Karenina*, who leaves her husband and son for a lover and loses him too. With nothing left, she throws herself in front of a train.

In June 1935 Garbo was back in Sweden despite George Brent's pleas not to go. She was seen with Noel Coward on numerous occasions. A homosexual, the brilliant and witty Coward was one of her few acquaintances who managed to get her out to parties. In October Garbo invited Mercedes to Stockholm and was shocked when she got on the next boat for Sweden. According to Greta's letters to a friend she did not expect Mercedes to accept her invitation. After her lover's departure, Garbo came down with influenza. When she was able to get out of bed she was too weak to return to California. Mayer told her to stay put and get well. It was during her illness that Garbo heard about Gilbert's death and this slowed down her recuperation. In June 1936 Garbo returned to Los Angeles. Apparently she didn't need George Brent any longer since she had a ten-foot fence built around her own house.

Garbo was anxious to do *Camille*, an Irving Thalberg production. Though his heart condition was no secret, his death from pneumonia so suddenly was a shock. On 17 September 1936, the American flag at MGM was lowered to half-mast and a black-on-black velvet mourning band wrapped around the base of the pole. Studio activities came to a halt, but MGM's fleet of 75 limousines were being prepared to pick up their galaxy of stars. Each car had a black flag of mourning in contrast to its distinctive blue MGM logo. Greta Garbo, wearing a black jersey dress, appeared late, but the fact she bothered to come at all is a tribute to the great Thalberg who had guided her career quietly. And his efforts to save John Gilbert were not forgotten by her. Thalberg had been a pallbearer at Gilbert's funeral and shed tears for his fallen star nine months earlier.

Garbo would face production of *Camille* without him. The consensus has always been that her performance as Marguerite Gautier, lady of the camellias, in love with young Armand, portrayed by Robert Taylor, was her greatest ever performance. Her masterpiece. Her zenith. In one scene with Armand, she surprised young Robert Taylor by kissing him all over his face. Amazingly she managed it without body contact. Director George Cukor described it as 'tremendously erotic. By suggesting passion, Garbo caught the eroticism beneath the surface.' Taylor, like Gable, was nervous working with Garbo, but Cukor had great faith in the 25-year-old actor. 'Bob was hurt that Greta ignored him,' Cukor said, 'but I explained she would warm up to him as she warmed up to Armand.' Not fully recovered from her recent illness, Garbo's portrayal of Marguerite dying in the arms of Armand was a difficult scene for her, so more lines were given to Taylor at the last minute. Cukor said, 'I think Greta was deeply affected by Thalberg's death so soon after Gilbert. Her brother was in ill health, too. I'm not sure she was up to doing *Camille* but her talent and the aura of death on and off the set gave this gifted actress the capacity for greatness beyond our wildest expectations.'

Garbo was not one to watch daily rushes, but she asked to see the last ten minutes of *Camille*, according to Cukor.

Greta liked Robert Taylor though they did not socialise and he always kept his distance if he saw her on the MGM lot. She would have to make the first gesture. When he died in 1969, she wept.

Nominated for an Academy Award for Best Actress in *Camille* Garbo lost to Luise Rainer for *The Good Earth*.

She might have lost the Oscar race, but Garbo was more popular than ever. If she thought her privacy was invaded before, it was even more precious after the tremendous success of *Camille*.

Charles Boyer was Greta's choice to play Napoleon in *Conquest*. She is his mistress, Marie Walewska, who bears him a child. Boyer steals this picture from Garbo. Not intentionally, of course, but his performance as Napoleon was so outstanding that the viewer's eyes were directed at him and not at Garbo. Boyer was nominated for an Academy Award but Spencer Tracy won for *Captains Courageous*.

Garbo had a chance meeting with director Ernst Lubitsch, who asked her why she had never done a comedy. She shrugged and said no one had suggested it. Lubitsch told her he was assigned to *Ninotchka*, a film about a Soviet woman commissar who goes to Paris and falls in love with a playboy (Melvyn Douglas). MGM publicised the film with two words, GARBO LAUGHS.

The dialogue was delightful. When Ninotchka meets her playboy she's studying a map on a Paris street. He tries to assist her, but she is annoyed by him.

'Must you flirt?' she asks.

'I don't have to, but I find it natural.'

'Suppress it,' she said, to his amusement.

The 'laughing' scene takes place in a restaurant where Douglas tried to impress her with a joke. She eats her soup without cracking a smile until he falls off his chair. Then GARBO LAUGHS.

Ninotchka was a wonderful movie and a smash success. Garbo was nominated for her fourth Oscar but lost to Vivien Leigh for *Gone with the Wind*. Garbo was, however, very pleased with her role as the stiff Russian commissar and regretted not doing comedy sooner. Is that why she agreed to do *Two-Faced Woman*? The plot was interesting until the censors stepped in and took the fun out of it. Garbo pretends to be her twin sister to test her husband's fidelity. The idea was that he didn't know he was having an affair with his own wife. Before the film's release the Legion of Decency condemned it as disrespectful to marriage. In one scene the husband finds out that the twin sister is really his wife, and the rest of the movie loses its mystery and zest. Though Garbo does a Latin dance, she is not comfortable with it, and the close-up of her shoes in step to the music gives the viewer the feeling Greta had big feet. This became part of her legend though she wore a size 8 shoe. She also appears in a bathing suit that was beneath Garbo's mysterious image.

Greta was devastated by the reviews and swore never to make another film even though she was obligated to make one more picture under the terms of her MGM contract. Whether she made it or not, the studio had to pay Greta, but she dropped out and Mayer paid her $250,000, much less than she was entitled to.

Though she had lost money during the stock-market crash, her real estate investments in Stockholm, Palm Springs and Los Angeles would afford her healthy monthly revenues. Garbo was very frugal, would hang on to her money and amass a fortune. While other actresses were forced to work for a living, at the age of thirty-six, Greta was financially secure for the rest of her life. In 1944 she began travelling abroad and living at the Ritz Tower in New York. Her small circle of friends consisted of Gayelord Hauser, Cecil de Rothschild and photographer Cecil Beaton with whom she was involved intimately. Her most serious love affair was with wealthy George Schlee who was married to fashion designer Valentina. Garbo's attraction to Schlee was his resemblance to Stiller and his determination to guide and take control of her life. Schlee told his wife, 'I love her, but I'm quite sure she won't want to get married. And you and I have so much in common.'

With Valentina's knowledge, the lovers dined at fine restaurants in New York and often travelled in Europe. In 1951 Schlee suggested that Greta buy a seven-room apartment on the fifth floor at 450 East 52nd Street in Manhattan. He and Valentina lived one floor below. She called Greta 'the vampire'.

Schlee became Garbo's manager and began looking for film projects and settled on Balzac's *La Duchesse de Langeais*. There was a successful screen test in Italy, contracts were signed and costumes were being fitted, but lack of financing ended the first and last comeback of Greta Garbo. She was almost as devastated as she was over the failure of *Two-Faced Woman*. Many people connected with *La Duchesse de Langeais* fiasco blame Schlee, who had little knowledge of the film industry. Others, who were reminded of

Stiller's interference that led to his dismissal from Garbo's productions, speculate that Schlee's dominance of Greta presented the biggest problem. She had not asked for too much money and her screen test was magnificent. Garbo was excited about doing another film, but when her hopes were dashed she said, 'Never again. It's over.'

Frequently Greta was a guest of Aristotle Onassis on his yacht *Christina*. She enjoyed chatting with 'Ari' and Winston Churchill, and relished the privacy afforded her as it did for Jackie Kennedy.

On 3 October 1964, Garbo dined with Schlee and Cecile de Rothschild in Paris. Schlee suffered a fatal heart attack and Greta panicked. Cecile took over and Garbo vanished, finally emerging at Kennedy Airport three days later. Valentina claimed her husband's body, banned Garbo from Schlee's funeral and had a priest exorcise her apartment to get rid of 'the vampire'. For the next twenty-five years the two women would avoid each other entering or leaving the building. They had one brief encounter. Garbo hurried on her way while Valentina crossed herself.

Ray Daum in his book *Walking with Garbo* said he met Greta on New Year's Day 1963 at a cocktail party. He knew Schlee, who introduced him to Garbo. Daum, who was working as a film and television producer at the United Nations, agreed to take Garbo on a tour. A year later he sent her a condolence note after Schlee's death and Greta asked if she could pay him a visit. This was the beginning of a friendship that consisted of long walks in New York City. She'd call him and say, 'Let's trot.' Fortunately Daum jotted down their conversations that are related in *Walking With Garbo*. She refused to discuss her movies and why she left Hollywood, but her outlook on the simple aspects of life are revealing:

> Anyone who has a continual smile on his face conceals a toughness that is almost frightening.
>
> One has to be an idiot to talk to me, no matter where I am. They mustn't find out that I don't know grammar in any language.
>
> Mine is a real bachelor's existence. Every day I have lunch on top of my bed, never anywhere else.
>
> Can you make good coffee? I don't perk . . . I throw the coffee in a boiling casserole, and let it stand for a few minutes with a cover on . . . then I strain it . . . . Delicious.

> I'm not a normal man so I can't do what other people do. If I could, I would be tossing around like the rest of the world and have something out of life.
>
> If I don't drink alone I'd never get a drink . . . It's very necessary to drink . . . I have it every day . . . But only a certain amount . . .
>
> I smoke all day long . . .
>
> You call the airlines yourself? How do you do that? I'd be so scared, I'd be so nervous . . .
>
> The story of my life is about back entrances, side doors, secret elevators and other ways of getting in and out of places so that people won't bother me.
>
> I can't imagine not having black telephones . . .
>
> If something happened to me over the weekend, no one would know. My girl [maid] doesn't come on the weekend. Nobody in the world would know.

In 1984 Greta survived a mastectomy. In 1987 she tripped and fell in her apartment, suffering a severely sprained right ankle. Not being able to take her daily long walks was the beginning of the end for her.

The following year Garbo suffered a mild heart attack and in 1989 she began taking dialysis treatments three times a week for kidney failure.

On 11 April 1990, Greta was admitted to New York Hospital where she developed pneumonia. Her niece Gray Reisfield was with Garbo when she died at 11.30 a.m. on Easter Sunday, 15 April 1990. A private memorial service was held at Frank E Campbell Funeral Chapel. Her wish to be cremated was observed but where she is interred isn't known.

Garbo left her $32,000,000 estate to Gray Reisfield and her family.

In November 1990 a huge placard with the initials G.G. was displayed in Sotheby's window. Among Greta Garbo's assets that amounted to $19 million were two Renoirs. Ray Daum, who was invited by the family, walked into the crowded auction room and left. It was almost like going to her funeral that had never been held, he thought. She is gone, out of our lives.

The more Greta Garbo hid from us the more we wanted to seek her out. Catching a glimpse of her in New York was a sighting like no other. Over the years she had us trained not to approach or she'd vanish into thin air like a U.F.O.

I was looking in a shop window on Madison Avenue and saw her reflection. I didn't know what to do. If I looked at her would she hit me with her pocketbook? I wondered why she didn't move on. She never wore dresses so why was she looking at them? Finally, I walked to the kerb waiting for the light to change and there she was standing next to me. Why did she make me so nervous? I let her go ahead so I could observe this mysterious woman. I was young, you see. If the movie stars of my generation weren't recognised, they'd throw themselves in the East River. I wondered why Garbo was different from Joan Crawford and Lana Turner who would never leave home without looking their best. And here was Garbo at her worst, looking like Garbo in a drab raincoat and walking shoes. Can you imagine Crawford walking on Madison Avenue in anything but designer heels? Would she be caught wearing a rain hat? I don't think so.

And so Garbo walked ahead of me. Nobody paid any attention so it was a good day for her. I was so busy observing I didn't see anything. She stopped at another shop window and we nearly collided so I pretended to be interested in women's winter suits also. Again that reflection. This time she looked at me and I yawned to prove I was totally disinterested.

The story goes on for many blocks. Nothing exciting to report except that it was Greta Garbo, and I was eligible to join an exclusive group of people who had actually experienced such a sighting. I wish she had hit me with her pocketbook because I would have been elected president of this club.

I remember thinking that Garbo and I had something in common. We were both wearing hats.

The Films of Greta Garbo

Peter the Tramp (Erik A Petchler, 1922)
The Saga of Gösta Berling (Svensk Filmindustri, 1924)
The Joyless Street (Sofar-Film, 1925)
Torrent (MGM, 1926)
The Temptress (MGM, 1926)
Flesh and the Devil (MGM, 1927)
Love (MGM, 1927)
The Divine Woman (MGM, 1928)
The Mysterious Lady (MGM, 1928)
A Woman of Affairs (MGM, 1928)
Wild Orchids (MGM, 1929)
The Single Standard (MGM, 1929)
The Kiss (MGM, 1929)
Anna Christie (MGM, 1930)
Romance (MGM, 1930)
Inspiration (MGM, 1931)
Susan Lennex: Her Fall and Rise (MGM, 1931)
Mata Hari (MGM, 1931)
Grand Hotel (MGM, 1932)
As You Desire Me (MGM, 1932)
Queen Christina (MGM, 1933)
The Painted Veil (MGM, 1934)
Anna Karenina (MGM, 1935)
Camille (MGM, 1936)
Conquest (MGM, 1937)
Ninotchka (MGM, 1939)
Two-Faced Woman (MGM, 1941)

4

Harlow

She is remembered for her husband's suicide and her own untimely death at the age of twenty-six. This is unfortunate because she was a gifted comedienne whose roles of the wise-cracking tramp brought her to the attention of MGM's production chief Irving Thalberg, who put her under contract despite the protests of mogul Louis B. Mayer.

She never wore undergarments, the thrust of her nipples always apparent. Before filming she rubbed her ample breasts with ice cubes to give them prominence. 'I love people to think I came up from the gutter,' she said. 'Wouldn't it be dull to know my grandpa's present to me on my fifth birthday was an ermine bedspread?'

It was Howard Hughes who discovered her. In her first major film *Hell's Angels* she uttered this famous line to Ben Lyon – 'Do you mind if I slip into something more comfortable?' He didn't and she did.

She was divorced twice and widowed once. Her second husband was reportedly impotent but she wasn't interested in sex. In fact she relished being married to a man who was more interested in her mind than in her body. He rewarded her by committing suicide and making sure she was the one to discover his puny nude body.

Not long before her death she found happiness with a man who refused to marry her.

Jean Harlow had a short and unfulfilled life. Was it illness or hunger for love that killed The Blonde Bombshell?

She was born Harlean Harlow Carpenter on 3 March 1911 in Kansas City. Her mother, Jean Harlow, was a beautiful woman, tall, blonde and regal. Her father, 'Skip', was determined that Jean marry the right man, overruling the suitors she preferred. His choice was a handsome dentist, Mont Carpenter, and Jean married him, in 1908, with little enthusiasm. When she becam pregnant, Jean conceived a child as perfect as she was. Baby Harlean, weighing nine pounds, had white porcelain skin, platinum hair and green eyes. If Grandpa wanted a boy, he soon changed his mind, lavishing Jean with a new house and servants. From the day she was born Harlean was referred to as 'The Baby' and did not know her real name until she went to school.

Though the Carpenter marriage had been in name only for a long time, Jean divorced Mont in 1922. Skip took over and enrolled The Baby in the exclusive Miss Barstow's School in Kansas City.

Free to be and do what she wanted, Jean went to Hollywood with The Baby to pursue a career in films in 1923. While Mother Jean chased her dream, Harlean attended The Hollywood School for Girls. Classmates said the eleven-year-old was sexy even then, with a swaying walk and worldly attitude like her mother. Thirty-four-year-old Jean Carpenter did not succeed in her quest to be a movie star but she had a good time with several dashing gentlemen. Skip, lonely for The Baby, ordered Jean to return to Kansas City or lose her inheritance.

Fifteen-year-old Harlean was back at Miss Barstow's School and went to summer camp at Michigamme. She hated outdoor activities until she met a boy who stole her heart and her virginity. The romance ended when Harlean was quarantined with scarlet fever. Mother Jean rushed to be with her precious daughter and stayed until Harlean recovered. When she returned home Harlean met her mother's new boyfriend, Marino Bello, a married Italian gigolo whose European charm captured Mother Jean from the moment he kissed the palm of her hand. She had never experienced good sex before and became addicted to Marino. Harlean and Skip disliked the phony Bello, but Mother Jean refused to give him up.

Because Marino lived in Chicago, Jean cleverly enrolled Harlean at a girl's academy, Ferry Hall, in Lake Forest, Illinois. A classmate said, 'She was stunning at sixteen. She was about five-feet-two, curvacious and had the most beautiful white skin and hair. She was an earthy girl, but very sweet. Everyone liked her. No one liked her mother, though. She was a possessive bitch.'

On a blind date Harlean met wealthy twenty-year-old Charles McGrew II whose parents had perished in a boat accident. It was love at first sight. She became closer to Chuck when Mother Jean married Marino Bello in January 1927. Nine months later Harlean and Chuck eloped. A few months later he received the first of his inheritance to the tune of $200,000 on his twenty-first birthday. The newlyweds travelled around the country ending up in Los Angeles. To distance The Baby from her domineering mother Chuck bought a house in Beverly Hills.

There is some speculation as to how Harlean got into films. Some claim it was as a dare and she got a job as an extra. This was all the encouragement Mother Jean needed to relocate to Los Angeles. Others insist she had followed Harlean to California and urged her to get into the movies. Whichever version is true, Chuck McGrew resented his wife's working and his mother-in-law's intrusion into his happy marriage. One wonders why Bello wasn't satisfied with McGrew's money instead of looking to his stepdaughter for support.

Harlean had registered at the casting office under her mother's name Jean Harlow, allowing Mother Bello to bask in the spotlight. As an extra, Jean appeared in Paramount's *Moron of the Marines*, *City Lights* with Charlie Chaplin at United Artists, and several Laurel and Hardy films for Hal Roach. With her mother in charge of her career, Jean tried to settle down with Chuck when she got pregnant but the Bellos were too persuasive, and Jean had an abortion. Chuck said her mother broke up the marriage. Marino claimed that he and Mother Bello came to live with Jean when McGrew abandoned her.

While filming as an extra at Metropolitan Studios, Jean was spotted by agent Arthur Landau. She was leaning over a drinking fountain with her breasts overflowing. Landau asked a cameraman, 'Doesn't that girl wear anything underneath her dress?'

'Never,' was the reply. 'That's her trademark. In a slapstick comedy her dress was yanked off and there she was, completely naked. Didn't bother her at all. But she's a very nice kid.'

Landau made friends with Jean and offered to represent her. She agreed after he loaned her money to pay some overdue bills. However, it wasn't Landau who suggested her to Howard Hughes, who was looking for an actress to appear in his World War I aerial film *Hell's Angels* also in production at Metropolitan Studios. In his book *Bombshell*, David Stenn suggests it was actor James Hall, who had a brief affair with Jean during *The Saturday Night Kid*. He was working on *Hell's Angels*, which started out as a silent film until Hughes realised that it would have to compete with talkies and shut down production until he could replace Norwegian actress Greta Nissen whose accent was unacceptable. Hughes met Jean and ordered a screen test. The following day she signed a five-year contract with Hughes for $100 a week in October 1929. She was eighteen years old.

Out of her element, Harlow was a dreadful actress. No one took the time to coach her, but Hughes wasn't interested in her talent. She looked the part of the tramp with a heart of gold who went to bed with fliers who were going into battle. To Ben Lyon she said, 'Would you be shocked if I put on something more comfortable?' Her gowns were low cut because Hughes had a fetish for women's breasts. And so did male audiences. Jean had no idea what an impact she would have in *Hell's Angels*. With six months between the end of filming and the premiere, she anguished over her forthcoming debut, pondering how to make any changes to the way she had looked. She was consoled by MGM executive Paul Bern, a strange little man with a brilliant mind and warped psyche. He was referred to as 'the father confessor' since many stars took him into their confidences. Occasionally he got too involved and fell in love. Barbara La Marr, known as 'The Girl Who Is Too Beautiful', was a hopeless drug addict and died at the age of twenty-six. Bern tried to help her and proposed marriage. She turned him down and he attempted suicide by sticking his head in the toilet bowl. He changed his mind but was stuck in the toilet seat and had to be rescued by a plumber. Bern soothed Joan Crawford, too, when others at MGM wouldn't give her a chance. What their 'affair' consisted of isn't clear since Bern was rumoured to be impotent or gay.

Bern escorted Jean to the premiere of *Hell's Angels* at Grauman's Chinese Theater on 17 May 1930. A mob of 50,000 people gathered outside, tying up traffic and terrifying celebrities who feared their cars would be tipped over. Jean arrived late and was asked to say a few words to the radio audience. She approached the microphone and thanked Howard Hughes 'for giving me this opportunity'. Hollywood had never seen a premiere as big as this one. *Hell's Angels* was a celebrated success but Jean received dreadful reviews except for *Variety*. 'It doesn't make any difference what degree of talent she possesses,' they wrote, 'for this girl is the most sensuous figure to get in front of the camera in some time. She'll probably always have to play these roles, but nobody ever starved possessing what she's got.'

Jean hated every word of it. Hughes raised her salary to $150 a week and sent her around the country to appear at theatres showing *Hell's Angels*. Meanwhile, Paul Bern convinced Hughes to loan Jean out to MGM for *The Secret Six* with Wallace Berry and newcomer Clark Gable. *The Iron Man* with Lew Ayres at Universal followed. Jean was overlooked in *Public Enemy* at Warner Brothers because her role was a small one. It was James Cagney's film from beginning to end and highlighted when he shoved a grapefruit in Mae Murray's face. A Harlow fan, however, would be quick to note Jean's affected speech in *Public Enemy*. Trying to improve herself, she was taking drama lessons that did nothing for her. Jean's casual approach to acting was part of the Harlow package that made her famous.

In Chicago Jean met gangster Abner 'Longy' Zwillman through Marino Bello. He fell for her and she liked the intrigue of dating a mobster. Zwillman would advance her career and treat her like a queen. He got Jean a two-picture deal at Columbia Pictures. When Hughes refused to give Jean a raise, Zwillman backed her with his own money. She played a socialite in *Gallagher* with Loretta Young and directed by Frank Capra. When Hughes labelled Harlow the 'Platinum Blonde', he urged Harry Cohn, head of Columbia Pictures, to use this as the title instead of *Gallagher*. Jean was forced to lighten her hair from ash to platinum. Her hairdresser said he used ammonia, clorax and peroxide every week to maintain the colour that every girl in America wanted. With her usual humour Jean said this meant bleaching her pubic hair as well. Observing her in a see-through dress, a cameraman commented, 'Now I know she's for real.'

Harlow might have kept her hair colour a secret but she was frank about icing her breasts before she went on camera. 'That's how I keep 'em up!' she told Clark Gable.

Paul Bern got her the part of a mobster's mistress in *The Beast of the City* and she set off on tour to promote the film. Since she couldn't dance or sing, Jean was featured at the top of a staircase in a white satin gown against a black background. She actually got encores for just standing there looking absolutely stunning. Thanks to Zwillman's influence, Harlow did not have to suffer the humiliation of appearing on stage with nothing to offer but a deep cleavage.

With three Harlow films playing simultaneously around the country combined with her personal appearances at theatres in major cities, she became a box office sensation. Paul Bern, who had kept in touch with Jean while she was on the road, suggested her to Irving Thalberg for *Red-Headed Woman*, a raunchy story about a small-town girl who has an affair with a married man, marries him after his divorce, sleeps with another man to break into society, marries him and has an affair with his chauffeur, shoots her husband and ends up living in luxury with a marquis while continuing her affair with the chauffeur. Censors balked at any film that preached 'sex pays off'.

Thalberg had the ability, however, to find a love story in obscene books. He hired the talented Anita Loos to write the screenplay with humour. 'We want to laugh off the bad girl's bad behaviour,' he said.

'That's not going to be easy,' Loos exclaimed.

'I think I know what a love story can be. Our heroine must be deeply in love with herself. The poor girl frightens off most men so who is there to love, except fools?'

'Who's going to play her?'

'Paul Bern wants me to test Jean Harlow. I've seen some of her films and she's the type but can she be funny? That's what you and I are going to find out when we talk to her.'

Jean was fitted with a red wig before being ushered into Thalberg's office. 'How did you make out with Howard Hughes?'

'Well, he offered me a bite of his cookie,' she said.

Thalberg hoped for a bit of gossip and was so surprised by her response he laughed out loud.

'Don't underestimate that,' Jean said. 'He's so afraid of germs, it could darn near have been a proposal.'

'Do you think you can make an audience laugh?'

'With me or at me?'

'At you.'

'Why not? People have been laughing at me all my life.'

Loos said, 'when Jean breezed out of the office, she stopped at the door to give us a quick, bright little nod, a gesture I wrote into the script.'

Thalberg smiled and remarked, 'I don't think we need to worry about Miss Harlow's sense of humour.'

Louis B. Mayer was opposed to *Red-Headed Woman* and Jean Harlow, but Thalberg bought her contract from Howard Hughes for $60,000 and signed Jean to a seven-year contract for $1250 a week in April 1932.

During production Jean was to start taking off her jacket at the end of the scene but the boy in charge of the clapper-board failed to give her the signal to cut, so Harlow removed the jacket and was nude to the waist. MGM technicians were not used to such a treat. The lighting crew almost fell off of their flies. Visitors on the set gasped. Jean wasn't the least bit embarrassed, but told director Jack Conway no one told her to cut. With an innocent wide-eyed look, Jean got away with it.

MGM initially premiered their films in Pasadena to get an idea of how audiences felt about them. Thalberg and Loos noted that no one laughed until the end of *Red-Headed Woman*. 'We need a prologue that will tip off the audience that it's a comedy,' he said. So Harlow opens the film at the beauty parlour, admiring herself in the mirror with, 'So gentlemen prefer blondes? Sez who?' She then puts on a dress in a department-store fitting room. 'Is this dress too tight?' she asks the salesgirl.

'It sure is.'

'Good. I'll take it.'

This time audiences got the idea. They were watching a comedy. *Red-Headed Woman* got rave reviews that concentrated on Harlow who, critics agreed, gave an electric performance. The film made history because it brought on more stringent censorship and caused massive difficulties to the industry for years to come. *Red-Headed Woman* outraged women's clubs and religious groups, but not because of any episode in the film. They objected to the sexy heroine not paying for her sins and living happily ever after. Eventually, MGM would withdraw the picture from distribution, but not before Harlow was acclaimed and well into her next box-office hit.

French actor Charles Boyer made his film debut in *Red-Headed Woman* as the chauffeur. Just in time, too, because he considered himself not good enough as an actor and was on his way back to France.

In April 1932 Jean and Paul Bern attended the premiere of the Academy Award-winning *Grand Hotel*, a Thalberg achievement with Bern's valued production assistance. After the premiere, Paul drove Jean to his new home in Beverly Hills, off Benedict Canyon. It was his intention to live there as a bachelor. It had one bedroom above the living room and kitchen. In a wooded area there was a patio strung with Chinese lanterns and a swimming pool. Sipping wine with classical music wafting through the air, Paul told Jean how much he appreciated the solitude of his first house.

No one thought much about Bern's appearing with Harlow at premieres, but when they began to attend parties together, Jean was asked why she was seeing so much of Bern. 'Because he likes me for my mind,' she replied.

'We listen to music and discuss books. He doesn't have his hands all over me. Most men talk then fuck, fuck, fuck, but not Paul. He's above that.'

Paul Bern was born in 1889. Like Thalberg he was German-Jewish and from New York City. He attended the American Academy of Dramatic Arts, tried acting but was more talented as a writer. His father died in 1908 and his mother drowned herself in 1920. With nothing to keep him in the East, Paul headed for Hollywood where he worked as a writer and producer at several studios before working with Thalberg at Metro-Goldwyn-Mayer. He was short, pot-bellied and balding, but was usually in the company of beautiful women. Though he had the respect of Hollywood insiders and a deep friendship with a few, there was something odd about him. It was Barbara LaMarr who said, 'No one should marry Paul Bern.' Did she know he was impotent?

No one claimed to have had sex with Paul so Hollywood insiders were suspicious. If he preferred men, this would have been a well-guarded secret. Anita Loos referred to Paul as a 'German psycho' because he had extreme mood swings. Today he would be considered a manic depressive. But associates, like Thalberg, believed that intellectuals were subject to this malady. Bern was a kind and patient man who had compassion for women like Harlow who were being exploited for their sexuality. He hoped to help them rise above this image. Actor John Gilbert, who was a good friend, said, 'Paul has a Magdalen complex. He does crazy things for whores.' Bern had a weakness for women who were down and out, offering to help until they got on their feet. Though he was desperately in love with the luscious Barbara LaMarr, his offer of marriage was to get her off alcohol and drugs. She was a major star in 1923, and her downfall hurt Paul deeply.

It was Irving Thalberg's friendship with Bern that gave him substance and credibility in Hollywood. Thalberg was also an avid reader of Freud, the subject of many a conversation. They confided in each other and 'did the town' before Irving's marriage to Norma Shearer. But what Thalberg knew about the very private Bern, he didn't say.

The big question is, how much did Harlow know about the man whose marriage proposal she accepted? More than most people thought, apparently, but not enough for a successful marriage. Jean had sex written all over her persona so the thought of her as the wife of a puny little man shocked Hollywood. Thalberg was also concerned. Though Jean did not have many boyfriends, how long could she go without sex? And, he wondered, was Paul capable of consummating the marriage? Even Bern's best friend wasn't sure, though Thalberg did not think his friend was impotent.

Mother Bello stayed out of it. She was delighted that Jean was marrying an MGM executive who could only further her daughter's career. After all, Norma Shearer had married Irving Thalberg who starred her in MGM's biggest productions. But, Mother Bello wondered – was Bern neurotic and dysfunctional as rumoured?

On the evening of 2 July 1932, Jean and Paul were married by a judge at his house. If she was a disillusioned bride on her wedding night, she didn't show it at the reception the following day held in the garden at Bern's home. MGM publicity chief Howard Strickling knew more than most. Jean had told him that sex wasn't important in her marriage. Bern had the same attitude at the start, but living with Jean frustrated him. She walked around the house and slept in the nude. Not being able to get an erection began to frustrate him, especially when he heard Jean telling friends she wanted a child. Was she living in a dream world, too?

That summer Jean began filming *Red Dust*. She plays a prostitute who is stranded in Indochina on a rubber plantation owned by Gable. After they have an affair, he falls in love with a married woman (Mary Astor), but changes his mind about breaking up her marriage and settles down with Harlow. In one scene, Jean takes a bath in a rain barrel. As usual she was nude and took gleeful pleasure in standing up when the camera wasn't rolling. Gable adored Jean and many suspected they were involved. Only author Charles Highham says they were. Because Jean was married to a man who could not perform, it's easy to root for her having an affair with the handsome roguish Gable, who was also married and having a torrid affair with Joan Crawford.

While Jean was filming *Red Dust* during the summer of 1932, Paul busied himself with future projects for her. On Saturday 3 September, he had dinner with MGM producer Bernie Hyman and actress Barbara Barondess at an Ambassador Hotel bungalow. Since Hyman was married, Bern was acting as a 'beard' for the lovers. After dinner he went home while Jean decided to spend the night at the Bellos since their house was closer to the studio.

On Sunday Jean resumed filming and plannd to spend U.S. Labor Day with Paul, but Mother Bello said Marino was going marlin fishing with Gable very early the next day. Could Jean spend the night with her? Precisely what happened on the night of 4th September isn't known in the exact sequence. The butler and chef claimed Jean wanted Paul to have dinner with her and the Bellos, but he refused. Bern did not appreciate Mother Bello's possessiveness, and Bello's pestering him about investing in a Mexican gold mine. Jean and Paul got into an argument. He told her to leave and she did.

During the night a limousine arrived at the Bern house with his common-law wife, Dorothy Millette. They drank wine on the patio and she went for a swim. In the early morning hours of Labor Day Jean returned home. Finding Millette with Paul, Jean said, 'When you find out who you're married to, let me know.' Then she left them alone. A gun shot woke her up. When Mayer was notified he told Jean, 'You know nothing because you were at your mother's home all night.'

Mayer found a note Paul had written to Jean:

> Dearest Dear,
>
> Unfortunately this is the only way to make good the frightful wrong I have done you and to wipe out my abject humiliation. I love you,
>
> Paul
>
> You understand last night was only a comedy.

MGM said this was a suicide note but maybe it wasn't since it was found in a notebook. It might have been Paul's intention to send Jean flowers with these words. There is no date on the paper so it's very possible it was written at some other time. On that Labor Day, however, MGM determined it was to be a suicide note, though there was no explanation forthcoming from Jean.

On Friday, 8 September, Jean sobbed at Paul's funeral held in the Grace Chapel of Inglewood Park Cemetery. Irving Thalberg wept also and he would suffer another heart attack brought on by grief. Bern was cremated and his ashes interred at the Golden West Mausoleum in Inglewood Park.

As the investigation into Bern's death continued, MGM did everything to protect Jean at all costs. Doctors testified that Paul had undersized genitals and was most probably impotent. Already there was enormous sympathy for Jean, but then Dorothy Millette's identity was confirmed after her body was found floating in the Sacramento River. Paul had been supporting her for many years. They had met at the Academy of Dramatic Arts in New York and lived together. He referred to her as his common-law wife. In May 1932 Millette moved to San Francisco to be near her sister.

There was speculation that she killed Bern, but the gun was clutched in his hand with his finger on the trigger. Police had a difficult time dislodging the pistol from Paul's grip.

That Bern was a bigamist might have been a scandal but the public's sympathy for Harlow did not wane. Jean paid for Millette's burial and tombstone (engraved Dorothy Millette Bern). Harlow used her own money because Paul's estate was insolvent.

Jean told Anita Loos that Bern thought he could overcome his impotency being married to her but he couldn't. He tried to assuage his guilt by practices which Jean was too normal to accept. Loos said Jean understood. 'Do whatever you want, sweetheart, but count me out of those sessions,' she told Paul. Loos speculated that Paul killed himself after approaching his wife about his sexual desires. This makes sense since Jean knew about Dorothy Millette. Though we know more today than we ever did about Paul Bern's suicide, there are still a few missing links. Unfortunately, Harlow was subjected to hearing the shot that killed her husband, finding his body, and trying to live with that memory subsequently. Why did he make sure she was in the house before he put the gun to his head in front of a full-length mirror? Was she being punished for being the sexiest woman in the world, but not sexy enough to produce the miracle he wanted?

It's no wonder Jean began to drink. At first she needed liquor to relax and forget. Then it became a habit, though she never appeared drunk. Mother Bello nagged her about it so Jean had to sneak her drinks, making matters worse.

Meanwhile *Red Dust* was a smash hit and broke all records at the box office. MGM teamed Harlow and Gable again in *Hold Your Man* about a con artist and a hussy. He accidentally kills her boyfriend and allows her to take the rap. But when Gable finds out she's carrying his baby, he attempts to marry her and is arrested. In the end, mother and son are waiting for Gable at the prison gates.

In *Dinner at Eight* Harlow plays the dizzy wife of a rich businessman (Wallace Berry) who spends her days in bed eating bonbons and waiting for her lover. She attends a high-society dinner party and tells Marie Dressler, 'I was reading a book the other day . . .'

Dressler is stunned and asks 'Reading a book?'

'Yes, it's all about civilisation or something. Do you know that the guy said that machinery is going to take the place of every profession?'

Dressler takes a good look at Jean in a tight satin dress and says, 'Oh, my dear, that's something you need never worry about.'

Then they proceed into the dining room as the movie ends.

Harlow was in awe of such great stars as Marie Dressler and the Barrymore brothers who were also in *Dinner at Eight*. She said it was an honour to be on the same movie set with them.

In *Bombshell* Jean plays a Hollywood star whose family takes advantage of her by living in the same house and doing nothing while she works hard at the studio. This mirrors Mother and Marino Bello who bragged a lot and then asked Jean for more money.

In the summer of 1933 Jean was having an affair with boxer Max Baer who was filming *The Prizefighter and the Lady*. She hung around the set to be with him and often drove past his residence to find out if he was at home with his wife or out with someone else. Baer tired of Harlow but that didn't prevent his wife from naming Jean in her divorce. Louella Parsons got wind of it and mentioned the affair in her column. L.B. Mayer was concerned that another scandal might hurt Jean. With the anniversary of Bern's suicide approaching, he did not want her involved in Baer's messy divorce. Mayer decided Jean should have a husband and chose cameraman Hal Rosson who had worked with Jean on most of her movies. On 18 September 1933, they were married in Yuma, Arizona. Rosson, who was 38, bore a slight resemblance to Paul Bern because of the moustache but any similarity ends there because Hal was very masculine and known for his skills in bed.

The newlyweds returned to Jean's mansion on Beverly Glen. Mother Bello had built it with her daughter's money and Marino somehow convinced Jean to sign over title to them. Rosson refused to live in the same house with the Bellos so he and Jean moved into the Chateau Marmont hotel on Sunset Boulevard. But this did not prevent Marino from going to Mayer and demanding that Harlow's weekly salary be increased from $1500 to $5000. Mayer refused and put Jean on suspension without pay on 13 November 1933. The Bellos were able to manipulate Jean after her appendicitis operation and her mother's insistence that Jean stay with her to recuperate. Hal Rosson had to be content to live at the Chateau Marmont alone, seeing Jean when the Bellos chose to let him in. Hal sought revenge by abusing Jean who occasionally showed up at the studio with bruises on her face.

In the spring of 1934 MGM offered Harlow $3000 a week and she returned to work. She also divorced Hal Rosson, who blamed the Bellos.

Anita Loos said, 'Mother Bello had an amazing hold over Jean. What she couldn't accomplish was getting Jean to stop drinking. If you think about it, who could blame a 23-year-old movie goddess whose three marriages had gone wrong. Jean blamed herself and that's a shame.'

The Girl from Missouri presented Jean as a gold-digger, but one who remains pure and is rewarded when she finally marries the son of a millionaire. This was not one of Harlow's best films. The audience, apparently, liked her better when she was openly promiscuous. But the public was hungry for a Harlow film after such a long wait and flocked to see *The Girl from Missouri*.

Jean was dating suave 42-year-old actor William Powell, known best for his role of Nick Charles in the *Thin Man* films. Writer Adela Rogers St Johns said, 'Jean was mad about Bill Powell. He was the perfect man for her. She called him "Poppy". He was father and lover, but I think Bill was lukewarm about the romance because he'd been married to zany Carole Lombard and didn't want another nutty blonde, though Jean was always the lady in his company. She was known to expose her breasts if anyone made fun of her low-cut gown, but not with Bill. He didn't approve.'

William Powell was born in Pittsburgh in 1892 and was living in Kansas City when Jean was born. He went to the American Academy of Dramatic Arts in New York City, played in stock companies and on Broadway. In 1915 he married actress Eileen Wilson, and had a son William David in 1925. William divorced Eileen when he met Carole Lombard whom he married in 1931. But he was a shy, private person in contrast to Lombard who was gregarious and much younger. They were divorced two years later but remained friends until her death in 1942.

Powell signed a contract with MGM in 1934 and met Jean on the set of *Manhattan Melodrama* when she visited his co-star Clark Gable. She had 'found him', Jean told friends. She had found the love of her life at last. Powell did not date Jean until she announced her divorce from Rosson, however. He was a very neat person with fine manners and a sense of decency. He was charming, witty and practical. He would venture to a nightclub now and then but was not a party fellow. That was all right with Jean. She would be anything he wanted.

Mayer took advantage of the romance and put Harlow and Powell in *Reckless* about an actress whose husband shoots himself. The theme was too close to home – that of a woman hearing a gunshot and finding her husband's dead body. Jean got through it because of Bill but was hampered by Mother Bello who was on the set every day to make sure her 'baby' did not go off her diet. Powell was privy to the control Jean's mother had over her and he didn't like it one bit.

Reckless was a disappointment, however. Harlow's starring in a musical was nonsense. Her singing was dubbed and someone else did the dancing, but Jean was required to know the routines. Audiences didn't like it or buy it.

But Harlow's next movie, *China Seas*, had been Bern's idea and was an Irving Thalberg production. Jean is in her element with Gable as captain of a steamship from Hong Kong to Singapore, who gives up his blonde mistress (Harlow) for a more refined woman (Rosalind Russell). But in the end Gable can't let Harlow go, and all ends well. Jean was marvellous in *China Seas*, proving once again the power of the Harlow–Gable combination.

Jean had been dating Bill Powell for a year, but he, like Bern and Rosson, refused to be in the same room with the Bellos. He was appalled by their demands on Jean and how she gave in to them. Harlow would spend her time at Bill's house if she wanted to be with him.

In August 1935 Jean Harlow made the cover of *Time* magazine. She wore a white negligée with ostrich-trimmed sleeves. The article was very revealing and truthful, especially regarding Marino and his Mexican gold mines. William Powell did some investigating and found out that Marino was taking a huge chunk of Jean's weekly salary for gold mines that did not exist. The money was used for his own folly and to support a mistress. When Mother Bello found out, she divorced Marino. He asked for $250,000 but settled on $22,000. Jean had to borrow the money from MGM to pay him. From then on Powell helped Jean with her finances, urging her to invest wisely. At this stage, Harlow should have insisted her mother sell the big house and move into a smaller one, and refused to support her until she did, but Jean was a softie. Powell loved her for her loyalty but he did not want a wife who was dominated by her mother.

Jean never told Mother Bello about Marino's advances and love letters to her when she was living under the same roof with them. When she married Bern, she told Anita Loos, 'I'm glad to be away from my stepfather, believe me!'

But Marino was always on the movie set, seducing starlets and boasting that he was responsible for Jean's booming career. What came as a suprise to everyone was that Mother Bello knew about Marino's affairs, but was so infatuated with him she looked the other way. As usual, it was Jean who paid.

So did her hair from too much bleaching. It began to fall out during *Reckless*, forcing Jean to wear wigs. Her hairdressers wanted to tone down the colour and save her hair, and Mayer agreed. Maybe it was time for a new Harlow image, anyway. Mayer hoped William Powell, with his conservative ways, would seriously consider marrying a brunette.

Jean's new hair colour made its debut in *Riffraff* with Spencer Tracy, a tuna fisherman who falls in love with a cannery worker, played by Harlow. The film received rave reviews and was popular at the box office, proving Jean's appeal as a brunette. She was happy with her new image. 'I never liked platinum,' she said, 'or the roles that went with it.' MGM rushed her into *Wife vs. Secretary* with Clark Gable and Myrna Loy. Jean plays it straight in this film, but Loy suspects she is having an affair with Gable, who plays her husband. Jean gets them back together. The *Hollywood Reporter* said, 'This is the beginning of a whole new career for Harlow. Her secretary is among the finest things she has ever given us.'

In March 1936 Jean's divorce from Hal Rosson became final. Louella Parsons hinted that Harlow and Powell would get married and the *Hollywood Reporter* predicted the same thing, but Jean said, 'Poppy doesn't think we should get married. Maybe two people who make movies can't make a go of it. But I'd like to settle down with Bill and have a family. I love him very much.'

Jean finally sold the big house and rented a smaller one. Mother Bello detested Powell for convincing her daughter to go through with it over her protests. But this was a big move on Jean's part and perhaps the first time she had gone against her mother's strong will. Myrna Loy, who was Nora Charles to William Powell's Nick in the *Thin Man* films, said Powell could not forget his being 'Mr Carole Lombard'. He would never go through that again. Though he was a star in his own right in 1936, it was Harlow who was the superstar and he was not going to walk in her shadow.

Jean, who wanted Bill's child very much, had to submit to another abortion . . . another reason for Harlow to lose herself in a bottle of gin that was her constant companion off the set.

Jean's next film, *Suzy*, with Cary Grant was a hit. As a chorus girl stranded in Europe, she was low key. Reviews were only fair, but audiences flocked to the box office, as always, to see Harlow.

In *Libeled Lady* Jean is again a floozy who wants to marry Spencer Tracy but is forced to wed William Powell in order to frame heiress Myrna Loy.

In this complicated plot, Jean steals the picture and proves once and for all what a gifted comedienne she really was.

Harlow accompanied Bill to San Francisco where he was filming *After the Thin Man* with Myrna Loy, who spent a lot of time with Jean. 'I felt so sorry for her,' Loy said. 'We sat up and talked all night about many things but mostly about Bill. I knew he would never marry her. Maybe he wanted to but he was very reluctant. Her mother had a boyfriend so I was hopeful Bill would change his mind. Jean wasn't one of those dedicated actresses who wouldn't give up her career. She would have quit in an instant. Fame meant nothing to her.'

Bill gave Jean an 85-carat star sapphire ring for Christmas. It was huge and Harlow flaunted it. She considered this an engagement ring, but Powell said nothing so she wore it on her right hand. Anita Loos thought Powell was forced into giving Jean a 'friendship' ring because he was practically living with her. 'I know she was drinking heavily,' Loos said. 'A mutual friend told me she downed a bottle of gin by herself. She looked terrible – bloated and puffy. But she didn't drink when she was working.'

After doing *Personal Property* with Robert Taylor, the cast of the movie went to Washington D.C. for a round of parties celebrating President Roosevelt's fifty-fifth birthday. It was a hectic schedule that drained Jean of her energy. She returned to Hollywood with influenza, but recovered in time to attend the Academy Awards on a double date with Powell, Gable and Lombard. Maybe it was being in the company of Bill's vivacious ex-wife that convinced Jean to get out of the relationship.

During the filming of *Saratoga* with Clark Gable, Jean heard from Powell and their relationship resumed. She became ill during production and was sent home but she went to Powell's mansion instead because Mother Bello was on Catalina Island with her boyfriend. Concerned about Jean's health, Bill got in touch with her mother who took Jean home on 31 May 1936. Much has been written about Mother Bello's Christian Science beliefs and her not giving Jean proper care, but a doctor and two nurses were attending to Harlow.

When Gable found out she had to leave the movie set early he remarked, 'Probably drunk again'. He was criticised for saying this but, in fact, Jean was drinking during *Saratoga*, a first for her. She needed it to dull the pain, she said.

Mother Bello believed Jean was suffering from alcoholism and tried to keep visitors away until her daughter dried out. But Harlow was afflicted with kidney disease (chronic glomerulonephritis) secondary to scarlet fever. Apparently she had been in decline since her bout of scarlet fever at summer camp when she was fifteen. The first doctor who treated Jean diagnosed her illness as inflammation of the gall bladder and treated her with dextrose injections rather than diuretics. By the time another doctor was summoned it was too late. L.B. Mayer had come to see Jean, offering the help of his personal physician, but Mother Bello refused to let him in. He told Howard Strickling, 'The next time one of our valuable properties gets sick, the studio's got to find out what's the matter.'

On Sunday 6 June, Bill Powell paid a visit to Jean, his first. He thought she looked pale but assumed she would be all right. That night an ambulance took her to Good Samaritan Hospital. On Monday newspapers reported Harlow was dying and Powell rushed to see her. He was devastated, sick to his stomach and sobbing outside her hospital room.

The nurse who was tending Harlow said, 'She has no desire to live. She said so.'

At 11:38 a.m. she died.

The offices and movie sets at MGM suddenly became silent. No one spoke in the noisy chatty canteen. Mickey Rooney said, 'It wasn't a star passing away. It wasn't a legend. It wasn't Jean Harlow. It was one of our family.'

On 8 June, the day of Jean's funeral, every studio in Hollywood observed a minute of silence. At the Wee Kirk O'The Heather chapel at Forest Lawn Cemetery in Glendale, flowers overflowed. Mayer sent a heart of red roses five feet tall pierced by a golden arrow, and Howard Hughes sent roses. But there were hundreds of other floral arrangements from stars and technicians and fans. It appeared that the flowers were worth more than Jean's estate that was said to be insolvent. However, she had taken Powell's advice and invested in non-taxable bonds amounting to $100,000 to be paid in monthly sums to Mother Bello who tried in vain to get the whole amount up front.

Jeanette MacDonald sang 'Indian Love call', and Nelson Eddy, 'Ah, Sweet Mystery of Life'. The funeral lasted less than twenty-five minutes.

Jean was laid to rest in her coffin wearing the pink negligée from *Saratoga* and a blonde wig. Powell placed a rose on her breast before the coffin was closed and covered with a spread of gardenias and lily of the valley paid for by MGM. Mother Bello made sure her Baby was entombed like a queen. She announced that William Powell had bought a room in Forest Lawn's luxurious Sanctuary of Benediction mausoleum. It's not known what Powell had offered to buy for Jean's resting place, but surely not a site that cost

$25,000. Tight with a dollar, he was stunned. Mother Bello pointed out there was room for three in the crypt, ensuring a place for herself and Bill. The third one remains empty to this day. Jean Harlow's name is etched over the entrance, and in the middle is simply inscribed 'Our Baby'.

Saratoga, featuring a double to complete the film without Harlow, attracted a big audience. MGM had pondered whether to release it, but Jean's fans wanted to see her last performance. Despite her bad health, Harlow was convincing as the daughter of a horse breeder in this race-track drama, but it will always be best known for being Harlow's last film.

Two years later William Powell married Diana Lewis, a 21-year-old starlet. He recovered from rectal cancer and lived to be 91. Did he regret Jean's abortion when his son by his first wife committed suicide?

Mother Bello married her boyfriend Heinie Brand and divorced him two years later. In June 1958 she died of a heart attack at the age of 69.

Today Jean Harlow has a whole new legion of fans who love and appreciate her as much as the ones who lined up to see her latest picture. But it's fair to say she envied them more than they did her . . .

The Films of Jean Harlow

Moron of the Marines (Paramount, 1928)
Fugitives (20th Century-Fox, 1929)
Close Harmony (Paramount, 1929)
Love Parade (Paramount, 1929)
The Saturday Night Kid (Paramount, 1929)
New York Nights (United Artists, 1929)
Hell's Angels (United Artists, 1930)
City Lights (United Artists, 1931)
Secret Six (MGM, 1931)
Iron Man (Universal, 1931)
Public Enemy (Warner Brothers, 1931)
Goldie (20th Century-Fox, 1931)
Platinum Blonde (Columbia, 1931)
Three Wise Girls (Columbia, 1932)
The Beast of the City (MGM, 1932)
Red-Headed Woman (MGM, 1932)
Dinner at Eight (MGM, 1933)
Hold Your Man (MGM, 1933)
Bombshell (MGM, 1933)
The Girl from Missouri (MGM, 1934)
Reckless (MGM, 1935)
China Seas (MGM, 1935)
Riffraff (MGM, 1935)
Wife vs. Secretary (MGM, 1936)
Suzy (MGM, 1936)
Libeled Lady (MGM, 1936)
Personal Property (MGM, 1937)
Saratoga (MGM, 1937)

5

Joan

She was the first star created by a motion-picture studio. She was manufactured by the newly formed Metro-Goldwyn-Mayer in 1925. Author F. Scott Fitzgerald described her as '. . . the best example of the flapper, the girl you see in nightclubs, gowned to the apex of sophistication, toying with iced glasses with a remote, faintly bitter expression, dancing deliciously, laughing a great deal with wide hurt eyes – a young thing with a talent for living,' hardly a candidate for stardom at MGM known for its genteel roster of contract players. Discovered when she was twenty-one (she claimed to be seventeen) she swore like a sailor, chomped on gum and told dirty jokes that delighted the grips and cast members who enjoyed a bawdy break in the staid atmosphere of MGM.

She slept with influential men, pleading with them for a chance to prove herself. She worked harder than other young starlets and grabbed every minute opportunity with gusto. Never satisfied, she spent her spare time with those who could teach and advise her. Make no mistake about it, she'd been around. She'd had passionate love affairs, her share of abortions and posed for pornographic pictures. But Joan Crawford turned her life around gallantly and became everything that Hollywood thought exemplified 'Movie Star'.

She was born Lucille Fay LeSueur on 23 March 1904 in San Antonio, Texas. Her father, Thomas, was a French-Canadian labourer who married Anna Bell Johnson around the turn of the century. They had three children – Daisy, who died as an infant and Hal in 1902. Thomas deserted his family before Lucille's birth. Anna, broke and desolate, moved with her family to Lawton, Oklahoma, where she married Henry Cassin, owner and operator of the Opera House that featured vaudeville, operettas and classical ballet. Lucille, who assumed Henry was her real father, spent most of her time backstage watching performances.

> It was then I decided to be a dancer and Daddy Cassin encouraged me,' she said. 'I'll always be grateful to him for that. Those were the only fond memories I have of my childhood and they were short-lived because Henry was charged with gold embezzlement. He was acquitted but blackballed in Lawton so we moved to Kansas City where he bought a seedy hotel. But again Henry came to my rescue by enrolling me in St Agnes School to get me away from the cheap hotel transients. Then I came home one day and he was gone. I wish he'd taken me with him. My mother was a nagging bitch and my brother was a lazy good-for-nothing. I cried when I found out Daddy Cassin wasn't coming back and that's when Hal told me Henry was not my real father.

Lucille waited on tables and washed dishes at St Agnes to pay her tuition, dreading the weekends with Anna who was now managing a laundry and living with a delivery man, Harry Hough, whom she later married. Lucille wanted to keep her distance but was expelled from St Agnes for running around with boys after hours. Anna never asked her daughter why she came home. Her only comment was, 'We need help in the laundry.' Stories vary as to why Lucille was sent to Rockingham Academy in

1919. She claimed her stepfather tried to seduce her and a suspicious Anna decided to send her to Rockingham, a detention school for homeless, unwanted and unruly children, many of whom came from wealthy homes. Lucille cooked, cleaned and cared for the younger children. If her work displeased the headmistress she was beaten with a broom handle. Lucille wanted to run away but she had nowhere to go. The headmistress took it easy on her when one of the wealthiest boys at school wanted to take Lucille to a school dance. She had to borrow a faded blue taffeta dress but felt very royal when her date pinned a corsage on her shoulder.

> After three years at Rockingham they said I graduated,' Crawford recalled. 'Hell, I hadn't learned anything. They passed me because I'd served my purpose as a domestic. I didn't want to go home but my salvation was a swell guy, Ray Sterling. He was my first beau and I was in love but I wasn't good enough for him. He never said so and tried very hard to make a lady out of me. Ray changed my life like Daddy Cassin by encouraging me. Because of him I got into Stevens College in Columbia, Missouri, 125 miles away from my mother, thank God. I waited on tables to pay my tuition but I wasn't qualified for college. My grades had been rigged at Rockingham so when I faced final exams at Stevens, I spoke to the principal and told him the truth because I'm not a quitter. He understood and I left Stevens with no regrets. My mother assumed I left because of money. She always thought about the almighty dollar and always thought of me as a workhorse, someone to help pay the bills. She had faith in Hal and failed to see he couldn't get along without her. I leaned on Ray Sterling. I was never intimate with him. I would never have gotten to Hollywood if he'd wanted me but he didn't.

He didn't because it was no secret she was sleeping around . . .

Lucille worked at the telephone company, as a package wrapper and sales clerk in a department store. She entered amateur dance contests, hoping for a train ticket out of Kansas City. In 1923 she succeeded and joined chorus lines in Chicago and Detroit where she caught the eye of Broadway producer J.J. Shubert who signed her for his show *Innocent Eyes* that opened in May 1924, in New York City. 'What a thrill!' Crawford exclaimed. 'I was a nobody in a New York show! The money wasn't bad and men admired chorus girls. They took us to the best places, lavished us with gifts like candy, jewellery, flowers – the works!'

Innocent Eyes went on the road in November but Lucille opted to remain in New York for *The Passing Show of 1924*. MGM executive Harry Rapf noticed Lucille and arranged a screen test for her.

'We'll let you know,' he said.

'Yeah? Well, I'm goin' home for the Christmas holidays,' she exclaimed.

'Give me your address in Kansas City just in case.'

Lucille forgot about the screen test. She wasn't an actress and was very happy dancing in a New York show. On the train home she was thinking about Ray Sterling with whom she had corresponded regularly. 'I never got to see Ray,' Crawford said. 'He was out of town visiting relatives. I was very depressed. I sat around feeling sorry for myself until that telegram came. MGM offered me a five-year contract for $75 a week. I ran down to their office in Kansas City to pick up my train fare and expense money, bought a seat in a coach and spent the rest on clothes and Christmas presents.'

On a frosty New Year's Day 1925 Lucille LeSueur boarded the Missouri Pacific west. For almost three days she shivered from the cold in an uncomfortable, narrow seat. She cursed herself for spending her expense money on clothes instead of the comfortable sleeper paid for by MGM. She washed her hands and face only once because the water froze in the lavatories. On 3 January she stepped off the train and thawed out in the bright California sunshine, expecting to find Harry Rapf waiting for her with a bouquet of flowers. She stood alone on the platform wondering if she was on another planet. Was it actually seventy degrees in January?

'Are you Lucille LeSueur?'

'Yeah. Who are you?'

'Larry Barbier, MGM publicity. I'll get your luggage.'

'This is it,' she said, picking up the suitcase.

'Please, allow me. The limousine's right over here. We'll go to Mr Rapf's office after you check into the Hotel Washington. It's not swanky but it's cheap and only six blocks from the studio.'

Lucille stepped out of the plush limousine into a shabby hotel that reminded her of the cheap dives in Detroit and Chicago. 'Maybe I had no big ambition to be an actress,' Crawford said, 'but making enough money to get out of that dump was incentive enough.'

Harry Rapf extended his hand. 'Welcome to MGM. Did you have a nice trip?'

'Not bad.'

'Those sleepers are very comfortable, aren't they? I always feel like a million bucks when I get to my destination. Lucille, we're going to do more tests of you. I don't think the others did you justice.'

'I came all the way out here just to do another test?'

'This time you'll have access to our make-up department, hairdressers, wardrobe and professional cameramen. You'll have a chance to rehearse and . . .'

'I thought you offered me a job,' she said, feeling tears welling in her eyes.

'As you can see in our agreement, MGM has the option to break your contract after six-month intervals.'

'You bastard. Why didn't you tell me?'

Rapf liked her spirit. He liked her legs, too. 'I wouldn't worry about it, Lucille.'

'I'm nervous as hell,' she told one of the stagehands.

'Listen. When the director tells you to do something, concentrate on an incident in your past. Relive it.'

She was posed by the director, who asked her to smile, tilt her head, and turn right and left. When he told her to show anger, she thought about her mother. 'Cry, Lucille.' She thought about Rockingham and the tears flowed. 'Fun. You're having fun, Lucille.' But she couldn't stop crying until she heard another voice. She looked up at Tommy Shagrue, an electrician. 'Hey, Lucille, can you do the cakewalk? Fun, isn't it?' he smiled, doing a few steps. She smiled and then laughed out of sheer relief, knowing the test was over.

'I think you passed,' Shagrue said.

'I'll never forget what you did. Thanks.' Joan Crawford gave Shagrue a job on all of her movies and faithfully befriended stagehands during her career. They would prove invaluable to her transformation from common chorus girl to respected movie actress.

Lucille's screen test showed promise. She was kept on salary but ignored. With only six months to prove herself she got up early every morning and reported to the studio. Her favourite pastime was watching the handsome, all-American movie actor Billy Haines, who became a lifelong friend. MGM knew Billy was a homosexual but they cleverly made him the darling of the ladies and occasionally hinted he was headed for the altar. He did marry, eventually, but to his boyfriend, Jimmy Shields. Meanwhile, it was Billy whose funny antics and down-to-earth personality helped Lucille get through her first year at MGM.

It was Haines who suggested she talk to Rapf about getting some experience in front of the camera. She took his advice and was assigned as a double for Norma Shearer, who was playing a dual role in *Lady of the Night*.

'But we don't look alike,' she complained.

'They'll only see the back of your head.'

'Shit.'

Rapf might have been offended by Lucille's cursing during their chats but he was a former vaudeville booking agent with a large nose that earned him the nickname The Anteater. Though he held the prestigious job of production assistant, Harry and Lucille spoke the same language. He was attracted to her and she was intimate with him. As a stepping stone, she could do worse. Harry got her a small part as a chorus girl in *Pretty Ladies*. She was billed for the first and last time as Lucille LeSueur.

'We're changing your name,' Rapf said. 'It's too stagy and besides, it rhymes with sewer. We're going to put your picture in *Movie Weekly* and sponsor a contest to find a new name. It's great publicity and we'll make a big deal over the winner. Movie fans will identify themselves with you.'

The winning name was 'Joan Arden', but a few days later it was discovered that a bit player went by that name. 'Joan Crawford' was second choice.

'It sounds like crawfish!' she told Billy Haines.

'Could have been worse,' he laughed. 'Suppose they chose "Cranberry" and served you every Thanksgiving with the turkey?'

'Harry's puttin' me in *Old Clothes* with Jackie Coogan.'

'You're on a first-name basis?' Haines winked

'Isn't everybody around here?'

'Not with Louis B. Mayer, honey.'

'I haven't gotten around to him yet.'

Haines threw his head back and laughed. 'No one gets around to Mr Mayer, my dear Cranberry. When he gets around to you, it means you've been accepted as part of the MGM family. Meantime, you should be seen around town with your new name. Get to know the right people. It'll pay off.'

Haines was right. One reporter wrote, 'Everything about the young hotcha girl from MGM is real. Her energy is abundant. She dances through lunch, tea, and dinner, long into the night. Joan Crawford is the hottest and most daring girl in town. She hasn't a care in the world and is frank about how she mastered the Charleston. Saying she learned the sizzling steps in Harlem is a devilish admission, but no one can keep up with her. She is to the Charleston what Valentino is to the tango.'

Mogul L.B. Mayer was sceptical. This was not the reputation he expected of his contract players. 'MGM is not a flophouse for flappers,' he told Rapf. 'I want a clean image for this girl. Can she act?'

'She got good reviews in *Old Clothes*. One critic said she stole the picture from Coogan.'

'Put her in *Sally, Irene, and Mary* with the fairy Haines.'

Playing a chorus girl once again, Joan received good notices but it was cameraman Johnny Arnold who went out on a limb and told her to lose weight. 'You have marvellous bone structure,' he said. 'You photograph well from every angle but let's get rid of the baby fat.'

'I've never been on a diet in my life.'

'Steak and vegetables three times a day. Nothing else. You'll be broke but thin.'

'I've been broke but never thin. Okay. I'll do it!'

Rapf, pleased with *Sally, Irene, and Mary* gave Joan a $25 weekly raise and a kiss. She kissed him back and cooed, 'With this money I can rent a tiny bungalow.'

Joan felt better about herself after losing twenty pounds. Living in her own place was a new and rewarding experience, also, though Haines said it looked like a bordello. 'Take back those dreadful pink taffeta drapes,' he scowled. 'And get rid of the frills, tassels and sequins.'

'I think it looks swell,' she replied. 'I finished decorating just in time because I'm having dinner with Paul Bern tomorrow night at Montmartre.'

'Cranberry, meet him there. Bern is a very conservative man. He'll die when he sees this gaudy mess.'

'He's interested in me, not my decorating.'

Paul Bern was one of the most influential men at MGM. He worked with his good friend, Irving Thalberg, vice-president in charge of production. Bern was the intellectual responsible for putting theatre on film in such classics as *Grand Hotel* and *Camille*. Known as 'Father Confessor and Advisor to the Stars', Bern was short, balding and middle-aged but seemed to tower over the beautiful and stately actresses he dated. He was bisexual and suffered from bouts of depression and impotency due to underdeveloped genitals.

> 'Paul took me to a white-tie and violins night at Montmartre,' Joan said. 'I was wearing a low-cut flapper dress and too much make-up. I felt very cheap sitting opposite this soft-spoken, quiet-mannered, well-groomed gentleman who reminded me of Henry Cassin. We discussed my future in talkies. This was a scary subject but Paul said I had nothing to worry about. In the meantime he was going to select dresses from the wardrobe department for me to wear to elite parties, premieres, plays and concerts. I was on my way, thanks to this dear man.'

It's not known when Joan's intense affair with Bern began. She brought out the best in him sexually but wanted more than he could manage, according to Haines who saw Paul crying on her shoulder in a dark corner on the movie set. When Billy asked her about it she replied, 'Sometimes he gets despondent . . .'

Trying to cheer her up Haines said, 'Yes, like the time the gorgeous Barbara La Marr turned down his marriage proposal. He tried to drown himself in the toilet and his head got stuck in the seat. When they got him out he looked like a derby winner.'

'He gave me an ermine coat and I wouldn't take it.'

'Why, Cranberry?'

'Because I'm seeing other men.'

Bern made it possible for Joan to star opposite the great Lon Chaney in *The Unknown*, about an armless knife-thrower in a circus who used his feet to hurl knives at his assistant, played by Joan. The *New York Evening World* commented, 'Miss Crawford's one of the screen's acknowledged artists, and each picture seems to merely justify the characterisation. Her performance in this picture is a most impressive one.'

This review opened the golden door to L.B. Mayer's office to her. 'Congratulations,' he exclaimed. 'I thought it was time we got to know each other. We're a family here at MGM. I want you to think of me as the father you never had. Your problems are my problems. My door is always open to you.'

'Thank you, sir.'

'On my desk is a new contract. Does two hundred fifty dollars a week sound good to you?'

'How much? I mean, yes, I can manage on that.'

'Paul tells me you send money home to your mother who lives in Kansas City.'

'Yes, even though she doesn't deserve it.'

'Joan, never talk ill of your mother. She is to be honoured and loved. Motherhood is the life of this great country of ours. Did you know our canteen chef uses my mother's recipe for chicken soup? You'll love it.'

'Can't wait to try it,' she said, signing the contract.

Mayer was not only impressed with Joan's acting ability. He relished the publicity about Bern's escorting her to every major event, not to mention her dates with Mike Cudahy, alcoholic heir to a Chicago meat-packing fortune. Then there was Tommy Lee, son of auto and radio millionaire Don Lee. Mayer knew Joan was intimate with heart-throb John Gilbert but this was a dressing-room affair because he was living with Greta Garbo. If this intimacy went public, Mayer would stop it because he despised Gilbert, who referred to his mother as a whore. Renowned for his harsh language and threats, Mayer was also famous for his tender approach and solemn promises. With Joan he would use all the tactics. In her he saw a workhorse, a go-getter, a hustler, and a beautiful tramp. '. . . as long as she doesn't get laid on Sunset, I don't care,' he told one of his spies who jotted down, 'at sunset', and the story got around.

Joan asked Haines, 'Did he mean on Sunset or at sunset?'

'Mayer's saying he knows you're sleeping around.'

'Does he know you like boys?'

'Sure. He'll get around to arranging a marriage if there are any concrete rumours.'

'Maybe we have a chance after all,' she teased.

'Not unless you're a lesbian. That's how it's done.'

When Joan got top billing in *Rose-Marie* with James Murray she bought a box camera to take pictures of her name on the theatre entrances. She was not making quality films, however, and when she was cast opposite Ramon Novarro in the potboiler *Across to Singapore*, Joan decided to take matters in her own hands. She was tired of Bern's classical music and preaching, tired of Mayer's father hugs while he pinched her right breast and tired of being called the most promising newcomer when there was nothing new that was worthwhile.

Joan did the unthinkable by approaching Irving Thalberg on the set. She made small talk and he paid little attention to her until she blurted out, 'Why does your wife get the choice parts? It's not fair.'

He said nothing at first. Nor did he look at her. It was a long minute before he said, 'You're progressing nicely and will continue to do so.'

'I'd like to know how long it takes to get a good part in a good picture, that's all . . .'

'You wouldn't want to make a fool of yourself, I'm sure,' he said.

Before she could challenge him, Thalberg walked away without a glance. Joan could not remember an emptier feeling.

'You did what?' Haines exploded.

'I had to do it,' she said. 'Norma Shearer doesn't deserve the parts she's getting.'

'You'll pay a high price for what you did. Thalberg could put you on suspension without pay. But he's a decent guy despite what you think, Cranberry.'

'So?'

'He'll probably put you in a film you'll try to forget the rest of your life.'

The name of that picture was *The Law of the Range*, a western with Tim McCoy. The first day on the set Joan said to McCoy, 'I'm going to enjoy working with you and your cowboys if it kills me.' She was the first one to report for work and made friends with everyone as if she were having the time of her life.

To make matters worse, Anna and brother Hal appeared on her doorstep. Joan used what influence she had to get Hal work as an extra and bit player at MGM. Bern, who was still squiring Joan around town, was worried about her. 'I know all about Tim McCoy and your family problems,' he said calmly. 'But I've had a bit of luck getting you Hunt Stromberg's *Our Dancing Daughters* and the part of Diana is you, Joan . . . the misunderstood flapper who dances the nights away with a broken heart.' She read the script and there was no doubt it had been written for her. With fine support from Johnny Mack Brown and Nils Asher, *Our Dancing Daughters* was a smash. The *New York World* wrote, 'Of Miss Crawford it may be predicted that in case her managers continue to find such breezy little comedies for her, she will realise what apparently has been her ambition for at least two years, and get going as a star in her own right. She has good looks, sprightliness, intelligence, and a good sense of humour. She dances with great grace and versatility and she knows when – and how – to call a halt.'

Mayer doubled Joan's salary and loaned her the down payment for a new house on Roxbury Drive that cost $18,000. She would support Anna but not live under the same roof with her.

Bern invited Joan to the opening night of *Young Wooley* at the Vine Street Playhouse. After the performance he took her backstage to meet the leading man, Douglas Fairbanks Jr. The next day she invited him for tea but was not available when he called for a date. 'That aroused my curiosity,' he said.

Douglas Fairbanks Jr was born on 9 December 1907 in New York. His mother, Beth Sully, was heiress to a cotton fortune, and his father, Douglas Fairbanks Sr, was a well-known stage actor. His parents' divorce in 1918 was blamed on his father's success in Hollywood. America's Sweetheart Mary Pickford became Junior's stepmother in 1920 though he saw very little of Mary and his swashbuckling father or their Pickfair mansion, the Buckingham Palace of Hollywood. Young Doug pursued a career on the stage and film producers thought he had a chance in films. It was at this stage in his life that he met Joan, who managed the romance very cleverly by keeping her distance but not for very long. Two months after they met, he proposed marriage and their engagement was announced on 8 October 1928. Mayer was so delighted he paired them in *Our Modern Maidens*, gave Joan another raise and another loan to buy a white stucco Moorish house at 426 North Bristol Avenue in Brentwood for $40,000. Her decision to buy a house had nothing to do with her impending marriage. It was simply a case of the bigger the star, the bigger the house. Mayer did not quibble with Joan about money because he didn't want it known that the Prince of Pickfair was in debt.

The elder Fairbanks was sick over the fact that his son was involved with Crawford and refused to discuss Junior's engagement with reporters. The press sided with Joan, the poor young girl who'd worked her way through school and danced to stardom. Poor Joan. She had suffered starvation, worn hand-me-downs, was beaten bloody by a nasty headmistress and was abused by her stepfather. By the time fan magazines printed the heart-rending stories of her pitiful background, moviegoers hoped Pickfair would burn to the ground.

Mayer's silent message to Fairbanks Sr was the success of *Our Modern Maidens*. Translated it went, 'If we've accepted your son, why can't you accept our daughter?' Then it seemed only fitting that Joan place her footprints in the forecourt of Grauman's Chinese Theater.

Metro-Goldwyn-Mayer's famous introduction logo Leo the Lion roared for the first time in 1928 and their first sound film *Broadway Melody* won an Oscar for Best Picture of 1928–1929. It was publicised as 'All Talking, All Dancing, All Singing'. Irving Thalberg, though a film production genius, did not think talking pictures would endure, so MGM lagged behind the other studios but, once they caught up, their movies were unsurpassed.

In the Oscar-nominated *Hollywood Revue of 1929*, Joan sang and danced to 'I've Got a Feeling for You'. Norma Shearer played Juliet to John Gilbert's Romeo. The film was a revue without a plot, featuring skits by MGM contract players. The finale brought all the stars on stage for a musical number 'Singin' in the Rain' in Technicolor. Joan, wearing a yellow raincoat and hat, joined the chorus line of stars with her arm around Marion Davies, mistress of millionaire newspaper mogul William Randolph Hearst.

The stock-market crash in 1929 changed the attitude of moviegoers at a time when sound was causing expensive havoc and transition in Hollywood. But motion pictures would play a big part in uplifting the saddened heart of a nation. Movie themes would blend tears with laughter, there would be romance in a meadow or in the arms of a gangster, and westerns would mosey along. MGM was so concerned that Garbo, Shearer, Haines and Gilbert would not make the transition to sound that Joan was almost forgotten.

'I had tap-danced and sung on the screen but not talked,' she said. 'I was scheduled to do my first talkie, *Untamed*, with Robert Montgomery. Someone gave me a diction book and told me to study it. Mostly, I read out loud to myself.'

Joan expressed her concern to Bern who said she would make the transition to sound with no problem. Before she started *Untamed*, Joan married Doug in the rectory of St Malachy's Roman Catholic Church in New York City on 3 June 1929. She gave him a wafer-thin platinum watch with diamond-studded hands. His gift to her was a gold cigarette box and lighter.

Joan's telegram to Mayer read, 'If I have worked hard in the past watch me now.' Doug's wire said, 'Joan and I were married yesterday. Now that I have a wife to support need raise in salary.'

The press felt betrayed at not having the pleasure of covering a lavish church wedding in Hollywood. They blamed Pickfair for the couple's elopement and, once again, Mayer was elated. After all, the occupants of Pickfair were not members of the MGM family. Though Mary Pickford had won an Oscar for Best Actress in her first talkie, *Coquette*, in 1929, America's Sweetheart was finished in Hollywood as was Fairbanks Sr, whose flamboyant antics on screen were passé. As they descended the ladder, Joan was rushing past them on her way up, thanks to MGM who boasted they had 'More Stars Than There are in Heaven'.

In *Untamed*, Joan plays the daughter of an oilman who is killed and makes her an heiress. Brought up in the wilds of South America, she moves into a New York mansion and falls in love with a struggling young engineer. He won't marry her so she shoots him in a jealous rage when he elopes with someone else on the rebound. But love conquers all and the ending is a happy one. Critics agreed that Crawford's voice was alluring, her diction clear and unaffected.

Although MGM and Joan's fans were relieved that she succeeded where ninety per cent of the silent screen stars failed, most of her publicity centred around her fairy-tale marriage. One of Joan's first guests was Billy Haines who was in a faint when he saw the rose, ivory, and green brocaded silk drapes, gold brocaded settees and a Burmese cover draped over the grand piano. The sun porch was crammed with toy gifts – Doug's electric train, Joan's teddy bears and dolls. She called the ten-room home 'El-Jodo'.

'El joke!' Haines barked. 'How the devil did you come up with that name, Cranberry?'

Unfazed, Joan sighed, 'Jodo stands for Joan and Doug, silly, and this house reflects our dollhouse marriage.'

'I'm surprised your fans aren't picketing Pickfair.'

'I've been snubbed all my life,' she said, 'so I'll be damned if I'll allow a 36-year-old Goldilocks and a flabby Robin Hood get under my skin.'

But eight months after the wedding, an engraved invitation arrived at 426 Bristol Avenue – 'Mr and Mrs Douglas Fairbanks Sr request the honor of your presence at a dinner honoring Lord and Lady Mountbatten at Pickfair.' Apparently Lord Mountbatten was unaware of the tension and asked to meet 'Our Dancing Daughter', and his wish was granted.

Joan fretted for a week about choosing an appropriate dress and hairdo. She wore a virginal white gown and almost regretted it on the way to the dinner party. 'I'm going to throw up,' she moaned. When the limousine pulled up to the entrance, Joan gagged and leaned forward. The chauffeur opened the car door and Doug took his pale wife's trembling hand. 'Please take me home,' she pleaded. But Doug took her arm firmly and, as if the director had said 'Action!' Joan Crawford stood erect, and with her chin up, she entered the sacred portals of Pickfair.

As Joan approached the unsmiling host and hostess, she stopped. 'My shoelace is untied, darling,' she whispered. 'Do you mind?' Doug got down on his hands and knees while Mary Pickford waited and the elder Fairbanks grinned. This pause gave Joan a chance to get her bearings and catch up to her heartbeat. Mary Pickford, also in white, but shrouded in diamonds, extended her gloved hand. 'Joan, dear, welcome to Pickfair.' Crawford said the occasion was a total blank to her in later years. Though she and Mary said very little to each other during her marriage to Fairbanks, Joan got along very well with 'Uncle Douglas', who became very fond of his daughter-in-law, playing jokes on her at dinner. His favourite was distracting her while she concentrated on which knife and fork to use. 'When I used the dessert spoon for the fish course,' Crawford recalled, 'he burst into gales of laughter.'

Following the successful dinner for Lord Mountbatten, Joan and Doug spent every Sunday at Pickfair. While the men played golf and Mary napped before dinner, Joan sat alone with her knitting in the living room.

The fan magazines were filled with stories about Joan and Doug. The big question was when Joan would have a baby. Mary Pickford made it clear that her 'Little Mary' image must be maintained, and becoming a grandmother would surely shatter the illusion. There were rumours of Joan's miscarriages, but she admitted to a close friend that she'd had an abortion because her marriage was in trouble.

'I was doing all right until I hit Pickfair,' Joan said. 'My informal happy little gatherings at home turned into formal affairs with the European set. Doug thrived on social life with the upper class. I was uncomfortable and bored at my own parties.' Unable to handle the dual role of actress and hostess, Joan acquired domestic help.

Doug signed on with First National for several trivial films while Joan's career took off like a skyrocket when Norma Shearer became pregnant with her first child in 1930.

'How did that happen?' she asked L.B. Mayer, who swallowed a smile.

'Irving would like to postpone *Paid* for his wife but I suggested you for the role of the innocent convict.'

'I read the script and I want the part very much.'

'You'll have to talk to Irving,' Mayer said, as if testing her willpower. 'He's stalling.'

This time, Joan's approach was professional and demure. She told Thalberg how proud she would be playing a role good enough for his beautiful Norma.

'Sam Wood is a very demanding director.'

'That's why I want to work with him.'

'We'll give it a try,' he said unenthusiastically.

For her role as the innocent convict who gets even with those responsible for her incarceration, Joan wore no make-up in the jail sequences and refused to comb her hair. She concentrated on camera angles, lighting and timing, and relied on the technicians. A nod meant she was on target.

Critics hailed Joan in *Paid*. *Variety* wrote, '. . . she impresses us as about ready to stand up under any sort of dramatic assignment.'

Drained after a long day of filming, Joan came home to find Doug entertaining. 'All I wanted was a refreshing swim, a light dinner and a quiet evening with my husband,' she said. 'Instead of our being touchy-touchy all the time, we lost touch with each other. He didn't want me to work. Isn't it strange how a man marries a woman for certain qualities and then wants to change them?'

The year 1931 was approaching and, after a tally of their incomes, Doug made $72,790 while Joan earned $145,750.

Crawford was terrified of working with thirty-year-old Clark Gable in *Dance, Fools, Dance*. The future 'King of Hollywood' had not been crowned yet. He wasn't even a star but he'd had stage experience on Broadway and was discovered in the play *The Last Mile* at the Majestic Theater in Los Angeles. He was married to his second wife, wealthy Houston socialite, Ria Langham, seventeen years his senior. When he was cast in *Dance, Fools, Dance*, MGM had not yet decided what to do with Gable. He wasn't suave or handsome enough to replace Gilbert or Valentino. Nor was he the boy-next-door type. But since he had played a vicious criminal on death row in *The Last Mile*, MGM knew he could fill in as a convincing gangster.

Gable said he wasn't looking forward to working with Joan Crawford. 'She was a star and knew the ropes in pictures,' he commented. 'I was afraid she'd laugh behind my back.'

Joan felt inferior to stage actors. 'I was a wreck,' she said. 'I kept thinking he knows how to read lines. I'm suffering in comparison. I recall vividly how, in one scene, he grabbed me and threatened the life of my brother.

Clark's nearness had such an impact, my knees buckled. If he hadn't held me by both shoulders I'd have dropped. Every girl on the set remarked about him.'

After making *A Free Soul* with Joan's rival, Norma Shearer, America had a new hero and star. Gable balanced the tipped scales of the sexes. It was the beginning of the diamond-in-the-rough image – the man who was raw, crude and hardened but had a heart of gold. If he couldn't win over his woman any other way, Gable carried her over his shoulder to a cave she'd never leave. After an hour with Gable, no woman was immune to his charms. Men cheered and women swooned.

Joan kept an eye on Gable's soaring career. She had never requested a leading man before but he had a considerable effect on her. She discussed her feelings with Haines.

'I remember him six or seven years ago,' Billy said with a snicker. 'He was an extra and always hanging around. He'd do anything for a job so . . .'

'What?'

'Cranberry, I fucked him in the men's room at the Beverly Wilshire Hotel. He was that desperate. He was a nice guy but not a fruitcake. As I recall he was married to his drama teacher who was old and ugly. He dumped her for his present wife.'

'Who else knows that you had sex with Gable?' she asked.

'No one. I have more to lose than he does.'

Joan let it be known she wanted Gable to co-star with her in *Possessed*, the story of a small-town factory girl who heads to New York and becomes the sophisticated mistress of a wealthy Park Avenue attorney. 'I knew when Clark walked on the set,' Joan remembered. 'I didn't know which door he came through, but I knew he was there. He had presence even then. I knew I was falling into the trap that I warned young starlets about – not to fall in love with your leading man. Leave the set and forget about it. Get laid by someone else. Get drunk. But brush it off. Boy, I had to eat those words, but they tasted very sweet.'

And so the affair began. Though it was physical at the start, they leaned on each other for support. They shared the frustration of unhappy childhoods and disagreeable parents. They worked at menial jobs and had no place to call home. 'We were nobodies transformed into somebodies by MGM,' Joan said. 'We were scared shitless. Could we hold on to what we had?' She cried every morning on her drive to the studio and wept all the way home. She feared for her marriage and she feared for her passionate love for Gable. If one or the other couldn't sleep at night, they had a pact to meet at the beach. 'Maybe that's why I couldn't sleep,' she said. 'I hoped he had insomnia, too, and would be there.'

In *Possessed*, one of Gable's lines was, 'The surest way to lose a woman is to marry her, and I don't want to lose you.' Crawford's line read, 'A woman can do anything and get anywhere as long as she doesn't fall in love.' For sure, *Possessed* was a preview of what lay ahead for Crawford and Gable.

And L.B. Mayer was well aware of it.

'Do you have any idea what I went through when your first wife made herself known? What I had to go through to shut her up?'

'I'm paying for it,' Gable mumbled.

'If you think two hundred dollars a month is payment due, my friend, you're wrong. The woman lives in a slum. But your present wife is a smart lady.'

'I guess my next line is "What's that supposed to mean?"'

'When it comes to lines, you've got 'em!' Mayer exclaimed. 'But I thought Joan had heard them all. I know her better than you do, my friend, and she's good for only one thing.'

'I love her,' Gable said.

'There's no such thing as love in this town.'

'Joan and I are going to get married.'

'What about the others you sleeping with?'

Clark frowned. 'You have a lively imagination.'

'Not as lively as your sex life.'

'That's my business.'

'As long as you work for MGM it's my business, and don't you forget it! You and Joan are finished or you'll never work for this or any other studio in Hollywood. Don't put me to the test.'

Possessed was acclaimed by *Photoplay*: '. . . you really don't care if the story is old and some of the lines are shopworn. For the Gable boy and the Crawford girl make you believe it . . . It's the best work Joan Crawford has done since *Paid* and Clark Gable – he's everybody's big moment. If Joan weren't so good, he'd have the picture. You'll like it. But while you're seeing it the kids should be doing their homework.'

L.B. Mayer congratulated Joan and offered her a part in their forthcoming all-star production *Grand Hotel* providing she did not see Gable again.

'Calm down,' she smiled. 'We're in love, that's all. It isn't shady or dirty.'

'I suppose he takes you out for an ice cream soda now and then.'

'My career always came first above anyone and everything else but I don't want *Grand Hotel*!'

Mayer stood up and pointed his finger at her. 'Give him up or you're fired, Joan, and you'll be blackballed from films. That goes for your cocksman, too. He can go back to the lumberyard and you can go back to the laundry.'

Joan broke down and sobbed. Mayer dabbed her cheeks with his handkerchief. 'Dry those pretty eyes, powder your nose, promise the affair is over. Finished.'

She moaned and wept. He handed her the *Grand Hotel* script. 'Tidy up now and look this over.' With moist eyes she read a few pages and burst into tears again. 'You want me to play a fucking whore?'

'I prefer to think of your character as a stenographer with ambition.'

'Who goes around screwing old men?' she cried.

Mayer smirked. 'Why don't you discuss that with your girlfriend, Billy Haines?'

Joan sighed, put on another layer of lipstick and mascara very carefully, and straightened out her wrinkled skirt. As she was leaving Mayer's office she turned around and asked, 'Don't you ever lose?'

'Pray that I don't, my dear. When I lose, everybody loses.'

Joan and Clark were shaken but not defeated. They knew that Mayer had spies everywhere and gossip columnists had their pencils sharpened, but somehow the lovers managed to see each other. Joan went so far as to invite Mrs Gable for lunch even though rumours of the affair were rumbling in Hollywood. A reporter spotted the two women and rushed over to their table. He complimented Joan on *Possessed* as an intro to, '. . . the way you looked at Clark, anyone can tell you're crazy about him.'

Joan looked up at the reporter and said, 'May I introduce you to my good friend, Mrs Clark Gable?'

Grand Hotel was a major part of Crawford's life these days. She was proud to be part of the great cast of players that included Lionel and John Barrymore, Wallace Beery, Jean Harlow and Greta Garbo.

Joan wanted Clark for her leading man in *Letty Lynton*, and had the nerve to ask Mayer, who called her a brazen hussy. She fought back with, 'We're good box office. I hope you aren't thinking of keeping us apart on the screen.'

'You'll work together when I say so,' Mayer responded. 'He's doing *Red Dust* with Jean Harlow. Meanwhile, you're going to have our best couturier for *Letty*. I saw the sketches and, as always, Adrian is a genius. He's emphasising your broad shoulders with padding. Something new and I expect it will catch on.'

And it did. *Letty Lynton* had the most influence on fashion in the film industry. American women demanded shoulder pads after they saw Joan Crawford wearing Adrian's creations, and she asked him to design her personal wardrobe, also.

Paul Bern married Jean Harlow on 2 July 1932. Two months later he put a gun to his head and committed suicide. Harlow resumed *Red Dust* two weeks later and Gable was there to console her on and off the movie set. Crawford knew about the affair but did not confront Clark because Mayer shipped her off to Catalina Island to do *Rain* for United Artists. 'I hated working for another studio,' she said. 'I didn't know the technicians and I thought Lewis Milestone's direction was so bad I did my own Sadie Thompson and it was a disaster.'

Depressed and tired, she retreated to Malibu. Douglas was sympathetic, but did not join her. Gable did and they discussed divorcing their spouses. Joan was adamant about going through with it but Clark balked for financial reasons.

Mayer cleverly released *Rain* while *Letty Lynton* played the circuit, to balance the reviews. He proved how important Joan was to the studio by sending her to Europe with Douglas, compliments of MGM. In New York, Mayor Jimmy Walker sent police escorts to make sure the famous couple arrived at the pier in time to board the SS *Bremen*. Once at sea, their second honeymoon was romantically private and, for a while, fulfilling. Without forcing it, Joan was comfortable and loving with Doug.

Once she arrived in England Joan was too busy to think about anyone else but her husband. Noel Coward was at Southampton to accompany them to their suite at the Savoy. Then came a round of plays and theatre suppers. Joan was totally unaware that she had so many fans in England. 'There is no other movie audience in the world to compare with the English,' she said. 'At Noel Coward's *Cavalcade*, they tore my evening coat off my back, and I basked in their fond attention. A corps of bobbies carried me into the theatre on their shoulders. This is the public without which an actress cannot exist. I had a ball.'

At first the crowds who chanted, 'Our Joan! Our Joan!' gave her a feeling of satisfaction, but she soon tired of being followed everywhere in Paris. 'Doug was able to shop and study painting at Montmartre,' she said, 'but I didn't have this freedom. While he dined with his elite friends at romantic cafés, I stayed by myself. Doug could not fathom what was happening. How difficult it was to be a star and a wife.'

When they returned home, Doug was the target of a $50,000 alienation-of-affection law suit. A man by the name of Dietz claimed Fairbanks had stolen 'the love and affection, comfort and assistance' of his wife. Joan planned to give her separation exclusive to *Modern Screen* but Louella Parsons got the scoop. Joan told the columnist, 'My God, Douglas doesn't even know. I wanted to ease out of it gracefully.'

'If you don't tell him, I will,' Parsons exclaimed.

'Give me time to pack his things,' Joan said.

Fairbanks was amused and told Louella, 'I'm going to send Joan flowers, call her every day, and send her telegrams when I can't get her on the phone. We're still in love.'

But Joan filed for divorce on 13 May 1933. Mayer was satisfied she was able to handle it without MGM's interference. He decided to reward her by casting Clark Gable in *Dancing Lady*, in which Fred Astaire made his screen debut. Franchot Tone portrayed the rich playboy who tried to lure her away from her stage director, played by Clark.

1933 was a year not to be forgotten. Billy Haines was arrested for soliciting a sailor again, and though Mayer hushed it up, he said it was time for Billy to get married. Billy said he was in love with Jimmie Shields, his live-in lover. Mayer gave him a choice – MGM or Jimmie. Haines opted for love and Mayer let his contract run out. Billy bounced back by decorating Carole Lombard's house. She invited all of Hollywood to see Billy's genius and he was in the decorating business for life.

In the same year, Gable, drunk at the wheel of his car, killed a pedestrian. Once again, Mayer was able to hush it up and a loyal MGM employee took the rap.

Irving Thalberg had a heart attack and would lose much of his power when Mayer hired his son-in-law, producer David Selznick, to handle special projects. And the Hays Office was bearing down with censorship, stating that films containing '. . . overt sexual freedom, loose morals, unnecessary displays of the female body, will hereafter be subjected to careful scrutiny by this office in advance of distribution.'

Jean Harlow's affair with Gable prompted Mayer to marry her off to cameraman Hal Rosson who abused her black and blue.

And, much to Crawford's distress, 'Uncle Douglas' was having an affair with Lady Sylvia Ashley that would lead to his divorce from Mary Pickford whose comeback in films failed. Joan became friendly with Mary who finally broke down and complimented 'that flapper' on a job well done. 'You not only set yourself a great goal, you surpassed that goal,' she told Joan.

Crawford changed the toilet seats in her Brentwood home and asked Haines to redecorate. 'This isn't a dollhouse any longer,' he said. 'You're a sophisticated woman and an accomplished actress. Your house should reflect that. We should also take Franchot Tone into consideration.'

'We've only had a few dates.'

'You went to New York with him.'

'Franchot wants me to go into the theatre.'

'It'll never happen, Cranberry. Remember that speech you were supposed to give to your fan club in England?

'What about it?'

'You took one look at the audience, said, "God bless" and ran off the stage.'

'I was behind schedule,' she said. 'Hear any new gossip lately?'

Haines laughed. 'Yes, Cranberry. Clark's having a hot affair with Loretta Young.'

'What else is new?' she sighed. 'He's not that good in the sack anyway.'

Joan continued her affair with Gable off and on, but was falling in love with 28-year-old Franchot Tone, who had come to Hollywood to raise money for the Group Theatre in New York. He co-starred with Joan in *Dancing Lady*, *Sadie McKee*, *No More Ladies*, *The Gorgeous Hussy*, *Love on the Run*, and *The Bride Wore Red*, most of which were forgettable films. In 1934, Joan and Clark were splendid in *Chained*, but critics agreed they couldn't lose on screen together.

Gable separated from his wife, Ria, and set up residence at the Beverly Wilshire Hotel. He was involved with Loretta Young and rumour had it she was pregnant with his baby when she took a sabbatical. Loretta gave birth in a secluded house outside Los Angeles, put little Judy in a Catholic orphanage, and adopted her nineteen months later. Because everyone in Hollywood knew the truth, Loretta was reluctant to be seen in public with Gable. She might have given birth to a child out of wedlock, but he was still a married man and Loretta was a devout Catholic.

Despite her affection for Gable, Joan had a sense of humour about Loretta. During one of her parties, a friend was about to sit down in a chair. Joan grabbed him just in time. 'Can't sit there,' she said. 'Loretta Young just got up, and the mark of the cross is on it!'

An evening spent with Alfred Lunt and Lynn Fontanne convinced Joan that Franchot Tone was the man for her. On 11 October 1935, they were married by Mayor Herbert W. Jenkins of Fort Lee, New Jersey. Their wedding night at the Waldorf-Astoria Hotel was destroyed, however, when she received an anonymous phone call from someone who said he possessed a pornographic film made by her. She had received similar calls in the past but this time she told the man to contact L.B. Mayer or J. Robert Rubin, an MGM attorney. Joan denied it but MGM paid $100,000 for the negatives. Most probably the film in question was a risqué vignette made in 1923. According to Joan, she was only fifteen at the time, but it's been proven that she was nineteen. Reliable sources claim she danced in the nude to earn the train fare from Kansas City to Chicago. Robert Slatzer, a newspaperman from Ohio, saw the film at a stag party and casually mentioned it to a friend at a Hollywood gala. 'A few minutes later,' Slatzer said, 'I saw Joan headed in my direction. She wanted to know if I was the reporter from Ohio and when I nodded she motioned for me to follow her out on the balcony. She told me to stop spreading rumours about the film and "keep your fuckin' mouth shut". We ran into each other at parties from time to time and Joan always made an effort to ask me about my screenwriting career. She was sincere about it, too. Strange woman.'

When Joan and Franchot arrived back in Hollywood, hundreds of reporters were waiting. 'Thank God I'm in love again,' she beamed. 'Now I can do it for love and not for my complexion.' Tone had not given up the idea of returning to the theatre, but he loved Joan enough to wait until she was ready to live in New York. During their first year of marriage she earned $250,000 and he made a mere $50,000.

According to Joan, *The Gorgeous Hussy* was the beginning of the end of her marriage to Tone. On the set, he stayed by himself and didn't speak to anyone. He was late reporting for work and stayed out all night occasionally. 'He was terribly bored with Hollywood,' Joan said, 'and he leaned on his theatre friends for consolation.' There was also the problem of Joan's star status and his lowly one. His ego was deflated further when *Life* magazine proclaimed Joan Crawford the 'First Queen of the Movies' in 1937. Believing, and rightfully so, that her fan clubs were responsible, she refused to sneak in a side door and out the back at premieres. Tone felt she was promoting herself and resented it. 'My fans put me where I am,' Joan said. 'If it wasn't for them I'd be back in Kansas City. Twice a year I go to New York specifically to see my fans. My schedule is no secret. They know where I plan to shop and where I'm having dinner. I answer all my fan mail personally.'

When Franchot finally got the message that Joan was not about to leave MGM for Broadway, he became abusive. The verbal battles became physical and she had the bruises to prove it. He turned to the bottle and other women.

It was typical Crawford to put her marriage on the back burner when the *Independent Film Journal* labelled her Box-Office Poison in 1938 – 'Among those players whose dramatic ability is unquestioned, but whose box-office draw is nil, can be numbered Mae West, Edward Arnold, Greta Garbo, Joan Crawford, Katharine Hepburn, Marlene Dietrich, and Fred Astaire.'

Joan cried on L.B. Mayer's shoulder. He told her not to worry about such silly nonsense, and handed her the script of *Mannequin* with Spencer Tracy. Shop girl marries rich man. Joan perked up. 'Like old times!' she cheered.

'And a new one-year contract,' he said.

'One year?' she gasped. 'L.B., I was Miss MGM when you started out thirteen years ago! How about five years?'

He shook his head.

'Three?'

'If you'll settle for $100,000 a picture,' he said with a stern smile. 'Joan, I'm taking a chance on you.'

'L.B., I'm supporting my mother and brother,' she wept.

'Don't forget your husbands.'

She nodded.

'And the butler and chef and upstairs maid. . . .'

'Damn you, L.B.! I live like a fuckin' star should. My fans sit on the kerb where I live. I serve them cookies and milk. They expect Joan Crawford to look like a million bucks. I do it for my image, yes, but MGM reaps the harvest. If Irving Thalberg were alive . . .

'Irving bowed to talent. I use it.'

Joan had a brief affair with Spencer Tracy while filming *Mannequin*. They parted company during a rehearsal for a radio show when she stuttered. 'For Christ's sake,' Tracy snarled. 'I thought you were supposed to be a pro!' She burst into tears, dropped the script and ran from the studio.

It was a bad year for Joan. She found Franchot making love to a starlet in his dressing room and asked him why. 'To prove to myself I'm still a man,' was his reply. She insisted he leave the house immediately and, like Fairbanks, Tone was gone without a trace a day later, and Joan changed the toilet seats at 426 North Bristol Avenue once again. Franchot had little to say about his ex-wife other than, 'She's like the old joke about Philadelphia. First prize, four years with Joan, second prize, eight.'

Famous child-star Jackie Cooper, in his classic memoirs *Please Don't Shoot My Dog*, wrote that he was seventeen when he began going to Joan Crawford's house to play badminton. One day when she bent over to pour him a Coke, he looked down her dress.

'You're growing up, aren't you?' she said.

Fresh and romantic, Jackie came back with a sexy remark that prompted Joan to say, 'You had better get out of here, young man.'

But he didn't go home. Instead he made a move toward her. She looked him over, closed the drapes, and he made love to her. 'Or, rather, she made love to me,' Jackie said. 'She was a very erudite professor of love . . . She was a wild woman. She would bathe me, powder me, cologne me. Then she would do it over and over again.'

Then one night Joan ended the affair. 'It never happened,' she said. 'But we'll always be friends.'

Because of her affair with Gable, who was cast as Rhett Butler in *Gone With the Wind*, Joan lost her chance to audition for the role of Scarlett O'Hara. But she forged ahead with *The Women*, playing Crystal, the girl who almost steals Norma Shearer's husband. They had only one scene together, a confrontation in a dressing room. Norma tells Joan's character her husband wouldn't like the revealing dress she's wearing. Joan's retort was, '. . . when he doesn't like what I'm wearing, I take it off.'

Since Miss Shearer had higher star status than Miss Crawford, Joan had to deliver lines to Norma, who complained that Joan's knitting needles made too much noise. Director George Cukor took Joan aside and told her to apologise, was refused and she left for the day. A week or so later the two feuding actresses were scheduled for publicity pictures. Though Joan's dressing room was across the street from the photographers, she always had a studio limousine at her disposal. When she saw Norma approaching, Joan departed, but neither wanted to be the first to arrive. Both limousines went round and round until publicity director, Howard Strickling, played traffic director and escorted the widow Thalberg into the photo studio. Then came the upstaging-each-other incident, each trying to pose higher than the other on the staircase.

When the session ended, Joan's chauffeur, immaculately uniformed, complete with puttees, opened the door of her limousine and closed the door on the Crawford–Shearer battle for power.

Strange Cargo with Gable and *Susan and God* with Fredric March were fine projects for Joan, but *A Woman's Face* gave her renewed enthusiasm. She hoped Mayer had changed his mind and was giving her good scripts to prove she was worthy of another contract. The attack on Pearl Harbor on 7 December 1941, however, put all that was petty aside. Gable's wife, Carole Lombard, was killed in a plane crash returning from a war-bond drive in Indiana on 16 January 1942. 'Clark came to me that night,' Crawford said. 'He was drunk and in tears. He was never the same again. He joined the Air Force and told me he had no intention of coming back.' Joan volunteered to take Lombard's assigned role in *They All Kissed the Bride* for Columbia Pictures, and donated her salary of $125,000 to the Red Cross.

Joan was appalled when Mayer put her in the forgettable *Reunion in France* with John Wayne. Maybe she resented co-starring with him but that did not stop Joan from trying to seduce Wayne. 'She called me often,' he said in later years. 'I wouldn't take her calls. She was dating her next husband, Phil Terry, when we made *Reunion*. When she made her entrance on the set, first came Joan, then her secretary, and then Philip, carrying her dog.'

Again and again Crawford begged Mayer for *Madame Curie*, *Mrs Miniver*, or *Random Harvest*, but Greer Garson was the chosen one now that Norma had retired from films.

'I'm getting married,' Joan told Mayer.

'To that bit player?'

'Who cares what he is if I can make the marriage work, and in order to do that I'm leaving MGM.'

'I wish you all the best, Joan, and I want you to think of me always as your father – the one man you can talk to and lean on, the one man who . . .'

'. . . let me down,' she exclaimed, extending her gloved right hand. L.B. Mayer clutched it with both of his. Tears flowed down his cheeks as he whispered, 'I love you, Joan. God bless you.' She turned and walked regally to the door and left it wide open.

Two days later Joan signed with Warner Brothers for two pictures a year at one-third the salary she had received from MGM. Billy Haines told her, 'That is Jack Warner's way of keeping Bette Davis in line. You're both suited for the same roles.'

'He doesn't have anything for me yet, but I'm delighted to be a housewife for a change.

'You'll get bored with it,' Billy sighed. 'But what about this obsession with adopting children? Honestly, Cranberry, isn't two enough?'

'Christina and Christopher are my life!' she cooed. 'But I have a chance to adopt two adorable girls, as well. They look like twins but were born two months apart . . . Cynthia and Cathy.'

Joan would eventually adopt all four children, two would later claim abuse, the other two disclaimed this. The details will remain unclear.

'Your fans are going to make you a saint or burn you at the stake when they read about you packing Philip's lunch pail every morning and waving goodbye to him as he leaves for the aircraft factory.'

'Billy, you must join us for cocktails some evening. My beloved husband's an expert bartender.'

'I've never known you to have more than one or two glasses of champagne, Cranberry.'

'Ain't love grand?' she laughed, planting a big kiss on his forehead and leaving a gash of bright red lipstick.

At the age of forty, Joan began drinking hard liquor, and only she knows when she started abusing it.

Two years passed before Jack Warner offered *Mildred Pierce* to Joan. She attended the gala premiere in New York City with Philip, who was shoved into the background while his wife once again basked in the spotlight. He had given up his job to run the household when Joan resumed her career. She expected him and the nurses to follow her instructions that were jotted in fifteen-minute intervals. Potty time indicated clearly how the children were to 'perform'. Philip said Joan's rigid schedule extended to their personal life. 'I had to check my allotted time for sex,' he said. The day after Philip left the Bristol Avenue house there was not a trace of him left anywhere. All three of Joan's marriages had lasted four years.

On 25 April 1946, Joan emerged from the courtroom and told reporters,

'Never again.'

'Does that mean you'll never listen to "The Wedding March" again, Miss Crawford?'

'Maybe that's the trouble,' she replied with a crooked smile. 'I never had any music at my weddings.'

But music to her ears was hearing she had been nominated for an Oscar for her performance in *Mildred Pierce*. Joan did not attend the Academy Awards ceremony due to a mild case of pneumonia. The real reason was sheer fright – such terror, in fact, that she was forced to stay in bed. With a radio on her night table Joan held her breath when Charles Boyer read the nominees for best actress: Ingrid Bergman in *The Bells of St Mary's*, Joan Crawford in *Mildred Pierce*, Greer Garson in *The Valley of Decision*, Jennifer Jones in *Love Letters*, and Jean Tierney in *Leave Her to Heaven*, and the winner is . . . Joan Crawford in *Mildred Pierce*!

Joan jumped out of bed, stepped into the shower, put on an exquisite negligée, applied make-up and had her hair styled. Michael Curtiz, who directed *Mildred Pierce* arrived with the Oscar and found Joan looking healthier and more beautiful than she had in years. 'Your front lawn is packed with fans,' he said. 'Wave to them from the window.'

'They deserve more than that,' she said, heading for the front door and stepping outside. She waved weakly, blew a kiss, and exclaimed, 'God bless you.'

The famous picture in the newspapers the following morning showed Joan asleep in bed with Oscar, Kleenex, nose spray, and telephone.

Many celebrities have said winning an Oscar is a curse, and so it was with Joan, though close friends firmly believed she was never the same after Mayer let her go. At MGM she believed she was Joan Crawford. Lucille LeSueur never existed. But then her creators let her down and she began slipping backward. She went out with Billy's gay friends, stayed out all night with Rock Hudson and dated his best buddy, George Nader. Yul Brynner was seduced before they went to dinner, and she had Kirk Douglas on the floor before he had a chance to close the front door.

'I was a highly sexed woman,' Crawford admitted a few years before her death.

There were many social occasions that Joan chose to attend alone. During dinner she looked over the eligible gentlemen and would ask one of them to escort her home. The chosen one would either return to the party very late or not at all.

Then Joan met handsome attorney Greg Bautzer, who treated her like a

Hollywood star. When they entered a room he remained a few steps behind carrying her dog or her knitting bag. He placed her dinner napkin on her lap and lit her cigarettes. One of Bautzer's habits was climbing up a rose trellis to Joan's bedroom during the night. 'It was very romantic when he forced himself on me,' she cooed. They had many royal battles but were very much in love. Then Greg did the unthinkable. He danced with another woman at a dinner-dance. No matter that Joan was doing the foxtrot with someone else. That night she offered to drive for a change and, in the middle of nowhere, asked Greg to get out and check one of the tyres. He did and she drove off, leaving him three miles from town.

Billy Haines said, 'To be Joan Crawford's boyfriend, a man must be a combination bull and butler.'

After making *Humoresque* with John Garfield, Joan signed a seven-year contract with Warner Brothers for $200,000 per picture. She was nominated for an Oscar as Best Actress for her performance in *Possessed* with Van Heflin and Raymond Massey, and for *Sudden Fear* with Jack Palance. Joan didn't win, but she was making quality films at long last. When Bette Davis left Warner Brothers in 1948, Joan was Queen of the Lot. *Flamingo Road*, *The Damned Don't Cry*, and *Harriet Craig* were 'Joan Crawford Films'. She remained in character – the strong-willed, gutsy bitch who refuses to accept defeat.

Regrettably, Crawford turned down the role of the army officer's faithless wife in *From Here to Eternity* because she insisted on using her own costume designer. So it was Deborah Kerr who lay on the sand in Burt Lancaster's arms as the ocean waves bathed them in passion. If Joan made a big mistake she never spoke of it because MGM wanted her for *Torch Song*. Even though L.B. Mayer was gone, she wanted more than anything else in the world to return 'home'. Above the gate at MGM flew a huge banner – 'WELCOME BACK, JOAN'. A red carpet was laid from the street to Joan's dressing room filled with flowers. Gable sent a market basket full of chocolate from Italy. Fred Astaire sent roses, and the technicians gave her orchids and violets. Telegrams arrived from all over the world. Dore Schary, who had replaced Mayer, reserved three connecting dressing rooms for Joan who made it known she planned to live at the studio for the duration of *Torch Song*. Christopher and Christina were away at school. With only 'the twins' at home she had nothing to worry about.

Esther Williams, MGM's 'Million Dollar Mermaid', thought Joan looked marvellous and still had a wonderful figure. One evening, as Esther was about to leave the studio, she saw Joan on Stage 4, all alone and talking to an imaginary audience of fans: 'Why have you left me? Why don't you come to my movies? What did I do? What did I say? Don't turn your back on me.' Esther was determined not to let this happen to her and walked out of her studio contract a short time later.

Joan, fortified with vodka, forged ahead with her first Technicolor film. She hadn't danced in fourteen years and the training was gruelling, but she managed with the help of the brilliant choreographer, Chuck Walters, who was gay but not immune to her advances.

Joan's co-star in *Torch Song* was Elizabeth Taylor's second husband, Michael Wilding. Liz was a frequent visitor on the set and paid no attention to Joan. After one too many snubs, Crawford told Wilding, 'You'd better teach that little bitch some manners. Next time I expect her to acknowledge my presence!' It's unlikely the mild-mannered Wilding said anything to his wife.

The *New York Herald Tribune* gave *Torch Song* a rave review:

> Joan Crawford has another of her star-sized roles . . . playing a musical comedy actress in the throes of rehearsal and in love with a blind pianist, she is vivid and irritable, volcanic and feminine. She dances, she pretends to sing: she graciously permits her wide mouth and snappish eyes to be photographed in Technicolor. Here is Joan Crawford all over the screen, in command, in love and in color, a real movie star in what amounts to be a carefully produced one-woman show. Miss Crawford's acting is sheer and colorful as a painted arrow, aimed straight at the sensibilities of her particular fans.

While making *Female at the Beach* in 1954, Joan elected to live at the studio. Production continued through the Christmas holidays, but she settled down with her vodka and caviar and fan mail by herself on New Year's Eve. That night a good friend Earl Blackwell called from Las Vegas. 'I'm at a very gay and intimate party,' he said. 'Someone here wants to talk to you.'

It was Alfred Steele, president of Pepsi-Cola. Joan had met him at a dinner party four years ago and though they were attracted to one another, he was a married man living on the East Coast, and she was a movie actress living on the West Coast. Steele, five years older than Joan and now divorced, pursued her with vigour, and on 10 May 1955 they were married by a municipal judge in the penthouse suite at the Flamingo Hotel. They sailed for Europe on the *SS United States* later that month. Joan referred to the sailing as a royal battle. She said Alfred wanted her to know right from the start who was boss. In later years she said their torrid fights came to an abrupt end with a stinging slap across her face that rattled her brain. The tension between them abated as Joan became more involved in his business. They were now living in a New York City penthouse apartment at Two East Seventieth Street, elegantly decorated by Billy Haines, who commented, 'I hear you're sitting in on Alfred's business meetings, Cranberry.'

'That's right,' she beamed. 'And I love every minute of it.'

'It's also rumoured you walk several steps behind him.'

'Yes,' she exclaimed. 'And I stand behind his decisions!'

When Alfred became chairman of the board, he was determined to 'beat the shit' out of Coke. He and Joan travelled the world on behalf of Pepsi whose executives considered her a prime asset to the company. Not only did she know the inner workings of the business but she was still the famous Joan Crawford and crowds greeted the couple everywhere. 'It was a very rough start for Alfred and me,' she said, 'but my years with him have been the best – the happiest of my life. He's been the strong one, and I learned to lean as well as comfort and protect.'

Steele died of a heart attack in April 1959, and two days later Joan was elected to the board of Pepsi by stockholders of the corporation. Steele was broke when he died. His estate was valued at around $600,000, but after taxes and debts, Joan was left with nothing. She had loaned him $100,000 without a note shortly before his death. They had essentially 'wiped out' each other. The biggest blow was Pepsi's refusal to reimburse the Steeles for the $500,000 spent on the penthouse that Alfred claimed was a business investment.

Joan sold her antiques, the Bristol Avenue house in Los Angeles and made *The Best of Everything* for 20th Century-Fox. She was paid $60,000 of Alfred's annual salary, according to his will, and would be paid for her services as board member and spokeswoman.

Joan opened thirty bottling plants a year and represented Pepsi around the world. Her business trips, like everything else in her life, were very well organised and Pepsi's publicity team were told to check her lists very carefully. Upon arrival at her hotel suites, she expected to find cracked ice, menus, a professional hair dryer, steam iron and board, a carton of Alpine Cigarettes, red and yellow roses, Old Forester bourbon, Beefeater Gin, 100-proof Smirnoff vodka, Chivas Regal Scotch, Dom Perignon champagne and a personal maid.

A memo to all concerned at her destination read, 'Miss Crawford is to be met at the airport in an air-conditioned limousine with a nonsmoking chauffeur who is not to exceed forty miles an hour.'

The same instructions were given to those in charge of her accommodation when she was making a film, with an added notation: 'Miss Crawford is a star in every sense of the word, and everyone knows she is a star in this film. Miss Crawford will not appreciate your throwing away money on empty gestures. You do not have to make empty gestures to prove to Miss Crawford or anyone else that she is a star of the first magnitude.'

Before Bette Davis committed herself to *What Ever Happened to Baby Jane?*, she asked director Robert Aldrich, 'Have you slept with Miss Crawford?'

'No,' he lied.

Bette agreed to $60,000 and five per cent of the net profits. Joan signed for $40,000 and ten per cent of the take. There was no love lost between these two great actresses and the tension mounted when Bette referred to her and Joan as 'we two old broads'. Joan sent her a note on her traditional blue stationery: 'Dear Miss Davis. Please do not refer to me as an old broad. Sincerely, Joan Crawford.'

The first day on the set Joan approached Bette's daughter B.D., and asked her not to bother Cindy and Cathy. 'You see, dear, they have been carefully brought up. You, obviously, have not and I don't want your influence to corrupt them.'

Bette complained about Joan's falsies. 'I keep running into them like the Hollywood Hills. She must have a different set for every day of the week!'

What Ever Happened To Baby Jane? grossed $9,000,000 and Davis was nominated for an Oscar. Joan was livid, but she got revenge on the night of the Academy Awards. Anne Bancroft, who was nominated for Best Actress, could not attend, and asked Joan to accept the Oscar if she won. When Bancroft's name was announced, Joan elbowed Bette aside and exclaimed, 'Excuse me!' before walking on stage.

Baby Jane put Joan on her feet financially so she was anxious to do *Hush, Hush, Sweet Charlotte* with Davis. Instead of travelling on the chartered flight with the others, Joan arrived in Baton Rouge, Louisiana, with 25 pieces of luggage and had to wait for her rooms to be properly set up, as dictated. She complained to Bette, who slammed the door in her face. From then on they were not on speaking terms except on camera, but even the dialogue exploded when Joan spoke her lines and Bette howled, 'Jesus, is that the way she's going to play it?' Under stress, Crawford became ill and was replaced by Olivia de Havilland.

Joan did five more films, all of which were dreadful and not worth mentioning.

Pepsi retired Joan in 1973 without warning. She would receive a pension of $40,000, but the fringe benefits were discontinued. In the same year Billy Haines died. His 'wife' Jimmie committed suicide a year later. The changes taking place were depressing ones for the great Crawford. She moved into a small apartment in the Imperial House at 150 East 69th Street. Both married, Cindy moved to Iowa and Cathy to Pennsylvania. Joan's relationship with Christina was strained and she refused to see Christopher. Taking a deeper interest in Christian Science, Joan refused to see a doctor when she became ill. The end came quickly on 10 May 1977. Death was attributed to acute coronary occlusion though it's been established Joan had cancer for two years. She was cremated and interred next to Alfred in a cemetery in Ferncliff, New York. Her estate was estimated to be $1,300,000.

Joan bequeathed both Cathy and Cindy $77,500, to be given in increasing amounts at five-year intervals, and $5000 to each of her four grandchildren, Carla, Casey, Jan and Joel. The rest went to her favourite charities. In the will Joan stated, 'It is my intention to make no provision herein for my son Christopher or my daughter Christina for reasons which are well known to them.'

A year later Christina and Christopher contested Joan's will, claiming she was subject to monomania, and under the influence of Cathy and her husband. Christina and Christopher received a total of $55,000 to be shared by them. Christina also requested a plastic bust of her mother and Cathy obliged.

In 1978 Christina's *Mommie Dearest* became a bestseller. She made more than a million dollars from the book that was denounced by Joan's friends and her enemies. Betty Barker, who was Crawford's secretary for 35 years, said Christina wrote the book for money, and that she neither saw nor heard any of the incidents described. Barker preferred not to discuss the 'other side of the story' because Christina and Christopher were still alive, but she was adamant about 'the hell those kids put Joan through over the years'. In an interview Douglas Fairbanks Jr commented, 'I'm not sure that what the daughter had to say was so accurate.' Cathy and Cynthia said they were unaware of any abuse, only kindness and fairness on the part of their mother.

At the Hollywood memorial for Joan, Christina was one of the last to arrive. Myrna Loy, one of Joan's closest friends, got up and left the room. Why? *Mommie Dearest* hadn't been written yet.

Nine actresses turned down the part of 'Mommie' for fear of offending Joan's powerful Hollywood friends. Faye Dunaway, whom Joan admired most, played the role. 'Of all the actresses, only Faye Dunaway has the talent and the class and the courage it takes to make a real star,' Joan told writer Roy Newquist.

Director George Cukor remarked at the Hollywood memorial for Joan that '. . . she was the perfect image of the movie star . . . the nearer the camera, the more tender and yielding she became – her eyes glistening, her lips avid in ecstatic acceptance. The camera saw, I suspect, a side of her that no flesh-and-blood lover ever saw.'

This author interviewed Joan Crawford several times in 1970. I remember her as kind, bitchy, amusing, frustrating, regal, generous and selfish. But whatever crumbs she threw my way were priceless jewels. She was the abused not the abuser . . .

The Films of Joan Crawford

Pretty Ladies (MGM, 1925)
Old Clothes (MGM, 1925)
The Only Thing (MGM, 1925)
Sally, Irene and Mary (MGM, 1925)
The Boob (MGM, 1926)
Tramp, Tramp, Tramp (First National, 1926)
Paris (MGM, 1926)
The Taxi Dancer (MGM, 1927)
Winners of the Wilderness (MGM, 1927)
The Understanding Heart (MGM, 1927)
The Unknown (MGM, 1927)
Twelve Miles Out (MGM, 1927)
Spring Fever (MGM, 1927)
West Point (MGM, 1928)
Rose-Marie (MGM, 1928)
Across to Singapore (MGM, 1928)
The Law of the Range (MGM, 1928)
Four Walls (MGM, 1928)
Our Dancing Daughters (MGM, 1928)
Dream of Love (MGM, 1928)
The Duke Steps Out (MGM, 1929)
Hollywood Revue of 1929) (MGM, 1929)
Our Modern Maidens (MGM, 1929)
Untamed (MGM, 1929)
Montana Moon (MGM, 1930)
Our Blushing Brides (MGM, 1930)
Paid (MGM, 1930)

Dance, Fools, Dance (MGM, 1931)
Laughing Sinners (MGM, 1931)
This Modern Age (MGM, 1931)
Possessed (MGM, 1931)
Grand Hotel (MGM, 1932)
Letty Lynton (MGM, 1932)
Rain (United Artists, 1932)
Today We Live (MGM, 1933)
Dancing Lady (MGM, 1933)
Sadie McKee (MGM, 1934)
Chained (MGM, 1934)
Forsaking All Others (MGM, 1934)
No More Ladies (MGM, 1935)
I Live My Life (MGM, 1935)
The Gorgeous Hussy (MGM, 1936)
Love on the Run (MGM, 1936)
The Last of Mrs Cheyney (MGM, 1937)
The Bride Wore Red (MGM, 1937)
Mannequin (MGM, 1938)
The Shining Hour (MGM, 1938)
The Ice Follies of 1939 (MGM, 1939)
The Women (MGM, 1939)
Strange Cargo (MGM, 1940)
Susan and God (MGM, 1940)
A Woman's Face (MGM, 1941)
When Ladies Meet (MGM, 1941)
They All Kissed the Bride (Columbia, 1942)
Reunion in France (MGM, 1942)
Above Suspicion (MGM, 1943)
Hollywood Canteen (Warner Brothers, 1944)
Mildred Pierce (Warner Brothers, 1945)
Humoresque (Warner Brothers, 1946)
Possessed (Warner Brothers, 1947)
Daisy Kenyon (20th Century-Fox, 1947)
Flamingo Road (Warner Brothers, 1949)
It's a Great Feeling (Warner Brothers, 1949)
The Damned Don't Cry (Warner Brothers, 1950)
Harriet Craig (Columbia, 1950)
Goodbye, My Fancy (Warner Brothers, 1951)

This Woman is Dangerous (Warner Brothers, 1952)
Sudden Fear (RKO, 1952)
Torch Song (MGM, 1953)
Johnny Guitar (Republic Pictures, 1954)
Female on the Beach (Universal-International, 1955)
Queen Bee (Columbia, 1955)
Autumn Leaves (Columbia, 1956)
The Story of Esther Costello (Valiant Films for Columbia, 1957)
The Best of Everything (20th Century Fox, 1959)
What Ever Happened to Baby Jane? (Warner Brothers, 1962)
The Caretakers (United Artists, 1953)
Strait Jacket (Columbia, 1964)
I Saw What You Did (Universal, 1965)
Berserk (Columbia, 1968)
Trog (Warner Brothers, 1970)

6

Lana

She was discovered sipping a five-cent coke in a Hollywood coffee shop, attended MGM's 'little red schoolhouse', and was dubbed the Sweater Girl. She had seven husbands, countless amours, lost the one man she loved, and wiped blood off the knife that killed her gangster boyfriend. She was dimpled and sexy, and retained a natural breathless quality in her voice, which blended with her baby face.

She was MGM's divine creation, gloriously pampered by L.B. Mayer, who often had cause to scold her soundly. She whimpered and purred. He melted and purred. But she defied him in ways that made her mother blush when Mayer laid it on the line. 'Your daughter comes on like a romantic teenager and then turns into a feverish, passionate tiger who can't get enough. She's only eighteen and reporters call her the Nightclub Queen. This I hardly the clean all-American image that we demand from our family. MGM abides by the rules that society dictates.'

Mayer was both charmed and frustrated by his darling dimpled beauty. Even the hardened columnist Walter Winchell bowed to her: 'She is made of rays of sun, woven of blue eyes, honey-coloured hair and flowing curves. She is Lana Turner, goddess of the screen . . .'

Her mother, Mildred Frances Cowan, came from Arkansas; her father, John Virgil Turner, was from Alabama and spoke with a thick Southern accent. They met at a dance in Picher, Oklahoma. Mildred was fifteen and travelling with her father, who disapproved of the relationship. But 24-year-old Virgil would not be put off. Mildred eloped with him to Wallace, Idaho, and a year later Julia 'Judy' Jean Turner was born on 8 February 1921.

Virgil was a happy-go-lucky guy who preferred making a living at bootlegging or at the poker table. Mildred was very much in love with the man she referred to as 'Mr Turner', but she was not prepared for life with a drifter. Virgil predicted new beginnings when they moved to San Francisco, but his compulsive gambling did not put food on the table. Mildred left Virgil and got work as a hairdresser. Judy stayed with friends whom she referred to in later years as 'foster parents'. To pay for bed and board Judy shared household chores, but after two years Mildred noticed bruises and cuts on Judy's body where she had been whipped with a stick. In desperation, Mildred was reconciled with Virgil, but living conditions were worse than before. Drinking and gambling, he would disappear for days, forcing Mildred to go begging for food and lodging.

On 14 December 1930, Virgil was robbed, beaten and killed after winning big at the crap table. His body was found on the street with one sock missing – the sock where he stashed his money. Lana recalled, 'The shock I suffered may be a valid excuse for me now. It may explain things I myself do not understand.'

Mildred and Judy shared a friend's apartment and were grateful for whatever they had at the height of the Depression. By 1935 the Turners were living a fairly normal life until a persistent cough began taking its toll on Mildred. When doctors suggested a drier climate in southern

California, Mildred called her friend Gladys Taylor in Los Angeles. 'Stay with me,' Gladys said. 'I have plenty of room.'

After only a month at Hollywood High School Judy cut class to have a coke at the Top Hat Café across the street. As she was sipping her soda a well-dressed gentleman with a moustache approached and asked if she wanted to be an actress. She shrugged.

'Every pretty young lady wants to be in the movies and I think you'd be perfect,' he said, handing her his business card.

'I'll give it to my mother.'

'Have her call me,' he said, tipping his hat.

Mildred was exhausted by the time she got home from work that evening and paid no attention to Judy's story about the man who thought she should be in the movies. But Gladys Taylor knew right away that Billy Wilkerson published a well-known newspaper, the *Hollywood Reporter*.

Wilkerson introduced Mildred to Zeppo Marx, who had a talent agency. Judy earned twenty dollars as an extra in *A Star is Born* with Fredric March and Janet Gaynor. There were no other offers until director Mervyn LeRoy decided Judy was the girl he'd been looking for to appear in *They Won't Forget*. 'It wasn't a big acting role,' he said, 'but the whole plot revolved around the girl's unsolved murder. She had to be young and sexy, but cute and innocent at the same time. This combination in a girl is almost impossible to find.'

LeRoy later described that first glance of Judy in December 1936.

> Her hair was dark, messy, uncombed. Her hands were trembling so she could barely read the script. But she had that sexy clean quality I wanted. There was something smouldering underneath that innocent face.' LeRoy said the only thing wrong with the girl was her name. 'I liked Judy and I liked Turner, but they didn't go together. She reminded me of someone I knew many years ago. Her name was Donna. So I went down the alphabet. When I got to the Ls, that was it. Lonna, but we'd spell it Lana. I signed her to a contract for fifty dollars a week on 22 February 1937.

The bra that Lana wore in the movie was made of lined silk with no uplift, allowing her breasts to move freely. Her hips were slim, but she strutted them effectively, and a tight skirt did the rest. Lana and Mildred went to the preview of *They Won't Forget* and were shocked when 'that thing' walked on the screen. Mildred crouched down in her seat. Lana did too when she heard the men in the audience react with howls and whistles. 'We snuck out and jumped into a taxi,' she said.

Billy Wilkerson reviewed the movie in the *Hollywood Reporter* – 'Short on playing time is the role of the murdered schoolgirl. But as played by Lana Turner it is worthy of more than passing note. This young lady has vivid beauty, personality, and charm.'

In 1937 Sam Goldwyn borrowed Lana for *The Adventures of Marco Polo* with Gary Cooper. She played an Oriental handmaiden in two brief scenes with Alan Hale. Part of her make-up consisted of black slanted eyebrows that were glued on with fishnet and pulled off after filming each day. By the time the movie was finished Lana's brows had disappeared completely and would never grow back, forcing her to paint them on for the rest of her life.

In 1938 Mervyn LeRoy accepted an offer from MGM and took Lana with him, raising her weekly salary to a hundred dollars a week. The extra money made it possible for Lana and Mildred to rent a furnished three-bedroom house in Laurel Canyon. For fifty dollars, Lana bought an old car, a Willys Knight.

LeRoy had no problem selling Lana to MGM. She signed a contract with the studio on 20 February 1938, and attended MGM's 'little red schoolhouse' with Judy Garland and Mickey Rooney. They were supposed to attend classes five days a week, but the studio got around this by having them tutored in their dressing room in the afternoons.

Lana's first film at MGM was with Mickey Rooney in *Love Finds Andy Hardy*. According to Rooney, he was pleasantly surprised to discover Lana was 'as oversexed as I was'. They dated for a while and then, suddenly, she stopped seeing Mickey. A few years later Lana told him she had aborted his baby. 'When my autobiography was published,' Rooney said, 'Lana was furious that I'd written about her and she denied it. All I can say is if it didn't happen it was the most beautiful dream I ever had!'

MGM girls were carefully taught to deny such stories.

Lana's big break in films came when she was chosen as one of Clark Gable's blonde chorus girls in Robert Sherwood's *Idiot's Delight*, filmed in 1938 and released the following year. Lana was not happy about bleaching her hair but contract players did what they were told. But she never made it into *Idiot's Delight*. Instead she was hospitalised for the removal of scar tissue from her ovaries and colon, the result of a botched appendectomy at the age of fourteen. The operation described by Lana was by no means an emergency, which led to speculation that she was the chorus girl who was fired by Carole Lombard for trying to make out with her husband, Clark Gable. The people who claim she was the one base their speculation on the fact that *Idiot's Delight* was Lana's big chance. The reason is not as important as the fact that Lana became a blonde, which not only changed her screen image but gave her an outgoing, swinging personality. Hollywood labelled her the Nightclub Queen.

Mildred was upset that Lana stayed out all night and came home just to change her clothes and make it to the studio on time. When Mildred failed to discipline Lana, Mayer took over. 'We can't keep up with your social life,' he said. 'We don't care if you drink and smoke, but let's not flaunt it. We can't airbrush every photograph taken of you, my dear. Besides, nice girls don't go out dancing with a different man every night.'

Lana pouted and pretended she was about to break down. She knew that always got him. He couldn't bear to see her cry. Then he told her the story about the little girl who walked through the golden gates of MGM and became a star, and lived happily ever after because she was rich and famous. If, that is, she behaved like a lady.

Lana might have been flighty, but she wasn't stupid. She was not an established star as yet and though some fan mail was trickling in, she had not proved her worth. So behave herself she did – for a little while.

After producing *The Wizard of Oz* at MGM, Mervyn LeRoy realised how much he missed sitting in the director's chair. He would do many films for Metro over the years, but in 1939 he decided to become a freelance director. Before leaving MGM he asked agent Johnnny Hyde to represent Lana in negotiating a new contract, for $250 a week. She received fifth billing in *Calling Dr Kildare*, and auditioned for the part of Scarlett O'Hara in *Gone With the Wind*. Years later she said, 'To my horror, they began showing the auditions on TV, mine included, and I was surely no threat to Vivien Leigh.'

Lana insisted she was a virgin when she met and fell in love with thirty-year-old attorney Greg Bautzer, painting a more romantic picture than giving in to Andy Hardy in the front seat of his convertible on Mulholland Drive. Lana's dates with Bautzer were well publicised. Mayer was delighted. He admired Bautzer's legal tactics and considered him a rare catch for any woman. Mildred, too, was thrilled. Greg brought Lana home at a respectable hour with only a goodnight kiss at the front door. Tall, tanned, handsome, brilliant and single, Bautzer knew how to handle women. He waited until Lana was ready and willing, but after they were intimate she expected a marriage proposal. To pacify her, Greg gave Lana a small diamond ring, and she took it for granted that they were engaged. Fortunately, she didn't make a formal announcement because MGM made it clear to her that, single and available, she was a good investment; married, her male fans might lose interest.

When Lana received a phone call from Joan Crawford, she thought nothing about it because she and Greg had attended several of Joan's parties. 'Why don't you come over to my place for tea and a chat, dear?' Joan asked. When Lana arrived, her hostess fawned over her and then, with a sweet smile, said, 'Now, darling, you know I'm a bit older than you, and I may know some things you haven't learned yet.'

'Like what?' Lana asked, thinking Joan was quite a bit older.

'Well, dear, when you're young you see things a certain way, but that's not always how they are.' Joan went on and on dramatising the complexities of life – her hand to her forehead, then to her heart – and then finally, after inhaling deeply from a cigarette, she pounced. 'Darling, I feel it's only fair to tell you that Greg doesn't love you anymore – that he hasn't for a long time. I couldn't let you go on believing. Greg loves me and he hasn't quite figured out how to get rid of you. So, Lana, dear, why don't you be a good girl and end it. He doesn't want to hurt you.'

Stunned and hurt, Lana managed, 'I don't believe you.'

'Why don't you ask Greg where he goes after he drops you off, dear?'

Lana did just that and Bautzer denied it, but he was never at home after he said good night to her. She continued seeing him for a while because it took her a long time to get Greg out of her system. When she went out with another man, a cosy table in the corner or a romantic ballad would remind her of Bautzer. When he fell off a rose trellis climbing up to Joan's bedroom and broke his leg, Lana laughed out loud. Meanwhile, she buried herself in work and it paid off. Her performance as a dancehall girl in *These Glamour Girls* was hailed by critics. The *New York Times* said, 'We like Lana Turner.' The *London Evening News* described her as 'beautiful, full of life, impish and sensitive . . . and on her way to stardom.'

L.B. Mayer rewarded Lana with her own dressing room and top billing in *Dancing Co-ed*. America's King of Swing, Artie Shaw, made his screen debut in the film, but he was not popular at the studio. Lana thought he was very egotistical and kept her distance. 'Artie thought Hollywood was beneath him,' she said. 'He complained about everything and was always primping. That was funny because he wasn't too good-looking to begin with.' Artie didn't have anything nice to say about her, either.

Lana's stardom was sealed when she made the cover of *Life* and *Time* magazines.

Six months after completion of *Dancing Co-ed*, comedian Phil Silvers brought Artie Shaw on the set of *Two Girls on Broadway*, where Lana, wearing a revealing green satin gown, was rehearsing. Shaw didn't recognise her at first, but he liked what he saw. 'Remember me?' she winked.

'I sure do,' he said, looking her over with a grin. 'How about dinner sometime?'

'Call me,' she replied, jotting down her phone number.

It was Mildred's birthday on 12 February 1940. Greg had invited her and Lana for dinner, but called to say he was sick. A few minutes later Artie phoned, and Lana went out with him alone. They drove along the ocean, talking. Artie said he was surprised that the beautiful girl sitting beside him wanted a home and family. But Lana said it was Artie who talked about settling down in a little house with a wife and lots of children. He was tired of running and wanted someone to come home to. Once again, Lana was taken in by a sweet-talking womaniser. She thought Artie was proposing marriage.

That they never got around to having dinner is one thing, but not sealing the 'marriage proposal' with a kiss is almost laughable. Looking back, Lana said she did it to spite Bautzer. As for Artie, who'd already been married twice, he described marriage as one way to get a girl into bed.

They flew by private plane to Las Vegas. The cab driver, who met them at the airport, called George E. Marshall, Justice of the Peace, who greeted them at the door in his bathrobe. After the brief ceremony, Artie took off his blue star sapphire ring and put it on Lana's finger. Then the bride and groom kissed for the first time. Before flying home, Lana sent a telegram to her mother, saying she had eloped to Las Vegas without mentioning the groom's name. Mildred thought it could be Bautzer and, if so, his servants might have some information. To her distress, Greg answered the phone. When Mildred mentioned Shaw, Bautzer made several calls and confirmed the awful truth for Mildred.

Reporters were waiting at Shaw's house. Lana, who was taught to be polite to the press, answer a few questions, make a brief statement, smile and disappear, was dragged into the house by a growling Artie, who raged at reporters and came close to using his fists. Lana begged him to set up a press conference for the next day, but Artie refused. She called MGM's head of publicity, Howard Strickling, who sent members of his staff to deal with the press.

Lana was so exhausted she hoped her wedding night could be postponed for one day and more romantic circumstances. But Artie quickly consummated their marriage and went to sleep. 'It was horrible and meaningless,' she recalled. 'I lay there thinking about Greg . . .'

'How could you?' Mayer sighed over the phone.

'I'm very happy,' Lana said.

'With a man you've known less than twenty-four hours?'

'Yes.'

'Poor Judy is brokenhearted.'

'Judy who?'

'There's only one Judy,' Mayer hissed. 'She was under the impression your husband was going to marry her.'

'Well, I . . .'

'And I hear from reliable sources that Betty Grable's pregnant with Shaw's baby. He gets around.'

'Mr Mayer, I called because we want to go on a honeymoon . . .'

'You're in the middle of a film and I won't shut down production. Be back here in three days.'

'But . . .'

'Next time give me some notice that you're getting married.'

'There won't be a next time,' Lana said.

'Tell your husband to use condoms. We don't want you getting pregnant like poor Betty.'

'But . . .'

'Three days,' Mayer repeated coldly and hung up the phone.

Apparently Artie's line about wanting to settle down was well known. It would work eight times. When a friend referred to him as a wolf, Artie said, 'Well, I'm not a wolf. I marry 'em.' His relationship with women was complex. He demanded perfection but always managed to find fault. Possibly he was too learned and too eager to change the world

MGM arranged for an informal press conference at Artie's house the morning after the wedding. While Lana, who had no change of clothes, tried to pull herself together, Artie handed her a lead pencil and said sternly, 'Put on your eyebrows.' He made no effort to help Lana move her clothes to his house and was appalled when he saw her vast wardrobe. True to form, the bride painted her face and put on an expensive daytime frock. Artie told her to change into a blouse, skirt and loafers. 'And take off your lipstick!' he barked.

It was bad enough that Lana didn't know Artie had been married twice before, but he expected her to clean the house, do the washing and cooking, have his shoes shined and be home when he walked in the door. He threw dinner on the floor in front of guests when it wasn't to his liking. There was no doubt that Shaw was master of the house. He resented Mildred and refused to let her in if she didn't give him plenty of notice in advance.

In June 1940, Lana left Artie. To gain public sympathy, MGM let it be known she was in a 'highly emotional state' and close to a nervous breakdown. Actually, Lana wasn't a bit concerned until, that is, she found out she was pregnant. Artie told her on the phone, 'It's not my baby.'

'You rotten son of a bitch,' she screamed.

Again, their stories differ.

Artie stated that Lana only confided in Louis B. Mayer and Johnny Hyde. When she was hospitalised for 'nervous exhaustion', she aborted their baby. He insisted he knew nothing about Lana's pregnancy, although he suspected something because he knew she was not having a nervous breakdown. 'Lana wasn't the type,' he said.

About her marriage to Artie, Lana said, 'He was my college education.'

He retorted that she had no interest in expanding her knowledge – that she lacked depth and wassn't very bright. 'If divorce is inevitable,' Artie remarked, 'my advice is to call a cab. A lawyer will do the rest.'

Lana was earning close to a thousand dollars a week and did not ask for alimony.

Fan magazines had a field day now that the Sweater Girl was single again, and dancing the nights away with dreamy-eyed crooner Tony Martin, handsome hunk Victor Mature, bandleader Tommy Dorsey, and drummers Buddy Rich and Gene Krupa. Anxious to cash in on the publicity generated by Lana's brief marriage to the King of Swing, MGM put her in *Ziegfeld Girl* with Hedy Lamarr and Judy Garland. Lana was cast as the doomed showgirl who cannot cope with fame and adulation. She snubs her beau, played by Jimmy Stewart, becomes an alcoholic and dies at the end. The *New York Times* raved, 'The girls, especially Lana Turner, who must have been born on Olympus, are breathtaking. She gives a surprisingly solid performance.'

Mildred and Lana moved into a beautiful house in Benedict Canyon,

Mayer put a star on Lana's dressing-room door and increased her weekly salary to $1500 a week. In *Dr Jekyll and Mr Hyde*, Lana got third billing and was barely mentioned in the reviews, but playing opposite Spencer Tracy and Ingrid Bergman was good exposure for her.

Clark Gable liked a script called *Honky Tonk*, about a ruthless gambler in the old West. His wife, Carole Lombard, thought it was a lousy idea and L.B. Mayer agreed, but Gable was determined. 'I know I'm sticking my neck out on this one,' he said, 'but I'm gonna fight for it.' Finally Mayer relented and chose Lana as Gable's leading lady. Lombard saw red when she heard the news. She said that Lana's role as the sweet young Bostonian virgin in *Honky Tonk* did not reflect Miss Turner's reputation, and a few days into filming, rumours of a romance were so rampant that Carole threatened to confront the 'lovers' on the set and 'kick them both in the ass'. Her fights with Clark were bitter and explosive. 'I'll have her fired,' she told him.

'You can't do that,' he argued.

'Then I'll have you fired!'

Carole went directly to Mayer and threatened to keep Clark from reporting to work if Lana tried to 'get her hands on him'. A quiet alert was called on the set of *Honky Tonk* whenever Carole drove through the MGM studio gates. Her visits ceased after Lana, rehearsing a scene with Clark, spotted Carole glaring at her and ran to her dressing room in tears. From then on the set was off limits to outsiders, including Lombard.

Gable was a humble guy, but he would tell his cronies that he had been intimate with most of his leading ladies. He had hundreds of flings that meant nothing more to him than morale boosters. Mayer observed the chemistry between Lana and Clark on and off the screen, and demanded that *Honky Tonk* be finished in short order to separate them.

Clark and Lana, who got equal billing, made the cover of *Life* magazine together as the 'hot new team'. His hunch about *Honky Tonk* proved to be right. *Variety* summed it up. 'Miss Turner, who is graced by tremendous sex appeal, proves she can act as well as turn the boys on. She clicks with Gable in this lusty Western that makes you wish you were there.'

Lana was then rushed into *Johnny Eager* with Robert Taylor, Edward Arnold and Van Heflin, who won an Oscar for Best Supporting Actor. Taylor told a close friend, 'Lana wasn't very career-minded, and preferred men and jewellery over anything else. She wasn't as busty as her pin-up pictures, but her face was delicate and beautiful. I've never seen lips like

Jeanette MacDonald *(left)* was MGM's prima donna. Below, with Allan Jones in *The Firefly*, 1937.

Norma Shearer *(inset)* personified glamour through sheer determination.

A young Norma Shearer in *A Slave of Fashion*, 1925.

Norma Shearer, the wife – at her wedding to Irving Thalberg in 1927 and getting ready to play the divorced woman in her husband's film *The Divorcee* in 1929.

A young Greta Garbo.

The mysterious Greta Garbo, *(left and below)* who retired at age 36, never won an Oscar, but remains the screen's greatest actress.

Jean Harlow, with Cary Grant *(left)* and Franchot Tone in *Suzy*, 1936.

Joan Crawford with Douglas Fairbanks Jr *(below left)*, whom she married in 1929, and with Walter Hudson in *Rain*, 1932.

Joan Crawford in *The Gorgeous Hussy*, 1936.

Goodbye, My Fancy, 1951, Joan Crawford with Frank Lovejoy *(top)*
Lana Turner *(above)* with Mary Beth Hughes, on her way to stardom in *These Glamour Girls*, 1939, and with *(right)* John Garfield in the memorable *The Postman Always Rings Twice*, 1946.

Hedy Lamarr with Edward Everett Horton and Tony Martin *(top)*, in *Ziegfeld Girl*, 1941. *Above*, Debbie Reynolds with Frank Sinatra in *The Tender Trap*, 1955.

A star at 17 and a legend at 27, Judy Garland appeared with Margaret Hamilton in *The Wizard of Oz,* 1939 *(top)*, with James Mason in a *A Star Is Born*, 1954 *(below)*.

Judy Garland with George Murphy and Gene Kelly in *For Me and My Gal*, 1942.

Ava Gardner *(left)* was perfect for her part in *The Snows of Kilimanjaro*, 1952.

Grace Kelly in *High Society*, 1956, with Bing Crosby and Sidney Blackmer *(below)* and Bing Crosby and Frank Sinatra *(right)*.

Katharine Hepburn *(right)* – nominated for 12 Academy Awards and awarded 4 Oscars. *Above*, with Cary Grant and James Stewart in *The Philadelphia Story*, 1940.

Elizabeth Taylor with Robert Taylor *(above)* in *Ivanhoe*, 1952, and with James Donald and Stewart Granger *(below)* in *Beau Brummel*, 1954.

Elizabeth Taylor, Hollywood legend, in *Giant*, 1956.

hers, and though I was not one to run after blondes, Lana was the exception. I couldn't take my eyes off her. There were times during *Johnny Eager* that I thought I'd explode. When she said "good morning", I melted. She was the kind of woman a guy would risk five years in jail for rape.'

When Taylor realised Lana was making no effort to discourage him, he had to have her, 'If only for one night'. Their affair went beyond that, however, because Taylor asked his wife, Barbara Stanwyck, for a divorce so he could marry Lana. The Taylors separated for a few days and reconciled in name only. Press agent George Nichols said, 'Turner did not want to be the one responsible for Taylor's divorce, especially when she heard Stanwyck tried to commit suicide.'

Critics said that Lana Turner and Robert Taylor were the most striking couple on the screen. They played well together, and MGM wanted to team them again, but it never happened. When Taylor remarried in 1954, he and his wife Ursula socialised with Lana and her fourth husband, Lex Barker. But Barbara Stanwyck was not as forgiving. Years later Lana was at the opening of a hotel in Lake Tahoe, heard Barbara was there and called her for a drink. The answer was an icy negative. Stanwyck disliked any woman who dated Bob before and even after their divorce and made it known.

By now Lana's power over men was well known in Hollywood. Carole Lombard could not let her guard down because Lana and Clark were on the same MGM lot every day. Gossip columnists knew that Gable did not attend premieres of his films and took note that he and Carole were visible at the *Honky Tonk* opening, she with her arm wrapped around his and traces of lipstick on his neck after the movie. But a few weeks later, Lombard went into a rage when she found out Clark and Lana were going to make *Somewhere I'll Find You* together. The bickering and battling began all over again. Gable asked her, 'If my affairs with other women mean nothing to me, why should it bother you?' His so-called logic added fire to her fury, but Carole would have to live with the dictates of MGM. The fact that the public clamoured for more of Lana Turner in the arms of Clark Gable was good business. But Lombard was more concerned about her marriage than Metro's box office.

On 7 December 1941, Lana was having a party. Her guests included Frank Sinatra and Tommy Dorsey. Mildred returned from a visit to San Francisco and, hearing the laughter and loud music, took Lana aside. 'Don't you know Pearl Harbor was bombed? We're at war.'

Male stars volunteered for the military, and those celebrities who stayed home sold war bonds, and entertained servicemen at the U.S.O. Bette Davis organised the Hollywood Canteen where the stars mingled with the boys in the armed forces. Carole Lombard was one of the first to volunteer. She boarded a train with her mother, Bessie, and Gable's personal public-relations man, Otto Winkler, for her home state of Indiana and sold $2,000,000 in war bonds. Carole begged Clark to go with her but MGM refused to postpone *Somewhere I'll Find You*, a film about war correspondents. Concerned that Lana would use her absence to seduce her husband, Lombard told her mother, 'I'm anxious to get home to Clark. Let's fly back.'

Winkler didn't like the idea and tried to talk her out of it. He knew that she and Clark had quarrelled bitterly over his attentions to Lana, and he thought a few days apart would bring them closer together. And he didn't want Gable caught off guard, just in case. Carole refused to back down. 'Let's flip for it,' she said. They did and she won the toss. Early on 16 January 1942, Lombard and her party boarded a plane. She sent Clark a telegram telling him to meet her at the airport that evening.

Where was Gable while his wife was away? The press and his friends did not give the same account of what he did or where he was, other than filming *Somewhere I'll Find You*. He wasn't at the airport to meet Carole either. Her plane was late so he sent someone else to wait it out. It was MGM publicity chief Howard Strickling, who got the call that Carole's plane had crashed into a mountain near Las Vegas. There were no survivors.

Carole's brothers never spoke to Gable again. Not only had they been eliminated from her will, but they also resented the quarrels over Clark's fondness for Lana, the obvious reason Carole had rushed home to her death.

Gable was a broken man. MGM considered scratching *Somewhere I'll Find You*, but he volunteered to return to work on 23 February. L.B. Mayer told everyone on the set to pretend nothing had happened. Above all, no pity or tiptoeing around. He had a private talk with Lana and told her to go along with Clark's moods. 'If he wants to work, work. If he wants to leave, that's all right. If he wants to talk, talk. I hear he doesn't like to eat alone, so if he asks, join him.' Clark invited her for dinner at the ranch he had shared with Carole. Lana said there was no mention of the tragic plane crash or his wife's death.

Somewhere I'll Find You was not a very good film, but by the time it was released, news of Gable's induction in the Air Force generated publicity, and the movie made millions. Critics applauded his ability to perform so soon after Lombard's death. Of Lana, they said she was another Jean

Harlow. *Time* magazine wrote, 'Lana suggests she is looking up from a pillow.'

When filming was completed, Lana and Mildred went on an extensive war-bond tour, with a stopover at her birthplace, Wallace, Idaho. Lana sold kisses to anyone who bought a $50,000 bond and she raised $5,000,000.

In April 1942 Lana was introduced to Stephan Crane at the Mocambo nightclub. She was instantly attracted to the tall, good-looking, charming fellow who looked and talked like a millionaire. He referred to himself as Joseph Stephan Crane III, tobacco heir. Lana should have been suspicious after one glance at his small apartment but she wore blinkers when she was in love. L.B. Mayer warned her about the relationship. 'Crane has close bonds with the underworld, Lana. Don't associate yourself with a gangster. He's a phony.'

Mayer had done his homework. Crane lived off gambling profits from a pool hall in Indiana. As this was illegal, he collected the money in cash. This afforded him the chance to mingle with Hollywood's café society. He was accepted as a wealthy playboy and not even mafia boss Bugsy Siegel knew the truth. He and Stephan became such good friends that Bugsy trusted him to squire his moll, Virginia Hill, when he was out of town.

Three months after Lana met Crane, they eloped to Las Vegas on 17 July 1942, and stood before the same justice of the peace that had married her and Artie Shaw. 'Tie the knot tighter this time, Judge,' Lana giggled. The next day Mildred gave the newlyweds a small reception at home and Stephan moved in. While Lana toiled in *Slightly Dangerous* with Robert Young, her husband slept late. They went out every night and Lana picked up the tab. If she was too tired, Crane went out alone and arrived home as she was leaving for the studio.

In November, Stephan told Lana that the divorce from his previous wife wasn't final. She ordered him out of the house and had the locks changed.

'I'm a bigamist,' she told Mayer.

'Tell Crane to keep his mouth shut and you do the same. Lana, your marriage isn't legal so forget about it and him!'

'I can't do that,' she cried. 'I'm pregnant.'

'Again?' Mayer barked. 'Well, we'll arrange for an abortion.'

'I can't do that, L.B. Stephan tried to commit suicide and he's been drafted. Don't you see? He's going off to war and I'm carrying his baby.

The least I can do is marry him again.'

Mayer took a deep breath. 'Your life will be riddled with scandal if you don't.'

'My life has been a series of emergencies!' she wept.

Mayer was too concerned about her reputation as a bigamist to scold Lana. MGM took over, covered up the truth, and on 15 March 1943, she and Stephan were married in Tijuana, Mexico. On 25 July 1943, Lana gave birth to Cheryl Christina 'prematurely'.

Crane received a medical discharge from the army and took up where he left off at the nightclub scene with or without Lana. The good life ended when Lana realised there was no money in the bank after paying her medical bills. She was on maternity leave from MGM and off their payroll temporarily, but Stephan did not offer to help. In April 1944 Lana sued Crane for divorce, and began dating Turhan Bey, the dapper Turkish actor remembered for *Arabian Nights* and *Ali Baba and the Forty Thieves*. Crane's jealousy got the best of him when he saw Lana dancing with the Turk. He broke in and demanded she return the diamond ring he had given her. Bey came to her defence, and the two men stepped outside to settle the matter with their fists.

Though Lana continued dating Bey, Rory Calhoun, Victor Mature and Ricardo Mantalban, she set her sights on Howard Hughes. Supposedly she was engaged to him for eight hours while on a cross-country flight with Howard at the controls. Lana was so sure he would marry her, she had silk sheets monogrammed 'HH'. But Howard had no intention of marrying Lana and when she pouted over the monogramming Hughes said, 'Why don't you marry Huntington Hartford?'

Peter Lawford fell madly in love with Lana, but he was immature and lacked the depth that she required in a man. Then there was Frank Sinatra, and there were rumours that Lana was responsible for his marital problems, but Frank was on a dating spree and not ready for an involved affair. He did, however, flaunt his romance with Lana by dancing with her all night, meeting her in Palm Springs, her snuggled up next to him.

MGM was now paying Lana $4000 a week. She was living in the fast lane and loving it. Her career was in high gear, she was rich and famous, and she had a beautiful little girl. She had the world at her feet.

The Postman Always Rings Twice co-starring John Garfield is one of Lana Turner's most memorable films. 'I loved the all-white wardrobe I wore,'

Lana said. 'The role of Cora gave me something to work with. I understood her yearning for security and respect – yet it led her to do things that ruined her chances of getting what she wanted.' The *NewYork World Telegram* said, 'One of the astonishing excellences of this picture is the performance to which Lana Turner has been inspired.'

Because Lana portrayed an adulteress in the movie, MGM offset any bad feelings the public might have by publicising Lana as the model mother of two-year-old Cheryl. They were photographed together at home and on the movie set. Fan magazines wrote about Lana' devotion to her daughter. This was typical of the studio system Occasionally a star's children were taken away from their nurse and dolled up for the press. Though Lana adored her little girl, she was too busy making films and dating until all hours of the night to spend much time with Cheryl. Keenan Wynn's ex-wife Edie was responsible for Lana's meeting one of the handsomest actors ever to grace the screen, Tyrone Power. She invited him home for a drink and their very intense romance began. Not since her affair with Greg Bautzer had Lana fallen head-over-heels in love. The problem was that Power was separated from his wife, French actress Annabella, and had not yet filed for divorce.

Coincidentally, Power had been deeply in love with Judy Garland, who became pregnant. He pressed Annabella for a divorce but she procrastinated and Judy was forced to get an abortion. There were some Hollywood insiders who think Judy lied about her pregnancy, hoping Annabella would have pity and give Ty his freedom. It didn't happen.

It never occurred to Power that he was bisexual until he fell in love with a handsome actor in New York. He could be faithful to a woman, but eventually the urge to be with a man got the better of him. For years, rumours persisted that he and Cesar Romero were not only best friends, but lovers as well. Bisexuality was so common in Hollywood that it was ignored. If Lana suspected the truth, she was too much in love to give a damn.

L.B. Mayer's daughter Edie Goetz said, 'Whenever I saw them together, they took my breath away. When they entered a room everyone was dumbstruck. Lana had platinum hair and Ty's was curly black. I've never seen a more beautiful couple.'

Power was a frequent guest on the set of *Green Dolphin Street*, a masterful epic that Lana was making with Richard Hart, Van Heflin and Donna Reed. Her maid was played by Linda Christian, who would play a big part in Lana's life . . .

When Power left for Mexico to do *Captain of Castile,* Lana had no intention of being separated from him for long. With three days off for the New Year's holiday, she decided to surprise him and flew to Mexico City. Told that the roads were closed to Patzcuaro where Ty was filming, she called him.

'How's the weather in Los Angeles?' he asked.

'Darling, I'm in Mexico City. I wanted to surprise you.'

Power cursed under his breath and tried to be civil. 'You stay put and I'll try to get a plane,' he said.

Lana could tell he was annoyed, but when he met her at the small airport in Patzcuaro, he seemed to have a change of heart. 'New Year's Eve was the most beautiful night of my life,' she said.

Lana followed the success of *Green Dolphin Street* with Spencer Tracy in *Cass Timberlane*. She had never been as beautiful on the screen. She had a special glow, blossoming with love for Tyrone Power, who was on her set if he wasn't working. But Lana had become too possessive of Ty, who told a friend, 'She's smothering me'. Whether he planned a flying press junket and long vacation to get rid of her isn't known, but it couldn't have happened at a worse time. When Lana told Ty she was pregnant, he had mixed feelings because he wanted a son to carry on the Power name. But at what price? Yes, he loved Lana, but not enough to marry her. He hemmed and hawed about the baby. 'I'm going to be away for quite a while so you'll have to decide what to do,' he told her.

Lana had another abortion, and Ty married Linda Christian. When he died of a heart attack in 1958, Lana was shattered. She confessed that he was the love of her life. 'He was the one who broke my heart,' she said.

After his divorce from Linda, Ty married a young Southern girl. Proudly he announced she was expecting a baby but he did not live to see his son, Tyrone, born in January 1959.

Of *Homecoming*, Lana's next film, critics said, 'Gable and Turner are Gable and Turner, and that's all their fans want.' Lana gave a very good performance as the army nurse nicknamed Snapshot, but moviegoers were annoyed at having to sit for over an hour before experiencing the thrill of a Turner–Gable kiss. 'And then it was in the dark,' one critic complained.

Still reeling from the loss of Tyrone Power, Lana fled to New York City and into the arms of millionaire Bob Topping. The slightly overweight, balding, 33-three-year-old wasn't Lana's type but he had social standing and a charm all his own. On their first date he gave Lana a pair of diamond earrings. She declined, but he insisted she wear them as a favour to him. After several more dates, Lana accepted his invitation to spend the Christmas holidays at his Connecticut mansion. 'My family and your family,' he said.

Topping's Round Hill estate in Greenwich, Connecticut, was awesome even for a movie star who had grown accustomed to the magnificent Hollywood mansions. Before returning home, Lana dined with Bob at the '21' club in New York. Sipping a dry martini, she suddenly caught sight of something sparkling in her cocktail glass. She dipped her finger into the martini and there, in all its splendour, was a fifteen-carat marquise diamond ring. 'What's this for?' she gasped.

'I'm asking you to marry me, Lana.'

'Yes,' she exclaimed, putting the rock on her engagement finger.

Lana said it might have been the martinis or the biggest diamond she had ever seen that convinced her to marry Topping. But there were other reasons as well. And she needed Bob's financial backing in case MGM suspended her without pay for turning down *The Three Musketeers*.

Louis B. Mayer was appalled by Lana's outrageous behaviour in recent months. Rumours were rampant that she'd broken up Frank Sinatra's marriage, but she went out with him anyway, ignoring repeated warnings from MGM. Then she became 'engaged' to Tyrone Power, who also had a wife. And, just prior to meeting Topping, Lana had had a brief but public affair with tycoon John Alden Talbot whose wife named Lana as co-respondent in her January 1948 divorce suit.

Mayer was prepared to suspend Lana for misconduct before her romance with Topping became front page news. When his wife, Arline Judge, claimed her marriage to Bob had been fine until Miss Turner came along, Mayer cringed. 'How nice to see you, Lana,' Mayer said sarcastically.

'Sorry I'm five days late,' Lana cooed, waving her fifteen-carat diamond before his eyes.

'You may have to hock that to cover production costs for *The Three Musketeers*. And I'm suspending you without pay for reporting late and not abiding by the morals clause in your contract.'

Lana was shocked but not beaten, knowing Topping would bail her out. 'L.B., you've been very good to me.'

'I've spoiled you rotten,' he said.

'So that makes you responsible, too, doesn't it?'

'Yes, it does. Putting up with your indiscretions is one thing, but I will not tolerate any member of my family who refuses to appear in a film.'

'L.B., you made me a star so I think like a star. The part of Lady de Winter in *The Three Musketeers* is too small. It's an insult. If you'd build it up . . .'

'I'll think about it,' he said sternly. 'Meanwhile, you're suspended.'

A week later Lana had her revised script and was put back on salary at $5,000 a week. She told columnist Louella Parsons, 'I could never disappoint Louis B. Mayer.' MGM proudly promoted *Musketeers* in bold letters: **LANA TURNER FIRST TIME IN TECHNICOLOR**. *The Three Musketeers* with Gene Kelly and June Allyson was a success. The *New York Times'* Bosley Crowther called it a 'splendiferous' production, adding that '. . . more dazzling costumes, more colors or more of Miss Turner's chest have never been in a picture like this one.'

Bob Topping rented a house in Beverly Hills and waited out his divorce from Arline Judge, which became final on Friday 23 April 1948. MGM announced that Lana would marry Topping the following Monday at Billy Wilkerson's mansion on Sunset Boulevard. After two elopements, Lana was determined to have a proper wedding. Her gown of champagne-coloured Alençon lace over champagne satin was designed by Don Loper. The altar was a mass of five thousand gardenias, and the bride carried a cluster of magnificent orchids, flown in from Hawaii. L.B. Mayer, Greg Bautzer and Joan Crawford were among the 65 invited guests who feasted on a lavish buffet surrounded by lakes and rivers filled with live goldfish.

Following the two o'clock ceremony, the bride and groom kissed. He said in a loud whisper, 'This is forever.' She smiled tenderly and replied, 'Yes, darling,' as she glanced down at the dazzling two-inch diamond bracelet that Bob had given her for a wedding present.

Though Lana wanted a dignified wedding, there was little she could do to prevent MGM press agents and 75 reporters from attending the champagne reception. This was the price she paid for being a movie goddess and allowing MGM to share the expenses. So Lana's wedding turned into a sideshow and was reported as such, columnists poking fun at a ham decorated with 'I love you' and a roast beef adorned with 'She loves him'. *Life* magazine said Lana wore heavy pancake make-up, the colour of her dress was unflattering, and she was so nervous that the bouquet of white orchids trembled 'as if they were in a storm. In a way they were.'

Louella Parsons hinted in her column that Lana was on the rebound from Tyrone Power.

The newlyweds honeymooned in Europe and returned to Round Hill in Connecticut. When Lana became pregnant, she hinted that Topping might buy up her MGM contract. Waiting for the baby, Lana played hostess to parties that often lasted for days. But her life was never blissful for long. In January 1949 she went into premature labour and gave birth to a stillborn baby boy. When Lana felt strong enough, she and Bob spent a leisurely few months in the Caribbean, but this turned out to be the pinnacle of her marriage to Topping.

Thirty pounds overweight, Lana returned to MGM for *A Life of Her Own* with Ray Milland. Being on a very strict diet made her nervous and abrupt. Unable to afford the maintenance and taxes on Round Hill, Bob began drinking heavily. While Lana counted calories and he counted his financial losses, their marriage was deteriorating and so was Lana's screen career. *A Life of Her Own* was panned by critics. Bosley Crowther wrote, 'Two years absence from the movies obviously did not improve Lana Turner's talents as an actress or her studio's regard for what she can do.' Crowther was right about MGM. L.B. Mayer was busy with his racehorses and the courtship of a new young wife. Dore Schary was brought in as production head to put MGM in the black again after a $6,500,000 deficit. Mayer was gradually losing control over his beloved studio and would be forced to resign in June 1951. His stars were not fond of Schary or his projects. He infuriated Lana by putting her into *Mr Imperium* with Ezio Pinza. The film was so bad that Radio City Music Hall cancelled the booking. But on 24 May 1950, Lana placed her hands and feet in wet cement on the sidewalk entrance of Grauman's Chinese Theater on Hollywood Boulevard.

Lana's second miscarriage and a pile of overdue bills prompted Mildred to speak up. 'Face it, Lana. You can't afford to support a millionaire.'

Bob's disappearing at night made Lana suspicious, so she had him followed and found out he was seeing both another woman and his attorneys in New York about a separation. On 11 September 1951, MGM announced that Lana was divorcing Bob Topping. Lonely and depressed, she had a few drinks, took some sleeping pills and slashed her wrist with a razor. Mildred found her in a pool of blood in the bathroom. Lana's life was never in danger, however. She didn't cut her wrist deep enough or take a lethal dose of sleeping pills. Her attempt at suicide was a classic cry for help.

Lana's depression and feelings of hopelessness faded away in the arms of her leading man in *The Merry Widow*, 36-year-old Fernando Lamas, who was dubbed the Latin Lover, and indeed he was. Lana was in love again. Kirk Douglas, who co-starred with her in *The Bad and the Beautiful* said, 'I was ready for Lana, but she was going with Fernando Lamas who was very jealous. He was always around so nothing happened.'

MGM announced that Lana would co-star again with Lamas in *Latin Lovers*, but shortly before production began she went to Benny Thau, head of MGM talent, who was shocked by the black-and-blue marks on Lana's body, inflicted by Lamas. Ricardo Mantalban was cast instead of Lamas in *Latin Lovers*. Though Benny Thau assured Lana she would not be harrassed by Lamas, she wanted to get out of town after the film was finished. Frank Sinatra, who was married to Ava Gardner, gave Lana the key to his house in Palm Springs. But Frank and Ava had another of their famous fights. He stormed out and told Ava, 'I'm leaving. If you want to know where I am, I'll be in Palm Springs fucking Lana Turner!' Ava thought about what he said. She and Lana were pals, but Ava knew about Lana's affair with Frank and she made up her mind to catch them in the act. When she got to Palm Springs, Frank was nowhere to be found, so she had a drink with Lana and her agent, Ben Cole. Frank barged in and accused the girls of 'really cutting me up'. Another loud fight ensued and neighbours called the police. Louella Parsons reported in a headline that 'Frank Sinatra and Ava Gardner separate after he finds her with Lana Turner.' The wording implies that he found the girls in bed together, which was far from the truth, though rumours persist to this day.

Lana began dating Lex Barker, who was separated from actress Arlene Dahl. When they divorced, Arlene wed none other than Fernando Lamas. Lex, who played Tarzan, was a handsome, blond, six-foot-four actor who tired of swinging through the jungle with Cheetah, and was offered films abroad because he could speak several languages fluently. In April 1953, Lana decided to join Lex in Italy where MGM arranged for her to do *The Flame and the Flesh* as a brunette. Critics thought the film was corny, but Lana couldn't have cared less. She married Lex Barker on 8 September 1953, at the city hall in Turin, Italy, and honeymooned on the isle of Capri before making *Betrayed* with Clark Gable and Victor Mature in Holland. Critics panned the movie. The *Hollywood Reporter* said, 'Seeing Gable without sex is like seeing *Ben Hur* without horses.' *Newsweek* reported that 'Miss Turner plays her part of a spy with no conviction.'

Lana and Lex returned to Hollywood before Christmas and went through another marriage ceremony when Barker found out his divorce had not been final when he married Lana in Italy. She wanted to use her influence at MGM to get Lex a contract, but he signed with Universal 'because if anything happens to my marriage, I don't want to be thrown out like Fernando Lamas.'

Lana's first picture in CinemaScope was *The Prodigal* with Edmund Purdom, who was having an affair with Tyrone Power's wife, Linda Christian. With her hair bleached again, Lana was very fetching in the scanty costumes that barely got by the censors. One publicity shot used to promote *The Prodigal* showed Lana in nothing but G-string and beads. It had to be airbrushed before theatre owners would display it. Lana wasn't pleased with the picture, or with Purdom, whom she described as an egotist with garlic breath. Critics weren't impressed, but there was much to be said for Lana's goddess of the flesh. Sidney Skolsky wrote in his column, 'That long walk that Miss Turner takes through the Temple of Love is the best reason for seeing the picture. Pure poetry in motion.' But Bosley Crowther of the *New York Times* viewed the film as a pompous, ostentatious, vulgar and ridiculous charade. 'Miss Turner conducts the rituals as though she were Little Egypt at the old Chicago's World Fair.'

The day after she completed *The Prodigal*, Lana was rushed into *The Sea Chase*, filmed in Hawaii with John Wayne. Lex stayed in Hollywood and, according to ten-year-old Cheryl, he was abusing her. His 'lessons in sex' began with him exposing himself and masturbating in front of her. Then he repeatedly raped Cheryl. These sessions continued for three years, whether Lana was away or at home. Lex convinced Cheryl she would go to a Detention Centre if she told anyone.

In 1955 Lana made a costume epic entitled *Diane*, about the mistress of King Henry II of France. Under her contract with MGM, she owed them one more picture, and she was loaned to 20th Century-Fox for *The Rains of Ranchipur* with Richard Burton whom she described as a supreme egotist. *Redbook* chose *Rains* as the picture of the month in December 1955.

MGM did not renew Lana's contract in February 1956. It was a sad day when she packed her belongings and left after eighteen years. She had to pay back sizeable loans to MGM, leaving her short of money. Lana became pregnant but the baby girl was stillborn in the seventh month. While she recuperated in the hospital, Lex was seeing other women and, according to Cheryl, sneaking into her bedroom at night. In 1957, she told Mildred, who in turn confronted Lana. They had Cheryl examined, and the doctor confirmed that the thirteen-year-old had been injured internally. Lex, relaxing in bed, did not see Lana come into his room with a gun. She gave him twenty minutes to get out of the house. She turned her back on him and filed for divorce.

Lex told the press he blamed Cheryl for the break-up of his marriage. 'She told lies about me,' he said. 'She's a bad girl and will end up in trouble one day.'

In 1973 Barker collapsed and died of a massive heart attack on Lexington Avenue and 61st Street in New York City at the age of fifty-three. When Lana heard the news she said, 'What took him so long?'

In April 1957, Lana signed with producer Jerry Wald to play Constance MacKenzie, the mother of an eighteen-year-old girl, in *Peyton Place*, based on a novel filled with rape, vicious gossip, sex, love and murder. Today the book and the film would be run-of-the-mill but in 1957 it shocked the world that such scandal could take place in small-town America. *Peyton Place* was nominated for nine Oscars, among them a Best Actress for Lana Turner, reviving her career and stature in Hollywood.

Johnny Stompanato introduced himself to Lana as John Steele. He filled her dressing room with flowers and called her every day. Intrigued, she agreed to go out with him. Before he arrived she received a diamond bracelet from Steele, who refused to take it back 'because it's engraved'. They began seeing each other off and on, and each time he presented her with another piece of expensive jewellery. Then a friend told Lana, 'You're dating Johnny Stompanato. He has connections to gangster Micky Cohen.'

Lana wanted to know why he lied to her. 'Because I knew you wouldn't see me if I gave my real name,' John replied. 'That's true, and now I have my doubts,' she said. 'It's too late,' Stompanato exclaimed. 'You're mine now.'

When Lana fell in love she made allowances, and clearly she was deeply involved with Johnny Stompanato. He was right. It was too late.

He was a good-looking Italian with piercing brown eyes, black wavy hair and a strong physique, and he was a cocksure lover at the age of thirty-two. Lana lavished expensive gifts on him but knew her reputation was at stake if she flaunted her affair with Stompanato so they were rarely photographed together.

When Lana went to London for *Another Time, Another Place*, Johnny followed. Suspecting her of having a romance with her leading man, Sean Connery, Stompanato confronted him on the set. Connery landed a right to Johnny's nose, knocking him helplessly to the floor. When *Another Time, Another Place* was completed, Lana headed for Mexico and though she claimed Johnny followed without her consent, reliable sources said she picked up the tab for his airline ticket and their vacation in Acapulco. By now he was growing tired of hiding in the shadows. He wanted to marry Lana and share the limelight, controlling her body, soul and bank account. Back in Hollywood, columnist Louella Parsons wrote, 'I hope it isn't true that Lana Turner, who is now in Acapulco, is going to marry Johnny Stompanato.'

A week before the Academy Awards, Lana and Johnny flew back to Los Angeles. Mildred and Cheryl were at the airport to meet them. The press was there too, but this time Stompanato took Lana's arm and smiled broadly for photographers. The next day newspapers headlined Lana's affair with Mickey Cohen's former associate. She denied a romantic involvement and made it clear to Johnny that he would not accompany her to the Academy Awards. He turned on the charm, but she was adamant. Stompanato fumed, watching Lana being pampered by her hairdresser and seamstress for the Oscar ceremony on 24 March 1958. She was a vision, in a clinging strapless white-lace sheath, diamond earrings, diamond bracelet, diamond necklace and diamond rings on several fingers.

At the Pantages Theater, Lana trembled and held Cheryl's hand when the names for Best Actress were announced. But it was Joanne Woodward who won for *Three Faces of Eve*. Lana accepted defeat graciously and went to the ball at the Beverly Hilton Hotel. Like old times, she held court at her table and danced with Clark Gable and Sean Connery. For Lana this was an evening for reminiscing with old friends and she drank in every minute of the Hollywood splendour that was slowly fading for great stars of the Golden Era.

When Lana returned to the Bel Air Hotel where she was staying before moving to a house at 730 Bedford Drive Johnny was waiting for her. Why was she so late? Hadn't he told her not to attend any parties after the award ceremony? They argued and he slapped Lana so hard her diamond earrings cut into her cheeks. He punched her body, knocked her down, picked her up and socked her once more. Weak and sick to her stomach, she got into bed and pretended to be asleep. Johnny kissed her on the cheek and left.

Lana confided in Mildred, who called their friend Chief Anderson at the police department. 'I can't do anything unless Lana makes a formal complaint,' he said. 'Please ask her to call me.' But Lana never did.

Good Friday, 4 April 1958, was a dreary rainy day in Beverly Hills. Johnny helped Lana move to the house on Bedford Drive. Several friends dropped in for cocktails and, by an odd coincidence, one of the guests remembered going to military school with Stompanato. Lana said that was impossible (the guest was 43). But the look on Johnny's face when he saw his former classmate told Lana he had also lied about his age. When the guests left, she confronted him.

'So what?' he said with a smirk. 'I thought we were going to the movies.'

'I'm not in the mood.'

'I guess you'd rather stay home and get drunk again.'

'Leave me alone,' she said, going upstairs to her bedroom and locking the door. Stompanato pounded on it with his fists. 'Open up, bitch, or I'll break the fuckin' door down!'

Lana knew he was strong enough so she let him in. 'You'll never get rid of me,' he threatened. 'I'll cut you up first.'

'Johnny, this is a new house – a new beginning for me. I don't want you here. Please go.'

He spun Lana around and grabbed her by the shoulders. 'You can't order me around,' he ranted, 'I give the orders. If I say jump, you'll jump. If I tell you to hop, you'll hop! If you try to get away I'll find you. I'll cut up your face so you'll never work again. I'll get your mother and daughter, too.'

Cheryl, in the adjoining bedroom, heard everything. She ran downstairs, not knowing what to do. Call the police? Call her father? No, they might not get here in time. She went into the kitchen and saw a butcher's knife on the counter. That's it. I'll warn him, she thought. I'll frighten him away. Cheryl took the knife upstairs and heard her mother crying hysterically 'Get out!' she screamed.

'You're dead, bitch!'

Cheryl knocked on the door and Lana opened it. Her hand was on the knob as Johnny raised his arm to hit her. Cheryl stepped into the room with the knife in her hand. 'Johnny ran on the blade,' she said. 'It went in. He looked straight at me and said, "My God, Cheryl, what have you done?"' He took three tiny steps backward, his eyes frozen on Cheryl, and then he fell on to the floor.

Lana called Mildred. She rushed to Bedford Drive with their physician,

Dr McDonald, who said Johnny Stompanato was dead. 'You'd better call a lawyer,' he told Lana. 'I suggest Jerry Geisler. He's the best.'

It took the jury only 25 minutes to come up with the verdict of justifiable homicide. The judge asked Cheryl which parent she preferred living with if it were up to her. Lana and Crane were shocked when their daughter replied, 'I want to live with my grandmother.' The judge determined that Cheryl would be a ward of the court until she was eighteen. For the next sixty days she would live with Mildred.

Lana had won the battle but lost the war. She was heavily in debt to MGM and to Jerry Geisler. Without the power and prestige of MGM behind her, she wasn't sure how to proceed with her career. Would anyone in Hollywood take a chance on her after the Stompanato scandal? Producer Ross Hunter did, but he had a difficult time convincing Lana to do *Imitation of Life* about an actress who gives up her daughter and the man she loves for her career. 'I can't do it,' she said. 'The theme is too close to home.'

Hunter replied, 'It's a good role and I think people will admire you for doing it.'

Lana accepted a small fee up front and fifty per cent of the profits. If the picture failed, her career would most likely be finished. But Lana liked and trusted Hunter, and she forged ahead with the task of reliving her life on the screen. Co-starring in the film were John Gavin as her lover and Sandra Dee as her daughter, who falls in love with him.

Imitation of Life was a smash hit at the box office, making more money than any other film at Universal Studios, and it got Lana back on her feet.

In the summer of 1958 Lana met 43-year-old millionaire, Fred May. Though she had moved into a house on Roxbury Drive, Lana was soon living with May at his ranch where he raised thoroughbreds for racing.

Ross Hunter's production *Portrait in Black* with Lana and Anthony Quinn was another financial bonanza, despite what the critics had to say. Like old times, however, they raved about Lana's lovely blonde coif and her magnificent wardrobe. Though she was not often seen in public with Fred May, they attended the premiere of *Portrait in Black* on 29 June 1960, and the following November they were married at the Miramar Hotel in Santa Monica. 'He's a wonderful guy,' she said. 'I wish I'd met him years ago.'

Fred May proved to be a good stepfather to Cheryl, who had run away from home several times. She was sent to El Retiro, a reform school in San Fernando Valley. Now that Lana was married, Cheryl was allowed to live with her, but she was arrested at a drunken party. Lana convinced Cheryl she needed psychiatric help. 'Fred and I will fly with you to the Institute of Living in Hartford, Connecticut,' she said. 'It comes highly recommended and is rather like a country club.' Cheryl would remain at the institute for a year.

Lana's marriage and her film career were thriving. *By Love Possessed* with Jason Robards Jr, and *Bachelor in Paradise* with Bob Hope were well received. But for how long could Lana live a normal life? Without a challenge, she bored easily. When asked why she stayed with Johnny Stompanato, Lana replied, 'His consuming passion was strangely exciting. Call it forbidden fruit or whatever, but this attraction was very deep – maybe something sick within me – and my dangerous captivation went far beyond lovemaking.'

Lana claimed the end came when Fred borrowed money from her because his was tied up. But he bought her a new Lincoln Continental with part of the borrowed money and Lana blew her stack. On the night of the argument, she fled in her new auto to a bar on the Pacific Coast Highway called the Cottage. She made a date with a bartender and parked the Lincoln in front of his apartment building. Worried about her, Fred May cruised the area and spotted her car. As it happened, Mildred was passing by, saw her daughter's Lincoln and a very angry Fred May. She testified against Lana at the divorce hearing on 15 October 1962.

Fred and Lana remained friends, and when he urged her to buy a Malibu house with ninety feet of beach front, she took his advice and lived there for seven years.

In 1962, a novel by Harold Robbins entitled *Where Love Has Gone* became an instant bestseller. It was loosely based on the Stompanato case. In the book Lana's character stabs her lover and allows her daughter to take the blame. The novel had such an impact readers were convinced that it revealed the truth about Stompanato's death. For Cheryl, it was reliving that dreadful night all over again. She began drinking heavily, became despondent, and took an overdose of sleeping pills. Fortunately, her roommate found Cheryl in time. During her recovery, she came to terms with herself and made up her mind to straighten out her life. She approached her father about working for him at his restaurant, the Luau. Crane gave her a job and taught his 21-year-old daughter the restaurant business.

Lana made one of her best films, *Madame X*, for Ross Hunter in 1965. As her character grows older in the movie, Lana became depressed, spending more and more time with her make-up man. She and Hunter clashed during production because she was wasting valuable time getting ready for the camera. He claimed she was staying up until all hours having fun, and at 45, she could not expect to party all night and be fit to work early the next morning.

The reason for Lana's strange behaviour was Robert Eaton, ten years younger, handsome, smooth, and divorced. His credentials? Aspiring actor/producer and stud. Eaton was the first man to satisfy Lana sexually. She told a friend they locked themselves in her bedroom for days, making love. 'He's the first man to keep up with me in the sack,' Lana confessed. As for Eaton, he had found a famous woman who could afford the expensive habits he was beginning to get used to. And so they were married on 22 June 1965, at his family's home in Arlington, Virginia.

A year later Lana had a face-lift. It was a guarded secret, of course, and the difference was barely noticeable. But if one takes the time to study pictures of her after the surgery, the eyes are slanted slightly and her 'little girl' features have lost their lushness.

For Lana there were many movie projects that never got off the ground, but she had fun appearing on TV doing skits on *The Milton Berle Show*, *What's My Line?*, and *The Carol Burnett Show*. Her income from Ross Hunter's movie projects had made her a millionaire so she could afford to wait for a worthwhile film to come along.

And she could afford to keep Bob Eaton dressed in expensive suits from the finest shops in Beverly Hills. She bought him a car, paid to have his teeth fixed and gave him a monthly allowance. But when she went to Vietnam on a U.S. tour in June 1967, Eaton entertained other women in the Malibu house, and Mildred had the stained sheets to prove it! Lana filed for divorce and then changed her mind, and concentrated on a television series Eaton was working on for her. ABC-Universal announced that Lana would appear in *The Survivors* with Kevin McCarthy as her philandering husband, Ralph Bellamy as her banking-czar father and George Hamilton as a playful half-brother. 'In the beginning we hated each other,' Lana said. 'At the end we simply disliked each other.'

Lana's salary was $12,000 per episode, while George Hamilton made $17,000. She said it was a matter of top billing or the money and MGM had taught her that top billing was more prestigious than the almighty dollar. Actually top billing was more prestigious, but the sponsors thought George Hamilton would attract more viewers. They were wrong and the show was cancelled.

Bob Eaton, who urged Lana to do *The Survivors*, contributed very little to the television series. He was too busy playing around with other women and Lana divorced him in April 1968. A year later, shortly after her divorce from Eaton became final, she met nightclub hypnotist Ronald Dante. She said it was love at first sight. On their first date, Dante showed up on his motorcycle and a playful Lana got on behind him. Speeding through the hills of Hollywood was a thrill for Lana, who had experienced just about everything else in her lifetime. When she turned down his marriage proposal, Dante stopped calling her. Lana knew this was an old trick, but loneliness got the best of her, and they were married in Las Vegas on 9 May 1969.

The press wasted no time checking into Dante's background. His real name was Ronald Peller and he was born in Chicago in 1930. Supposedly he'd swindled one of his previous wives out of her life's savings. She sued for an annulment claiming Peller had hypnotised her into getting married. If he was looking for publicity when he married Lana, it backfired because Santa Ana police were looking for him on a grand theft felony charge that was eventually dropped.

Lana appeared with Dante at his out-of-town nightclub appearances as a hypnotist but she soon tired of that and gave him $35,000 to invest in a business that would keep him at home. Dante disappeared with the money. Lana sued him for divorce. He, in turn, wanted $250,000. It would take three years before the case was settled in Lana's favour, except she never got her $35,000 back. 'I'm so gullible,' Lana said. 'I always thought I was being loved for myself.'

In February 1970 Lana was spending a week in Palm Springs when she got a call from Dante, who said he missed her and hoped they could remain good friends. She wasn't prepared for his call in the middle of the night, nor the romantic one-way conversation. Seemingly desperate to see her, he asked how long she would be in Palm Springs, and she replied, 'Two or three more days'. Dante wished her a good time and hung up. When Lana returned home from Palm Springs, she noticed the sliding doors to the swimming pool were open. While she waited for police, Lana discovered that $100,000 worth of jewellery was missing. The thief and the jewellery were never found, but it was obvious to Lana that Dante had taken advantage of her once again.

In 1971 Lana toured in the stageplay, *Forty Carats*, as a forty-year-old divorcee in love with a man half her age. The reviews were mild. Many critics said Lana Turner was playing Lana Turner, while others were delighted to see the great star as herself. Then there was her quick change into a glittering ball gown while the audiences were preparing to leave the theatre. One critic considered this corny and pretentious. To others it was class and glamour personified. Lana's attitude was that the public had come to see an MGM star and, by God, they were going to have the opportunity to see the stunning actress as she had appeared on the screen.

Exhausted after doing *Forty Carats*, Lana lazed about, sipped vodka and watched television. Occasionally she saw Cheryl who was living with Joyce 'Josh' LeRoy, but it would take a while before Lana accepted the fact that her daughter was gay, despite the fact it was Josh who helped Cheryl put her past where it belonged.

Four years off the screen, Lana signed for the lead in *The Terror of Sheba*, a horror movie to be filmed in England. She played a deranged mother who gets revenge on her son for drowning her favourite cat in its milk. At the end he drowns his mother in Sheba's milk. This movie was a dreadful comedown for Lana. Her excuse for doing it was the success of Bette Davis in *What Ever Happened to Baby Jane?* and *Hush, Hush, Sweet Charlotte*. Lana should have known she could not play horror films like Bette Davis.

Before Lana left for England, she bought a condominium at Century Park East on Santa Monica Boulovard in Century City. She did not move again.

In 1974 she had another face-lift and remained dedicated to looking her very best. Even if Lana did not go out of the condo, her hairdresser and manicurist came every week.

In the spring of 1975 Lana was asked to attend a tribute in her honour at Town Hall in New York. Two thousand people showed up to see the one and only Lana. Beginning to feel more comfortable in front of a live audience, she appeared on stage in *The Pleasure of His Company* with Louis Jourdan for three weeks in Arlington Heights, Illinois. The play might have continued for another few weeks but Jourdan had another commitment. Lana refused to play with an unknown, but rather than admit the truth, she managed to get sick and returned to California.

In 1976, Lana went on tour with *Bell, Book and Candle*. The play was successful and she received rave reviews. But the temperamental Lana would not perform if there were many empty seats in the theatre

The following year Lana was hospitalised with a liver ailment. When she recovered, doctors told her to give up drinking or suffer the consequences. She obeyed orders as long as she could stand it, telling friends, 'I can't face the day or an audience without vodka.'

Murder Among Friends, in Chicago, was another hit play for Lana and the ultimate plan was for her to appear on Broadway but success went to her head. She showed up later and later for her performances. Audiences either booed her or left the theatre. Lana got away with it in Chicago, but Broadway wanted no part of her.

Taylor Pero, who had formerly worked for Johnny Mathis, had been Lana's secretary and public relations representative since 1969. He was remarkably handsome, and though he attracted women of all ages, he never strayed from Lana's side at business functions. During their ten years together she enjoyed flaunting him so many observers assumed Pero was Lana's stud. She said the very idea that they were lovers was absurd. According to Pero, they became intimate not long after her marriage to Dante ended, and it was she who made the first move. 'Pandora's box had been opened,' Pero said, 'jumbling and intertwining sex and love, work and friendship, hope and hate. It was the end of a great platonic relationship. It tore down the barrier of employer and employee in my mind, though not in hers.'

Taylor Pero saw Lana through her stage plays, trying his best to get her to the theatre on time which was too often a frustrating task. Eventually, they fought bitterly and she fired him in November 1979. Lana flew to Hawaii to spend Thanksgiving with Cheryl, who had settled in Honolulu with Josh. Nervous and argumentative, Lana cut short her visit.

When she found out that Pero was writing a book entitled *Always, Lana* about their ten years together, Lana decided to publish her memoirs, *Lana: The Lady, the Legend and the Truth*, a bestseller in 1982. But Hollywood columnists who had been around a long time got a chuckle over Lana's book. Sheila Graham said, 'When a Hollywood queen claims she's telling the truth and nothing but the truth, she's "hiding behind" the truth.' In contrast Pero's book was far more interesting, even though he wrote about Lana with great compassion. He kept her on the throne and removed her crown only when the occasion warranted.

Though Lana wrote very little about Taylor Pero in her book, she fell apart when they went their separate ways. Her weight dropped to under a hundred pounds, and she admitted she was drinking heavily and not eating. At the advice of a close friend Lana turned to holistic medicine and pulled herself together. 'When you've found God, you're never alone,' she said.

To heal old wounds and to be near Cheryl and Mildred, Lana spent several months a year in Hawaii. In casual clothes and very little make-up, she had become humble and more understanding of the real world. She accepted Cheryl's homosexuality and embraced Josh as a daughter. The only dark cloud was Mildred's death from emphysema on 22 February 1982.

In October, Lana embarked on a tour to promote her book. Reporters noted that she wasn't travelling with trunks of gowns and furs. 'I'm an author,' she said, 'with only two suitcases and two garment bags.' Her companions on the tour were her devoted maid Carmen Cruz, and her good-looking hairdresser Eric Root.

In 1983 Lana retired from show business after appearing in the primetime soap opera, *Falcon Crest*. Jane Wyman, who was the star of the series, was miffed that Lana demanded star treatment. Her character was killed off at the end of the first season.

A year later Robin Leach asked Lana to be on his popular weekly television show, *Lifestyles of the Rich and Famous*. She agreed to appear if her segments were filmed in Egypt. With the Sphinx and Giza pyramids in the background, Lana and Eric Root took a camel ride in the desert. She endured it for the sake of the camera as she did dancing with Root on a cruise down the Nile.

'Looking back on your life, are you at the happiest point of it all,' Leach asked.

'Oh, yes,' Lana replied, sitting on a gilded chair that resembled a throne. 'I have a glorious life. I can do anything I want, go where I want, be alone if I want, travel if I want, and sometimes I don't want anything. Now isn't that a blessing?' Lana was rarely seen in public after that. Often she spent hours getting ready for an event and then decided not to go. 'I don't want people saying I look old,' she said. 'I want my fans to remember me as I was.'

Taylor Pero said, 'Dear Lana, selflessly saving Hollywood from decline. Image before truth, façade rather than fact, pride over all – that was Louis B. Mayer's and Hollywood's legacy to Lana Turner.' Bette Davis, who was quite the opposite of Lana, told Pero at a cocktail party, 'My basic interest was the performance, not the off-screen image. Lana was different. She consciously perpetuated the glamour thing.' Davis said she felt no obligation to anyone when she wasn't working, until her peers in Hollywood convinced her that an off-screen impression was just as important. 'That's how you come to be preoccupied with your appearance. I realised I owed the public something. People like Lana never appeared in public any way but put together. I think the public still wants that. Look the way you want to at home, live your own life, but give the American people their kings and queens.'

After suffering from a sore throat for months, Cheryl insisted that Lana check into Cedars-Sinai Medical Center on 13 May 1992. She was diagnosed with throat cancer, which was spreading to her jaw and lungs. One gossip columnist wrote, 'The blonde movie queen retained her royal status during radiation therapy. Instead of a hospital gown, she wore an off-the-shoulder peasant blouse.' On her birthday, 8 February 1993, Lana told friends in a hoarse voice that she was completely recovered. Two years later the cancer had spread to her lungs, but gallantly she travelled to San Sebastian, Spain, to receive a Lifetime Achievement Award. Lana Turner waved to her fans from the centre-stage spotlight for the last time.

On the night of 29 June 1995 she told her maid of 44 years, Carmen Cruz, 'I think I will go soon.' Carmen held Lana in her arms until the end. 'Nobody paid her attention,' Cruz said. 'Poor little thing . . .'

Lana Turner was cremated and, as of this writing, her ashes are in her daughter's possession. Cheryl inherited a small sum of money, jewels and furs from her mother. The balance of Lana's $2,000,000 estate was willed to Carmen Cruz . . .

In 1970 film historian David Shipman wrote, 'Lana Turner has no other identity than that of a film star – and that from a mould, a fabulous creature who moves on screen among beautiful furnishings, and who, off screen, is primarily noted for a series of love affairs and marriages. It is presumably due to this that she owes the longevity of her career, which has consistently triumphed over appalling personal notices. Even her admirers would admit that she couldn't act her way out of a paper bag.'

This author disagrees with Shipman. Lana Turner's career in films lasted *despite* her personal mishaps. Moviegoers paid to see a screen personality, not a great actress. She was a vibrant woman who lived life with the zest and passion that novelists attempt to emulate in fiction. She is a movie legend who would almost have us believe that the chiffon and tinsel still exist in Hollywood.

*

Lana Turner was cremated, and I understand, her ashes are still in her daughter's possession. Cheryl inherited a small sum of money, jewels and furs. The balance of Lana's £2,000,000 estate was willed to Carmen Cruz . . .

The Films of Lana Turner

A Star is Born (United Artists, 1937)
They Won't Forget (Warner Brothers, 1937)
The Great Garrick (Warner Brothers, 1937)
The Adventures of Marco Polo (United Artists, 1938)
Love Finds Andy Hardy (MGM, 1938)
The Chaser (MGM, 1938)
Rich Man, Poor Girl (MGM, 1938)
Dramatic School (MGM, 1938)
Calling Dr Kildare (MGM, 1939)
Dancing Co-ed (MGM, 1939)
Two Girls on Broadway (MGM, 1940)
We Who Are Young (MGM, 1940)
Ziegfeld Girl (MGM, 1941)
Dr Jekyll and Mr Hyde (MGM, 1941)
Honky Tonk (MGM, 1941)
Johnny Eager (MGM, 1942)
Somewhere I'll Find You (MGM, 1942)
Slightly Dangerous (MGM, 1943)
The Youngest Profession (MGM, 1943)
Dubarry Was a Lady (MGM, 1943)
Marriage is a Private Affair (MGM, 1944)
Keep Your Powder Dry (MGM, 1945)
Weekend At the Waldorf (MGM, 1945)
The Postman Always Rings Twice (MGM, 1946)
Green Dolphin Street (MGM, 1947)
Cass Timberlane (MGM, 1947)
Homecoming (MGM, 1948)

The Three Musketeers (MGM, 1948)
A Life of Her Own (MGM, 1950)
Mr Imperium (MGM, 1951)
The Merry Widow (MGM, 1952)
The Bad and the Beautiful (MGM, 1952)
Latin Lovers (MGM, 1953)
The Flame and the Flesh (MGM, 1954)
Betrayed (MGM, 1954)
The Prodigal (MGM, 1955)
The Sea Chaser (Warner Brothers, 1955)
The Rains of Ranchipur (20th Century-Fox, 1955)
Diane (MGM, 1956)
Peyton Place (A Jerry Wald Production for 20th Century-Fox, 1957)
The Lady Takes a Flyer (Universal-International, 1958)
Another Time, Another Place (A Lanturn Production for Paramount, Released 1958)
Imitation of Life (Universal-International, 1959)
Portrait in Black (Universal-International, 1960)
By Love Possessed (Mirisch Pictures with Seven Arts for United Artists, 1961)
Bachelor In Paradise (A Ted Richmond Production released by MGM, 1961)
Who's Got the Action? (Amro-Claude-Mea Production for Paramount Pictures, 1962)
Love Has Many Faces (A Jerry Bresler Production for Columbia Pictures, released 1965)
Madame X (A Ross Hunter Production for Universal Pictures, 1966)
The Big Cube (A Warner Brothers-Seven Arts Release of a Francisco Diez Barroso Production, 1969)
Persecution (later titled Terror of Sheba) (A Tyburn Film Production, 1974)
Bittersweet Love (Avco Embassy Pictures, 1976)

7

Judy

She was £2,000,000 in debt when she died of an accidental dose of barbiturates. The greatest shock about her death was that there was no shock. One simply wondered how she survived as long as she did. Ray Bolger, her co-star in *The Wizard of Oz* said, 'Her private life and all its problems were eating away her vitality and her strength. She was worn out.' The *New York Times* wrote of her as 'the glamorous Hollywood personality with the built-in destruct mechanism'.

A star at 17, a legend at 27, a corpse at 47. The years between included alcohol, lawsuits, divorces, suicide attempts and nervous breakdowns.

She had a drug problem that her abusive stage mother initiated and sanctioned at Metro-Goldwyn-Mayer. Taking Dexedrine to wake up and Seconals to sleep was common practice in Hollywood where contract players worked long hours and required more than coffee to keep them on their feet. But few had addictive personalities.

She tried to get over that rainbow with the help of five husbands, seeking the one to replace her meek homosexual father whom she adored. How many MGM starlets were looking for a father figure? Lana, Ava, Grace, Liz and Joan. No wonder L.B. Mayer told his girls to think of him as their father. They disliked him intensely when he was alive and spoke fondly of him after he died. All, that is, but Dorothy of Oz who cursed him to the end.

Sadly, Judy Garland was trapped by her talent. She wanted to sing and he wanted to hear her. But we became disenchanted by her tardiness at concerts. In the beginning we were happy she showed up at all. Eventually we asked for our money back.

Little did we know Judy began to die the day she was born . . .

Judy claimed that her battle with life began with her stage mother, Ethel Gumm, a frustrated domineering woman who sought fame through her. Judy's father Frank, whom she resembled, adored his 'Baby' and she worshipped him. He would prove to be the one person in her life whose affection was genuine. How much Judy knew about Frank is unknown. A homosexual, who was attracted to young boys, he was shunned for his preference before Judy was old enough to understand. Frank was, unfortunately, a meek man who, had he lived to enjoy his daughter's fame, would not have been able to save her.

Judy was attracted to homosexuals. She married two men who were gay and faced this realisation by attempting suicide. If she had inherited the steel nerve of her mother, Judy would have learned a lesson by choosing men with more discretion. By this time, however, her good sense was clouded by a desperate desire to get away from Ethel's domination.

Judy was born Frances Gumm on 10 June 1922 in Grand Rapids, Minnesota, the youngest of three daughters. Her parents met at the Orpheum Theatre in Wisconsin. Ethel's fingers at the piano provided background music for silent films. Frank, who had a vibrant tenor voice, sang for the audience between reels. After their marriage, they started a vaudeville act billed as 'Jack and Virginia Lee, Sweet Southern Singers', but as their family grew, the Gumms were forced to settle down. Frank managed a local theatre in Grand Rapids, but this was only a temporary arrangement because Ethel's ambitions in show business were unfulfilled. Daughter Mary Jane was born in 1915, Virginia in 1917, and Frances in 1922. Ethel prepared her older daughters for vaudeville, but their voices left a great deal to be desired. It was 'Baby' Frances who had the personality and talent. This was a twist of fate since Ethel wanted a boy and ignored Frances until Christmas Eve 1925 when three-year-old Frances decided, on her own, to sing 'Jingle Bells' with her sisters on stage at her father's theatre.

'I loved it,' Judy recalled. 'I wouldn't stop singing until Dad thought it was enough and led me offstage.'

From that day on, Baby Gumm's fate was sealed. Ethel could live out her ambitions through her youngest daughter and she set out to make this a reality. She convinced Frank to pack up and move to California because the warmer weather would be better for his health. What Ethel didn't say was that Frances deserved a chance to prove herself.

The Gumms moved to Lancaster, California, where Frank purchased a theatre in 1927. Ethel wanted to concentrate on Frances but, in need of money, she settled on 'The Gumm Sisters'. During a 1933 appearance in Chicago, the theatre billed them as 'The Gum Sisters'. Georgie Jessel, who was headlining the show, convinced her to change their name to Garland after his friend Bob Garland, the drama critic. Frances, who loved the lyrics to Hoagy Carmichael's song 'Judy', decided to change her first name as well.

Frank was trying desperately to keep his family together but lost his battle with Ethel, who thought nothing of taking the girls out of school and on the road. Often she took only Judy on the vaudeville circuit. 'My mother didn't know when to stop,' she said. Though Ethel never physically abused Judy, she punished her in ways that caused severe psychological problems. Packing her bags in a hotel room, she told a naughty Judy that she was leaving her behind. Judy pleaded with her mother not to leave, but Ethel went as far as to close and lock the door behind her, leaving the frightened child behind. She returned to a more obedient daughter.

In 1935, agent Al Rosen took an interest in Judy and arranged auditions for her at the studios in Hollywood. Metro-Goldwyn-Mayer had not shown any interest in her until L.B. Mayer's secretary Ida Koverman recognised Judy's talent as a singer. She summoned her busy boss who arrived in time to hear Judy's rendition of, 'Zing! Went the Strings of my Heart'. Mayer showed no emotion but ordered a seven-year contract drawn up on 27 September 1935, for £100 a week.

'We had come so far and finally succeeded,' Judy said, 'and then my world caved in. Daddy was the only person who really cared about me.' Frank died from spinal meningitis on 17 November. Suffering the agonies of watching people file past her father's coffin, she begged to have the lid closed. Ethel couldn't care less. Her only concern was getting Judy back to Metro-Goldwyn-Mayer's little red schoolhouse and a movie assignment. Unfortunately, MGM didn't know what to do with her.

Roger Edens, the studio's musical arranger, knew what to do, though he had no idea it would open the door for Judy. He arranged a special lyric of 'You Made Me Love You' into 'Dear Mr Gable' for Clarke Gable's 36th birthday party at the studio. Gable, who hated these parties, was so impressed he went over to Judy and hugged her. She broke down in tears and glanced over at Mayer who held out his arms to her. Judy climbed into his lap. This gesture on Mayer's part was for show. He was the best actor on the MGM lot and took great delight in proving this to his stable of stars who were obligated to attend these studio parties.

Though there was no question that Judy could belt out a song, she was no beauty like her idol, Lana Turner, who exemplified MGM's ideal. Judy had a stubby neck that blended into her shoulders, a plump short-waisted torso, long arms and legs. Mayer often referred to Judy as 'my little hunchback' because she had a stooped posture. But her frequent co-star, Mickey Rooney said, 'If I had not been tainted with the same phony Hollywood notions about who was beautiful and who was not, I would have fallen in love with her [Judy] myself.'

The day after Judy sang a birthday tribute to Clark Gable, Mayer put her in *Broadway Melody of 1938* with Robert Taylor, George Murphy, Eleanor Powell and Buddy Ebsen. She would sing 'You Made Me Love You' to Clark Gable's photograph in the film.

Thoroughbreds Don't Cry with Mickey Rooney was a mediocre picture with nothing for Judy to sing, but it proved their worth as a team. Following *Everybody Sing* and *Listen Darling* she teamed with Rooney in *Love Finds Andy Hardy*. Judy played Betsy Booth, the visiting girl next door, who became a regular in the very popular Andy Hardy films, Mayer's idea of the all-American family, a series that was very close to his heart.

Now that Judy's star was on the rise, the powers at MGM set out to make sure she did not gain weight. In the MGM canteen she was served only chicken soup with matzoh balls, a recipe handed down by Mayer's mother. Orders to serve her nothing else were strictly obeyed. So there she sat with the adults instead of the teenagers' table where juicy hamburgers and hot dogs were being gobbled down. Judy would, however, go on binges that prompted Ethel to give her Benzedrine pills to curb her appetite. These uppers gave Judy the energy needed to get her through a gruelling schedule seven days a week. Ethel had doled them out to Judy before she reached the golden gates of MGM, as well as sleeping pills if Judy was too keyed up.

When MGM bought the rights to *The Wizard of Oz*, they did not have Judy in mind for the role of Dorothy Gale, who flies to Oz in a dream.

Mayer's boss Nicholas Schenck, president of Loew's, wanted to borrow Shirley Temple from 20th Century-Fox but that was not to be. It's doubtful that Shirley was capable of singing the numbers planned for *Oz*, anyway.

Production began in October 1938 with Frank Morgan as the Wizard, Bert Lahr as the Cowardly Lion, Buddy Ebsen as the Tin Man and Ray Bolger as the Scarecrow. Ebsen, however, was allergic to the aluminium make-up and was replaced by Jack Haley. Richard Thorpe was to direct but was taken off the movie because his conception of the *Oz* story was unacceptable. George Cukor took over temporarily and undid the wrong. He was appalled that Judy, as the little girl from a Kansas farm, was made-up to look like an over-rouged Shirley Temple. Cukor removed most of her make-up, eliminated the blonde wig and put Judy's brown hair in pigtails. One of the hardships that Judy had to endure was wearing a corset that flattened her bosom and plump curves.

Director Victor Fleming eventually took over the reins. Judy had a crush on the handsome Fleming, who had to come down hard on her when she got out of line. On one occasion he slapped her out of the giggles.

The Wizard of Oz is the story of Dorothy Gale who hits her head during a Kansas tornado and dreams she is in the land of Oz with her dog Toto.

'Over the Rainbow', the song that would be forever identified with Judy Garland, was almost cut out of the film but Mayer would not allow it. With so many opposing views, it's a miracle that this movie became a classic. Today it ranks as one of the best motion pictures to grace the silver screen.

'Over the Rainbow' won an Academy Award for Best Song and Judy received a special juvenile Oscar for *The Wizard of Oz*. It was presented to her by Mickey Rooney who lent her support at the event. After she accepted the award, Judy sang 'Over the Rainbow' for her peers and recalled, '. . . the most sensational moment of my career . . . The lump in my throat was so big when I sang that I sounded more like Flip the Frog than the most excited girl in Hollywood. And I'll never forget how Mickey came to my rescue, for I was so nervous I thought I'd faint. He practically held me up through the second chorus.'

Judy made the list of the top moneymaking stars of 1940. Mickey Rooney was number one. As a result, MGM set out to maintain their teenage image. 'When Mickey and I were in production,' Judy said, 'they had us working day and night. They gave us pep pills to keep us going and then took us to the studio hospital. We were given pills to help us sleep, Mickey on one cot and me on another.'

When Judy made *Oz* she was making $500 a week. In 1940 she had a new contract calling for a weekly salary of $2000.

'No one asked me what I wanted,' Judy said. 'I didn't sign a contract and I didn't see the money.'

Unfortunately, Ethel did not invest wisely or save any of the half-million dollars Judy earned in her teen years.

Garland made five more films with Mickey Rooney: *Babes in Arms* (1939), *Andy Hardy Meets Debutante* (1940), *Life Begins for Andy Hardy* (1941), *Babes on Broadway* (1941) and *Girl Crazy* (1943).

Mickey's energy was boundless. He thrived on the rigours of show business and maintained his youthfulness well into his twenties. Judy, however, wanted grown-up roles on and off the movie set. Much to the distress of Louis B. Mayer and Ethel, Judy got married. At nineteen she had been madly in love with several men including bandleader Artie Shaw who eloped with Lana Turner in February 1940. 'He broke my heart,' Judy wailed.

Shaw was twelve years older than Garland. He was sophisticated, highly intellectual and charming enough to captivate women, including Pin-Up Girl Betty Grable, who also hoped to get him to the altar. Artie claimed Judy had a crush on him and he did not take advantage of her in any way.

Judy's puppy loves were juvenile stars Freddie Bartholomew and Jackie Cooper. She was more intimately involved with Dead End Kid Billy Haloop, who may or may not have been her first intimate encounter. Reliable sources claim Judy lost her virginity at the age of fifteen, pursuing and enjoying mostly older men. She was a romantic young lady who craved the affection that was sadly lacking after her father's death.

To the rescue came composer David Rose, recently divorced from comedienne Martha Raye, and a decade older than Judy. Rose was a good friend of Shaw's and tried to comfort her when Artie eloped with Lana. He sent Judy a large piece of chocolate cake as consolation and won her heart.

Rose was a pleasant-looking man with a quiet nature like Frank Gumm, but he lacked the electrifying personality to hold Judy's interest for very long. His friendship with Artie was the chief attraction for Judy and they became a steady couple. L.B. Mayer knew about the relationship and tried to end it. Ethel, who had married her long-term boyfriend, William Gilmore, was opposed at first and then relented so that she would not lose control of Judy's money. On the rebound from an imagined romance with Shaw, Judy eloped with Rose to Las Vegas on 27 July 1941, with Ethel in attendance. Judy cabled Mayer asking for a little time to enjoy a honeymoon. He flatly refused and she was back on the set of *Babes on*

Broadway with Mickey Rooney within twenty-four hours.

In the autumn of 1942, Judy learned she was pregnant. Though she was finding life with David a boring experience, she hoped to go through with the pregnancy. Ethel, however, managed to convince Rose it would be a mistake for MGM's little girl to have a baby. Judy's pregnancy was terminated and so was her marriage in January 1943. She shed no tears, however, because she had fallen in love before MGM announced her separation from Rose.

At 29 years old, Tyrone Power was one of the handsomest actors in Hollywood. Married to French actress Annabella, Ty may not have been faithful but he was careful not to jeopardise his marriage. The bisexual Power, who is known for his dashing screen presence in *The Mark of Zorro*, *Blood and Sand*, and *The Black Swan*, was well liked in Hollywood. He had his choice of beautiful women and chose Judy, with whom he fell deeply in love, enough so that he admitted the affair to his wife Annabella, but he did not come right out and ask for a divorce. Judy, in an attempt to nudge him into it, said she was pregnant with his baby. Most probably she was bluffing because she had not filed for divorce from David Rose, which would not become final for a year. How then could she have a baby without ruining her career? Power, who was in the Marine Corps, went overseas and corresponded with Judy faithfully. Mayer stepped in once again with Betty Asher, who became Judy's friend and confidante. MGM assigned studio publicists to 'look after' their stars, to take care of their needs and requests and, if necessary, accompany them on excursions, honeymoons and vacations. In all fairness their help was needed to keep the press at bay and to prevent avid fans from literally tearing the clothes off their idols. But these publicists were also spies for Mayer and expected to report back to him about his contract players.

There were rumours that Betty Asher and Judy were lovers since they spent so much time together. This may or may not be true. What is known for sure is that Asher filled Judy's head with lies about Power's sharing her love letters with his Marine buddies for entertainment. Judy should have known better, but she believed Asher and finished with Power, who was stunned and brokenhearted.

Judy's romance with producer-writer Joe Mankiewicz might have been considered on the rebound but it was the closest she came to a stable relationship. Joe was the ideal man in the opinion of Hollywood's most glamorous actresses, which included Elizabeth Taylor. Joe's attraction to Judy was a combination of fascination and compassion. He managed to get her into psychoanalysis and Judy was responding well. She was becoming independent and speaking up to Ethel who complained to Mayer that Judy was having an affair with Mankiewicz, a married man whose wife was at the Menniger Clinic suffering from a serious psychological disturbance. Mayer confronted Mankiewicz who responded, 'Obviously, this studio isn't big enough for both of us.' It was not Mayer's intention to lose this talented man to 20th Century-Fox, but the damage was done. Once again, Judy was determined to get her man one way or the other. She told Joe she was pregnant with his baby. And, once again, Judy was not thinking clearly. Joe could not leave his wife, but he would see her through the abortion that wasn't required, anyway. They drifted apart after that . . .

At twenty-one, Judy found satisfaction in her new image as a grown-up in *For Me and My Gal* with newcomer Gene Kelly, and *Presenting Lily Mars* with Van Heflin. The latter prompted the *New York Times* to comment, 'Perhaps MGM should let Miss Garland grow up and stay that way.'

Judy claimed that the role of Esther in *Meet Me in St Louis* was too young for her. Filming began in November 1943 but Judy's repeated illnesses held up production. She challenged director Vincente Minnelli by showing up late and complaining about his inability. He struggled through it and surprised her when she finally took the time to watch the daily rushes. Minnelli had managed to make her look beautiful on screen. Her hair, make-up and wardrobe blended with a softness not attributed to her in the past. Judy suddenly decided Minnelli was her saviour and, after a few months of dating, they were living together.

Vincente Minnelli was a brilliant director but a very unattractive man. He had thick lips, droopy eyes, a large nose and receding chin. His manner was limp, effeminate and prim. He was an unlikely candidate for Judy's affection after Tyrone Power and Joe Mankiewicz. She had pursued her co-star in *St Louis*, but couldn't arouse Tom Drake because he was gay. Now she was involved with another homosexual who became her second husband, 42-year-old Vincente Minnelli.

L.B. Mayer sanctioned the marriage because he felt the flighty Judy needed a husband who was gentle, but firm, reliable and established. That he was a homosexual didn't matter in a town as bisexual as Hollywood.

On 15 June 1945, Mayer gave the bride away in a simple ceremony at Ethel's house. His wedding present to the Minnellis was a three-month honeymoon in New York. Vincente said later that he and Judy were blissfully happy at this time. She threw her vial of pills into the East River and vowed that she was free of them at last. In September she announced her pregnancy for no other reason than it was true this time. Ethel was delighted, and L.B. Mayer said he couldn't be happier.

On 12 March at 7.58 a.m., Liza Minnelli was born by Caesarean section at Cedars of Lebanon Hospital in Los Angeles. She bore a striking resemblance to her father . . .

Judy had a difficult recovery, but felt well enough to begin filming *The Pirate* with Gene Kelly, directed by Vincente. This Cole Porter musical revolved around a girl in the West Indies who imagines a wandering player is a famous pirate, who is in fact her despised suitor. Judy began to fall apart almost immediately. She was jealous of Vincente's spending so much time with Kelly who, she thought, was trying to expand his role in *The Pirate*. She also suspected he and Vincente might be lovers. Judy was very fond of Kelly and hoped for a more intimate relationship with him. He adored her but had no intention of getting involved. Suffering from post-natal depression, Judy demanded too much attention, which was not forthcoming. She was back on pills, begging for Benzedrine, sobbing, laughing and often in a state of hysterics. Vincente had to shoot around Judy, but he remained calm by making the most of her infrequent appearances on the set. Kelly, who feigned illness to take the pressure off Judy, said, when *The Pirate* failed at the box office, 'Vincente and I honestly believed we were being so dazzlingly brilliant and clever, that everybody would fall at our feet and swoon clean away in delight and ecstasy – as they kissed each of our toes in appreciation for this wondrous new musical we'd given them. Well, we were wrong.'

Judy now believed that Vincente had failed her. With his approval she had signed another MGM contract that had resulted in the most disastrous movie of her career (*The Pirate*) with him at the helm. She had found him in bed with a man and made a feeble attempt to cut her wrists with a razor blade. The time had come for Judy to be admitted to a sanatorium for rest and psychoanalysis. Unfortunately, she chose to go home too soon and no one could stop her.

Judy's spirits lifted with Irving Berlin's *Easter Parade* on the horizon and asked that her husband be replaced as director of the film. Vincente was stunned and hurt, but he bowed out to Charles Walters. Judy's co-star Gene Kelly broke his ankle shortly after filming began in October 1947, and was replaced by Fred Astaire. To everyone's amazement, Judy was a professional during production of *Easter Parade*, because she knew Astaire would not have put up with her nonsense.

Astaire was a dedicated man who rehearsed his dance routines for many hours each day. He was also a compassionate man but only to a point. MGM decided to team them again in *The Barkleys of Broadway* and though Judy was elated, she failed to report for work. Her psychiatrist said her attitude toward MGM and the stress of going to the studio every morning would result in another breakdown. MGM suspended Judy without pay and replaced her with Astaire's former dancing partner, Ginger Rogers. Hoping to gain sympathy, Judy visited the set of *The Barkleys of Broadway*, sending Ginger to her dressing room. In short order, Judy was asked to leave but not before babbling abusive words about Ginger.

In September 1948, Judy informed the studio she was ready to go back to work. *In the Good Old Summertime* was a remake of the delightful comedy *The Shop Around the Corner*. Her leading man was friend Van Johnson. Though she was often late, the cast and crew greeted her with respect and made sure there was a fresh red rose in her dressing room every day. When the film was finished ahead of schedule, Mayer asked Van Johnson how the miracle was accomplished. 'We made her feel needed,' Johnson replied. 'We joked with her and kept her happy.' As a result, *In the Good Old Summertime* was a hit.

It was becoming apparent that Judy could not handle two films without sufficient rest in between, but she wanted to do *Annie Get Your Gun*. The film clips that Judy managed were horrible. Needing the money, she tried to go with it but failed. Her contract was suspended on 10 May 1949, and the part of Annie went to Betty Hutton. Columnist Louella Parsons wrote, 'Certainly after all the breaks she has had at MGM they have a right to expect her to co-operate and not fail to report for work.'

'I've been a bad girl,' Garland said.

Louis B. Mayer was having his own problems in 1949, contending with production head Dore Schary who would take over in 1951. It was Mayer who sympathised with Judy and tried to convince the studio to loan her the money to pay for her stay at a Boston hospital. This request was rejected at first so Mayer promised to pay her hospital bills out of his own pocket. 'She is in a terrible way,' he said. 'She has made millions for us. We should be able to help her.' MGM finally agreed with Mayer and loaned her the money.

After three months at Peter Bent Bringham in Boston, a plump and contented Judy returned to Los Angeles in August. Mayer, who had visited her in the hospital, paid her doctor to be with Judy during *Summer Stock* with Gene Kelly, who outdid himself to make sure she received love and respect from everyone connected with the film. 'We need to be patient,' Kelly stressed, '. . . to understand what she's been through.'

But Judy was convinced everyone was against her. On drugs, she didn't know where she was occasionally, looking around at people she knew but not recognising them. MGM did not stop production, however, and in the spring of 1950, *Summer Stock* was almost finished. While Chuck Walters worked on a finale, Judy went to Carmel for a rest and to lose weight. A slim and sexy Judy returned to do the 'Get Happy' number that is so often identified with her. In a panic, she locked her dressing-room door and refused to come out. MGM hair stylist Sydney Guilaroff, a confidant of Judy's, offered to help and Judy let him in. 'I was in shock,' he said. 'She had been tearing out her hair. It was strewn all over the floor.'

'I know they're trying to get rid of me,' she cried. 'Nobody cares about me, nobody! What am I here for, anyway? What do they want out of me?'

'The "Get Happy" number, remember?'

'What am I supposed to do?'

'Let's tell everyone that you want to do the song and then we'll get you ready,' he said.

While Judy was being made up, Sydney chose a pair of black tights, black jacket and black high heels for her to wear. There was nothing he could do about her hair so he tucked it under a black fedora hat. He got her in place on stage and pointed to the camera, 'Can you see it, dear?' he asked. She nodded, and to everyone's surprise Judy went through the entire number to perfection.

Summer Stock was a successful film. Viewing it one can tell that Judy was heavier before doing the 'Get Happy' finale that made you forget she was the overweight farm girl who fell in love with Gene Kelly's character and it appeared in his summer stock show. It all came together.

Judy returned to Carmel where she received a call from the studio. June Allyson, who was Fred Astaire's leading lady in *Royal Wedding* was pregnant. Did she feel well enough to take her place? Regrettably, she agreed. Regrettably, because the studio was on a tight schedule. Delays cost money and MGM was on a strict budget. Judy paid no attention to such details. It's very possible the new regime at MGM knew this and needed an excuse to get rid of her. She took the bait and was fired for the last time on 17 June 1950. Judy went home, locked herself in the bathroom and attempted to cut her throat. It was Vincente who broke the door down and was relieved that the cut needed only a Band-Aid.

In December 1950 Judy told the press that her marriage to Minnelli was finished. It had been over for a long time, but fear of being alone held her back from filing for divorce. Vincente continued to look after her when she needed him. Then there was Liza who had to be considered and he was willing to give her some sort of security with or without an unstable mother.

When Judy met Sid Luft she was warned to stay away from him. He was a self-indulgent promoter who thought only of his own desires and needs. At 38, Luft was looking around for a sucker like Judy who fell for him like a ton of bricks. He was a very handsome guy with a great deal of persuasive charm and guile. From a middle-class Jewish family in rough and tough Bronxville, New York, Luft learned the hard way to fight for what he wanted even if it involved using his fists. After a stint in the Royal Canadian Air Force, he was a test pilot for Douglas aircraft, which qualified him as a consultant for the 1940 B-movie, *Charter Pilot*, at 20th Century-Fox. Three years later, he married the film's leading lady, Lynn Bari, who never made it beyond the 'other woman' roles in B-films, though she could be considered beautiful with a degree of talent. Sid managed her career, which didn't go far though he had convinced Lynn that he would make her a big star. They had one child, John Sidney Luft, before she filed for divorce. 'During our marriage,' she said, 'I was the only breadwinner in the family.' She went on to say that Sid preferred gambling and nightclubbing over any kind of home life.

When Luft met Garland, he was in the process of getting a divorce and looking for a job that would make him rich with little or no effort. In contrast to Vincente, Sid was outspoken, blunt and very often crude in his dealing with others if it put him in the winner's corner. Judy fell under his spell immediately and was determined to make him a permanent part of her life. She met Luft at the Little Club in New York. Her date was old friend Fred Finklehoffe who rebuffed Sid when he approached their table. 'I don't want any traffic from you, Sid,' Fred spoke up. 'Get lost.'

'Oh, let him sit down,' Judy said.

In front of Luft, Fred called him a dirty, low-down S.O.B., on the move. 'You'd better watch yourself,' he told Judy, 'because he's going to nail you.' She ignored the advice and asked Sid to call her.

Judy moved into an apartment in Los Angeles and was seen publicly, but discreetly, with Luft. Minnelli commented that Sid apparently had the ability to keep Judy sane and content. He would not stand in the way of her filing for divorce in March 1951. She charged Vincente with mental cruelty, the most common complaint in Hollywood divorce suits. Judy was awarded custody of Liza, who would spend six months of the year with her and six months with Minnelli, who was ordered to pay $500 a week in child support when Liza was living with her mother.

Since Hollywood wasn't interested in Judy these days, she accepted an offer from London's Palladium for $20,000 a week. Though terrified of performing on stage, Judy needed the money to pay her debts. She begged Luft to sail with her on the *Ile de France* on 30 March. He declined but did not say he wouldn't join her later. Judy called him repeatedly. She was a nervous wreck. Recognising her vulnerability, Sid wanted Judy to find out how much she needed him. He showed up in London shortly before opening night on 9 April.

Aside from stage fright, Judy was concerned about her weight. Only five feet tall, she had gained forty-five pounds and appeared heavier than she did in *Summer Stock*. Before the British press made a point of it, Judy told reporters that she was too fat, but she felt very, very good. It didn't matter to the British how she looked. Judy Garland could sing and she had chosen to perform for them in her first major concert. On opening night, everyone concerned was afraid Judy would collapse or try suicide or get on a plane and disappear. Maybe she had to be nudged on stage but once the audience showed how much they loved her before she opened her mouth to sing, Judy belonged to them. The *Daily Express* wrote, 'Judy Garland walked into the biggest welcome yet for a Hollywood star . . . the audience opened eyes wider to drink all the big girl in. Bigger still for wearing yellow, with spangles, and with diamond ice at her ears, throat, waist and wrist – an ensemble that cheerfully upholds her reputation as the worst-dressed woman on the screen . . . Backing out, she accidentally falls down and sits on the stage. "That's probably one of the most ungraceful exits ever made", she grins . . . She may be a heavyweight, but she hits her stuff home . . .'

The *Evening Standard* said, 'We saw a brave woman on Monday, but more than that we saw a woman who has emerged from the shadows and finds that the public likes her as she is, even more than what she was.'

For the four-week booking, the Palladium was sold out for every performance. Not so in Glasgow and Edinburgh. Exhausted at times, Judy did not want to perform but Luft made sure she did despite her drinking. In Manchester he gave her a shove and said bitterly, 'Get out on stage, you drunken bitch!' But Sid could do no wrong in her eyes. She wanted him to be her manager and he took over with gusto. In October 1951 Judy Garland appeared at the Palace in New York and broke all records for nineteen weeks. In April 1952 Judy gave a concert at the Philharmonic

Auditorium in Los Angeles that was attended by a roster of celebrities that included L.B. Mayer, who cried when Garland sat on the edge of the stage and sang, 'Over the Rainbow'.

Judy's career was back on track and her bills were paid. Now she wanted to marry Sid, who was against the idea. He had learned from one bad marriage and did not want to risk another, he said. Luft had spent a year with Judy and doubted that he could put up with her possessiveness. Getting her to sober up and perform was enough, not to mention the constant vigil to make sure she didn't overdose on pills.

As usual, Judy solved the problem her way. She was pregnant. Whether Sid tried to convince her to have an abortion isn't known, but if he did it was to no avail. On 8 June 1952, they were married at a friend's ranch in Paicines, California, and on 21 November Judy gave birth to a daughter, Lorna, at St John's Hospital in Santa Monica. When she emerged to take her baby home, Judy was alone. Sid was at the racetrack. 'I know what he is,' she told a friend, 'but I love him.'

Suffering again from post-natal depression, Judy spent her time in bed, taking pills and crying. It was just a matter of time before she tried to kill herself. This time she cut her throat with a razor and the gash needed stitches. The doctor told her, 'Judy, you keep this up and you're going to hurt yourself.'

News of Garland's attempted suicide got around. This time it was Jack Warner, not Louis B. Mayer, who was concerned because Luft was negotiating with Warner Brothers for Judy to appear in the musical version of *A Star is Born*. Sid got her out of bed for a round of parties in Hollywood and New York. Wearing a high-necked dress to hide her bandaged throat, Judy proved she was fit and ready for *A Star is Born*.

In January 1953, Ethel had a fatal heart attack after parking her car at Douglas Aircraft where she worked. Her body was found wedged between two cars. Judy felt no remorse that her mother had to work in a factory and could barely make ends meet. She felt no remorse that she refused to loan her mother a few measly dollars. She felt no remorse that she refused to allow her mother to see Lorna. She felt no remorse at all until a friend pointed out, at Ethel's funeral, that 'She was, after all, your mother.' Judy locked herself in her sulking place, the bathroom, and cut her wrists.

The Hollywood press was not sympathetic to their stars who made big money and refused to take care of their parents. Judy answered back with a false claim that she was in the process of buying Ethel a house shortly before her death. She did not deny, however, that she and her mother were estranged.

In *A Star is Born*, Judy played Esther Blodgett, a small-town girl, who tries her luck in Hollywood. At a benefit she meets matinée idol Norman Maine (James Mason), who not only marries her but gets her a movie contract. With a new name, Vicki Lester, she outshines his star and he turns to alcohol. Thinking he is a burden, Maine commits suicide by walking into the ocean. At the end she attends a benefit, broadcast around the world, and introduces herself as 'Mrs Norman Maine'.

James Mason and Judy managed an affair during filming. 'I always fall in love with my leading men,' she said. He was prepared to put up with her lateness, absences and bad temperament. Sid Luft was prepared but vowed she would not get away with it this time. He hired someone to get her to the studio at all costs, but Judy still managed to hold up production. Director George Cukor said, 'This is the behaviour of someone unhinged. She's devious and untrustworthy and has no regard for anyone.'

A Star is Born premiered at the Pantages Theater on 29 September 1954 to rave reviews.

> *Time* magazine said, *Star* is a massive effort. The producers took astonishing risks with . . . the Star. Judy Garland was a 32-year-old has-been as infamous for temperament as she is famous for talent. What's more, all the producers' worst dreams came true. Day after day, while the high-priced help – including Judy's husband, producer Sid Luft – stood around waiting for the shooting to start, Judy sulked in her dressing room. In the end *Star* took ten months to make and cost $6,000,000. But after Judy had done her worst in the dressing room, she did her best in front of the camera, with the result that she gives just about the greatest one-woman show in modern history . . . an expert vaudeville performance was to be expected from Judy; to find her a dramatic actress as well is a real surprise – although it should not be.'

Judy was nominated for Best Actress. Her competition for the 1954 Oscar were Dorothy Dandridge in *Carmen Jones*, Audrey Hepburn in *Sabrina*, Grace Kelly in *The Country Girl*, and Jane Wyman in *Magnificent Obsession*. James Mason, nominated for Best Actor, was up against Humphrey Bogart in *The Caine Mutiny*, Marlon Brando for *On the Waterfront*, Bing Crosby in *The Country Girl*, and Dan O'Herlihy in *The Adventures of Robinson Crusoe*.

It was a big disappointment to Garland, Luft and Warner Brothers that *A Star is Born* was not mentioned for Best Picture.

Columnist James Bacon wrote for the Associated Press that the Best Actress award was

> . . . a class struggle. It's Judy Garland, born in a vaudeville trunk, versus Grace Kelly, born into a Philadelphia mansion. At this writing, the contest between Little Miss Showbusiness and the debutante actress looks like a draw. Hollywood, perhaps unconsciously, is taking sides strictly on the class basis. Performance-wise, both were superb. Sentiment, perhaps, is on the side of Judy. One of the greatest of child actresses, she has led a heartbreak life – a has-been and a near suicide at 28, and Oscar favourite at 33. It's the kind of story Hollywood loves and one that needs an Academy Award for the happy ending.

But did Garland's peers in Hollywood feel the same way? Working with her had not been a pleasant experience, to put it mildly. She had been given more chances than other actresses, and rewarded generously when she showed an ounce of professionalism. Louis B. Mayer was a prince compared to Jack Warner who refused to take Judy's whining calls during production of *A Star is Born*. While most studios went all out to campaign for their nominated stars, Warner Brothers did not. Why waste their money when they did not plan another film with Garland, a sure sign that she was a costly risk.

The Grace Kelly factor had nothing to do with class. Her part in *The Country Girl* was a first for the beautiful Grace who chose to play the dowdy wife of a washed-up singer. Under contract to MGM, Kelly made *The Country Girl* at Paramount, giving her the backing of two studios.

It would be a close race between the two actresses for the coveted Oscar though the prediction was that sentiment would prevail in Garland's favour.

Judy, pregnant for the third time, agreed to sing 'The Man Who Got Away' at the Oscar ceremony, but she went into labour two weeks earlier than expected and gave birth to a son, Joey, on 29 March 1955, the day before the Academy Awards. Joey had a collapsed lung and was placed in an incubator with a fifty per cent chance of surviving. Twenty-four hours later, he was out of the woods.

N.B.C. who was airing the Oscars, received permission from Luft to set up their equipment in Judy's hospital room to televise her if she won.

Though not that confident, she had to rehearse her thank-you speech, which undoubtedly made it all the more difficult for her to sit through the long ceremony on 30 March. 'The Man Who Got Away', nominated for Best Song, lost to 'Three Coins in the Fountain', and James Mason lost to Marlon Brando. Then came the big moment when William Holden walked on stage at the Pantages and read the nominees for Best Actress. If Judy won, it was friend Lauren Bacall who would accept the Oscar on her behalf. Holden opened the envelope and announced that Grace Kelly was the winner. As she was giving her tearful acceptance speech, N.B.C. technicians were frantically moving their equipment out of Judy's hospital room. 'They were so gracious when they arrived,' she said, 'but when I lost they couldn't get out fast enough.'

Jack Warner was only concerned about the $30,00 he had loaned Sid during filming of *A Star is Born* that would not recoup production costs. He sued but said, '. . . trying to collect from Sid Luft was like finding a popsicle in the desert. I finally got $500 as full settlement.'

The Lufts were in debt regardless of how much money Garland made, but they were always one step ahead of bill collectors. Though Judy was accustomed to the good life she had enjoyed at MGM, she had never handled money and was more than willing to led Sid handle their finances. They bought a large house in Holmby Hills, an exclusive area of Los Angeles, a few doors away from Humphrey Bogart and his wife Lauren Bacall. The Lufts became members of the Holmby Hills Rat Pack with Bogie as their leader. Others in their group were Frank Sinatra, Mike Romanoff, David Niven and agent Swifty Lazar. Bogie adored Judy but recognised Luft for what he was. 'Do you sing?' he asked Sid, who didn't have a chance to respond. 'No, you don't,' Bogie spoke up. 'Then why the hell are you living off a singer?'

In September 1955 Judy did a ninety-minute television show on C.B.S. for $100,000. Excellent ratings prompted C.B.S. to offer her a $300,000 contract for three more TV specials. To make fast money, Sid convinced her to face the gambling crowd at the New Frontier Hotel in Las Vegas for $55,000 a week in July 1956. In September Judy returned to the Palace in New York for a percentage. Garland broke all records wherever she entertained but the money came in and disappeared. Why then did she argue with C.B.S. over the format of her future TV shows that would earn her a quarter of a million dollars? Whatever the reason, the lucrative contract was cancelled.

On New Year's Eve 1957 Judy tried to get out of her engagement at the

Flamingo in Las Vegas, but she was forced to honour it. Upset that drinks were being served while she struggled with a touch of laryngitis, Judy introduced eleven-year-old Liza who sang a few songs. The crowd was not pleased but Judy said it was important that her children understand show business. One has to wonder why Garland would do such a thing after complaining so bitterly about Ethel's taking advantage of her as a young girl. Had she forgotten how her first appearance on stage deprived her of a normal childhood, resulting in a life of sheer hell?

To what extent would Garland go to get out of appearing at the Flamingo? She tried to break the $100,000 contract that night because waiters were serving food and drinks during her act. Luft tried to reason with her but she refused to give in. He charged $5000 in chips to the Flamingo, played a few hundred dollars, cashed in the remaining chips and snuck out of the hotel in the middle of the night with Judy and Liza.

Luft was so furious over the loss of $100,000 that a royal battle ensued and he walked out. She filed for divorce. Regardless, Sid set out to find work for Judy – not an easy task after the Flamingo fiasco. He settled for the Town and Country in Brooklyn, quite a comedown for Judy. Worse was a warrant issued for her arrest in New York. With the Sheriff at her door, she called Sid who met her in the State Collector's Office where she answered charges that she owed over $8,000 in back taxes. Judy agreed to pay this debt over a period of three weeks from her salary of $75,000 at the Town and Country. She showed up for the first two nights but on the third she arrived an hour late after the audience had been informed she would not appear. Management told her to go home but she went on anyway and sang a few songs before her mike was silenced. When Luft arrived, Judy was out of control. With no money to pay taxes due, she handed over her jewellery to the State of New York until she could satisfy the debt with borrowed money.

> MGM press agent George Nichols commented, 'Maybe Judy hated MGM, but she was no different than the others who were lost souls without the studio's protection. In Judy's case, she was determined to make things difficult for everyone to gain attention. That's all she ever wanted was attention. Everyone at the studio loved and pampered Judy but they couldn't hold her hand every minute. The problem with her didn't start with pills, it started with her obsession to be beautiful like Lana Turner. Judy had a crush on Mickey Rooney who had eyes for Lana and then married the beautiful married Ava.

> Tyrone Power was in love with Lana. The first man who made her look beautiful was the man she married, Vincente Minnelli, whom she humiliated. No other studio offered her work after MGM fired her. Whose fault was that?'

Writer Anita Loos was harsh about Garland. 'She was a compulsive weeper,' Loos said. 'She moaned all the time that she was unloved, persecuted and neglected. She was a great big bore.'

> Joan Crawford was just as unsympathetic. 'We were all under pressure at MGM,' she said. 'It wasn't so much L.B. Mayer as it was Nicholas Schenck who laid down the law and Mr Mayer had to comply using methods that were hard to accept. Judy took uppers and downers, but a lot of celebrities did. It was the thing to do. Let me tell you, Judy was given more chances than anyone else except Spencer Tracy, who went on drunken binges and no one could find him. He was fired, too, and rightfully so. I was a big fan of Judy's and attended her concerts, but I know for a fact that she lied to her psychiatrists. Is this progress? If Judy wanted to get well, she would have succeeded. She didn't want to. How many times did MGM send her to sanatoriums and pick up the tab? Why didn't she try to overcome her addiction? I'll tell you why. She craved sympathy. If you're sincere about wanting to get on with life, the one thing you don't want is sympathy.'

In 1959 Judy worked a gruelling schedule until she collapsed from acute hepatitis. When she recuperated, Judy formed her own production company with former M.C.A. representatives, Freddie Fields and David Begelman, squeezing out Sid Luft as her manager. Judy made appearances in Europe and America, but is remembered for her Carnegie Hall concert on 23 April 1961. She had lost weight and gained strength. Critics agreed that this was the greatest night in show-business history.

Judy's first film after several years was *Judgment at Nuremberg*, a fictionalised version of the 1948 trial of the Nazi leaders for crimes against humanity. Judy played a German housewife testifying for the prosecution. She received an Academy Award nomination for Best Supporting Actress but lost to Rita Moreno for *West Side Story*.

Judy's last two films, *A Child is Waiting* and *I Could Go On Singing* were box-office disasters.

In September 1962 Judy sued Luft for divorce at Lake Tahoe, Nevada, and took another overdose of barbiturates. When Sid called to find out how she was, Judy told him to 'get lost'. The divorce, however, was put on hold until their financial matters were straightened out. As for her career, she said,

> I'm at my best . . . Also, I just turned forty, and when you hit that stage you feel that maybe people won't think of you as a stupid backward child that you wind up and send out on a stage to sing. I'm not a half-child any more. Before, nobody ever let me do anything for myself. First my mother, then my husband. Oh, the early days at MGM were a lot of laughs. It was all right if you were young and frightened – and we stayed frightened. Look at us – Lana Turner, Elizabeth Taylor, Mickey Rooney and me – we all came out a little ticky and kooky. Now I'm getting too old to be towed around. I'm out of debt, and it's a nice feeling to have money in the bank. I have inner satisfaction and peace of mind for a change.

Fields and Begelman went for the gold in 1963 with *The Judy Garland Show*, a weekly C.B.S. television series on Sunday nights at 9.00 p.m. Judy's weekly salary was over $25,000. But, as *TV Guide* said, it was a risk: 'The big question mark and the one that set C.B.S. nerves twanging like banjo strings, was Judy Garland, whose efforts to hoist herself over the rainbow to happiness have been headline news for twenty years. C.B.S. knew, its affiliates knew, what almost everyone else knew about Miss Garland – that she was a woman in an almost constant state of emotional turmoil; that, as a result, her career as a movie superstar had been cut short because the studios deemed her undependable (which she denies); and that she had suffered several breakdowns.'

Singer Mel Tormé was hired to write special numbers for Judy who wanted to know why he took the job. Tormé, who knew she had to be pampered and complimented, said it was an honour to work with her. Judy believed he was putting her on and let him know that it was her show and he would be working for her. 'It's not going to be like the old Metro days,' she said. 'For once, I'm running things. You know how Mayer treated me in the old days . . . I had to take it then but not any more.' Judy went on to say that grown men were afraid of her now.

Tormé told Garland she was full of shit.

Luft, who would shortly be out of Judy's life for good, gave her proof that she had been swindled out of more than $200,000 by David Begelman, with whom she was having an affair. Her response was, 'So what? I'm going to make millions from my television shows.'

On 29 September 1963 *The Judy Garland Show* made its debut and was praised by the critics, but C.B.S. president James Aubrey Jr became disenchanted within a few weeks. He didn't want a 'Palace' performance every Sunday night. He felt weekly viewers settled in to watch a more relaxed programme. Aubrey wanted Judy to be more comfortable with her audience in contrast to the lavish productions on tape. He said Garland would have to learn to adjust to television, not the other way around. Following the Kennedy assassination, Judy wanted to dedicate her show to the fallen President. C.B.S. said no. She was also determined to tell her viewers how she had been used by MGM. Mel Tormé said L.B. Mayer was dead. What was the point? Judy said she always swore to get even with him and now she was going to do it. Tormé commented at the time that Judy was behaving erratically and was more disturbed than anyone realised.

By the end of 1963, *Bonanza* on N.B.C. at 9.00 p.m. on Sundays blew *The Judy Garland Show* away. As one N.B.C. executive said in early 1964, 'We didn't expect her to last that long.' And neither did anyone else.

The television series that was going to give Judy financial security failed. She found herself so heavily in debt that she would never recover. Bombarded with law suits and running from the sheriff, Garland decided to flee once again, this time to Australia.

During her ill-fated TV series, Judy did not find consolation in love. She'd had affairs with actor Glenn Ford and lawyer Greg Bautzer. She'd been swindled by lover David Begelman and suffered through failed reconciliations with Luft.

The new man in Judy's life was a 33-year-old gay actor Mark Herron whom she'd met at a party. Maybe they could appear together in the legitimate theatre. Why not? She was tired of travelling the world doing concerts. With no one to accompany her on the long plane flight to Australia, she asked Herron go to along. Her concerts in Sydney were a success, but in Melbourne, Judy arrived two hours after curtain time. The audience was outraged. They shouted 'You're late!' and 'Have another brandy!' Judy told them she couldn't get out of her hotel because of the crowds. As if undecided what to sing, she took the orchestra leader's baton and pretended to take over. The audience was not pleased. When she started to sing, Judy complained that her microphone squeaked. Then she complained about the air conditioning. The audience booed and many walked out. She burst into tears and tried to tell them she was lonely by herself, followed by 'Good Night'. More boos followed. The management said they would never bother with Garland again. At the airport she was delighted that a crowd was there to see her off. They booed and hissed so viciously that she burst into tears and boarded the plane.

Judy and Mark flew to Hong Kong where she took an overdose of sleeping pills and had to have her stomach pumped. When she returned to the United States, Judy was granted a divorce from Sid Luft in May 1965. In September, she performed at the Greek Theater in Los Angeles, fell over and broke her arm. *Variety*, who had usually supported Judy in the past, wrote, 'There's no arguing with a broken arm, but the long-term effects of the occurrence will, unfortunately, compound an impression that exists in the minds of some promoters and fans that Miss Garland cannot be relied upon to completely fulfil a commitment.'

It was now obvious that Judy had lost the support of her Hollywood peers who bought tickets to her concerts in Los Angeles faithfully. It was no secret that she had been drinking the night she broke her arm. And it was no secret that Judy was sneaking out of hotels in the middle of the night to avoid paying the bills.

With few friends left, the lonely Judy was desperate enough to marry Mark Herron in Las Vegas on 14 November 1965. They separated a few months later. About her fourth husband she said, 'I used to hear from him once in a while. I think he called from a phone booth on castors.'

Peter Lawford said he received a frantic call from Judy who claimed Mark was abusing her. Lawford rushed to Judy's house and found her with razor cuts on her face. 'Mark did this to me,' she said, but her maid told Lawford she saw Judy inflict these facial cuts on herself.

Few people were able to cope with Judy as Luft had done. He was the love of her life and the one who paved the way for a comeback when all the doors were closed to her. He was fairly successful in limiting her pill intake that had escalated to 25 amphetamines and 45 Ritalin a day. Observers said they saw her pleading for one more pill before going on stage. Sid refused to give it to her. Part of his motivation in their marriage was money, but his real problem was how to manage it. Luft's ability as a father was never questioned and it's a miracle the court gave Judy custody of Lorna and Joey who eventually fled to him when Judy took her wrath out on them. Had Ethel been as abusive?

Liza distanced herself from Judy, too. Her career was soaring and her marriage to Peter Allen appeared to be a happy one. According to Gerald

Clarke, author of *Get Happy*, Mark Herron had discovered Allen in a Hong Kong nightclub. Mark and Peter were intimately involved in Hong Kong and eventually got together in the United States. It was through Judy that Liza met Peter Allen whom she married. Clarke writes that Liza found Peter in a compromising position that mirrored Judy's shock on finding Vincente in bed with a man. But Liza not only loved Peter, she needed him to keep her mother at a safe distance.

Judy continued to sing to full or half-empty houses. If she made good money, it went for back-taxes and unpaid bills that now amounted to half a million dollars. Forced to sell her house, Judy had nowhere to live. Those friends who took her in were glad to get rid of her.

She had affairs with several men for the sex or for a place to sleep. In December 1968 Judy met 34-year-old Mickey Deans, the manager of Arthur's, a discotheque owned by Richard Burton's ex-wife, Sybil. The good-looking Deans had met Judy previously, but this time around they became very close very fast. In need of a manager and a husband, Judy asked Mickey to accompany her to London for an engagement at a large cabaret called Talk of the Town that had once been the Hippodrome Theatre. Here again, we have Judy about to go abroad alone and in need of someone to take charge. Columnist Earl Wilson was the first to get the news that Judy and Mickey were engaged to be married. 'I don't want to be alone anymore,' she told him. Deans said he wanted to protect her from further humiliation and disappointment. 'There was hope for the future,' he said. 'I wasn't exactly naive. I know that in our profession love has about as much of a chance as a snowball in hell. But sometimes love begins with an unspoken cry for help. And a response.'

On 27 December they flew to London and checked into the Ritz. About her appearance at Talk of the Town, the *The Times* said, 'No logic, no analysis, no judgment in the world can completely explain the phenomenon of Judy Garland's performance . . . She walks the rim of the volcano each second. Miraculously she keeps her balance. It is a triumph of utmost improbability.'

Variety reported Judy's five-week engagement at Talk of the Town as a 'troubled success'.

In an interview Judy said, 'I don't have to live for applause any longer. I could give it all up tomorrow without a single regret or heartache. I'm happier than I've ever been, and the future promises that I will be happier still. I want to be loved by one man, and Mickey is that man. I don't have to fight any more and that's a great feeling. No more pressures and no more decisions. I can sit back and be a lady. I don't even have to answer the telephone or worry about who's calling or what they want. Mickey takes care of everything. And me.'

Judy's reputation followed her wherever she went, however. When she was really ill, no one believed her. Battling the flu, she showed up late for a show at Talk of the Town. The audience turned on her, throwing things on stage. A man stood up and shouted, 'If you can't show up on time, why show up at all?' Garland walked off the stage in tears. On closing night, however, she was twenty minutes late but forgiven by the audience who showered her with bouquets and flowers.

Judy had to wait for her divorce decree from Mark Herron before she could marry Deans, but they decided to go through with it anyway on 9 January 1969 at St Marylebone parish church in the wee hours of the morning. On 15 March they made their marriage legal at Chelsea registry office. Judy looked radiant but very frail. The reception was held at Quaglino's but, of all the celebrities invited, only singer Johnny Ray showed up. Judy told reporters who drank the champagne and ate the wedding cake, that she was surprised and disappointed that her friends weren't there. 'They said they'd come,' she sighed.

After a brief Paris honeymoon, they embarked on a concert tour with Johnny Ray. Sceptics predicted that Garland and Ray would not draw an audience but they did in Stockholm, Malmö and Copenhagen. Those who applauded Judy saw a pathetic figure struggling to please them. And struggling to stay alive. Insiders said she was on hard drugs while others thought she was suffering from a lifetime of amphetamines, seconals and alcohol. Deans attributed her wasting away to insomnia, but he was alarmed when he found Judy locked in the bathroom talking to people who weren't around. On the plane bound for London, she was rolling an imaginary ball of yarn and carrying on a conversation with people who did not exist. Her strange behaviour was attributed to a change in medication in an attempt to get her off Ritalin.

In June 1969 MGM hair stylist Sydney Guilaroff and Ava Gardner were delighted to run into Judy at a party in London. After they reminisced for a while, Judy invited them to her place for a drink. Sydney recalled in his memoirs, 'Her home was in a narrow two-storey mews, very dreary and practically devoid of furnishings. The walls were bare, without a single hanging on them. With one glance I knew that she was down and out financially, and that saddened me. In all the years we had known each other I had never seen her in such poor condition.'

On Saturday 21 June, Judy and Mickey had planned to go to the theatre but stayed home because both had head colds. At 10.40 a.m. the following day Mickey woke up when the phone rang. Charlie Cochran and John Carlyle, friends of Judy's, were calling from California and wanted to speak to her. The bathroom door was closed and locked from the inside. When Deans knocked there was no response. He climbed on to the roof, peeked through the bathroom and saw Judy on the toilet, her head slumped forward and her hands on her knees. She had been dead for several hours. Accidental overdose of barbiturates was the cause of death.

Judy Garland's body arrived in New York on 26 June and was taken to the Frank E Campbell Home on Madison Avenue. 22,000 people paid their respects before the funeral. James Mason, who gave the eulogy said, '. . . she was the most sympathetic, the funniest, the sharpest and the most stimulating woman I ever knew. She was a lady who gave so much and richly both to the vast audience when she entertained and to the friends around her whom she loved that there was no currency in which to repay her. And she needed to be repaid, she needed devotion and love beyond the resources of any of us . . .'

Mickey Rooney, who was devastated by Judy's death, wrote in his memoirs, 'Judy turned to drugs because she was in pain and because drugs made her feel good. As one of the MGM kids, she'd been treated for most of her life to magical, instant, solutions to everything . . . She could never accept herself so she was always on the run.'

Thinking she might write her story one day, Judy recorded her thoughts on tape between 1964 and 1967. Drugged and angry she said, 'I wanted to believe and I tried my damndest to believe in the rainbow that I tried to get over and I couldn't. So what? Lots of people can't . . .'

The Films of Judy Garland

Pigskin Parade (20th Century-Fox, 1936)
Broadway Melody of 1938 (MGM, 1937)
Thoroughbreds Don't Cry (MGM, 1937)
Everybody Sing (MGM, 1938)
Listen, Darling (MGM, 1938)
Love Finds Andy Hardy (MGM, 1938)
The Wizard of Oz (MGM, 1939)
Babes in Arms (MGM, 1939)
Strike Up the Band (MGM, 1940)
Little Nellie Kelly (MGM, 1940)
Andy Hardy Meets Debutante (MGM, 1940)
Ziegfeld Girl (MGM, 1941)
Life Begins for Andy Hardy (MGM, 1941)
Babes on Broadway (MGM, 1941)
For Me and My Gal (MGM, 1942)
Presenting Lily Mars (MGM, 1943)
Girl Crazy (MGM, 1943)
Thousands Cheer (MGM, 1943)
Meet Me in St Louis (MGM, 1944)
The Clock (MGM, 1945)
The Harvey Girls (MGM, 1946)
Ziegfeld Follies (MGM, 1946)
Til the Clouds Roll By (MGM, 1946)
The Pirate (MGM, 1948)
Easter Parade (MGM, 1948)
Words and Music (MGM, 1948)
In the Good Old Summertime (MGM, 1949)

Summer Stock (MGM, 1950)
A Star is Born (Warner Brothers, 1954)
Pepe (Voice only: Columbia, 1960)
Judgment at Nuremberg (United Artists, 1961)
Gay Purr-ee (Voice only: Warner Brothers, 1962)
A Child is Waiting (United Artists, 1963)
I Could Go On Singing (United Artists, 1963)

8

Ava

Mogul Louis B. Mayer viewed her screen test and remarked, 'She can't act. She can't talk. She's terrific.'

From a lazy town in North Carolina, she had such a thick Southern drawl, no one in Hollywood understood a word she said. But this beauty had a figure and face to die for, and Frank Sinatra almost did. He lost everything to possess her.

She bears the distinction of being MGM's final mould of a screen legend. Her image was that of the independent-minded, worldly-wise, and sexually knowledgeable good/bad dame who fascinated men and worried women. She was the girl from the wrong side of the tracks who crossed over in her bare feet from the tobacco fields of America's South to a Dream Factory in Culver City – Metro-Goldwyn-Mayer – the grandest motion-picture studio in the world.

London, 1953.

Lana Turner and Clark Gable lounged on the couch sipping cocktails, discussing a winter storm expected to blitz London that night. Robert Taylor said the aroma of fried chicken was making him ravenous. 'What the hell are we waiting for?' he asked. 'Let's eat.'

'My wife forgot to make gravy,' director Tay Garnett said. 'Can't have fried chicken without gravy.'

The doorbell rang and when Garnett answered it, there stood Ava Gardner in a clinging, shimmering gown. 'I don't give a shit what everyone else is wearing,' she said. 'I bought this dress today and I had to spring it!'

Mrs Garnett hugged her and sighed, 'I forgot the gravy, Ava.'

'Stand aside, honey. I'll whip some up and I don't need an apron.'

If Ava was casual about her cooking, it wasn't an act. She came from a large family who suffered through the Great Depression. Before she was ten years old, Ava was preparing meals for twenty people and making it look easy.

Mary Baker Gardner named her daughter after her mother, Ava, who died giving birth to her nineteenth child, Lavinia. Mary, known as Molly, had been ten days overdue in her seventh pregnancy. The doctor delivered the child by Caesarean section on Christmas Eve 1922, in Grabtown, about fifty miles from the state capital of Raleigh in North Carolina. Molly was forty, robust and barely over five feet tall. Her husband of twenty years, Jonas Bailey Gardner, was a tall, lean Irishman, with dark hair and green eyes. A year after Molly and Jonas were married, his father died, leaving them a white clapboard four-bedroom house on three hundred acres of rich tobacco land in Boon Hill. This was Ava's first home. Her eldest sister was Bappie, nineteen. Then came Elsie May, eighteen, Inez, sixteen, Melvin, fourteen, and Myra, seven. Another boy, Raymond, was killed at sixteen months when a rifle shell exploded. He would have been fifteen when Ava Lavinia was born.

Molly was a religious, overly protective mother. Her Victorian principles were strictly enforced in the family. The only book allowed in the Gardner house was the Bible.

Ava's first recollection as a child was the aroma of tobacco. Her playgrounds were the fields of dark, tarlike sticky soil that oozed between her toes. For a few cents to spend at the candy store, she picked larvae and worms off the tobacco leaves. She knew when it was time to fertilise and when the harvesting was about to begin. The pink, white and red flowers she wore in her hair were from the tobacco plants. Ava rolled her first cigarette when she was five.

When the Great Depression hit in 1929, tobacco prices tumbled and Jonas sold the Gardner home and property, forcing the family to break up. Jonas was in ill health so Molly, at the suggestion of a friend in Newport News, Virginia, rented a boarding house there, and, with Ava's help, she cleaned the rooms and cooked meals. When Jonas became bedridden with a streptococcus infection of the chest, Molly cared for him while Ava, aged ten, took over the kitchen duties. Jonas died two years later.

Yearning to be closer to her family, Molly got a job at another school in Rock Ridge, North Carolina, where Ava attended high school. 'Mama was so busy working she hadn't noticed I was growing up,' Ava said. 'Suddenly I had breasts and Mama didn't know what to do about it except to keep boys away from me. One time she found me sitting in a boy's car near Holt Lake. Nothing was happening, but Mama literally dragged me out of the front seat. Another time one of my dates dared to kiss me on the front porch. When Mama came after him, he ran for his life and I was severely punished. Nobody wanted to take me out.'

Ava loved her mother dearly, but at sixteen she needed more freedom. And there was the desire to help out Molly financially. Ava's brother Melvin offered to pay her tuition at the Atlantic Christian College in Wilson. She studied shorthand and typing, but soon lost interest. 'I never had any ambition to be anything but dead in those days,' Ava said. But underneath the altered and faded hand-me-down dresses was a tall, beauteous woman with a tiny waist and full, uplifted breasts. All that Jonas bequeathed Ava were his green eyes, lean figure, and heavy dimple in his chin. These traits would be valuable assets some day, but at that time she had no confidence in her appearance. Not to wear make-up like the other girls, Ava could not comprehend why men stared and whistled. Molly said they wanted one thing, and sex was dirty.

Ava's only glimmer of hope was sister Bappie. She had married Larry

Tarr, a photographer from New York City, and in 1940 decided it was time for her little sister to get away from home for a few days. For Ava it was the thrill of a lifetime. Even Tarr's tiny apartment over his photo studio at Forty-ninth and Fifth Avenue was heaven to a shy hillbilly girl. Bappie made sure Ava saw New York, and Larry, who was very impressed with his sister-in-law's striking face, took photographs of her. She had no idea how to pose but, as Tarr said, she was a natural beauty with hair that had a healthy chestnut glow, smooth pale skin, straight white teeth and an innocent smile.

For Ava the excitement of seeing New York City soon faded. Molly was suffering from breast cancer and only time would determine her fate.

It was a messenger boy who was responsible for discovering Ava Gardner. Barney Duhan, who ran errands for Loew's legal department, saw her picture in the window of Tarr's photo studio and wanted to date her. Posing as a talent scout for Loew's MGM, he managed to meet many attractive women by promising them a screen test. At Barney's request, Larry delivered pictures of Ava to the MGM offices on Fifty-second Street. When Duhan realised Ava was out of reach in North Carolina, he gave the photos to Marvin Schenck in charge of talent at MGM.

'They liked those pictures,' Ava said. 'When Bappie called to tell me, honest to God, I was not excited. Everyone else was, so Mama and I went to New York. Because I had such a rolling Southern accent, MGM did a silent screen test. In Hollywood George Sidney saw it and told the New York office "to ship her out, she's a good piece of merchandise".'

MGM offered Ava a contract for fifty dollars a week, but she was reluctant to leave her mother. Molly agreed to let her baby go to Hollywood if Bappie went along as chaperone.

On 23 August 1941, Ava and her sister arrived in Los Angeles by train and were greeted by Milton Weiss from MGM's publicity department. After a tour of the studio, the Gardner girls checked into a 'two-by-four' room at the Hollywood Wilcox Hotel. 'We had only one little bed and a small kitchen,' Ava recalled. 'For the first three weeks I was there, I didn't get paid. Bappie went to work for I. Magnin and I got up before dawn every day to catch two buses to the studio.'

*

'What kind of a name is Ahvah Gahdnuh?' L.B. Mayer wanted to know after viewing her screen test.

'It's Ava Gardner,' Milton Weiss said.

'Perfect. We'll change it.'

'It's a lovely name . . .'

'That's why we're going to invent it, Milton. Make up some shit about her real name. You know, Mary Lou or Lucy Ann, the Southern Belle crap. What's her background?'

'Secretarial school,' Weiss said.

'We can't use that in our press releases. Even I don't believe it.'

'How about the Powers model routine?'

'That's good. Meanwhile, get the usual stills of her in a bathing suit.'

'Who's Lucy Ann Johnson?'

'That's you,' Weiss replied. 'You might say MGM gave birth to Ava Gardner.'

'Bappie wants to know about these six-month options. She says you can let me go if I don't work out. If that's true, I want no part of it.'

'Do you have train fare back to New York?' Weiss asked.

'We can't even pay our hotel bill,' Ava replied.

'Then I suggest you stick around for a while. What do you have to lose?'

'That's what Bappie said.'

'Sign here, Ava. Then you'll meet Mr Mayer.'

The Thalberg Building was buzzing with hundreds of clerks and secretaries scurrying from room to room and floor to floor. There were private dining rooms, a canteen, conference rooms, kitchens and bathrooms. Aside from the public elevator, there were private ones used by executives.

Mayer's office was surrounded by rows and rows of desks occupied by secretaries and their secretaries. It was hectic but well-organised. If Ava was impressed with her boss's staff, it was nothing compared to what she felt when she was ushered into his office. It was a large room with white leather walls. At the far end was Mayer's huge, horseshoe-shaped desk and behind it a big chair that had been custom-built to make the short, chunky mogul appear taller. Many MGM players said the walk from the office door across the room was the longest they had ever taken. Mayer had his reasons for arranging the office in this manner. Those who paid homage to their master were ushered into a great room where the throne loomed at the far wall. In

Mayer's case, he wanted a full-length view of those who entered, and perhaps it was a test of their endurance as well.

Mayer was very businesslike with Ava, warning her about staying out late at night, drinking too much, and dating indiscriminately. 'If you need an escort,' he said, 'we can arrange one for you. I prefer, however, that you concentrate on getting to the studio on time every morning. Practise your diction faithfully. Read the newspaper aloud every morning. It'll pay off. You'll see. And remember, Ava, there is always someone here at MGM who can solve your problems, answer your questions, and assist you in every way to get settled in Hollywood. Think of me as your father. Anything we discuss in this office will go no further.' With pride he stressed that she was in the hands of the greatest designers and make-up artists in the world. Her diction and dramatic coaches were the best. Ultimately Louis Burt Mayer was telling Ava that if she failed it would be her fault and no one else's.

She was taken aback when Weiss told her, 'Mayer is the highest salaried person in America.' It never occurred to Ava that anyone earned more than the President of the United States.

Living at the dreary Hollywood Wilcox was Ava's reality as she and Bappie tried to cook Southern fried chicken in the tiny kitchen and night after night they stayed in the shabby room with its stained rugs and dirty walls. According to what Ava said in later years it was Bappie who urged her on and had the confidence that she would succeed. Tarr was patient and understanding for a long time, but the separations from Bappie would end the marriage.

Though Ava found the MGM star system a bore, she did what she was told with the exception of allowing the make-up man to pluck out all her eyebrows. The custom in those days was to shave or pluck the brows and pencil them in. Ava made such a fuss they left hers alone. MGM's make-up supervisor Jack Dawn turned up her eyelashes with wave set, emphasised her cheekbones and toned down the dimple in her chin. Dawn enjoyed Ava's sense of humour and her spunk when an MGM executive made a pass at her. She told him off with a string of four-letter expletives that made his head spin. As a result of this tirade, Dawn wanted to accentuate this tempestuous side of Ava's personality by arching the eyebrows, and emphasising her almond eyes.

When Ava reported to Sidney Guilaroff, the best hairdresser in the business, she waited with a group of other starlets. Nervous because she was facing the possibility of becoming a redhead or a blonde, Ava chomped on a piece of gum to the annoyance of Guilaroff who heard the cracking and barked, 'Who's chewing gum in here? Take it out at once!' Ava swallowed it and waited. When he stood behind her, she cringed, but Guilaroff had made his point. He trimmed her hair below the shoulders and set it off the face, giving Ava the windblown look. But he kept her hair long enough to sweep up for the sophisticated effect.

Voice coach Gertrude Vogeler, who was responsible for ridding Ava of her Southern accent, said, 'You drop your "g"s like magnolia blossoms and we've got to teach you how to pronounce your "r"s.' Vogeler, by chance, overheard Ava singing and detected no accent. Putting words to music played an important part in erasing Ava's drawl.

Lillian Burns was MGM's best dramatic coach. She was strict but patient. Each newcomer was an individual to Burns and, in Ava, she detected the animal magnetism in her lackadaisical manner and carriage. Her voice was soft and low, and her husky laugh sexy and elusive. Burns's most difficult task was convincing Ava that she possessed these assets. In North Carolina it was the lazy attitude. In Hollywood, it was mysterious. At MGM it spelled . . . class.

Ava looked forward to her sessions with Lillian Burns, to whom she attributed her progress during these awkward months.

Modern dance and ballet lessons gave her poise and muscle co-ordination. Stretching, bending, and rhythmic body movements toned the legs and waistline. Just as important was getting through a night at the Mocambo by dancing a graceful waltz, fox-trot and tango.

Posing for publicity photos was the worst for Ava. In later years she told *Playboy* magazine, 'You could have carpeted Hollywood Boulevard with my pictures from kerb to kerb. I don't remember how many swimsuits I wore – without getting near the water. I shot enough sultry looks around the MGM photo gallery to melt the North Pole.'

Ava would never change her mind about being 'promoted'. She did, however, have an ally in Howard Strickling, chief of MGM publicity, who was not only loyal to and trusted by Mayer, but a man who had a warm and understanding relationship with the MGM family. Clark Gable told Ava, 'If it hadn't been for Howard, I'd probably be driving a truck.' When Strickling retired he gallantly refused to divulge studio secrets. Nor did he discuss the personal lives of the stars he promoted and protected. Ava was not in Strickling's league yet. He assigned Anne Strauss to look after her and explain the rules. During interviews, for example, swearing, gossip, religion and politics were taboo. Strauss would make certain that cocktail glasses, liquor bottles, and cigarettes were removed from the table in a restaurant or nightclub before any pictures were taken. Ava was expected to be well groomed at all times. For special occasions, Strauss would help her select clothes from MGM's wardrobe department. 'They were on loan, of course,' Ava said. 'I looked like a million bucks and I was flat broke.'

It was during her first week at MGM that Ava Gardner met Mickey Rooney. On a tour of the studio, Weiss took her on the set of *Babes on Broadway* where Mickey was doing an impersonation of the Brazilian entertainer Carmen Miranda. He was wearing a basket of fruit on his head, a bodice blouse with falsies underneath, a long samba skirt, high platform shoes, rouge, lipstick, and long false eyelashes. Weiss said, 'I introduced Ava to Mickey, who took one look at her and was horny as hell. He asked her for a date and she turned him down.'

That same day Mickey was having lunch in the canteen with his entourage when Ava walked in. 'Won't you join us?' he said, standing up. Ava was stunned. 'Jesus,' she commented later, 'I thought he must have shrunk since this morning. But then I remembered he was wearing those high platform shoes.' Though only five-foot-three, Rooney was 'King of the Box Office' and one of the hottest properties in Hollywood. He had as much power at the studio as Clark Gable.

Mickey called every day and was rejected every day. Ava was more interested in getting out of the Hotel Wilcox and finally found an apartment on Franklin Avenue, not far from the studio. It was one step forward, but she and Bappie could barely afford a night out at a café. So why did Ava turn down Mickey's daily invitations to dinner? 'For one thing,' she told Anne Strauss, 'he's not my type, but he won't give up. What should I do?'

'Go out with him,' was the reply. 'Being seen with Mickey Rooney will do you a lot of good.'

But Ava continued to resist until his determination won her over. 'I'd like to go out,' she told him on the phone, 'but I promised to have dinner with my sister.'

'Bring her along!' Mickey exclaimed, trying to contain his excitement.

They went to Chasen's, a favourite restaurant of the Hollywood elite. Mickey reserved one of the banquettes covered in red leather against a pine-panelled wall. He was greeted personally by owner Dave Chasen. The best champagne was on ice and the most expensive caviar served as an appetiser Mickey, holding Ava's hand, went from table to table, showing her off. 'I met more famous stars that night than during my two months in Hollywood,' she said.

Mickey offered to drive her to and from the studio every day. These short trips were not merely rides. They were vaudeville shows on wheels. Rooney entertained her with gossip and funny stories, and Ava began to find him rather amusing. Mickey knew he was progressing when she laughed at the same joke twice. He began a major courtship – dinner at Romanoff's, dancing at the Mocambo, cocktails at Don the Beachcomber. At premieres, he gave Ava the spotlight, but she gave him neither her heart nor her body.

Mickey decided that being chauffeured in his Lincoln would free both his hands. Ava held him off and slammed the car door in his face.

L.B. Mayer was growing uneasy. He told Howard Strickling, 'I know Rooney. All he wants is to get into her pants. Make sure he doesn't marry her to do it.'

'I understand he's proposed to her already.'

'That kid's got me by the balls. The Andy Hardy pictures are worth millions to us.'

'His teenage following might not be interested if he's married. We might stress that possibility.'

'We'll wait it out,' Mayer scowled. 'From what I hear Gardner's not biting. If she'd give him what he wants, we'd have no worries. Suppose . . .'

'Not on your life,' Strickling laughed. 'She wouldn't go to bed with Mickey if you threatened not to renew her option.'

'That's what I said. They've *both* got me by the balls.'

In November 1941, Ava was not avoiding Mickey's persistent marriage proposals because he had won over Bappie. Finally she said yes, but he had to get permission from L.B. Mayer, the greatest actor at the studio.

'You're breaking my heart, Mickey,' he sobbed.

'I'm in love,' Rooney choked, tears running down his face.

Mayer cried and Mickey cried. Their moans could be heard in the outer office where Ava was waiting. Mayer's secretary told her, 'You'll be sorry. Don't do this.'

Mayer finally consented. 'If I can't prevent you from getting married, Mickey, you'll do it my way – quietly and without fanfare. Les Peterson will handle everything and accompany you on the honeymoon in January sometime. I'll let you know.'

Mayer told Les Peterson, Rooney's MGM publicist, to make all the arrangements. He bought the wedding ring, obtained the marriage licence and found a suitable apartment for Mickey and his bride. Ava wanted to walk down a church aisle wearing a traditional white gown and veil, but Mickey explained, 'That's for everybody else. It can't be that way for us, honey. You wouldn't want a circus of fans and reporters spoiling our wedding day, would you?'

Ava considered buying a white dress anyway, but couldn't afford one, and she was too embarrassed to ask Mickey for the money. MGM gave her a small bonus to buy a trousseau that consisted of a sheer long white nightgown, matching slippers, a simple dark-blue tailored suit and shoes.

Very early on Sunday, 10 January 1942, Ava, Mickey, and Les Peterson drove north toward Santa Barbara. Squeezed in the second car were Mickey's parents, Bappie and an MGM photographer. At 11:00 a.m. they arrived at a little Presbyterian church, tucked away in the foothills of the Santa Ynez Mountains. The Reverend Lutz married the couple after Mrs Lutz played 'I Love You Truly' and Mendelssohn's 'Wedding March' on an upright piano. After the ceremony, Peterson rushed to a phone and called Howard Strickling. He then accompanied the newlyweds to the Del Monte Hotel in Carmel. Ava was terrified. She was about to engage in the act that Molly scorned and ridiculed. Was it a consummation of love to be cherished? Or was it the duty of a bride on her wedding night to be endured?

If Mickey thought his crowning achievement was in the tiny white church earlier that day, he was wrong. For he was the first man to possess Ava Gardner. 'I was proud,' he said in later years. He admitted being clumsy on his wedding night, but when Ava lost her shyness, she was warm and receptive – ready for more the next morning.

'Beautiful day, darling,' she sighed.

'Perfect for golf,' he said, hopping out of bed.

A set of new golf clubs was part of Mickey's trousseau. He was very proud of his woods and irons. 'I've been playin' in the seventies,' he cheered as they headed for the green. In shock, Ava tagged along. For the remainder of the honeymoon, she stayed at the hotel with Peterson, who was in the dining room when the newlyweds came in for breakfast, lunch and dinner. Mickey liked people and, though not overly fond of Peterson, a threesome was more entertaining. Ava said, 'On my honeymoon I saw more of Les than I did of my husband.' What Ava failed to notice were fans and reporters prowling the hotel grounds – without Peterson's help the four days might have been a total disaster.

From Carmel the threesome drove to San Francisco where they began a war bond tour and to promote Mickey's new picture, *Life Begins for Andy Hardy*. They attended President Roosevelt's birthday celebration in Washington and made a side trip to North Carolina. 'Mama was dying,' Ava recalled, 'but she was all dolled up for Mickey who put on a show for her with impersonations, songs and dances. He was very funny and made Mama laugh. He hugged and kissed her. I was so moved and grateful to him because I would never see Mama alive again.'

They returned to California and moved into the apartment Peterson had found for them in Wilshire Palms near Westwood. Ava resumed her lessons at MGM and came home every night to kick off her shoes, cook dinner and relax with Mickey who had other ideas. He came home raring to go or he was late without phoning. 'I went nuts sitting around,' Mickey said. 'I had to have people around. Action. I dreaded those long evenings at home.' Ava was bored to death with parties every night. Mickey did not appreciate her sulking alone in a corner, but he became a madman when she mingled. One evening she danced with actor Tom Drake and Mickey went into a rage, but Ava stood up to him. She called him a runt and a midget. Then she stormed out and went to Bappie's apartment on Franklin where Ava would often flee. Mickey always followed and they made up. She knew he was being unfaithful when she came home from the hospital after having her appendix removed. 'It was clear to me,' she said, 'that Mickey had been entertaining girls in my bed. . .'

In the autumn of 1942, the Rooneys unofficially separated. Mayer might have left the couple alone to sort out their own problems, but Mickey's performance in *The Courtship of Andy Hardy* was dull and listless. Mayer had a long talk with the Rooneys and urged them to reconcile. Ava thought she might give it another try, so Mayer increased Ava's salary to $150 a week and gave her a part in *Ghosts on the Loose* with the Dead End Kids at Monogram Pictures, a subsidiary of Allied Artists. Mayer also made sure the Rooneys were seen together in nightclubs to prove their togetherness, but Ava was no longer putting up with Mickey's one-ring circus.

'Would you do me a favour?' she asked on the drive home from the Mocambo.

'Sure, darling. What is it?'

'Shut up.'

On 2 May 1943, Ava filed for divorce in Los Angeles City Court. She accused Rooney of inflicting 'grievous mental suffering' and 'extreme mental cruelty'. Instead of demanding half of Mickey's holdings that she was entitled to, Ava asked for $25,000, a car, and whatever furs and jewellery he had given to her. The day after Ava appeared in court, she received the news that Molly had died . . .

Bappie moved into the Westwood apartment with Ava, who now concentrated on her career. She appeared in such forgettable films as *DuBarry Was a Lady*, *Young Ideas*, *Lost Angel*, *Spring Fever*, and *Music for Millions*. Mayer wanted to give Ava plenty of exposure before putting her into *Three Men in White*, one of the popular Dr Gillespie movies. Ava got her first billing. The *Hollywood Reporter* thought she was superb, but Bosley Crowther of The *New York Times* wrote that Ava was 'sultry but stupid'.

Before Mickey was inducted into the Army in June 1944, he and Ava were seen together at nightclubs and, according to her, they were intimate. Mickey hoped for a reconciliation but Ava told him, 'As a husband you're a pain in the ass.' She went out on dates arranged by the studio but met no one who interested her until Howard Hughes invited her out to dinner. Not only was he tall, dark and handsome, his bashfulness brought out the motherly instinct in Ava. That Hughes was a millionaire impressed her least of all, but his money bought Ava the freedom and privacy she wanted. His possessiveness, however led to bitter arguments, physical brawls and separations.

Hughes was particularly interested in recently divorced women, 'wet backs', as he referred to them. His faithfulness was always in question, but Howard was intent on possessing Ava and she did not resist. He had her watched by Mormon bodyguards twenty-four hours a day, and seemed to know what she was going to do before she did. 'Howard makes it easy for you by pressing a button and there's a plane to take you anywhere,' Ava said. 'Another button and there's a hotel suite waiting for you. If you want to be quiet and left alone, he arranges it. He's just the ticket for a simple girl from North Carolina.' Hughes gave her expensive presents, including a Cadillac. When he was away in December 1944, Ava went to the Mocambo with friends, including a Mexican bullfighter. After a night of dancing and drinking, they returned to the house Hughes had leased for Ava. She put the toreador to bed upstairs and dozed on the couch. Unfortunately, Hughes showed up just in time to see the bullfighter fleeing out the front door. He slapped Ava so hard she dislocated her jaw. When he turned and walked away, she picked up a large heavy bronze bell and knocked him out cold.

Hughes sent Ava hundreds of roses and gardenias by way of an apology. He offered Ava the world and when she consented to see him, he flew her to Tijuana, where an entire restaurant had been reserved exclusively for them. He gave her another new Cadillac and offered her anything she wanted. Knowing her request was impossible, but craving it anyway, she replied, 'I want a big tub of orange ice cream!' Two hours later a limousine pulled up in front of the Westwood apartment and a chauffeur brought Ava an enormous tub of orange ice cream with a simple card, 'Love, Howard'.

When her Cadillac needed repairing, he told her to take it to Hughes Aircraft and he'd see to it personally. They argued over something trivial, and before making up, Ava received a call that her car was ready. She picked it up, drove two miles, and the engine fell out. 'I was told he had it wired,' Ava said, 'That son of a bitch!'

Four years in Hollywood brought Ava little happiness other than Howard's flying her to romantic destinations. He wanted to support her, but Ava was too proud for that. She stayed in the house he leased for her only when he was in town.

One evening at the Mocambo, Ava was approached by producer Seymour Nebenzal who was doing *Whistle Stop* at United Artists. He asked her if she would be interested in playing the female lead opposite George Raft. Ava was not his first choice for the role, but everyone else had turned down the part, and MGM was asking only $5000 to loan her out. She played Mary, a woman with a mysterious and shady past who returns to a tiny whistle-stop Illinois industrial town where her lover (George Raft) has become a loafer and a drunk. The owner of a local hotel and saloon becomes strongly attracted to Mary, while her downbeat lover is almost forced into theft and murder by the bartender.

The film's director, Leonide Moguy, noticed right away that Ava was a product of MGM's Lillian Burns, but he hoped to get a natural performance out of her by rehearsing patiently until she was relaxed. It took Moguy longer than expected because Ava was consulting with Burns every morning before reporting on the set. He had the charm to pacify Ava into being herself. Burns was a great drama coach, he confessed, but an actress must learn to take over and use her natural abilities. For Ava it was mixing oil and water. But Moguy refused to give up. Screenwriter Philip Yordan realised that neither Ava Gardner nor George Raft knew anything about acting so he rewrote the opening scene with her standing on the station platform wearing a mink coat and diamond ring. 'They couldn't speak the lines,' Yordan said, 'so it was done in monosyllables.'

Raft: What's that?
Ava: A ring.
Raft: Where did you get it?
Ava: Chicago.
Raft: From whom?
Ava: A man.
Raft: What man?

Whistle Stop was finished in six weeks. United Artists decided to preview it in Pomona with no fanfare. Ava slipped into the theatre wearing a scarf and sunglasses. She was horrified. Her acting was stiff and bland but when she kissed Raft with her mouth open, men in the audience reacted. Throughout the film she had the male viewers sitting up. It was then Ava realised it wasn't only her acting that sold tickets at the box office. It didn't matter whether she talked or not. She didn't want to be a sex object in movies, but Ava knew she would have to accept this if she wanted to stay in Hollywood.

To everyone's amazement the reviews were good. *Motion Picture Herald* said, 'With the dynamics of Gardner and Raft in it, *Whistle Stop* is certainly not a dull place.' *Variety* wrote, 'Miss Gardner does her best work to date as the girl who must have her man.'

Ava returned to MGM with her head held high, but she remained on their loan-out list of players. 'They never took much interest in me,' she said. 'I can't say I blame them very much.'

Ava was introduced to band leader Artie Shaw at the Mocambo. She had been a big fan of his, danced to his music and collected his unforgettable records of 'Dancing in the Dark', 'Copenhagen', 'The Back Bay Shuffle', and 'Begin the Beguine'. Ava was completely under his spell after a few dates and moved into his house on Bedford Drive near Sunset Boulevard. Bappie, who wanted her sister to marry Howard Hughes, did everything she could to discourage Ava. MGM was disgusted, but the publicity department convinced gossip columnists not to print the truth because '. . . this is only a phase with Ava'. L.B. Mayer might have dropped her option had she not been married to Mickey Rooney, but MGM offered nothing in the way of good or bad roles to divert her attention away from Shaw, who considered the studio system degrading. He convinced Ava it was the basis for her insecurity, which, he emphasised, should be analysed by his therapist May

Romm. He set up appointments for Ava three times a week. 'It really fucked me up,' she said. Despite Shaw's effort to create an intellectual beauty, Ava became bored with his choice of books, friends and therapy.

The consensus in Hollywood was that Ava's affair with the band leader was coming to an end. Friends witnessed embarrassing fights at parties, though it was usually Shaw who verbally attacked Ava about not wearing her shoes or curling up her feet on the couch. 'That's uncivilised,' he hissed. 'You're not in the tobacco fields now!' Observers wondered why she didn't hit Artie over the head and knock him out cold as she'd done with Hughes. The reason was simple. She had loved Howard, but she was in love with Artie.

Bappie was appalled when Ava told her she was marrying Artie on 17 October 1945 at the home of Judge Stanley Mosk in Beverly Hills. Howard Strickling said it was the only thing they could do. 'The live-in affair was public knowledge. If Ava had stayed with her sister, marriage might not have been the only solution.'

The Shaws spent their honeymoon in New York because Artie was appearing with his band at the Paramount Theatre. With time on her hands, and to impress her husband, Ava browsed through bookstores with enthusiasm. She chose Kathleen Windsor's best seller, *Forever Amber*. Artie went through the roof. 'If ever catch you reading shit like that again,' he bellowed, 'I'll throw you out!'

Ironically, author Kathleen Windsor would be the next Mrs Artie Shaw.

When Ava returned to Hollywood she was approached by producer Mark Hellinger about a starring role in a film based on Ernest Hemingway's famous short story, 'The Killers.' Hellinger had seen Ava in *Whistle Stop* and thought she would be perfect as Kitty, a beautiful and treacherous gang moll. Newcomer Burt Lancaster was making his first screen appearance as the killer Swede.

When MGM refused to loan out Ava to Universal for *The Killers*, she made sure Mayer would hear about her ranting and raving to anyone within hearing distance. 'Bastards!' she cried to Lillian Burns. Hellinger knew it was only a matter of money. He convinced Universal to offer a thousand a week to MGM for Ava, who was making $350. The deal was made, and *The Killers* was applauded by critics. *Look* magazine chose Ava as the most promising newcomer of 1947 and Ernest Hemingway said it was the first film of any of his work that he genuinely admired. Ava would eventually appear in two more movie adaptations from his novels and she became one of Hemingway's very close friends.

Bouncy and happy, Ava came home at the end of each day with a cheerful, 'What's for dinner?' Artie put up with it for a few months until he finally sat her down. 'I pay the rent, the utilities, the gardener, the help,' he said. 'I buy the food, your clothes and take care of business. What do you do for me, Ava?'

'I take college courses and go to therapy and read every book you give to me.'

'Lana couldn't cook but the table was set when I got home. Why don't you tell me what we're having for dinner?'

The marriage didn't last long enough for Artie to find out. She left him on 8 July 1946, the day after Howard Hughes was critically injured in a plane crash. When he came out of surgery. he asked to see only a few friends, one of whom was Ava.

On 16 August, Ava quietly filed for divorce in Superior Court. She charged Artie with cruelty and 'grievous mental suffering'. She told the judge, 'He wanted me to contribute to the conversation with his friends. When I did he told me to shut up . . . that I didn't know what I was talking about. Everything had to be done his way. I was embarrassed. Everyone was.'

Two days after his divorce from Ava was granted, Artie married author Kathleen Windsor. When the marriage ended two years later, Windsor said, 'Never by any stretch of my own magination or anything I could find by research in any library, could I gain the knowledge brought me by being the wife of Artie Shaw. He told me what books to read and I read them. He told me what clothes to wear and I wore them. He told me what I must think on every subject conceivable and would tolerate no difference of opinion.'

Lana Turner, the third Mrs Shaw, commented sarcastically, 'Artie was my entire college education.'

Ava said, 'I left before he had a chance to flunk me.'

Six weeks after Howard Hughes's near-fatal plane crash, he and Ava resumed their torrid affair, but she was also involved with director John Huston, actors Peter Lawford and Fernando Lamas and singer Mel Tormé.

Then she got a call from Clark Gable, but not for a date.

'Ava, I wish you'd reconsider doing *The Hucksters* with me. I had a showdown with Mayer and he's cleaning up the script.'

'I'm tired of playing whores,' she said.

'She's not a whore, honey. She's lovable and sexy.'

'Bullshit!'

'You'd rather go on suspension than work with me?' Gable asked.

'When I first came to this dump called Hollywood I saw you driving down Sunset and I almost crashed into the car ahead of me.'

'Then you'll do it?'

Ava laughed. 'How can I refuse?'

'We'll have a good time. You'll see.'

In *The Hucksters*, based on a novel by Frederic Wakeman, Ava plays a sensuous singer in love with a Madison Avenue advertising man (Gable) who prefers a demure widow (Deborah Kerr). Ava and Clark were attracted to one another from the start. Though he preferred blondes 'because brunettes look dirty to me', he made an exception with Ava, who used profanity like his late zany wife, Carole Lombard. MGM press agent George Nichols said, 'If anyone says Clark and Ava didn't have a fling, they're crazy. To deny it would be like denying the birds and the bees. I remember Gable looking at a group picture of MGM actresses and he said, "Aren't they beautiful – and I've had every one of 'em . . .".'

Both Ava and Clark were unsure of themselves doing *The Hucksters* and fluffed their lines often. She took the blame because the love scenes with Gable made her nervous, but he apologised to her. 'I'm sorry. I wasn't thinking straight. I'm so damned concerned because you don't think you're an actress. Well, after all these years, I'm not sure I'm an actor.'

Ava, in turn, felt compassion for Gable because his hands and head shook. She assumed he suffered from hangovers but he said it was the Dexedrine he was taking to lose the weight he had gained from too much drinking.

'In *The Hucksters* I had to sing to him,' Ava recalled. 'Clark used to leave the set at five, but on this day he stayed so he wouldn't have to sing to an empty nightclub. He straddled a chair and sat just off-camera. He stole my heart.'

Near the completion of *The Hucksters* Universal made a frantic call to MGM. Their leading lady had been taken ill. Could they borrow Ava immediately? MGM agreed, for $5000. Ava was rushed from Gable, who was wearing a dark-blue Madison Avenue suit, to an Oriental setting where Fred MacMurray, in a white tropical suit, was waiting to be kissed! She changed costumes and was told by the director to walk in front of the camera and into Fred's arms. 'I didn't even know the story line,' she said. For several weeks Ava simultaneously played a sexy nightclub singer in *The*

Hucksters and a married woman with amnesia and two husbands in *Singapore*. A technician commented, 'I remember Ava running to and from MGM, sometimes at night. Rather than primp and preen like most actresses do on a hectic schedule, she was making out her grocery list. I got the feeling acting was just a job – not a career to her.'

The Hucksters established Ava not only at MGM, but at the box office. She was praised for her sultry beauty and acting ability by critics who predicted she was 'going places'.

When Ava went to New York to promote *The Killers* in the autumn of 1947, she was introduced to Howard Duff, the voice of Sam Spade in the radio series. He had appeared on the stage in *Brute Force* and made his movie debut in the film version. At the time Duff was involved with actress Yvonne DeCarlo, but was hooked on Ava instantly. Before returning to California, she had one date with Duff who followed soon after signing with Universal for *Naked City*.

Ava was busy at the bullfights in Mexico or hiding out with Howard Hughes, who had just acquired RKO Pictures. Ava changed considerably after her divorce from Artie. She was restless. Make love and run. She was like a rocket that was all fired up with no place to go. She became a night person, but was usually in make-up or wardrobe before the others arrived in the morning. Ava was beginning to drink heavily but maintained her enormous Southern appetite, one reason she didn't get drunk.

During production of *One Touch of Venus*, Ava had a brief affair with her co-star Robert Walker, who was carrying an alcoholic torch for his former wife, Jennifer Jones. Ava's dates with Walker were all-night binges. She held her own on the set the next day. He did not and the cameraman was forced to shoot the back of his head in love scenes. She mothered him and he fell in love with her. If she refused to go out with Bob he became abusive, calling her at all hours and showing up on her doorstep in a rage. If Ava was staying home, Howard Duff was with her, answering the door and the telephone.

One Touch of Venus failed at the box office, but Ava was identified with Venus. She had posed topless for the statue that was considered too risqué for the film. A Grecian gown off one shoulder was just as sexy and Ava's only costume in the picture. Her extraordinary beauty and sense of timing in *One Touch of Venus* could not be overlooked, and MGM gave her star status. She was given Norma Shearer's old dressing room, the largest occupied by an MGM actress. The three-room suite consisted of a boudoir, bathroom, kitchen and the actual dressing room, which was lined with mirrors, light bulbs and closets. The studio hiked her weekly salary to $1,250 and publicised her as 'Hollywood's Glamour Girl of 1948'.

The Bribe was a dreadful film but Ava remembers it fondly because of her leading man, Robert Taylor. He was unhappily married to Barbara Stanwyck and Ava was no longer seeing Howard Duff. 'It was a glorious few months,' Ava said. 'Bob was a warm, generous and intelligent human being. We knew our affair was just that and nothing more.' Taylor often took Ava to his mother's house in the afternoons. When his mother found out and complained Taylor asked her, 'Would you rather I go to a cheap motel and be photographed?'

The Great Sinner with Gregory Peck was the first bone thrown to Ava by MGM. She was cast as the daughter of a Russian general who saves Peck from gambling his life away. Her elaborate period costumes were magnificent, but the film was not. One critic said there was depth to Ava's acting, but no depth in the dialogue.

The Great Sinner, however, was a breakthrough for Ava who was learning her trade at last. She spoke up about the small key spotlight on her face and took notice of other details pertaining to camera angles. Rather than demand, she asked technicians to give her advice and important tips on lighting, no longer sitting around reading movie magazines between takes. Just as Ava was changing her attitude toward her craft, MGM executives were changing their attitude toward L.B. Mayer, who was paying more attention to his racehorses and the courting of new young wife than MGM's $6,500,000 deficit. For the first time the studio's contract players were not winning Oscars or making the prestigious 'Best Ten' lists. It was the man to whom Mayer reported, Nicholas Schenck, president of Loew's Corp, who hired Dore Schary as vice president in charge of production at MGM on 1 July 1948. Though he put MGM in the black again, Schary was not popular with many of Mayer's family. It was sad as well as frightening to watch Father Mayer fight to keep his mother's chicken soup in the canteen and a sense of dignity in Leo the Lion. Ava was not particularly fond of Schary. He did, however, make her a household name by casting her in MGM films rather than loaning her out to other studios.

Norma Shearer and Greta Garbo retired from films in the early forties, and Joan Crawford had signed a contract with Warner Brothers, leaving the door open for Ava if she chose to take a serious interest in her profession. Also in her favour was the realism of the post-war years that overshadowed Mayer's attitude that all women should be beautiful and virginal, all men should be handsome, and together they would inspire wedding bells and apple blossoms. Schary would produce message pictures such as *The Asphalt Jungle*, *Red Badge of Courage* and *Battleground*. These films were a disgrace to Mayer who refused to accept a generation of realists, but he stayed with his beloved MGM and tried to rule compatibly with Dore Schary.

Meanwhile, Howard Hughes wanted Ava at RKO to do *My Forbidden Past*. She balked until she got a phone call from her co-star.

'Ava, this is Bob Mitchum. I need a favour.'

'Honey, the answer is "no".'

'I guess you know about my arrest for possession of marijuana.'

'Yeah, but you came through it, baby, and I admire you for that.'

'I came through it with the support of Howard Hughes. I'd have been tarred and feathered without him, Ava. I owe him a lot of money so how about it. Will you do the picture with me?'

'Hell, why not?'

My Forbidden Past involved an impecunious aristocratic New Orleans family embroiled in mysterious goings-on. Ava was instantly attracted to Bob Mitchum and he to her. When he drove her home after work, they discussed the 'situation'. Bob was losing his grip and wasn't sure what to do about the woman who was his boss's girlfriend.

'Suppose something happened between Ava and me,' he asked Hughes over the telephone.

'Like what?'

'Should I go to bed with her, is what I'm asking?'

'If you don't, everybody will think you're a pansy.'

'If you want to discuss your problems, I'll discuss mine,' Mitchum exclaimed.

'You're like a pay toilet,' Hughes laughed. 'You don't give a shit for nothing, do you?'

Ava was determined to seduce Mitchum before the picture was finished. Her last opportunity was on tour to promote *My Forbidden Past* in Chicago, but she failed. It wasn't Ava's vanity as much as knowing Bob was deliberately holding back. 'If I could have gotten him in bed, I would have,' she said. Disappointed and depressed over the Mitchum affair, Ava got on a plane without telling anyone and returned to Los Angeles and Frank Sinatra whom she described as conceited, arrogant, and overpowering. This instant hostility was a precursor of a sudden romantic interest. Though Sinatra was a married man with three children, he had been involved with many women during his four years in Hollywood, but he could not get the elusive Ava out of his mind. After a few casual dates, they became intimate. 'Oh, God, it was magic,' Ava said. 'We became lovers forever – eternally. I truly felt that no matter what happened we would always be in love.'

In January 1950 her affair with Sinatra was exposed when he took Ava with him to the Shamrock Hotel in Houston, Texas, for a two-week singing engagement. A reporter spotted them in a cosy restaurant and approached their table with a camera. Ava screamed and covered her mink coat. Frank threw down his napkin and pushed back his chair. The owner of the restaurant hurried over to the table and asked the photographer to leave, but the incident was reported in the *Houston Post* and picked up by other newspapers around the world. As a result, L.B. Mayer negotiated a settlement with Sinatra, whose contract with MGM was terminated. Ava faced an angry Mayer, who called her a whore. 'You were denied permission to leave Los Angeles,' he said, 'because I knew where you were going and with whom. Have you read your fan mail? They're calling you a bitch and a Jezebel. The Catholic Church is up in arms, and the Legion of Decency has threatened to ban your films.'

'Frank's wife Nancy is filing for divorce.'

'They're Catholics. Don't bet on it. So I'm sending you to Spain for *Pandora and the Flying Dutchman* with James Mason. That's what you wanted, isn't it?'

'Mr Mayer, are you sending me abroad to get me away from Frank, or giving me a picture I requested?'

'I want you to get away until things quiet down,' Mayer replied.

On her way to Spain Ava decided to stop over in New York for Frank's all-important opening at the Copacabana. He faced an unfriendly crowd that did not fall silent when he made his entrance. With a blend of the sweet-and-sour he said, 'Hey, this is my opening night. Give me a break.' But Sinatra did not have 'that old black magic' that used to thrill the bobbysoxers. His voice was weak, and his nerves about to crack. The tightening in his throat was getting progressively worse knowing Ava was leaving for Europe. At this juncture he feared losing her more than losing his voice.

When Artie Shaw invited Frank and Ava to see him perform at Bop City and to a dinner party at his apartment after the show, Sinatra was enraged. He detested Shaw, who remarked, 'Yes, I think Frank hated me. He wanted to sing with my band, but I told him I didn't use boy singers.' Frank had warned Artie in the past not to see or speak to Ava – or else. Shaw pointed to Frank's bodyguard and cracked, 'If you're so tough, why do you need him?'

Coddling, consoling and mothering Frank's anxieties became a bore to Ava. When his daughter called begging him to come home, Ava saw him about to give in. She doubted his ability to live alone while she was in Spain, knowing he could easily go back to Nancy. So Ava turned to Artie Shaw, who was always available to counsel her. When a violent argument erupted with Frank about it, she went with another couple to see Artie perform at Bop City and returned to his apartment for the dinner party. Frank went back to the Hampshire House Hotel, expecting to find Ava there. Incensed, he called Shaw's apartment, got her on the phone and said, 'I just called to say goodbye.'

'Where are you going, Frank? Can't I come with you?'

'Not where I'm going, baby.'

Ava heard a pistol shot, a pause, and then another shot. She dropped the phone, screamed hysterically, and, accompanied by Artie and friends, rushed to the hotel where she found Sinatra sitting up in bed reading a book. Ava found out later that he had fired the bullets into his mattress and switched it with the mattress in another room with the help of Columbia Records chief Manie Sachs. The police were called by several people who heard the shots, but the truth was covered up quickly and cleverly.

The following day MGM demanded that Ava leave for Spain. She had delayed the trip several times because Frank needed her, but after playing the fool to Sinatra's fake suicide she wanted very much to busy herself with work. Frank's phone calls to her in Spain about the divorce proceedings were not encouraging. As Nancy Sinatra's future plans wavered so did Ava's moods vary from anger to relief to despair over the relationship. Her salvation was the role of Pandora, the lazy spirit in Spain, dancing the flamenco, and drinking with bullfighter Mario Cabre in the dark corners of unpretentious nightclubs. He serenaded her and wrote verses of everlasting devotion and love. To further his career in films, his odes to Ava were published. MGM took advantage of this and publicised the romantic twosome, hoping it would offset the Sinatra scandal.

Frank was so beside himself over Ava and the bullfighter, he suffered a submucosal haemorrhage of the throat and was warned by doctors to rest for two weeks. When word got out that Sinatra was on his way to meet Ava, Mario Cabre told reporters he would not leave Spain alive. MGM made sure the bullfighter was filming another segment of the film in Italy when Frank arrived with a $10,000 diamond and emerald necklace for Ava. His stay in rainy Spain did little to heal Frank's throat or relieve his anger over Mario Cabre. In later years Ava admitted getting drunk and being intimate with the bullfighter only once, but once was enough for Frank who never forgave her.

Ava flourished in Spain. She refused to use a double for the scene in which Pandora swims nude to the Dutchman's anchored schooner. In the moonlight the camera shot a rear view of Ava climbing aboard, but the final editing showed only her wet hair and bare shoulders.

In June 1950 Ava moved into a handsome London flat in Park Lane. Frank flew in for an appearance at the London Palladium on 12 July and was acclaimed by the British press. They were presented to Princess Elizabeth and Prince Philip after a movie benefit. It was a very special occasion for Ava, magnificent in a strapless ivory silk gown, and especially for Frank following his triumphant performance at the Palladium. British reporters were considerate and scarce, offering the famous couple peace and a good deal of freedom.

George Sidney, who was to direct the colourful musical *Showboat*, wanted Ava to play Julie, the tragic half-caste. She tested for the part, mouthing to Lena Horne's voice. 'Ava had a lilting accent that suited Julie perfectly,' Sidney said. 'It's been said that Ava's voice wasn't good enough. That's not true. She and Frank pleaded with me to let her do her own voice and it worked. It was deeply moving. But the studio insisted we use a professional singer. Ava was very disappointed. On the soundtrack album they used her voice, however. She was very proud of that.'

Producer Arthur Freed said, 'I knew we had it made when we got Ava for *Showboat*. She was wonderful. I don't think any close-ups were as breathtaking as those she did in the picture. Dore Schary wanted Dinah Shore to play Julie. She asked me point-blank why I didn't give her the part and I said, 'Because you're not a whore. Ava is. When she sings "Bill", she's every streetwalker you ever saw.' I don't mean to say Ava was a prostitute, but she had the heart of a prostitute in a way that would rip everybody else's heart out just watching her.' Critics liked Ava's Julie, too, but emphasised her beauty and that was unfortunate, because *Showboat* was a breakthrough for her as a fine actress.

Sinatra's career was not faring so well. Ava called Howard Hughes for help, and Frank sang two songs in RKO's *Double Dynamite* which led to *Meet Danny Wilson* at Universal with Shelley Winters who said, 'Frank was in the process of divorcing Nancy to marry Ava. I think he thought that's what he wanted. His children were quite young and there were always psychiatrists and priests and his kids visiting him on the set. Everyone in Hollywood knew of his struggle to divorce or not to divorce.'

Shelley and Frank fought bitterly. She walked out and refused to answer the phone until she heard Nancy Sinatra was trying to get through. In tears she asked a favour of her friend. 'Shelley, Frank doesn't get the $25,000 for the picture until it's finished. The bank might foreclose the mortgage on the house. My children are going to be out on the street. Please complete the picture, or they won't give me the $25,000.'

Ava wasn't thrilled about playing a tempestuous newspaper woman in *Lone Star* about Andrew Jackson's fight for independence against the Union. She might have gone on suspension to avoid doing it, but Ava needed the money. Besides, Clark Gable was her co-star and, like *The Hustlers*, he hated the film as much as she did. The King had aged considerably and rumour had it he was in first stages of Parkinson's disease. Ava's heart went out to him again, and she guided him through love scenes to conceal his head shaking. Spencer Tracy was a frequent visitor to the set and got a kick out of Ava who complained about a scene in the film that Schary cut out. 'All I was doing was happily walking down the street after spending the night with Clark.'

'Yeah,' Tracy said. 'Since Dore took over, nobody gets laid around here.'

Frank was on the set often, too, much to Ava's dismay because his gloomy aura disturbed her fun with Gable and Tracy. To get rid of him she announced plans to vacation in Mexico when *Lone Star* was finished. Not wanting Ava out of his sight, Frank begged Nancy for his freedom. 'If I cannot get a divorce, where is there for me to go and what is there for me to do?'

Hedda Hopper hinted in her column that Nancy was losing public sympathy and support from Hollywood insiders. It was time she considered the children after a year and a half of sizzling publicity.

On 22 June, L.B. Mayer told Nicholas Schenck to make a choice. 'Either Schary goes or I go.' Schenck was more than delighted to get rid of Mayer, who had used his contacts in Washington to get what he wanted over the years. Mayer's departure from MGM was the beginning of the end for the studio system in Hollywood. The reigning Golden Era stars were making too much money and their contracts would not be renewed. Clark Gable and Lana Turner were victims in the early fifties. 'I was an orphan,' Lana said. 'I didn't know how to make a hotel or airline reservation. For a long time I waited for my limousine that never came to pick me up. I was an orphan. MGM prepared us for stardom but not for life . . .'

Schary gave Ava a $20,000 bonus and promised her better roles. She took the money and shrugged off his pledge. She trusted only Howard Strickling who was there when she needed him but also very concerned about her image. He discussed Frank's outbursts of hostility with reporters and stressed the importance of good press relations. What he didn't say was that she was on her way up and Frank was on his way down.

After her long talk with Strickling, Ava tried to calm Sinatra on their flight to Mexico, but reporters were at every stop along the way. Frank, on the verge of a nervous breakdown, lost control. He called *Newsweek* reporters sons of bitches, and threatened to shoot a photographer in Acapulco. When they returned to Los Angeles their private plane landed in a noncommercial area of the airport where Sinatra's Cadillac was waiting. Behind the wheel, he was blinded by floodlights. 'Kill that light! Kill that light!' he shouted. He stepped on the gas and pinned reporters against a fence. The car's bumper grazed the leg of one newsman. Frank leaned out of the window and yelled, 'Next time I'll kill you!'

William Eccles, an airport photographer, described what happened to him. 'Sinatra turned the car into me to scare me away. I figured he'd swerve so I shot a picture and didn't get out of his way. He slammed on the brake, and at the last minute I jumped. I went up over the fender and rolled off on my stomach, dropping the camera. It was a case of hit-and-run. I could have sued.' Eccles did file a criminal complaint against Sinatra but withdrew it after Frank wrote a letter of apology.

Over the Labor Day weekend the couple went to Lake Tahoe with friends. On 1 September 1951, the *New York Daily Mirror*'s headline read: SINATRA FELLED BY SLEEPING PILLS. The story reported his attempted suicide after a violent quarrel with Ava who admitted that was the day she told Frank about spending one night with Mario Cabre. He exploded and called her names. Ava packed her bags, drove back to Los Angeles, got a call that Frank had taken an overdose and drove back to Lake Tahoe. 'He tricked me back to his bedside,' Ava said. 'They didn't even have to pump his stomach. It was all an act. I could have killed him.'

But when all seemed lost, Nancy Sinatra was granted an interlocutory decree of divorce on 31 October 1951 in Santa Monica, California. Howard Strickling offered to help Ava with her wedding, but Frank wanted nothing to do with the studio. He told Ava they would be married in Philadelphia at the Germantown mansion belonging to Isaac Levy, founder of C.B.S. Frank asked his close friend Manie Sachs to assist with the arrangements and give the bride away. On Friday, 2 November, they picked up their marriage license. Since Pennsylvania law required a three-day waiting period, they returned to the Hampshire House in New York. On Saturday night James Mason and his wife joined them at the Sugar Hill nightclub in Harlem. Ava became insanely jealous because Frank was flirting with an attractive woman sitting at another table. Ava looked at Pamela Mason and said, 'It looks like I'm through with him. I can't even trust him on the eve of our wedding.' She screamed at Frank and he yelled back. 'The fucking wedding is off!' Ava announced. With the help of Bappie and Frank's parents, she changed her mind. Finally on Wednesday 7 November, Ava Gardner, wearing a cocktail-length dress of mauve-toned marquisette with a strapless top of pink taffeta, started down the stairs leaned on the arm of Manie Sachs and married the love of her life Frank Sinatra. The bride and groom exchanged thin platinum wedding bands. His present to her was a sapphire-blue mink stole. She gave him a large, heavy, gold locket with a St Christopher medal on one side and a St Francis medal on the other. Inside was her photograph.

'Well,' Frank beamed, 'we made it.'

Ava, true to her MGM breeding, sent a wire to Howard Strickling and signed it 'Ava Sinatra'. The newlyweds left in such a hurry that Ava forgot her suitcase. Their chartered Beechcraft landed in Florida at dawn. The press respected their privacy at the Green Heron Hotel, but took some informal photos of them strolling along the beach in the Sunny Isles district on a chilly day. Hand in hand, they walked barefoot, Frank's trousers rolled up and Ava wearing his jacket over a casual blouse and skirt. When the trousseau suitcase arrived they flew to the plush Hotel Nacional in Havana where they managed to honeymoon without an argument . . . a record for 'The Battling Sinatras', as they would be dubbed by the press.

Reporting back to MGM, Ava was thrilled to find out Ernest Hemingway wanted her to do *The Snows of Kilimanjaro*, based on one of his short stories. She was perfect for the part of Cynthia, the twenties girl whom the big game hunter, played by Gregory Peck, loves and loses and finds again as she's dying in a Spanish Civil War battle. Frank, in a panic, said he needed her at his Paramount opening in New York. Ava spoke to director Henry King about her dilemma. 'If you can promise me I'll be finished with *Kilimanjaro* in time to go with Frank to New York, he says it's okay.'

'I'll do my best,' King replied.

'You'll have to do better than that. Frank's not doing very well. I must be with him.'

King revised the filming schedule and the pressure was on. Frank phoned every day to make sure there were no delays. These calls were nerve-wracking to Ava and others in the cast, who sensed not only her nervousness but fear as well. King had promised to film Cynthia's scenes in ten days, but the Civil War sequence took longer than expected. He told Ava, 'You'll have to stay on an extra day. I'm truly sorry.'

'You're sorry?' she exclaimed in tears. 'That motherfucker is going to give me hell when I tell him and I'm just going to sit there and take it.'

Sinatra *was* furious. He made her last day of filming sheer hell by phoning repeatedly to make sure she was finished. Under the circumstances, King considered Ava's performance superb. 'No one else could have given Cynthia the sensitivity and the bruised quality that Ava imparted.' *Variety* said, 'Miss Gardner makes the part of Cynthia a warm, appealing, alluring standout.'

Sinatra did not fare as well. The *New York World-Telegram* wrote about his Paramount performance: 'Gone on Frankie '42, Gone in '52 and what a difference a decade makes – empty balcony.' Reporters joked about an interview with a bobbysoxer at the Paramount. When asked how she liked Frankie, she replied, 'I think Frankie Laine is wonderful!' In Chicago, Sinatra appeared at the Chez Paree nightclub which seated 1,200. Only 120 people showed up.

Ava signed a new ten-year contract with MGM, calling for twelve movies at $100,000 per picture, and planted her feet and hands in wet cement at a special ceremony in front of Grauman's Chinese Theater on 21 October 1952. It would take Sinatra thirteen more years to achieve this honour. Jealous and resentful, he demanded Ava take a vacation with him in Hawaii instead of doing *Sombrero*. She was suspended without pay and punished with a mediocre western, *Ride, Vaquero* with Robert Taylor and Howard Keel. It was filmed in Kanab, Utah – a hot, dusty, dead town with one seedy hotel called Perry's. Without any air conditioning Ava found life unbearable. 'I wish I was dead,' she told Taylor, who tried convincing their hard-drinking womanizing director John Farrow to find Ava decent living quarters. He ignored the request. It was Perry, owner of the hotel, who offered Ava his small house near town. A typical (and very amusing) review of *Ride, Vaquero* was, 'Nothing could have been as static as the dusty shenanigans of such buckaroos as Taylor, Gardner, and Keel. In short, it rated not Tiffany's window but the old cat bin.'

Ava could afford a bad film and few moviegoers remember it. At this stage of her career she paid little or no attention to reviews. She said in later years that she continued making movies 'for the loot'. It was true that she needed it to support her and Frank. He was having recurrent problems with his voice. Friends referred to these throat infections as 'guilt germs.' He was spending too much time with his family as far as Ava was concerned. Her possessiveness of Frank extended to his children and his cronies, who were always hanging around. She put up with them until one night Frank ignored her for two hours in a restaurant while he carried on a lengthy conversation with his buddies. She left and wasn't missed until Frank was ready to go home. So it was no wonder that Ava went berserk when she thought he was singing 'All of Me' to his former girlfriend Marilyn Maxwell at the Riviera in New Jersey. Ava stormed out of the nightclub, flew back to Hollywood, and mailed her wedding band to Frank at the Riviera with a bitter note. 'I've got problems,' he told Sammy Davis Jr. 'That's what happens when you get hung up on a chick.'

Ten days later the Sinatras reconciled in Los Angeles and were seen holding hands at the bullfights in Tijuana . . . happier than ever – the calm before the storm. Within days they would be involved in a notorious incident that Hollywood insiders whisper about to this day. Tabloids, including *Confidential* magazine, were very explicit with their versions and shocked readers into believing the sordid rumour.

After one of his famous battles with Ava, Frank said he was leaving. 'And if you want to know where I am,' he shouted, 'in Palm Springs fucking Lana Turner.' Ava, soaking in the bathtub, thought that was very funny until she remembered that Frank and Lana had had a serious love affair. Hoping to get even and catch Frank 'in the act', Ava drove to his house in Palm Springs. As she was peering through the windows, Lana's business manager Ben Cole appeared at the back door. 'Ava, is that you?'

Lana explained that Frank said it was all right if she and Ben spent the weekend at his house. 'Let's have a party then,' Ava said, settling down next to Lana with lots of gossip and a bottle of booze. A few minutes later, Frank burst through the front door in a rage. 'You girls carving me up?' he yelled. Ava laughed and said, 'I thought you would be here fucking Lana.'

Sinatra sneered. 'I wouldn't touch that two-bit whore if you paid me!'

Lana burst into tears and left with Ben Cole as the Battling Sinatras went at it. 'Get out of my house!' he shouted.

Ava smirked. 'Ha! We're married so it's my house, too!'

'I'm going to call the police.'

'Call the fucking police,' Ava yelled, throwing her possessions in the driveway.

The police arrived and told Ava to 'calm down'.

'I'm very calm,' Ava smiled. '. . ..just getting my possessions out of this fucking house, that's all!'

The rumour of a lesbian relationship between Ava and Lana started with Louella Parsons, who headlined her column, FRANK SINATRA AND AVA GARDNER SEPARATE WHEN HE FINDS HER WITH LANA TURNER. The *L.A. Times* followed with: SINATRA–AVA BOUDOIR ROW BUZZES. TOO MUCH LEFT TO THE IMAGINATION.

After the Palm Springs incident, Ava refused to take Frank's calls and eventually changed her phone number. In desperation he called columnist Earl Wilson to print a plea on his behalf. When Ava read, 'Frankie Ready To Surrender; Wants Ava Back; Any Terms' she called Frank, and, together, they attended a rally for Democratic presidential candidate, Adlai Stevenson. Ava walked on stage in a black satin strapless gown, stepped before the microphone and said, 'I can't do anything myself, but I can introduce a wonderful, wonderful man. I'm a great fan of his myself. Ladies and gentlemen, my husband, Frank Sinatra.'

But Lana said the aftermath was very painful because rumours of her lesbian relationship with Ava lingered on. Years later, on a visit to London Lana invited Ava to her hotel for cocktails but asked her male secretary Taylor Pero to join them, '. . . because if I'm alone with her the rumours will start all over again.'

Mogambo was the remake of the 1932 film *Red Dust* with Clark Gable and Jean Harlow. The new version revolved around Gable, a big game hunter in Africa, a married woman (Grace Kelly) on safari with her husband, and Ava as chorus girl Honey Bear. Sinatra was jealous of his wife's leading men, especially the recently divorced Clark Gable who was dating a string of beautiful young ladies. Knowing Ava would be in Africa for five months tortured him even more. She wanted to be with Frank on their first wedding anniversary and urged him to accompany her to the Dark

Continent. Before he left, Sinatra approached Harry Cohn, the hard-bitten, blunt head of Columbia Pictures.

'I read *From Here to Eternity*,' Sinatra told him. 'I want to audition for the part of Private Maggio.'

'You're a singer, not an actor, Frank.'

'Yeah, but I have a feeling about this part. I knew Maggio. I went to school with him in Hoboken. I was beaten up with him. I might have been Maggio.'

'Eli Wallach's set to play the part,' Cohn said.

'But you haven't signed him yet, and I want the chance to audition. About the money . . .'

'Who's talking money?' Cohn laughed. 'I used to get $150,000 a picture.'

'Used to. I'll do it for a thousand a week.'

'Jesus, you really want the part, don't you, Frank? Well let me think it over.'

Sinatra knew Cohn wasn't interested in him. He called his agents and said, 'I'll do it for nothing.'

Cohn relished telling the story about Frank's pleading. 'He owes $110,000 in back taxes, but he offered to pay me if he could do Maggio.'

Ava spoke to Cohn's wife, Joan, explaining the seriousness of the situation. 'I'm afraid Frank might kill himself,' she said. 'All I'm asking is that Harry give him a screen test. That's all. Another thing. Frank must never know I spoke to you about this.' Joan promised to do what she could. This put a whole new light on the situation as far as Cohn was concerned. He might want Ava Gardner for a picture some day and she would flatly refuse if Frank wasn't given a chance to test for the part of Maggio.

On 7 November 1952, the Sinatras celebrated their first wedding anniversary on a stratocruiser bound for Nairobi. He gave her a diamond-studded dome ring, and her gift to him was a thin platinum wristwatch. Clark Gable was at the airport and drove them to the New Stanley Hotel. 'Enjoy this place,' Gable remarked, ''cause we spend most of our time on location.'

'Then let's have a party!' Ava exclaimed. 'After all, this is the first time I've been married for a whole year.'

While a phonograph blasted Sinatra singing 'All Or Nothing At All', Gable admired Ava's new ring. 'Very fancy,' he commented.

'And very expensive,' Ava cracked. 'I should know. I paid for it!'

The New Stanley Hotel was a luxury on an occasional weekend off. But MGM's budget for *Mogambo* provided a comfortable location settlement near Mount Kenya. The 1,800-yard landing strip was literally hacked out of the jungle. Tents were upholstered and lavish. Thirteen of them were dining rooms. There was a movie theatre, an entertainment section with pool tables and a hospital with an X-ray unit. Gable, who arrived in Africa ahead of the others, told Ava, 'We have hot and cold running water, too. That wood fire in the back of each tent serves two purposes. It heats the water and keeps the lions away at night.'

'Is that why everyone was given a gun?' Ava asked, taking out a .38 police special revolver from her handbag.

'No, honey. There's a Mau Mau uprising, but we have a large police force. No worries.'

'Says you with that high-powered hunting rifle.'

'If it'll help,' Gable said with a straight face, 'MGM's paying the witch doctors for favourable omens.'

Sinatra said sarcastically, 'Maybe I should talk to those guys!'

It was Ava who needed all the love and support she could get, however. Not only was Frank taking out his problems on her, but director John Ford was as well. He wanted Maureen O'Hara to play Honey Bear and resented Ava from the start. Nothing she did for the camera was right. Ford needled her relentlessly in the 120-degree temperature. When she'd had enough, Ava let him have it, using her most vile language, and stormed off the set. He followed and cornered her in a secluded spot. 'You're damned good, Ava. Take it easy.'

When she burst into tears, Ford sat down with her in a shaded spot. 'I'm pregnant and sick as hell,' she cried.

'Congratulations. Frank must be a very happy guy.'

'He doesn't know and you're not going to tell him. I don't want a baby now, John. This is not the right time. Frank heard from Harry Cohn who wants him in Los Angeles right away for a screen test. When he leaves, I'll have the abortion in London. Can you get permission from the studio without letting them know I'm pregnant? You know how these things get around.'

Ford contacted MGM officials in Hollywood requesting permission for Ava to fly to London for a checkup. The reply read: 'Feel Gardner's trip unwise for many obvious reasons. Suggest you use your persuasiveness and have lady stay put.' Ford wired back: 'Gardner giving superb performance . . . very charming and co-operative . . . however really quite ill since arrival in Africa and deem it imperative London consultation otherwise tragic results . . . will not affect schedule . . . weather here miserable but we are trying . . . repeat . . . believe trip imperative.'

On 23 November 1952, with her MGM publicist and wife of cameraman Robert Surtees, Ava flew to London and checked into the Chelsea Hospital for Women where she had the abortion. When the press found out she was ill, her publicist said Ava was suffering from dysentery and severe anaemia. Twelve pounds thinner she returned to Nairobi and a telegram from Frank saying he would be back in Africa for the holidays. As Christmas approached, the *Mogambo* company became a close-knit family.

In the beginning Ava and Grace Kelly had a strained relationship. Though the future Princess of Monaco had had her share of love affairs despite the strictness of her family, she was not a woman of the world. The 24-year-old beauty told a friend, 'I'm doing a picture in Africe with *old* Clark Gable and *old* Ava Gardner and *old* John Ford.' But the real Grace Kelly would surface in Africa under the tutelage of a lover, Clark Gable, a gal with a raw tongue from North Carolina, and a tough director who referred to Grace as perfect for the prudish Linda in *Mogambo*, 'You know, the frigid dame that's really a pip between the sheets.'

It was apparent that Gardner and Kelly were good friends when they walked past a group of Watusi warriors. Ava turned to Grace and said, 'I wonder if their cocks are as big as they say.' Grace blushed but giggled when Ava pulled up one of the Watusi's loincloths and a magnificent penis gleamed in the sunshine. Grace stared and Ava shrugged, 'Frank has a bigger one.'

The tables turned when Grace had a spat with Gable in the middle of the night and ran to Ava who said, 'I told Gracie her nose was pink and that meant she'd had too much to drink. She wanted a commitment from Clark who wasn't ready for that so Gracie ran out in the darkness. He was worried that a lion had had her for a late-night snack and showed up, rifle in hand, to take Gracie back to his tent. They were very cute together.'

Sinatra was also very romantic over the holidays despite his not hearing from Cohn about the screen test. He brought noodles and all the ingredients for his mother's home-made spaghetti sauce that Ava had achieved to perfection. She and Grace borrowed evening gowns from the wardrobe tent for Christmas Eve. The generator broke down but there was only laughter in the darkness. 'So we ate by candlelight,' Gable said. 'I thought it was a very warm and romantic setting. On Christmas Day we trimmed the tree, sang Christmas carols with the natives, and had a delicious dinner flown in by MGM – turkey, puddings, champagne and plenty of whisky. Ford recited "The Night Before Christmas" – something we never expected. We were a family and it was a very special feeling. I'll never forget it.'

Ava's recollection was how thoughtful Frank was, setting up a tiny tree in front of their tent and decorating it with little coloured lights. He rigged up a shower for Ava, too, consisting of a pump that took the river water through a pipe and a little wooden hut surrounding it. Ava was more thrilled with this effort than all the diamonds and mink coats in the world.

When Ford had a party for the British governor of Uganda, Sir Andrew Cohan, and his wife, the gruff director's joke on Ava backfired. 'Why don't you tell the governor what you see in that hundred-twenty-pound runt you're married to?' he asked her.

'Well,' Ava replied, 'there's ten pounds of Frank and one hundred and ten pounds of cock!'

Everyone, including the governor and his wife, thought it was hilarious. Ford was the only one who was shocked.

When Sinatra received word that the part of Maggio was his at $8000, he paced back and forth like a panther in front of his tent waving the cable. 'I'll show those mothers. I'll show them now!'

Ava celebrated her thirtieth birthday in a maze of confusion, happy for Frank but hating the return of egotist she had shunned in the mid-1940s when he was riding the crest of success. 'When Frank was on top he was a sacred monster convinced there was nobody in the world except himself,' she said. 'I liked him better when he was down and out.'

Shortly after Christmas, Gable asked Grace and the Sinatras to spend a weekend at a beach resort on the Indian Ocean. They had to take an old plane that Gable said was held together with baling wire. 'I kept thinking about the four of us – maybe the hottest properties in Hollywood – taking a chance like this. MGM would not have been happy.'

Perhaps it was during this peaceful interlude that Ava became pregnant again, but this time Frank knew about it and was so happy he began singing to her for the first time. 'There we were in a jeep,' she said. 'He was serenading me and I was throwing up.'

Before the *Mogambo* company settled in the desolate Isoila desert country in Uganda, the Sinatras flew to Paris for a few days. It was there that Frank received word to report for work in *From Here to Eternity*, which would be filmed in Hawaii. He said they would meet in London where Ava was scheduled to do *Knights of the Round Table*.

Following the completion of *Mogambo*, Ava and Grace stopped off in Rome. Cameraman Robert Surtees said, 'Ava wanted to see every whorehouse in the city one night. Grace wanted to go, too. At one dive we met a guy who became attracted to Grace and got in the back of the car to neck with her. Ava laughed till I thought she'd burst. We went from one place to another. Ava loved talking to the girls and exchanging raw and ribald jokes. We really tied one on that night.'

The girls flew to London to complete interior scenes for *Mogambo.* Grace, who was being groomed for stardom, stayed at the luxurious Savoy Hotel. Gable chose the quaint Connaught Hotel to avoid the press while Ava rented a place in Hyde Park Gate and kept open house day and night for her Hollywood peers who were in London for tax purposes.

In the spring of 1953 Ava checked into a nursing home near Wimbledon for an abortion. 'As long as I live I will never forget waking up and seeing Frank sitting next to the bed with tears in his eyes,' she said. 'But I think I was right. I still think I was right.'

Frank was booked on a three-month singing tour throughout Europe and asked Ava to accompany him. That he asked and did not insist was the new Sinatra. 'It will be a second honeymoon,' he said. 'I feel great and my voice is better than ever.' The trip got off to a bad start when their car broke down and they missed the flight to Milan. They were forced to fly to Rome where several Ava Gardner films were playing. Her fans and the press ignored Frank, who was booed midway through his concert in Naples because the crowd wanted, 'Ava! Ava!' The police were summoned and it was agreed that she should make an appearance to appease the angry crowd. She walked onstage, waved and walked off. The audience went wild – 'Ava! Ava!' When they booed Frank again, she boarded a train for Milan. A Neapolitan paper read, FRANK SINATRA BOOED AS AVA SKIPS TOWN.

In Denmark and Sweden, Sinatra sang to half-filled theatres. One Scandinavian newspaper said, MR SINATRA, GO HOME! Frank cancelled the rest of the tour and returned to London where Ava was finishing *Knights of the Round Table*. Impatient to rehearse for his singing engagement at the Riviera in New Jersey, he wanted Ava to leave with him. 'I'm almost finished with the film,' she said. 'What's the damn rush?'

'Finish your damn movie,' he shouted. 'I have a career, too, you know!' Their fight was so violent the other tenants called the landlord, who threatened to evict the Sinatras. Frank left without her and checked into the Waldorf Astoria on 12 August 1953. Ava went to Madrid for a few week's rest and kept her whereabouts secret. While on vacation, she was introduced to Spain's most famous bullfighter, Luis Miguel Dominguin, whom Hemingway described as a 'combination Don Juan and Hamlet'.

When Ava met Luis he was recovering from a bad goring in the stomach, but the tall, lean, handsome playboy attracted Ava, who wasn't ready for an affair just yet. When temptation almost got the better of her she flew to New York and checked into the Hampshire House. Frank read about his wife's arrival in the newspaper like everyone else. When Sinatra opened at the Riviera, Ava attended a Broadway show.

It was Frank's mother, Dolly, who got them together and Frank moved to the Hampshire House. But when he came in at four in the morning, Ava complained bitterly.

'Don't cut the corners too close on me, baby,' he said with his jaws clenched.

On 2 October they attended the New York opening of *Mogambo* at Radio City Music Hall and flew to Hollywood the next day. Frank went to Las Vegas to appear at the Sands Hotel and Ava attended the Los Angeles premiere of *Mogambo* without him. Newspapers described her as ravishing in a very low-cut clinging pastel satin gown with a slit in the skirt and a long white fox stole. The next day she left for Palm Springs and once again the Sinatras weren't speaking because he felt her place was with him in Vegas.

Everyone tried to effect a reconciliation – Dolly, Earl Wilson, Hedda Hopper, Louella Parsons and Bappie. Before either gave in, a picture of Frank with two Las Vegas chorus girls at a costume party appeared in the newspaper. Ava's attorney set up a meeting with Frank, who flew to Los Angeles, but did not keep the appointment. On 29 October 1953, MGM officially announced that the Sinatras had reluctantly exhausted every effort to reconcile their differences and could find no mutual basis on which to continue their marriage.

Frank couldn't eat or sleep. He told Earl Wilson, 'If it took seventy-five years to get a divorce, there wouldn't be any other woman.'

Ava laughed. 'Frank doesn't love me. He would rather go out with some other girl, almost any other girl. I'm on my way to Rome to do *The Barefoot Contessa* so the hell with it.'

On 18 November 1953, Sinatra slashed his wrists and was rushed to Mount Sinai Hospital in a shroud of secrecy. Doctors said Frank, whose weight had dropped to 118 pounds, was suffering from severe emotional strain. Ava had been through these suicide attempts before and did not respond this time. She was trying to let go, and only a complete break from Frank could clear her head.

Ava was completely engrossed in *The Barefoot Contessa*. She could identify with Maria Vargas, a Spanish dancer who becomes a famous movie star, falls in love and is killed by her impotent husband. 'One of my all-time favourite scenes,' Ava said, 'is when I perform a flamenco dance wearing a tight sweater and a cheap satin skirt. We shot this in an olive grove with one-hundred Gypsies beating time to a phonograph record. *The Barefoot Contessa* was the apogee of my life as a so-called star. MGM promoted me as "The World's Most Beautiful Animal", a label I couldn't shake.'

Ava's co-star was Humphrey Bogart, who was Sinatra's friend and sided with him. He nicknamed her the 'Boon Hill Gypsy' and asked her sarcastically, 'Do your bullfighter boyfriends know you're just a little hillbilly girl?' Without pausing Ava replied, 'That's what attracts them, honey.'

'I'll never figure you broads out. Half the world's female population would throw themselves at Frank's feet, and here you are flouncing around with guys who wear capes and little ballerina slippers.'

Bogart's wife, Lauren Bacall, joined him in Rome and brought Ava her favourite coconut cake from Frank. 'She couldn't have cared less,' Bacall said. 'She wanted me to put it down on some table she indicated – not a thank you, nothing. Her reaction had only to do with Frank – she was clearly through with him, but it wasn't that way on his side.'

Ava was looking forward to spending Christmas with Luis Miguel Dominguin in Madrid, but prior to leaving Italy she received a call from Sinatra, who said he would be in Spain to spend her Christmas Eve birthday with her. 'Why the hell does he do this?' she complained. Frank had a bad cold over the holidays, and when he was sick in bed, Ava slipped out to see her bullfighter. By the time she arrived back in Rome to finish *The Barefoot Contessa*, Frank was in a bad mood and she had caught his cold.

The beautiful Greek statue of Maria Vargas used in the cemetery scene was an exact replica of Ava's face and body. At first glance Frank wanted it, and the statue was installed in Sinatra's backyard as a shrine. Having failed to effect a reconcilation with Ava, he left Rome more downhearted than before, but on the night of 25 March 1954, Sinatra claimed his Oscar for Best Supporting Actor (*From Here to Eternity*). Ava, nominated for Best Actress (*Mogambo*) lost to Audrey Hepburn (*Roman Holiday*). Ava had bought a house in La Moraleja, Madrid's posh garden suburb, not in Hollywood for the Academy Awards. Two months later she rented a lodge in Lake Tahoe to establish residency for a Nevada divorce, but Frank refused to pay the legal costs so she did not pursue it until 1956.

Ava's next role was a halfe-cast in *Bhowani Junction* filmed in Pakistan.

Attracted to her leading man, Stewart Granger, who was married to actress Jean Simmons, Ava tried seducing him one night.

> 'She burst into my room,' he said. 'She was wearing a sari that clung to every curve of her body. I told her I was married to Jean. Ava said, "Oh, fuck Jean!" All I could manage was, "I'd love to, darling, but she's not here." Ava laughed and left. I took a lot of cold showers doing that movie, but I adored Ava with a passion, and we became very close friends. She called me a week or so before she died. She was watching *Bhowani Junction* on TV. "Weren't we beautiful then?" she said. I told her she was still beautiful and I meant it.'

Frank sent Ava a Facel Vega for her thirty-third birthday. She turned the car over twice, walking away uninjured . . .

On 19 April 1956, Ava attended the wedding of her good friend 'Gracie' to Prince Rainier of Monaco. As the bride walked down the aisle, she turned to her MGM publicist and whispered, 'Look at Grace's father. How I envy her. If only I had a father to lean on.' In deference to Ava, Sinatra did not attend the wedding. He did, however, see her in Spain when he was filming *The Pride and the Passion*. They spent one night together, hoping for a miracle to happen, but it was too late. Ava made the announcement that divorce papers had been signed in London.

After buying her house in Madrid, Ava was nearly broke. Whatever she earned, she spent. Saving money never occurred to her. Since she was one of the first celebrities to settle in Spain, bartenders never presented her with a bill. Restaurants and nightclubs were generous to her, also, because business flourished once word got around that Ava Gardner frequented their establishment. She soon found out there were few places to hide 'except in the caves where the Gypsies danced'. Ava remained a night person, getting out of bed in the afternoon. Lunch was around three, dinner at eleven, and supper at two in the morning. When the bars closed, she returned home with friends and continued partying long after dawn. A neighbour dropped by one morning and wasn't sure if the party was beginning or ending until he saw bodies lying around, some passed out drunk and others sound asleep. Not Ava. She was dancing by herself, the phonograph blasting.

In 1958 Ava was finally free of Metro-Goldwyn-Mayer. 'After seventeen years,' she said, 'it was a little frightening leaving the security I had with MGM. I hated it but they were there for me.' Now she wanted to make movies of her choosing and she considered a film about the life of Conchita Cintron, a woman who had been a famous bullfighter in Spain. In October Ava visited the ranch of Angelo Peralta, the celebrated trainer of bulls, and decided to try her hand at *torea a caballo* – fighting bulls on horseback. She was in the ring briefly before the horse reared and Ava went down. As she was trying to get on her feet, the young bull charged and struck her in the left cheek. The well known British plastic surgeon Sir Archibald McIndoe diagnosed the injury as a haematoma or blood clot. He recommended heat and massage treatments. 'You'll be back to normal in a year,' he said. Though the tiny, almost invisible mark could not be detected, she was convinced the beautiful Ava Gardner would never be the same again.

MGM would never be the same again, either. Many Golden Era stars believe the studio's demise began when their father Louis B. Mayer resigned in 1951. He died of leukaemia on 29 October 1957, uttering his last words to Howard Strickling, 'Nothing matters. Nothing matters.' Contract player June Allyson said, 'When Mr Mayer went he took the studio with him.'

After Dore Schary was released from his contract in November 1956, too many changes in management at MGM forced Leo the Lion into debt to the tune of $35,000,000 by 1969. There were no more seven-year contracts for beautiful nobodies like Ava because the studio system was dead.

In its prime, MGM's empire consisted of 117 acres, 6 miles of road for their 4,000 employees, 25 sound stages, a police force, hospital, fire department, and their own telephone exchange. It was a kingdom with its own rules and morals.

Robert Taylor stayed with MGM for 24 years and goes down in Hollywood history as having the longest running contract with a motion-picture studio. He collected a hefty pension, unlike Esther Williams who passed up her $3,000,000 pension because she refused to do the films assigned to her. Esther related in her memoirs how stunned she was to see Ava at a party in Madrid given by matador Luis Miguel Dominguin who married Italian actress Lucia Bose after Ava turned down his many marriage proposals. But that didn't stop her from crashing Dominguin's party and dancing the flamenco on the table. 'Ava was wearing a skirt that revealed everything as she twirled,' Esther said. 'She was not wearing panties. My heart went out to Ava and what she had become. Here she was, desperately self-destructive and keeping company with a drunken band of Gypsies. Sometimes she would just disappear with them for days.'

For Ava, however, these interludes between films were the life for her. 'I don't understand people who like to work and talk about it like it was some sort of goddamn duty,' she said. 'Doing nothing feels like floating on warm water to me. Delightful, perfect.'

In 1958, Ava flew to Australia for *On the Beach* with Gregory Peck. Sinatra arranged a concert in Melbourne where he and Ava went into seclusion. 'The truth was,' she said, 'we wanted to talk, to look at each other, to be together. With only two nights, we didn't have time to fight. Every once in a while Frank would call me in London or Madrid or wherever I was. "Let's try again", he'd say. Our phone bills were astronomical.'

After a string of bad films, Ava was reluctant to do *The Night of the Iguana* in 1963, but director John Huston flew to Madrid and convinced her to play Maxine, the happy-go-lucky proprietor of a seedy hotel. The international press flocked to Puerto Vallarta, Mexico, because Elizabeth Taylor was there with her boyfriend, Richard Burton, who was Ava's co-star in *Iguana*. Her reviews were smashing. *Life* thought Ava ran away with the picture. *Newsweek* commented, '. . . a great woman to play a great woman.' But she received criticism from *Show* magazine about her attitude in Puerto Vallarta: 'She was her customary self, as amiable as an adder. Both Elizabeth Taylor and Ava are as spoiled as Medieval queens. They expect men to fall at their feet, and they are accustomed to being catered to and having everything done for them.'

John Huston convinced Ava to play Sarah, the barren wife of Abraham, in *The Bible*. She began a turbulent affair with her leading man, George C. Scott, who beat her severely on numerous occasions. He made the mistake of following her to Hollywood where Sinatra hired two bodyguards to protect her. He told *Photoplay*, 'If there's one guy I can't tolerate, it's a guy who mistreats women. They need a real working over by a man of their own size.' Scott wasn't cut down to size, but his clothes were. When he returned to his hotel one night he found that all his shirts, sweaters and suits had been cut off at the shoulders.

In the summer of 1969 Ava took a flat near Park Lane in London while she looked for a permanent residence there. Rumour had it she was asked to leave Spain, but Ava's reasons were valid. She said taxes were very high and there were too many tourists in Spain now. She had a series of gynaecological problems in the late sixties and was hospitalised for minor surgery. She cut down on drinking and confined her social life to small dinner parties. When Ava found an apartment in a quaint old town house overlooking a private square in Knightsbridge, near Hyde Park, she said in an interview, 'I haven't taken an overdose of sleeping pills. I haven't been in jail, and I don't go running to a psychiatrist every two minutes. That's something of an accomplishment these days.' As for marriage, Ava said, 'I was mad about Artie, just as I was about Mickey and Frank. I married three exciting men, all very talented, and fascinating to the ladies, and, I might add, vice versa. But it's not all entirely my fault, when you consider that my three husbands have had a collection of twenty wives.'

On 11 July 1976, Frank Sinatra married Barbara Marx, but not before asking Ava repeatedly to come back to him. On the day of his wedding, Frank called Ava who told reporters, 'I'm glad he has found happiness with Barbara. Even though we were divorced long ago, I've always counted on Frank to advise me in business affairs. He's always been so generous with his time and interest. I'm sure his new wife won't object if I continue to call on him in the future.' Devastated by his mother's death in a plane crash, Frank turned to religion for consolation. In 1978 he had his marriage to Nancy annulled and, after Barbara's conversion to Catholicism, they were married by a priest. Marriages to Ava and Mia, outside the Church, were not recognised.

Ava made several bad films 'for the loot' and even ventured into television on *Knots Landing*. The press responded graciously with THE GODDESS ON THE LITTLE SCREEN – THE GRAND LADY SWEEPS KNOTS LANDING OFF ITS FEET – TIME LEAVES LITTLE TRACE ON FILM'S LOVE GODDESS – WORLD'S MOST BEAUTIFUL ANIMAL ON TV.

On 6 October 1986, Ava was flown from London to Saint John's Hospital in Santa Monica, California, suffering from a persistent virus that developed into pneumonia. During her illness she had a minor stroke that affected her walking and made her left arm useless. In January 1988, Ava went back to Saint John's Hospital, not returning home until May. Sinatra paid her enormous medical bills that came to over $1,000,000 and made sure she did not want for anything. He sent her a huge floral arrangement with a note signed 'Chi-Chi', her old pet name for him.

*

Ava Gardner died of pneumonia in London on 25 January 1990 at the age of sixty-seven. She was buried in Smithfield, North Carolina, in the Gardner family plot.

In her memoirs that were not finished before she died, Ava wrote, 'If I had my life to live over again, I'd live it the same way. The truth is, honey, I've enjoyed my life. I've had a hell of a good time . . .'

The Films of Ava Gardner

Three Men in White (MGM, 1944)
Maisie Goes to Reno (MGM, 1944)
She Went to the Races (MGM, 1945)
Whistle Stop (United Artists, 1946)
The Killers (Universal, 1946)
The Hucksters (MGM, 1947)
Singapore (Universal, 1947)
One Touch of Venus (Universal, 1948)
The Great Sinner (MGM, 1949)
East Side, West Side (MGM, 1949)
The Bribe (MGM, 1949)
My Forbidden Past (RKO, 1951)
Pandora and the Flying Dutchman (MGM, 1951)
Showboat (MGM, 1951)
Lone Star (MGM, 1952)
The Snows of Kilimanjaro (20th Century-Fox, 1952)
Ride, Vaquero (MGM, 1953)
Mogambo (MGM, 1953)
Knights of the Round Table (MGM, 1953)
The Barefoot Contessa (United Artists, 1954)
Bhowani Junction (MGM, 1956)
The Little Hut (MGM, 1957)
The Sun Also Rises (20th Century-Fox, 1957)
The Naked Maja (MGM, 1959)
On the Beach (United Artists, 1959)
The Angel Wore Red (MGM, 1960)
55 Days at Peking (Allied Artists, 1963)

Seven Days in May (Paramount, 1964)
The Night of the Iguana (MGM, 1964)
The Bible (20th Century-Fox, 1966)
Mayerling (MGM, 1968)
The Devil's Window (Commonwealth United, 1971)
The Life and Times of Judge Roy Bean (United Artists, 1972)
Earthquake (Universal, 1974)
The Blue Bird (20th Century-Fox, 1976)
Permission to Kill (Warner Brothers, 1975)
The Sentinel (Universal, 1976)
The Cassandra Crossing (AGF/CCC/International Cine, 1976)
City on Fire (Astral-Bellevue-Pathe, 1979)
The Kidnapping of the President (Sefel Pictures, 1980)
Priest of Love (Filmways Pictures Inc.– Enterprise Pictures, Ltd,1981)

9

Grace

Her type was a Hollywood rarity in the early fifties. She was a natural beauty with class and refinement. But actress Zsa Zsa Gabor saw another side to the millionaire's daughter: 'She had more boy friends in a month than I did in a lifetime. Though she had risen to stardom as a chaste iceberg queen, she went to bed with anyone she fancied at the time.'

The independent starlet did not want to be tied down with a seven-year contract at Metro-Goldwyn-Mayer but she changed her mind to work with Clark Gable with whom she fell in love. When the filming ended, The King walked away and broke her heart.

Her fans thought she was a debutante and MGM did nothing to discourage this image. In reality, her wealthy father was not one of Philadelphia's Main Line. As a former Irish bricklayer he wasn't eligible for the Social Register. She adored her father, who was not impressed with her accomplishments. She hoped he would be pleased with her Oscar but he wasn't. The more she achieved, the less he appreciated her.

And so she packed her suitcases, sailed to Europe, married a prince, moved into a palace, and lived unhappily ever after.

Grace Kelly made only eleven movies but many became classics. Like Greta Garbo, she did not intend to retire from films forever. Unfortunately, Grace underestimated her husband, Prince Rainier, and the people of Monaco who did not want their princess kissing other men on the screen.

She was puritanical in her role of a princess, but she never forgot how to let her hair down with Hollywood friends. 'She got ripped to the tits,' Rock Hudson said. At Elizabeth Taylor's fortieth birthday party, guests were amazed watching Grace doing wild Hungarian dances and leading the Conga line. All of this without Prince Rainier in attendance.

Grace Kelly was an American Cinderella but her glass slipper was shattered all too soon . . .

'As an unmarried woman in Hollywood,' Grace Kelly explained, 'I was thought to be a danger. Other women looked on me as a rival, and it pained me a great deal. The worst was when gossip-columnist Hedda Hopper started to persecute me with her hatred. She warned all the producers, directors and actors against me. Hedda referred to me as a nymphomanic.'

Grace arrived in Hollywood wearing white gloves and a virginal smile, and hypnotised director Fred Zinnemann, Gary Cooper and Alfred Hitchcock. She may not have been popular in the movie colony but the friends she had there were powerful and loyal. One of them was Hitchcock, who had been mesmerised by her in *Mogambo*. He saw fire beneath the purity of her lily-white skin. There was something about her sex appeal that fascinated him. She was his concept of the angel-whore. It was Hitchcock who taught Grace how to smoulder for the camera, and it was she who made him smoulder. He became a Grace-watcher, a smitten voyeur whose fantasies about her were never fulfilled. Hitchcock was the one who fought valiantly to lure his princess before the camera again. When his attempt failed, Grace went into a deep depression. Her fate had been sealed.

Grace had given and proclaimed her love for many men except the one she chose to marry, a man she had met only twice. Alfred Hitchcock said about her proposed marriage to a prince, 'Grace has bounced around with the ease of a girl on a trapeze. Whether the platform on which she has landed is too narrow, I don't know.'

Grace's ex-fiancé, couturier Oleg Cassini thought she was escaping the turmoil of life. Clark Gable said she was a smart girl to retire at her peak in movies: 'Actresses age on the screen and even faster in their mirrors.' Close friend Ava Gardner was certain that it was Grace's attempt at winning over her father.

But Grace told close friend Judy Quine, 'I don't want to be married to someone who feels inferior to my success or because I make more money than he does. The Prince is not going to be "Mr Kelly". What he does is far more important than what I do.'

Her father, Jack Kelly, wasn't impressed. 'Royalty means nothing to us,' he said. To a reporter he remarked, 'The Prince comes up to Gracie's titties.'

Behind closed doors Jack Kelly fumed over having to pay a dowry to his future son-in-law, Prince Rainier. 'Isn't my daughter enough?' he growled. The palace in Monaco was too big. He couldn't ask the servants where the bathrooms were because he couldn't speak French. When nature called on his first visit, Jack Kelly was forced to visit a friend in a nearby hotel to relieve himself. 'And my dress shirts,' he complained, 'come back pleated!'

The elite who attended the royal wedding were not pleased rubbing elbows with the Kellys. Even Winston Churchill's son, Randolph, complained to England's Lady Docker in disgust. 'I didn't come here to meet vulgar people like the Kellys!' he wailed

Columnist Dorothy Kilgallen was amused that Grace's sister Peggy drank milk with escargots. Kilgallen said, 'At least the Kellys aren't hypocrites.'

Grace Patricia Kelly was born on 12 November 1929, in Philadelphia. Her father Jack won the U.S. singles sculling championship in 1919. The following year he got an Olympic gold medal. A former bricklayer, Jack formed his own company, Kelly for Brickwork, in 1921. A handsome man with a healthy physique, he was considered one of the most eligible bachelors in North Philadelphia. Though sculling and business had taken up most of his time, he dated many women, who were his for the asking – all except one, that is.

He met sixteen-year-old Margaret Majer in 1914 at the Philadelphia Turngemeinde, an athletic social club. She said, 'He was nine years older than I, so we didn't take each other seriously.' Margaret pursued a career as a swimming instructor, graduated from Temple University, and became the first woman to teach physical education at the University of Pennsylvania. Always attracted to her, Jack finally got a date with Margaret and they were married in 1924. They had four children – Margaret ('Peggy'), Jack ('Kell'), Grace, and Elizabeth Anne ('Lizanne'). Peggy was the apple of Jack's eye, and Margaret doted on Lizanne. Neither had patience for a clinging Grace, who said in reflection, 'We were always competing. Competing for everything – competing for love.' Grace was a frail child in a family of robust and energetic athletes. Susceptible to allergies, lingering colds and ear problems, she did not wrestle in the backyard with her tomboy sisters. Jack commented, 'I don't get that girl. We're an athletic family, very good athletes, and she can barely walk. She's teased and abused but never fights back. Her younger sister can beat her up.' Peggy wasn't punished for dragging Grace by the hair across the front lawn. She was rewarded instead 'because children have to learn how to defend themselves', Jack said. In later years, Grace commented 'I don't like yelling and fighting, and I can't quarrel. Getting angry doesn't solve anything. I'd rather give in because bitter words tire me out. I'm not one to forget easily. The hurt lasts for a long time.'

As the middle sister, Grace had no identity. Born with a vivid imagination, she made up little plays with her dolls and learned to be quite content alone in her bedroom. As if they were devoted friends, she kept her doll collection into adulthood as a reminder of the many hours of happiness they had shared when there was no one else.

Grace was a fine swimmer and played a good game of tennis Her only desire to excel in sports was to please Jack, but she would never live up to his standard because, according to him, 'Gracie doesn't have the Kelly determination to win, win, win because she's enjoying herself too much. If you can't win at sports, you'll never be a winner at anything.'

A close friend of the family recalled, 'I felt sorry for Kell. Regardless of how many medals he won, his father expected one more or the kid was a failure. I take a more optimistic view of Grace's situation because Jack didn't expect the impossible of her. In fact, she didn't exist. The first time I met the whole family, Jack forgot to introduce Grace, and she was the one I noticed first because of her ethereal quality that the others didn't have.'

When she was five, Grace was enrolled at Ravenhill, a convent school a few blocks from home. With the other children, she took part in school shows. Her first role was as the Virgin Mary in the annual Nativity play, walking on stage and laying down Baby Jesus with reverence. It seemed unlikely that someone as timid as Grace would be at ease on the stage, but taking on the role of someone else was gratifying to her. She could make the transition with little effort. This inborn talent would eventually make her a fine actress.

In her teens, Grace had blossomed into a very pretty, willowy young lady with soft blonde hair. Because she was tall for her age, older boys were attracted to her and she quickly cultivated a flirtatious response. Harper Davis, a friend of Kell's, was Grace's first love, but in 1946 he became ill with multiple sclerosis. When he died in 1953. Grace flew to Philadelphia from Hollywood to attend his funeral.

Despite Margaret's insistence that all her children attend college, Grace avoided it, thanks to her uncle, Pulitzer Prize-winning playwright, George Kelly, a discreet homosexual. Uncle George arranged for Grace to audition at the American Academy of Dramatic Arts in New York. She was enrolled as a junior in October 1947. Getting out of Philadelphia was important to Grace. 'I had to find out who I was,' she said. Her parents made sure, however, that Grace did not have too much freedom. The Barbizon Hotel a 140 East 63rd Street was a proper place for wealthy young women in the

1940s. No men were allowed in the hotel after 10 p.m., and never in the girls' living quarters.

If the Kellys were preserving their daughter's virginity, it was too late. Grace planned her first sexual encounter before departing Philadelphia. 'I went to a friend's house to pick her up,' she said, 'but she wasn't there. I began talking to her husband and we became intimate.' What Grace did not say was that she wanted to know what sex was all about before moving to the big city.

Jack didn't think Grace would qualify at the American Academy of Dramatic Arts and gave his consent. 'I give her two weeks and she'll be back home.' Having predicted wrong, Jack challenged Grace by giving her little spending money, but this gave her more determination in a city that gobbled up attractive young attresses who needed a job. Grace, with her 'scrubbed look' was the exception in a generation of black-lined eyes and defined brows. Her wholesomeness landed her on the covers of *Redbrook*, *Ladies Home Journal* and the original *Cosmopolitan* that catered to housewives before Helen Gurley Brown revamped it for the single girl. Grace was also in advertisements for a variety of products that included Old Gold tobacco and Electrolux. She was soon earning more than $400 a week, which would relieve Jack Kelly of his 'financial burden'.

Photographer Ruzzie Green was sceptical about Grace's future in modelling. 'If she lacked anything, it was sex appeal,' he said. 'She was what we called "nice clean stuff" in our business. She would never be a top model because she had no glamour. She had lovely shoulders but no chest.' Grace hated modelling, anyway, and was doing it only for the money until she graduated and could concentrate on getting in a Broadway play.

When Grace returned home for a visit, the Kelly family made fun of her refined speech that was tinged with a British accent. Margaret noted other changes.

'There's a man in your life, Gracie?'

'Yes,' was the dreamy response.

'Who is he?'

'A director at the Academy.'

'Catholic?'

'No . . .'

'Are you in love with him, Gracie?'

'Yes.'

Most mothers would have been in a dead faint, but not Margaret Majer

Kelly. She wanted to meet the city slicker who was *not* going to marry her daughter.

Before Grace fell in love, she had been dating several men, including actor Alex D'Arcy who had twenty movies to his credit. A ladies' man, D'Arcy was, nonetheless, a gentleman who did not force a lady to have sex unless it was mutual. He described Grace as shy and demure. 'I touched her knee in a taxi,' he said, 'and she jumped into my arms.' According to D'Arcy, she was a tigress in bed.

But it was Don Richardson, a Jewish director at the Academy, who stole Grace's heart. Nine years older and separated from his wife, Richardson paid little attention to Grace in class. They became friendly during a snowstorm when she couldn't get a cab. He suggested taking a bus to his apartment to dry off.

After he finished making coffee, Richardson found out he had got dressed for nothing when he found a nude Grace in bed. She stayed the night and spent weekends with him from then on. In a sincere effort to help her, Richardson contacted Edie Van Cleve, an agent at MCA who agreed to represent Grace. Now a graduate of the American Academy of Dramatic Arts, she decided that it was time to take Don home to meet the Kellys. Over dinner he told the family, 'Your daughter's going to be a great movie star.'

The Kelly clan roared with laughter. Jack commented wryly, 'She'll get over that nonsense and settle down.' The next morning, Margaret had the gall to go through Richardson's belongings. Not only did she find legal papers pertaining to his pending divorce but several condoms as well. Richardson was told to leave and Grace was forbidden to see him again.

The summer of 1949 was a turning point for Grace. She had been torn from the man she loved, denied the right to look for a job in the New York theatre, and was more distant than ever from her family. Discussions about New York were tinged with Jack's threatening to have her followed. The revelation that Grace was no longer a virgin cast a dark shadow over the trusting relationship she'd had with her parents.

Uncle George came to the rescue with a part in his play *The Torch Bearers* at the Bucks County Playhouse, a short drive from Philadelphia. The Kellys were there on opening night and, much to Jack's surprise, his daughter's performance as the ingenue was applauded, even by him. Soon after, Grace got word that she was being considered for a part in *The Father* with Raymond Massey. After opening in Boston, the play was scheduled for New York in November 1949. Jack could hardly keep Grace locked in her room at this stage. He permitted her to return to New York, providing she did not see Don Richardson, but Grace was in his arms on her first night back in the big city. Rather than the staid Barbizon Plaza Hotel, she took an apartment in the Manhattan House on East 66th Street. It's possible, however, that Jack had had Grace followed since he called Richardson and offered him a Jaguar if he'd stop seeing Grace. Then came threatening calls from Kell. Richardson ignored the Kelly men and continued his affair with Grace for another two years.

The Father opened at the Court Theater in New York on 16 November 1949. The *New York Times* critic wrote, 'Grace Kelly gives a charming pliable performance as the bewildered broken-hearted daughter.'

At the cast party after the play, Raymond Massey approached Jack. 'What on earth are you doing here, Kelly?'

'My daughter's in your play.'

'Grace Kelly? What a delightful surprise!'

Jack changed the subject. 'Did you hear about my son winning the Diamond Sculls at the Henley Regatta?'

Grace went on to do more than sixty television shows including *Philco/Goodyear Playhouse*, *Studio One*, *Lux Video Theater*, and *Robert Montgomery Presents*. Doing live television was no easy task in the fifties. The actors had only one chance, camouflaging errors as they went along, but it was an excellent breeding ground for young performers such as Grace, who was eagerly looking for another play and, meanwhile, making a name for herself in more ways than one.

She continued to see Richardson but became involved with other men as well. Claudius Charles Philippe, banqueting manager of the Waldorf-Astoria Hotel, was forty years old and about to divorce his second wife. As Grace's love for Richardson was waning, her attraction to Philippe exploded. Jack Kelly was furious when he found out his daughter was spending romantic nights at the Waldorf with the banqueting manager. He forbid any thoughts of marriage and, once again, Grace continued see him, anyway. Then there was the Shah of Iran, who was in New York for only a week. Grace went out with him every night. The Kellys browsed through the newspapers daily to find out what a gay time their daughter was having with the Shah but were horrified over an article that mentioned he had given her very expensive jewellery from Van Cleef and Arpels. Margaret rushed to New York and confronted Grace. 'What did he give you?'

'Oh, mother . . .'

'Where are the jewels?'

'In my dresser drawer.'

'Get them!'

Grace showed the jewellery to her mother – a pin in the shape of a gold cage with a diamond bird inside, a gold vanity case with 32 big diamonds on the clasp, and a bracelet with a dome of pearls and diamonds covering the face.

'You'll give them back!' Margaret bellowed.

'That would be very rude, mother.'

'Your father says they have to be returned.'

'It just isn't done. I can't . . .'

Grace kept the jewellery.

Then there was Prince Aly Khan, who is best remembered for his marriage to actress Rita Hayworth. Don Richardson remembered seeing Grace wearing a bracelet that he recognised as the one Aly Khan gave to a girl after he slept with her. 'I dropped it in her fishbowl,' Richardson said, 'and I left in a huff. That was the end of our romance.'

Edith Van Cleve was responsible for getting Grace to Hollywood for her first movie role in the summer of 1950. Henry Hathaway was directing *Fourteen Hours* (1951) for 20th Century-Fox, a film based on a real-life drama of 1938 when a young man jumped to his death from a ledge of the Gotham Hotel in New York. Grace was cast as 'Mrs Fuller,' a neatly dressed young woman discussing divorce plans with her lawyer when the suicide takes place across the street. After witnessing the tragic event, she changes her mind about leaving her husband.

Actor Richard Basehart played the jumper, Agnes Moorehead portrayed his mother, Barbara Bel Geddes was the sweetheart, and Paul Douglas plays a good-natured cop. Grace's part was cut to a minimum and she received no screen credit. She bought herself a mink stole with the money earned and rejected an offer to sign a seven-year contract with Metro-Goldwyn-Mayer. 20th Century-Fox didn't waste their time on a screen test for her 'because she has no stove in her belly'.

Grace returned to New York and joined Sanford Meisner's acting classes at the Neighborhood Playhouse. Her agent called her there about a screen test for 20th-Century-Fox director Gregory Ratoff, who was casting the part of a plain Irish immigrant girl in *Taxi* (1953). Wearing a plain blouse and skirt, and no make-up, she rushed to Ratoff's office. 'She's perfect,' he said. 'I like her because she isn't pretty.' Grace was excited about *Taxi* because it was going to be filmed in New York and would not involve a studio contract, which was customary. But the English actress Constance Smith was chosen instead. Grace was very disappointed, but this setback was a blessing in disguise because her screen test for Gregory Ratoff was put to good use by her agents at MCA.

In the spring of 1951, Grace joined the prestigious Elitch's Garden Theater in Denver, Colorado, for a season of repertory. At the same time, Hollywood director Fred Zinnemann was considering Grace for a small part in *High Noon*, a low-budget Western with Gary Cooper. The two projects conflicted, but Edith Van Cleve advised Grace to go ahead with summer stock because Hollywood production schedules were unpredictable.

Grace flew in from Denver to see Zinnemann, who had never interviewed an actress wearing white gloves before. He never failed to mention this, but added, 'It wasn't the white gloves. She was a very, very pretty girl.' Grace was shy during the interview, answering 'yes' or 'no' to his questions. Not much for small talk, Zinnemann told her, 'You should learn to speak to people when you meet them.' It was a strained interview, but her shyness convinced Zinnemann that she was right for the part of Gary Cooper's sweet Quaker wife in *High Noon*.

The summer of 1951 was one of the happiest for Grace. She was thrilled with the prospect of acting in a film with Gary Cooper while working with one of the best directors in Hollywood, but Grace returned to Denver with just as much enthusiasm over her participation in repertory.

'We had a grueling schedule of eleven plays in ten weeks,' she said, '. . . closing in one, opening in another, and rehearsing something else.' When the Kellys came to Elitch, Grace told them excitedly, 'I could stay here for ever!' Margaret recognized the glow on her daughter's face and waited for the inevitable.

'Mother, I'd like you to meet Gene Lyons,' Grace beamed, looking up at the tall, reserved Irishman with reddish blond hair. As usual, Margaret did her homework and found out Lyons was in the process of getting his marriage annulled. 'What bothered me most,' she said, 'was Grace's marrying someone in her own profession. He was a pleasant fellow, but not stable enough.' Margaret wasn't overly concerned, however, because she felt Grace was in love with love, not Lyons. With *High Noon* about to begin shooting in California, the couple would have to separate anyway.

While Grace was enjoying the stage and her romance with Gene Lyons in Colorado, Gary Cooper checked into hospital for a hernia operation. He was legally separated from his wife, Rocky, and seriously involved with actress Patricia Neal. Gary was fifty years old and not in good health. An old injury to his hip made him limp in pain, and his recurring ulcer was giving him trouble. Professionally, he was considered over the hill, and was offered *High Noon* after John Wayne, Charlton Heston, Marlon Brando and Gregory Peck had turned it down.

The script was written by Carl Foreman after he was blacklisted by the House Un-American Activities Committee. He left the United States and settled in England. Producer Stanley Kramer approached John Wayne about playing Marshal Kane, who faces four outlaws alone when the townspeople refuse to support him. Wayne was bitterly opposed to the script and said years later, 'I'll tell you about Carl Foreman and his rotten old *High Noon*. Everybody says it was a great picture because Gary Cooper and Grace Kelly were in it. But it's the most un-American thing I've ever seen in my life! The last thing in the picture is ol' Coop putting the U.S. Marshal's badge under his foot and stepping on it. I'll never regret having helped run Foreman out of the country.'

Though Cooper agreed to do *High Noon* for a low salary, he was getting a percentage of the profits, making it possible for Kramer to produce the movie for only $750,000. Despite Cooper's ailments, he held on to the magnetism that women had found enormously attractive for over twenty years, but he wasn't sure about facing the camera with a young Grace Kelly. 'Everyone will laugh at me,' he scowled, looking at her photograph, but Kramer assured him she would be insignificant in the picture.

Production on *High Noon* began in September 1951 on location in California's Sonoma Mountains. In the first scene Marshal Kane kisses his attractive Quaker wife. It was not quite that simple, however. Hollywood kisses never are. He and Grace had to shoot the wedding scene over and over again. She counted at least fifty kisses. He was tired and she was nervous, but it was the beginning of a mutual attraction that almost erupted into a blatant affair. The truth became apparent to the crew when Grace was going over her lines with Zinnemann, who was both disappointed and surprised when Cooper ambled over and offered to rehearse with her. Gary was a sweet and humble guy, but he indicated from the start of *High Noon* that he needed plenty of rest. Every day, however, he coached Grace who often sat on his lap during rehearsals.

Fred Zinnemann was smitten by her, too, filming more of Grace than the script called for. His close-ups of her were endless, most of them ending up on the cutting room floor. But it was Grace and Gary who made the gossip columns, and the frantic Kellys sent their eighteen-year-old daughter Lizanne to room with Grace on location. This intrusion put a stop to her budding romance with Cooper, who took it all in his stride by taking Lizanne along for dinner, also.

Gary Cooper won an Oscar for Best Actor of 1952, and *High Noon* was nominated for Best Picture, thanks to film editor Elmo Williams who thought up the ticking clock idea to give an otherwise routine western the suspense that made the picture a classic.

Grace returned to New York and Gene Lyons who was working there to be near her. She told her mother they had been apart for several months and survived it. Margaret reminded her that Gene Lyons was a married man. 'His annulment will be coming through any day now,' Grace said. 'He's highly regarded as an actor. One day he'll be one of the greats in the theatre.'

Grace accepted Gene's heavy drinking but she was not aware that he was an alcoholic. They acted out their doomed affair in *The Rich Boy*, an F. Scott Fitzgerald story adapted for the *Philco Television Playhouse* that aired in February 1952. Grace played a debutante who leaves the man she loves because of his excessive drinking. When she marries someone else, she tells her former boyfriend, 'You see, I am in love at last. I was only infatuated with you.'

But Grace was very much in love with Lyons. She described him best when she said, 'Gene has a fragile psyche.' Her desire to marry him diminished with the realisation that there was nothing she could do about his drinking. Grace believed that love would replace his inner conflict and the fears that made him self-destruct. She was wrong. Fortunately for Grace, her film career began to skyrocket, leaving little time to cry over her doomed affair with Gene Lyons. He reached his professional peak in the popular weekly television program, *Ironside*, with Raymond Burr. When the series ended in 1975, Gene died an alcoholic down on his luck.

In the spring of 1952, Grace got her second role in a Broadway play, *To Be Continued*. It opened at the Booth Theater on 23 April and flopped. But Grace suddenly became famous when *High Noon* was nominated for Best Picture and Oscars went to Gary Cooper and to Dimitri Tiomkin for the theme music sung by Tex Ritter. Director John Ford, who was casting for *Mogambo* was not impressed by Grace. 'All she did was shoot a guy in the back,' he said. 'Cooper should have given her a boot in the pants and sent her back East.' MCA suggested Ford view Grace's *Taxi* screen test and he changed his mind. 'That dame has breeding and class,' he told MGM mogul Dore Schary, 'but I'd like to see her in colour.' Grace did the screen test that Schary described as 'stunning', and Ford agreed.

The reluctant one was Grace, who would lose the part if she did not sign a seven-year contract with MGM. Negotiations began with Lucille Ryman Carroll, head of talent at the studio.

'I insist on time off to work in the theatre,' Grace told her.

'One year off after three,' Carroll said. 'And you have the right to make New York your home base.'

'I also want it stipulated that I can choose my own parts.'

'That isn't possible.'

'Suppose the role doesn't suit me?' Grace asked.

'Trust me, my dear. We're the best judge of that.' Grace signed with MGM for $750 a week instead of the usual $1500 because she wanted to see Africa and work with Clark Gable.

It was actor Stewart Granger's idea to do a remake of *Red Dust* following his success in *King Solomon's Mines* (1950). Schary, who had replaced Louis B. Mayer, went ahead with the script but decided it was Clark Gable whose career needed a boost.

Schary told The King he could have Ava Gardner in the picture too. 'That's the good news.'

'What's the bad news?' Clark asked.

'The Mau Mau are rebelling.'

Mogambo is the story about Victor, a white hunter (Clark Gable), whose dalliance with Honey Bear (Ava Gardner), an American showgirl who has come on safari for fun, is interrupted by the arrival in their camp of an English anthropologist and his pretty wife (Grace). Honey Bear is the first to notice that Victor has melted the icy Linda, who decides to leave her unsuspecting husband, but Victor thinks twice and tells Linda she was only a diversion. She shoots Victor, who isn't seriously wounded. The English couple depart on the next boat, and Honey Bear stays in Africa with Victor.

In *Red Dust*, the original version of *Mogambo*, Gable had the male lead with Jean Harlow as the wisecracking trollop, and Mary Astor as Linda, the married woman who falls in love with him.

Grace was busy calling family and friends with the good news. 'I'm going to do a picture in Africa with *old* Clark Gable and *old* Ava Gardner and *old*

John Ford.' Her flippant attitude was soon tamed by shots for typhoid, paratyphoid, tetanus, cholera, smallpox and yellow fever. Sick with a touch of all six, she sweated it out in bed. It was worth the agony until her agent phoned with bad news. 'Actors' Equity won't grant you a permit to work in Africa, Grace.'

'I don't understand.'

'*Mogambo* is an MGM British production, and aside from John Ford and three principal stars, the entire cast and crew have to be British. Due to your lack of screen credits, Grace, you're not a principal star.'

'Never, never would I have signed that contract with MGM if it hadn't been for *Mogambo*,' Grace moaned. 'I'm not anxious to work in films. When I signed that damn contract I became nothing but a puppet.'

Virginia McKenna, a well-known British actress who had originally turned down the part of Linda was approached again. Waiting out the final decision was agony for Grace, but Margaret was relieved. 'How could I allow her to go to Africa by herself?' she said in later years. 'I was worried sick.'

Grace had to wait a week before her agent called with the good news that her permit had been granted. Now she faced the long and tedious journey from New York to Africa by way of England, Italy and Egypt. Gable had gone ahead of the others, but Ava Gardner and her husband, Frank Sinatra, met Grace in Rome. Photographers were falling over themselves trying to get pictures of the 'Battling Sinatras' while Grace sat quietly reading a book.

Gable was at the airport in Nairobi to meet the plane. On the drive to the New Stanley Hotel, Ava invited everyone to a party to celebrate her first wedding anniversary as Mrs Frank Sinatra. Grace checked into her room and within minutes could hear Ava's phonograph blasting, cocktail glasses clinking, and people laughing. Not sure whether she belonged with the close-knit group, she stood in the doorway until Gable asked her to sit down and have a glass of champagne. 'I must confess,' she said nervously, 'that I fell in love with you in *Gone With the Wind*.'

With a dimpled scowl, Gable said, 'I didn't want to play Rhett Butler, but I was under contract. I couldn't afford to go on suspension because I was getting a divorce.'

'And then you married Carole Lombard?'

'Yes,' he replied. 'How about more champagne before we have dinner?'

'I'm not much of a drinker,' she said.

'Africa changes people, Grace. Some grow up, some grow old, and some go mad. Hemingway said there were no exceptions.'

At dinner that evening, Grace spoke to the waiter in Swahili. Gable pretended to be impressed, but he considered the performance rather juvenile. The English-speaking waiter sighed, and Clark puckered his lips quizzically. The tall, slim blonde had class underneath that Swahili act, he said to himself, but she wasn't Philadelphia Main Line. If anyone knew the difference between the blue bloods and the nouveau riches, it was Gable.

Feeling the effects of too much champagne, Grace wanted to know why he had accepted the role of a man having an affair with a married woman since he'd frowned on these parts in the past.

'Because, my dear, the relationship between Linda and Victor does not go beyond infatuation.'

'I didn't get that impression,' she said, peeling a banana.

'Victor is a white hunter who plays by the rules on safari.'

'in the script he's described as a two-legged boa constrictor, Mr Gable.'

'Clark . . .'

'May I call you "Ba"?'

'Did you say "Pa"?'

'B-A. *Ba* . . .Swahili for "father".'

'I'm old enough to be.'

'*Ba* has nothing to do with age,' she explained. 'It refers to one who's admired and respected. Would you like some of my *ndizi*?'

'I've never turned down an offer like that in my life.'

She handed him half of her banana, and asked, 'Do you know what *mogambo* means in English? It means passion. So you see, there is more than infatuation between Linda and Victor.'

'That depends on one's interpretation of passion,' he said.

'You're rather old-fashioned about not playing a man who makes love to a married woman on the screen.'

'Maybe little girls from Philadelphia think it's old-fashioned, but I call it professional ethics.'

'Referring to your image?' She laughed. 'Hollywood amuses me. Holier than thou for the public and unholier than the devil in reality.'

'How many films have you done, Grace?'

'Two.'

'That explains it. After a few more, you'll be as holy as I am.'

Gable looked into her aqua eyes. She didn't blink. Very interesting girl, he concluded . . . smooth tawny skin, perky lips, sculptured nose with sensuous nostrils, and soft yellow hair pulled back from her square jaw line.

She was corny, innocent, brazen, flirty, childish and seductive. She reminded him of his love, Carole Lombard . . .

The following day, they flew to the MGM location near Mount Kenya. While the plane was making its descent, Gable said to Grace, 'Home sweet home on the banks of the Kagera River. Upholstered tents with all the comforts.'

'Signing my life away to MGM was worth it,' she said, looking around the camp site.

Cleaning his rifles, Gable said pensively, 'I've been under contract for more than twenty years and now they're planning to dump me. They offered me a two-year extension, but I'm getting out on my own terms, and if Metro ever wants me back for another film, they can shove it.'

'You're not giving me much to look forward to,' Grace said, forcing a smile.

'You didn't know Louis B. Mayer, but after he was squeezed out, nothing's the same. He and I never got along, but he *was* MGM. The old man made us all stars from Greta Garbo to our beautiful Ava. My advice to you, Grace, is to be on time, know your lines, and go home at six o'clock.'

John Ford, however, expected more than that. He was a rough, gruff, and abusive director of Westerns whose rude and uncouth manner could not be ignored. He referred to Grace as 'Kelly' and bellowed when she recited her lines. 'Don't you have any instinct, Kelly? We're doing a movie, not a goddamn script!' Grace might have been deeply hurt, but he was just as demanding and cruel to Ava and Clark, who walked off the set one day and refused to talk to Ford.

Being with Gable made everything all right for Grace. When they were not working, she got up early and went on safari with him. Holding hands they strolled along the riverbanks and did not try to hide their growing attraction for each other. Grace grew up fast in Africa. If Gable did not respond to her femininity, she'd find another approach just as Carole Lombard had done to win him over. He asked her, 'Why do you go on safari with me? It's hell to bounce around in a tin wagon with nothing but mosquitoes and heat.'

'I don't want to miss anything,' she replied. 'Besides, you don't have a choice. I'd come along whether you liked it or not.'

Though Grace was losing her inhibitions, she was shocked by Ava Gardner's running through camp in the nude. Clark explained that British officials complained about Ava's bathing naked in front of the native boys. Ford kept this to himself but when Ava found out she took off her clothes and ran through camp in front of everybody. Gable said she was a brave but bewildered girl.

'I'm not so sure I agree, *Ba*.'

'I'm not so sure I care,' he barked.

'You're angry.'

'No, but have you given any thought to how you looked the other night being carried from my tent to your tent – out cold from too much booze?'

'I wasn't out cold!' she snapped.

'You're right. Excuse me. You came to, threw up, and were *half*-carried back to your tent.

Grace found out it was Ava who was the sophisticate – the happy-go-lucky girl who wept inwardly but never gave up. She was Clark's pal and had been close to him for years. Grace felt guilty when she found out that Ava flew to England for an abortion because her marriage to Frank was breaking up despite deep love for each other. Once Grace understood Ava, they became lifelong friends.

Columnist Louella Parsons wired Clark about the romance and the 51-year-old King of Hollywood replied, 'This is the greatest compliment I've ever had, but I'm old enough to be her father. She's only a kid.'

Ava remembered how frantic he was when he returned from work and couldn't find Grace. 'They told him she took a walk and he was yelling at everyone about the Mau Mau guerrillas and wild animals,' Ava mused. 'Poor Clark grabbed his rifle and found Gracie sitting on a rock by the river reading Hemingway's *The Snows of Kilimanjaro*. He wanted to shake the hell out of her.'

Gable's fury was ignited when Grace told him she saw a lion. 'A beautiful lion,' she sighed.

'And you weren't afraid?'

'No, it was very moving. I had no fear at all.'

'Grace, from now on, if you want to take a walk, wait for me and we'll go together.'

They sat by the water until dark. Ava said this was a common occurrence. Grace read to him from Hemingway's book and he recited poetry to her. They were like an old married couple. A technician recalled,

> Grace was very plain. She wore frumpy clothes and her glasses and no make-up. She and Clark had their candlelight dinners alone or they'd sit in the lobby together. Grace kinda followed him around. It was taken for granted they were practically living together. I went to

> his tent late one night with a script revision. It was dark but I saw them in bed together. I think Clark was embarrassed but Grace wasn't. When they were in public he wasn't very affectionate, but she had a habit of resting her head on his shoulder. She was crazy about him. She was also fitting into the group. She remembered raunchy jokes and repeated them. Clark taught her how to use a rifle and she became a good shot. He admired her sportsmanship and guts in the bush.

Frank Sinatra, who had flown to Los Angeles to make a screen test for the part of Maggio in *From Here to Eternity* returned to Africa in time for the holidays. He surprised Ava with pasta and all the ingredients for homemade spaghetti sauce. She and Grace borrowed evening gowns from the wardrobe tent for Christmas Eve. The generator broke down but nobody cared as they feasted on Ava's spaghetti dinner by candlelight. On Christmas Day Gable found one of his socks hanging on the tent. Grace had stuffed it with goodies.

Soon after Christmas, they finished filming at Kagera. While the new location was being set up, Clark asked Grace if she'd like to spend a weekend at a beach resort on the Indian Ocean. 'It's cooler at Malindi,' he said, 'and we can swim without fear of crocodiles. I'm told it's a beautiful spot.'

'I'd love it,' she replied, 'but do you mind if Ava and Frank come along? I think they're on the verge of reconciling, and this might do it.'

Grace and Clark swam in the ocean and watched the sun rise from their veranda. They kept to themselves as did the Sinatras. For both couples, this would be their last romantic few days together. Grace did not want it to end and neither did Clark, but he knew only too well that the tender moments in Malindi were not real.

Rumours persisted about the Gable-Kelly affair in gossip columns almost daily. Whether it was the intimate trip to Malindi or their togetherness on location, word leaked out that they were in love. MGM was giving Grace an enormous publicity campaign in preparation for the release of *Mogambo*. Her role in *High Noon* was built up, emphasising her part as Gary Cooper's wife. Moviegoers began to recognise Grace when her pictures, many of them with Gable, appeared in newspapers and magazines. The studio took advantage of the romantic gossip and Gable no longer denied anything. Margaret had heard enough. She made plans to fly to London where her daughter would be filming interior shots before going home.

From the lovely beach resort, the cast settled into the desolate Isoila desert country in Uganda. 'This is Samburu country,' Gable explained. 'They're seven-feet tall, and live on blood and milk. They shoot an arrow in the necks of the cattle, drain some blood, and plug the hole with mud. I don't think they'll bother us but I suggest you don't take one of your famous walks my dear.'

Grace took his arm and whispered, 'I'll stay close, *Ba*.'

As filming of *Mogambo* was coming to an end, the cast sat around a campfire discussing their plans.

Ava said she was staying on in London to do *Knights of the Round Table* with Robert Taylor. 'And my door is open to one and all,' she said with a wink. 'Come for a drink at any hour.'

'My mother is meeting me,' Grace mumbled.

'I'm helping John Ford edit the film,' Gable said in a businesslike fashion. 'So I'll be pretty busy.'

'I thought you were flying to Rome to pick up your car.'

'I'm having it shipped to London, but you'll have fun with Ava. She knows all the out-of-the way places there.'

Hearing the news that Margaret Kelly was meeting Grace in England, Gable cooled off. He was not in the mood for a family affair. He checked into the Connaught Hotel in London to avoid reporters and MGM publicists, who booked Grace at the luxurious Savoy. They saw very little of each other. Always the gentleman, he took Grace and Margaret out to dinner and then refused to accept calls from the girl who called him '*Ba*.'

On 15 April 1953, Gable drove Grace to Heathrow Airport. Reporters were everywhere, but he ignored them as he led Grace to the gate and gave her a fond hug and kiss. She burst into tears and sobbed. He whispered something to her. She hesitated, kissed him again, and rushed for the plane bound for New York where she was interviewed by columnist Earl Wilson.

'How often have you been out with Gable?' he asked.

'I never counted,' she replied. 'We dated others.'

'Did he give you a diamond bracelet as reported?'

'Maybe he forgot to give it to me.'

'He must be twice your age.'

'He turned fifty-two in February. We celebrated his birthday in Africa.'

In the summer of 1953, Grace did a television drama 'The Way of an Eagle', a biography of American ornithologist John James Audubon. Her co-star was 44-year-old Jean-Pierre Aumont, the handsome French movie actor whose actress wife, Maria Montez, had died of a heart attack in 1951. He was attracted to Grace right away, but she kept her distance. Then one day they were doing a scene in a dance hall and there was graffiti on the walls. He told Grace there was something he wanted her to see. The graffiti read, 'Ladies, be kind to your men – after all, they're human beings, too.' Grace's laughter was the beginning of a tender romance that lasted for several months. They were together constantly until he returned to France. It was her close relationship with Aumont that ended Grace's affair with Gene Lyons once and for all.

With 3,000 miles between them, Gable felt it was safe to keep in touch with Grace who had been nominated for Best Supporting Actress in *Mogambo*. He wouldn't be back from Europe in time for the New York premiere but told Grace he'd escort her to the opening in Los Angeles. Ava was nominated for Best Actress in *Mogambo*, and Frank Sinatra for Best Supporting Actor in *From Here to Eternity*. It might have been a gala reunion, but the Sinatras were getting a divorce.

Mogambo was a hit at the box office. *Newsweek* said, 'Grace Kelly makes one of the loveliest patricians to appear on the screen in a long time. Her particular quality is the suggestion that she is well born without being arrogant, cultivated without being stuffy, and highly charged emotionally without being blatant.'

Alfred Hitchcock agreed. He was looking for a girl with the attributes of a debutante on the surface and the sexual appetite of a whore in her belly. Hitchcock had formed his own production company and signed with Warner Brothers to produce and direct *Dial M for Murder*. The film was based on Frederick Knott's play about an aging tennis player (Ray Milland) who discovers his rich English wife is having an affair with another man (Robert Cummings). The husband hires a school chum to kill her, but in the struggle, she stabs him in the back with a pair of scissors. Though the part of Margot was relatively dull, she had a dual personality, that of a staid wife and an adulteress. Hitchock thought Grace would be perfect. He could afford to be more colourful in love scenes with a lady than a trollop.

'Actors often make the mistake of giving too much of themselves at the start and winding down,' he said. 'Grace, as young as she was, had the ability to pace herself.' Hitchock would bring Grace to the forefront with what he referred to as 'sexual elegance'. He lowered her voice and taught her how to exude passion. It always helps if the director is in love with his leading lady, and Hitchock was a Grace-watcher – a smitten voyeur. For the screen, he supervised her wardrobe, her hairdo, and her make-up.

Everything had to be perfect because she was perfect.

Hitchcock studied Grace so intensely that he knew what she was thinking despite a cover of casualness toward her leading men. He took advantage of mutual attractions and ran with it.

In Hollywood Grace rented a small apartment on Sweetzer Street in North Hollywood. The press reported she was at the Bel-Air Hotel, but it was Gable who had a permanent suite there with his own private entrance. He and Grace were seen together, and rumours flourished again that they might marry. 'It would be all right for a few years,' he told Grace. 'But that's all – at best. I'd rather not pretend it will work out and risk losing what we have right now.' He confessed his love for her but wanted to trade marriage for a lifetime of friendship. Grace accepted the offer without shedding a tear.

He escorted her to the Academy Awards and the press went wild. Even though Grace lost to Donna Reed in *From Here to Eternity*, she said Frank Sinatra's winning an Oscar was such a delightful surprise that '. . . I didn't feel so bad'.

As for Clark Gable, she told the press candidly, 'We talked about marriage but the age difference was insurmountable.'

Then Grace Kelly fell deeply in love with Ray Milland, her co-star in *Dial M For Murder*. A married man for thirty years, he was separated from his wife, Mal, three times, twice due to his career problems and once for the love of Grace Kelly, who was twenty-five years younger than him.

Hollywood insiders knew about the affair before *Los Angeles Mirror-News* columnist Kendis Rochlen wrote, 'Miss Kelly's supposed to be so terribly proper, but then look at all those whispers about her and Ray Milland.' Director Henry Hathaway's widow told author James Spada, 'I have nothing good to say about Grace. She had an affair with my best friend's husband, Ray Milland. And all the time wearing those white gloves.' When asked if Grace had affairs with anyone else in Hollywood, Mrs Hathaway replied, 'You name it. Everybody! She wore those white gloves, but she was no saint.'

Jack Kelly was appalled though he should have had sympathy for Grace because he had been very much in love with divorcée Ellen Frazer, a socialite from Philadelphia. The Kelly children did not know about their father's girlfriend, but Margaret would not consent to a separation or a divorce.

When Grace was finished filming *Dial M For Murder*, Hitchcock asked her to do *Rear Window* with Jimmy Stewart as the bored photographer, confined to a wheelchair with a broken leg, who spies on his neighbours with a telephoto lens and believes one of them has murdered his wife. Grace played Jimmy's wealthy and playful girlfriend who stops by every day with food and kisses. Once again, Hitchcock played the sex game with his audience. The theme is based on murder and clues and neighbour-watching, but Stewart is so obsessed, one gets the impression that he should put away his lenses, put his arms around a very inviting Grace, and solve the murder some other time. But the press waited for clues of another kind. Would Stewart succumb to Grace, who had a perfect score to date? When asked how he felt about her, Jimmy said, 'Everything about Grace is appealing. I'm married but I'm not dead! She has those big warm eyes – and, well, if you ever have played a love scene with her, you'd know she's not cold . . . besides, has that twinkle and a touch of larceny in her eye.' He did not fall in love with Grace, but he brought her bouquets of flowers, mumbling that he had picked them from his own garden. When she married Prince Rainier, Jimmy commented, 'If Grace had married one of these phony Hollywood characters, I'd have formed a committee of vigilantes.'

Grace continued to see Ray Milland, Clark Gable and had occasional dates with widower Bing Crosby . . .

In *The Bridges at Toko-Ri*, Grace had a small part as the wife of a Navy pilot (William Holden) during the Korean War. When Holden heard that Grace had been cast in *Toko-Ri* he was anxious to find out if all the rumours about her were true. Theirs was a gratifying affair that was interrupted when she finished her few scenes and returned to New York. Before leaving she spoke to Dore Schary about doing *The Country Girl*. Jennifer Jones, who was in line for the part of Georgie Elgin, was pregnant and had to bow out. Schary said he was opposed to loaning her out to Paramount a third time. Grace's reply was, 'Then I'll give up making movies and go back to the theatre.' Schary, however, did not give in right away because he knew Grace wasn't the type to play the dowdy Georgie.

She decided to wait it out in New York – her only salvation because the love she shared with Ray Milland was a lingering threat to both of them. Ray did not want to go home until Grace sent him back. They were not seen in public any longer, cleverly hiding away in his apartment.

In New York, she sought out the company of Jean-Pierre Aumont. They were having dinner one evening at *Le Veau d'Or* on East 60th Street when fashion designer Oleg Cassini sat down at a nearby table. He had seen *Mogambo* that very night and was captivated by Grace, and there she was only a few feet away. Cassini described her as 'gorgeous, not striking. She did not stand out in a room; her beauty was subtle, the sort that required a second look.' For the next ten days Cassini sent her a dozen roses every day and signed the cards, 'The Friendly Florist'. When he called to introduce himself, Grace was reluctant to go out with him. 'There are other people I would like to see,' she exclaimed.

'Then we will see them together,' Cassini said, and he arranged a small party at E1 Morocco for Grace and her friends. That night she told him, 'I want you to know I happen to be in love.' Cassini suspected Ray Milland and complimented her on having good taste but added, 'I don't think his wife will divorce him.' Grace said it didn't matter. Then Oleg predicted within a year that he, himself, would be engaged to her.

'You're crazy, Mr Cassini!'

The next day she left for California to begin *The Country Girl*, the story of Frank Elgin (Bing Crosby), a singer and actor whose career is in the doldrums. When a Broadway director, Bernie Dodd (William Holden), offers him a comeback, Elgin blames his decline on his wife Georgie (Grace Kelly). Dodd tries to keep them apart until he realises it is Georgie who has kept her husband from total destruction. They fall in love and work together to rebuild Elgin's career. In the end, Georgie sacrifices her love for Dodd and remains with her husband.

In the beginning of the film, Grace as the drained and exhausted Georgie appears with greasy hair and wearing baggy, wrinkled clothes. She has no vitality. Her eyes are listless and she wears no make-up. As her husband makes a successful comeback, she takes more pride in herself.

Grace found herself in a sticky situation working with two men she was dating. Crosby told Holden, 'I don't mind telling you, Bill, I'm smitten with Grace. Daffy about her, and I was wondering if . . .'

'If I felt the same way?' Holden replied. 'What man wouldn't be overwhelmed by her. Look, Bing, I won't interfere . . .'

Crosby proposed marriage to Grace who said she'd talk it over with her family; but there wasn't time for that now because she was leaving for South America to do a film.

Green Fire, an MGM potboiler about emerald mining in Colombia, was the price Grace paid for the part of Georgie. 'It was a wretched experience,' she said. 'Everyone knew it was an awful picture . . . nobody had any idea how to save it.' Grace thought her leading man, Stewart Granger, was terribly conceited. She was less than thrilled when he grabbed her bottom with both hands in a kissing embrace during the last scene in pouring rain. MGM's publicity department went all out to publicise *Green Fire*. Grace was mortified when they placed her head on a bosomy body poured into a tight green strapless gown and displayed the blown up photograph prominently in front of the Mayfair Theater in New York. 'It made me mad,' Grace said. 'The dress wasn't even in the movie.'

Green Fire was insignificant when it opened in December 1954 following *Dial M For Murder*, released in May, *Rear Window* in August, and *The Country Girl* in December. Grace was nominated for Best Actress of 1954 for her portrayal of Bing Crosby's drab wife, Georgie. She was on the cover of *Life* magazine, a profile portrait with a wave of her shoulder-length hair brushing the corner of one eye. Underneath her name was the caption, 'Hollywood's Brightest and Busiest New Star'.

Hitchcock and Paramount postponed *To Catch a Thief* until Grace finished *Green Fire*. MGM was reluctant once again to loan her out, but she consulted dress designer Edith Head about her wardrobe for *Thief*. 'No matter what anyone says,' Grace exclaimed, 'keep right on making my clothes for the picture. I'll be in it.'

Fifty-year-old Cary Grant and his wife, Betsy Drake, were in Hong Kong when he received the script of *To Catch a Thief*. He was contemplating retirement at this juncture but was intrigued by the story of John Robie (The Cat), a reformed jewel thief. During an attempt to clear his name after a series of cat burglaries in Cannes, Robie meets and falls in love with a beautiful heiress (Grace Kelly).

Grant was delighted to find out Grace would be his leading lady and offered to use his influence if MGM did not consent to loaning her out for the fourth time. Ironically, MGM had a project with William Holden in mind so they traded Grace for her former lover. Leaving a string of broken hearts behind her, Grace returned to New York and began seeing couturier Oleg Cassini who had been married to Gene Tierney, the beautiful star of *Laura*. The son of exiled Russian nobility, Cassini lived a colourful life and was pursued by women everywhere, but he set his sights on Grace and refused to give up. After several casual dates in New York she asked him to join her in Cannes. His first evening there was anything but romantic. He went to bed alone that night and made up his mind to leave Cannes after a picnic outing with Grace the following day. 'Enough is enough,' he told her. 'We're alone here, on the raft in the Mediterranean. The sun is warm; the waves are lapping gently against the wood. There is no need for artifice any longer.'

When they returned to the hotel, Cassini had every good reason to stay on for two months.

Much like her stay in Africa for *Mogambo*, Grace found the same family atmosphere dining in the finest restaurants on the Riviera with the Hitchcocks, the Grants and Oleg. Much of the filming was set in or near Monaco where Grace inquired about the palace gardens. She had never heard of Prince Rainier.

In *To Catch a Thief*, Grace's character suspects Cary Grant is responsible for robbing rich women of their jewels. She deliberate flaunts her gems in his face during an intimate dinner in he hotel room.

The dialogue was sophisticated, suggestive, and very provocative:

Kelly — If you really want to see fireworks, it's better with the lights off. I have a feeling that you're going to see one of the Riviera's most fascinating sights.

Grant — I never doubted it.

Kelly — (As she reclines seductively on a divan.): Give up. Admit who you are. Even in this light I can tell where your eyes are looking. (Close-up of her necklace, revealing as well her inviting décolletage.) Look – hold them – diamonds! Ever had a better offer in your life?

Grant — You know just as well as I do this necklace is imitation.

Kelly — Well, I'm not. (The kiss, and cut to fireworks.)

Grace and Cary did not have an affair, but she fell in love with Oleg Cassini and accepted his marriage proposal. Grace wanted to notify her parents before there was any hint of it in the newspapers. Cassini said she discussed their wedding 'with the flushed enthusiasm of a typical American Junior Leaguer'. She was not concerned about her mother but told Oleg, 'I don't think you're my father's type. He might give us some trouble.' Shortly before they were scheduled to leave Europe, Grace decided it would be best if Cassini took a plane and she would sail with the Grants to New York. This sudden concern about the press and the reaction of her family gave Oleg his first clue that trouble was ahead. He was at the dock to meet her and got a peck on the cheek. With her sisters in town, Grace did not have a chance to see much of her fiancé, a very frustrating experience for

Cassini. It got worse. Over lunch, Margaret told him, 'Look here, Oleg. You're a charming escort, but in my opinion, poor risk for marriage.'

'Attractive men, including your husband, have been popular with the opposite sex,' Cassini said. 'Why am I being punished?'

Grace said nothing, but she invited him, on behalf of her family, to spend a weekend at the Kellys' beach house in New Jersey. The Kelly men did not say one word to Oleg, who told a friend, 'Having dinner with Grace's father was like eating a chocolate eclair filled with razor blades.'

The Kelly family thought it best that Grace did not see Oleg for six months but she defied them by dining with him at home or at a friend's place. At public functions, it appeared that Grace came without an escort to avoid being photographed with Cassini, who arrived before or after her.

To Catch a Thief received smashing reviews. The *New York Times* raved, 'The film comes off completely as a hit in the old Hitchcock style . . . Miss Kelly is cool and exquisite and superior. The picture does nothing but give out a good, exciting time.'

Without any film commitments, Grace was able to stay in New York with Oleg. When she turned down *Tribute to a Bad Man* with Spencer Tracy, MGM suspended her without pay. Dore Schary said, 'We feel that Miss Kelly has certain obligations to us. After all, we were the first to give her a chance. All her offers came after she appeared in *Mogambo*. Maybe she has a few complaints, but we are all willing to discuss whatever is wrong.'

When the Oscar nominations were announced and Grace Kelly was among them for *Country Girl*, Schary knew that MGM faced an embarrassment if she won an Academy Award while on suspension. Ten days before the Oscar ceremonies, MGM announced that Grace was back on salary. To make it appear as if they won the dispute, Schary said she agreed to do *The Barretts of Wimpole Street* but they did not bind her to any film commitments.

On 30 March 1955, Willian Holden walked on stage at the Pantages Theater to present the Oscar for Best Actress. When she heard her name, Grace rose from her seat slowly and glided majestically up the stairs to the stage. 'I will never forget this moment,' she said in a whisper. 'All I can say is thank you.'

In Philadelphia, Jack Kelly shook his head. 'I can't believe it! I simply cannot believe that Grace won. Of the four children, she's the last one I expected to support me in my old age.'

Oleg Cassini was lost in a maze of Grace's popularity. Short-tempered, he blew his stack when Grace said she was having dinner with Bing

Crosby, knowing how the crooner felt about her. Oleg was further enraged when she asked permission to go out with her agent and Frank Sinatra.

Cassini asked the help of Joseph Kennedy, the father of the future President of the United States. Oleg poured out his heart to Joe, who said, 'Don't worry about a thing. Set up a meeting and we'll settle everything. I promise you.'

Cassini was confident when they met for lunch at *La Cote Basque* in New York. The stage was set, and Joe reached out for Grace's hand. 'My dear,' he said, 'the Kellys, the Kennedys, people like us, we have to stick together.' Joe glanced at Oleg and then back to Grace. 'This fellow's a nice boy, but you'd be making a big mistake by marrying him.' Kennedy might have been teasing, but he never did get around to helping Cassini.

In the spring of 1955, Grace accepted an invitation by the French government to be the guest of honour at the Cannes Film Festival. She arrived in Paris on 4 May. On an overnight train to Cannes she met actress Olivia de Havilland and her husband, Pierre Galante, who was the movie editor of *Paris Match* magazine. 'How would you like to meet the Prince of Monaco?' he asked her. 'It would be a change of pace.'

'I guess it will be all right,' she replied.

However, when Grace arrived in Cannes, she looked at her schedule and knew there was no time for a trip to Monaco because she was the official hostess at a 5:30 p.m. reception the following day. Galante explained it was only a fifty-mile drive and they would be back in plenty of time. Grace declined and Galante called the Prince's secretary to arrange an earlier appointment. 'His Serene Highness will try to be back at the palace by three p.m.' was the reply.

Grace was forced to change her mind again but the next morning regretted it. There had been an electricity strike, which meant her wrinkled clothes could not be pressed, nor did her hair dryer work when she plugged it in. The only dress that was unwrinkled was a gaudy taffeta with large red-and-green cabbage roses splashed in the background. 'Oh well,' she told a friend. 'It's only for *Paris Match*. It's not like anyone will see those pictures again.' Little did she know that the awful taffeta dress would be immortalised.

Grace's entourage arrived at the palace in Monaco shortly after lunch. After an endless wait she told Galante, 'Let's go. It's getting late.' As they were preparing to leave, an apologetic Prince Rainier arrived.

Photographers took pictures of them in the palace gardens that she had admired during filming of *To Catch a Thief*. The Prince showed her his private zoo and, to Grace's amazement, he put his hand in the cages and petted the animals. 'This impressed me the most,' she said. Her visit to Monaco did not receive much attention. Those who knew about the visit asked what the Prince was like. 'He's very charming,' she commented.

It was not love at first sight, but Rainier was looking for a wife. Without an heir to the throne, Monaco would be swallowed up by France. He mentioned Grace to his spiritual leader, Father Francis Tucker, who took the reins from there. Rainier was delighted to receive a note of thanks from Grace. He responded and a regular exchange of letters followed.

In the fall of 1955, Grace went to Asheville, North Carolina, to film *The Swan*, a charming fable of a Ruritanian princess whose marriage to a rich prince (Alec Guinness) is arranged to save her father's kingdom from ruin. A handsome tutor (Louis Jourdan) is hired to teach the princess protocol in preparation for her marriage. The plan almost fails when she falls in love with her teacher, but duty prevails. Standing with the young princess on a balcony overlooking a lake, the compassionate prince explains, 'Think what it means to be a swan . . . to glide like a dream on the smooth surface of the lake and never go on shore. On dry land where ordinary people walk, the swan is awkward, even ridiculous. So there she must stay out on the lake, silent . . . white . . . majestic. Be a bird but never fly: to one song but never sing it until the moment of her death. And so it must be for you.' An omen, perhaps?

When Grace saw the Biltmore, a French Renaissance-style chateau built by George Vanderbilt in Asheville, she told her agent, 'It's like a palace. I love it.'

The setting was perfect for a young lady being courted by a prince whose letters to her were becoming more serious as the weeks passed. Then word came that Rainier wanted to visit her while he was in the United States, Grace told her parents that the filming schedule was indefinite, and they decided Christmas Day in Philadelphia would be best for all concerned.

When filming resumed in Hollywood, Grace had second thoughts about going home for the holidays, knowing Rainier was prepared to propose marriage. She was still in love with Cassini despite their many separations and marriage plans that never worked out somehow. She put off going home until 24 December, dreading Christmas Day when she would see Rainier again. In the past, she knew beforehand that her family would not approve of the men she'd brought home to be observed and rejected. This was a first for Grace and she wasn't facing it with ease.

Jack Kelly greeted Rainier, Father Tucker and Dr Robert Donat, the Prince's personal physician. Grace was shy during the introductions, but Peggy noticed 'sparks flying' between the Prince and her sister almost immediately. After dinner, Grace and Rainier went to Peggy's house. Jack drove Father Tucker to the rectory and returned home in a huff.

'The Prince wants to marry Grace,' he told his wife. 'He asked the good father to sound me out. I told him I didn't want any damn broken-down Prince marrying my daughter. I think he's after Grace's money. Father Tucker says he can prove otherwise.' Though he said his concern was Grace's welfare, Jack Kelly resented being upstaged by his daughter and replaced in her heart by a young, good-looking prince whose royal blood was far more impressive than a few Olympic Gold Medals.

On Wednesday 28 December, the Prince and Dr Donat drove Grace to New York for a meeting with MGM about her next film, *High Society*, a musical version of *The Philadelphia Story*. That evening, she accepted Rainier's marriage proposal.

Grace called Oleg Cassini and asked him to meet her on the Staten Island ferry. 'I want you to know first of all,' she said, 'that within my capacity for caring, I have cared more for you than anyone I have ever known and will probably continue to do so. However, for various reasons that should be apparent, I have decided to marry Prince Rainier of Monaco.'

'Are you going to marry someone because he has a title?'

'I will learn how to love him,' she replied.

Cassini wrote in his memoirs that he did not see it as a grand romantic gesture: '. . . I thought it had tragic aspects. I saw it as a capitulation decision to avoid the wondrous turmoil of life.'

There was turmoil in the Kelly family over a sizeable dowry that was traditional with European royalty. How much Jack paid isn't known, but it was estimated to be as high as $2,000,000. It's doubtful that Jack knew about Grace's taking a fertility test to ensure an heir to the throne.

On 5 January 1956, the Kellys held a luncheon party for relatives and friends at the Philadelphia Country Club. When the champagne was poured, Jack stood up, tapped his glass, and said, 'We are happy to announce the engagement of our daughter Grace to His Serene Highness Prince Rainier of Monaco. We drink a toast to them.'

Grace was accustomed to reporters rattling off questions while flash-bulbs nearly blinded her. But the Prince was not happy. He leaned over to Father Tucker and said, 'I don't belong to MGM!'

The famous couple made their first public appearance at the *Night in Monte Carlo* Charity Benefit at the Waldorf Astoria in in New York. The Prince wore white tie and tails with his royal decorations. Grace was never lovlier in a Dior white strapless gown, pearls and orchids. *Time* magazine reported, 'They sat uncomfortably in the royal box and nibbled crystallised violets while the press howled at the door. Later at the Harwyn Club, Grace nibbled Rainier's ear and danced until four a.m.'

Before leaving for Hollywood to make *High Society*, there was the matter of where the wedding would take place. It was assumed that Grace would be married in Philadelphia, but the people of Monaco were so outraged that Rainier changed his mind and the Kellys consented.

Dore Schary gave a luncheon for his biggest star and her Prince, who told the MGM mogul that the area of Monaco was five square miles. A stunned Schary blurted out, 'That's not as big as our back lot!' It was an embarrassing blunder but proof that few people knew anything about the tiny principality famous only for it's gambling in Monte Carlo.

The Prince rented a villa in Hollywood while Grace filmed *High Society*, the story of wilful socialite Tracy Lord (Grace Kelly), who plans to marry a stuffed shirt (John Lund). Complicating matters at the prewedding celebrations are Tracy's former husband, happy-go-lucky C.D. Dexter-Haven (Bing Crosby) and *Spy* magazine reporters (Celeste Holm and Frank Sinatra). Tracy has too much champagne the night before her wedding and embarrasses George by going for a midnight swim with reporter Sinatra. Dexter is on hand for the showdown and wins Tracy back.

Grace did her own singing with Crosby, 'True Love', which was Bing's last big record hit. Grace won a Gold Record Award for the romantic duet. In the film she wore the twelve-carat solitaire engagement ring given her by the prince instead of the one provided by the studio.

Margaret was so busy planning for the royal wedding she did not have time to edit a series of interviews with Hearst reporter Richard Gehman entitled, 'My Daughter Grace Kelly – Her Life and Romances by Mrs John Kelly'. Grace was mortified to see her private life exposed. She had overcome these scandals, had sought help from a therapist, and risen above the ridicule. Now her mother had dug up her romances with Clark Gable, Gary Cooper, Ray Milland, Gene Lyons, Jean-Pierre Aumont, and Oleg Cassini.

'How could you do this to me?' Grace asked.

'It's for a good cause,' Margaret replied. 'I'm donating the royalties to my favourite charity.'

Grace did not forgive her mother for a long time. MGM was incensed but powerless. They did, however, edit the articles before they appeared in European newspapers. When asked about her film career, Grace said, 'My contract with MGM is good for another four years. I've always been faithful to any agreement I've made.' Prince Rainier, however, told the press before boarding the *Ile de France* in New York, 'No more movies for Miss Kelly.'

Grace responded, 'If that's the way he wants it, that's the way it will be.'

MGM was in a dilemma over this. How could they sue a princess for breach of contract? Easing out of an awkward situation, they settled for exclusive rights to the royal wedding. They kept her on salary until after the honeymoon, gave her a bonus of $70,000 for 1956, paid a tidy sum of $7,000 for her wedding gown designed by Helen Rose, and assigned a publicity agent to manage the international press in Monaco. In return, Grace agreed that MGM could extend her contract until 1966, assuming she would change her future husband's mind.

Rainier III, Louis Henri Maxence Bertrand de Grimaldi, His Serene Highness, the Prince of Monaco, was born on 31 May 1923. His parents were divorced soon after his birth when his mother, Princess Charlotte, ran off with an Italian doctor. About her husband, Prince Pierre de Polignac, she said, 'To make love he needs to put a crown on his head.'

In 1947 Rainier fell in love with French actress Gisele Pascal with whom he shared an ice-pink villa at Cap Ferrat, a short drive from Monaco. When his grandfather died two years later, Prince Rainier became Monaco's ruler. It was taken for granted that he would marry Gisele whom the people of Monaco referred to as their 'invisible princess' and eventually their 'uncrowned princess'. Though details are sketchy, Rainier was forced to give up the woman he loved because she had failed two fertility tests. In October 1955 Gisele married French movie idol Raymond Pelligrin and later gave birth to a daughter, proving the palace doctors wrong about her ability to have children.

A 1918 treaty between Rainier's great-grandfather, Prince Albert, and the French government recognised Monaco as an independent principality exempt from taxes; but should the Prince die without an heir, Monaco would become a protectorate, ruled by France.

Aristotle Onassis, who had invested heavily in Monte Carlo in 1953, talked to Gardner Cowles, publisher of *Look* magazine, about the sagging economy of Monaco and how they might lure America's rich back there. One solution was to marry Rainier off to a beautiful movie star; the first one that came to mind was Marilyn Monroe, who did not know where Monaco was, but she said about the Prince, 'Give me two days alone with him and of course he'll want to marry me.' Cowles said he would arrange a meeting but before he could put his plan into motion Prince Rainier was engaged to Jack Kelly's daughter.

Marilyn called Grace with congratulations, adding, 'I'm so glad you've found a way out of this business.'

On 4 April 1956, Grace Kelly, her family and members of the wedding party, boarded the liner *Constitution* in New York.

'What do you call the prince?' a reporter asked.

'I call him Rainier.'

'How about your citizenship?'

'On my marriage, I shall become a Monegasque, but it will not affect my American citizenship. I shall have a dual citizenship.'

Peggy was to say that her sister's engagement was not a fairy-tale romance. Lizanne thought it was 'just a nice agreement'. The Catholic news agency D.I.S. wrote, 'The romance, if not an imposed one, was certainly advised by experts who had watched the Monegasque tourist trade dwindling and badly needed some unexpected sensation to put it back in the public eye.'

The Monegasques were excited over the forthcoming wedding, but the Grimaldis were less than enthusiastic about the family gathering in Monaco. Rainier's mother, Princess Charlotte, detested her former husband, Prince de Polignac. Nor did she approve of her son's marrying an American movie actress and was prepared to dislike Grace before they met. Rainier's sister, Antionette, was not only estranged from their mother but resented transferring her rank in Monaco society to the new princess.

Their bickering would seem less important when they had to contend with the Kellys who had no intention of 'putting on the dog' for anyone.

On 12 April at 9:45 a.m., the *Constitution* sailed into the Bay of Hercules near Monaco, where the prince was waiting at the bow of his white yacht, *Deo Juvante II*. Grace waved and he saluted. 'I see him!' she exclaimed to her parents. Wearing a navy-blue fitted coat over a matching dress, white gloves, and a huge white organdy hat, Grace held her black poodle, Oliver, a gift from Cary Grant and his wife, and walked down the gangplank. If this important part of the welcoming ceremony had been planned carefully, Grace would not have carried the dog because Rainier was thus unable to embrace or kiss her. Instead, she extended her gloved hand for the disappointing and unromantic meeting.

Another faux pas was her choice of hats for the occasion. The crowds, anxiously waiting for a glimpse of the future princess, could not see her face underneath the upside-down lacy saucer.

Onassis had arranged for a seaplane to drop red and white carnations on the harbour while boats blew their whistles and spouted fountains of water. 'I've never been happier in my life,' Grace told Margaret. Once off the yacht, she got into the prince's green Chrysler, which he drove up the hill to the freshly painted pink palace of Monaco.

The Kellys were introduced to the Grimaldis at a small reception before lunch. If Charlotte was cold with Grace, she was appalled when Margaret patted her firmly on the shoulder, shook her hand with gusto and cheered, 'Hi! I'm Ma Kelly!' Charlotte froze.

In a gesture of friendship, Grace asked Antoinette to be a bridesmaid, and further insulted her future sister-in-law by presenting her with an organdy gown and matching hat. Rather than explain that she was a member of the royal wedding party, Antoinette sent her lady-in-waiting with a note to Grace declining the offer.

Sixteen-hundred photographers and reporters descended on Monaco, making it almost impossible for Grace and Rainier to get to and from their destinations. The testy press booed her on more than one occasion when she ducked into a waiting limousine. Grace's nerves were so frayed she barely ate or slept. Still, the dark circles under her eyes and the loss of ten pounds did not detract from her beauty or stance.

Jewel thieves were more organised than the press. More than $50,000 worth of gems were stolen from wealthy guests at the Hotel de Paris. Margaret Kelly's loss was kept secret because she was staying at the palace. Insiders were suspicious of Charlotte's chauffeur and alleged lover, René Girier, a well-known 'retired' jewel thief. She was shocked by the rumours and defended him vehemently. Her feathers ruffled, Charlotte was not pleasant company at a dinner-dance hosted by Jack Kelly. She had to endure an obligatory dance with the bricklayer from Philadelphia and did not pretend to enjoy it.

The Kellys were not hypocrites, either. Peggy drank milk with escargots and ran about the palace with her two children wearing shorts. But Peggy's homespun frivolity was refreshing to the press for lack of exciting news stories.

As Princess of Monaco, Grace could not wear jewellery given to her by other men. She gave each piece away in private to her girlfriends but was handsomely rewarded. Each day preceding the wedding, Rainier gave her furs and jewels, among them diamond and ruby necklaces with matching rings, bracelets and earrings. The people of Monaco presented their Prince and his bride with a new Rolls-Royce, and the list goes on. Because the films of Grace Kelly would not be shown again in Monaco's three movie theatres, friends in Philadelphia gave her a Cinemascope screen and two 35mm projectors for a proposed viewing room in the palace.

On Wednesday 18 April 1956, eighty guests took their seats in the *Salle du trône* (the throne room in the palace at Monaco) for the civil ceremony. Rainier, serious and tense, wore a morning coat and striped trousers. Grace was elegant and poised in a rose-beige lace suit with a juliet cap trimmed with matching silk roses and white gloves. They exchanged their civil vows a second time for MGM cameras.

Sometime between the luncheon, lawn party, and the Opera House gala, Rainier bestowed the Order on Grace. Rather than waiting until after the religious ceremony, he proclaimed that Grace was Her Serene Highness, Princess of Monaco. That evening at the Opera House, she wore the Order of Charles, a red-and-white ribbon, across her bodice.

On Thursday morning, 19 April, six hundred guests assembled in Monaco's Cathedral of St Nicholas. Among them were David Niven, Gloria Swanson, King Farouk of Egypt, the Aga Khan, Ava Gardner, Somerset Maugham, Conrad Hilton and Aristotle Onassis with his wife, Tina. Frank Sinatra backed out at the last minute because his recent divorce from Ava had been highly publicised and he was afraid the press might focus on them. 'This is your day,' he told Grace. Cary Grant was filming at the time and could not attend. He sent the newlyweds an antique writing desk for a wedding present.

The altar was banked with white lilies, lilacs and hydrangeas to hide a battery of cameras and microphones that would provide live television coverage.

At 10:30 a.m. Grace walked down the aisle in the $7000 white wedding gown designed by Helen Rose. The lace for the bodice and ten-foot train, made of antique rose point lace, was 125 years old and had been purchased from a French museum. The skirt consisted of 25 yards of silk taffeta and 100 yards of silk net. Thousands of seed pearls had been sewn into the veil and also decorated the petalled lace headdress. The gown had long tight sleeves with scalloped wrists, a pleated taffeta cummerbund, and a stand-up collar. Grace's hair was pulled straight back into a chignon, and the only jewellery she wore were pearl stud earrings. It would be redundant to describe Grace as the personification of beauty that day.

When father and daughter reached the altar, Jack was told to sit down. 'No,' he replied. 'I'll wait until *he* gets here!' To the very end Jack Kelly had no intention of being ordered around or of giving up his starring role in this spectacular event.

Outside, trumpets heralded the Prince's arrival. He had designed his wedding uniform to resemble those of Napoleon's marshals – a decorated black tunic with gold leaf on the cuffs, sky blue trousers with a gold band down the sides, and a midnight-blue bicorne with white ostrich feathers. Rainier walked down the aisle followed by his three witnesses, and Jack Kelly finally sat down. The Prince told a reporter later, 'There was such a lack of intimacy . . . cameras and microphones were everywhere. Such lack of dignity and solitude.' On the way back to the palace, Grace followed tradition and laid her small lily-of-the-valley bridal bouquet at the shrine of the martyred virgin Saint Devote and prayed for her marriage.

The wedding reception was held in the Court of Honour, where guests sipped champagne and nibbled on caviar, cold lobster, shrimp and jellied eggs. The bride and groom cut a five-tier wedding cake with his sword and then disappeared to change their clothes for the honeymoon.

They waved from the bridge of the *Deo Juvante II* as it left the harbour; to the delight of the crowd, Prince Rainier hugged Grace at long last. They remained on deck until the royal yacht disappeared out to sea.

Variety reported the wedding with a notation: '. . . bride is film star, groom is non-pro.'

Less than an hour after leaving Monaco, rough water forced Rainier to lay anchor. Grace, who was not a hearty sailor, had agreed to a yachting honeymoon for the privacy of hidden coves and secluded beaches along the Riviera coastline. She attributed her daily nausea to seasickness, unaware that she had become pregnant a few days into the honeymoon.

On 2 August Rainier made the formal announcement: 'Her Serene Highness Princess Grace expects a child whose birth should take place in

February. The significance of this awaited event is clear to all of you . . .'

The people of Monaco did not see much of Grace during her pregnancy. She remained inside the dank and gloomy palace writing letters and making long-distance telephone calls. 'They told me about morning sickness,' she said, 'but they didn't tell me you could be sick all day every day.' She was also plagued with insomnia, sleeping late in the morning and napping in the afternoon. Estranged from her family and friends, the bewildered and lonely Grace was going through one of the most difficult and trying times in her life. She spent days crying and was plagued by moods of deep depression.

Since Grace was expected to give birth earlier than expected, Margaret arrived in Monaco shortly after the Christmas holidays. Mother and daughter had been estranged over Margaret's newspaper articles; however, it took a keen eye to notice the strain that existed between them at the wedding festivities. During the last few weeks of Grace's pregnancy, they became reconciled.

Following Grimaldi tradition, Grace gave birth at the palace at 9:27 a.m. on 23 January 1957. Caroline Louise Marguerite weighed in at eight pounds and eleven ounces. Grace had been in labour for six hours and delivered the baby without anaesthetic in the palace library, which had been converted into a delivery room.

Rainier told his people, 'Thank God and rejoice.'

In Philadelphia, Jack Kelly said, 'Aw, shucks. I was hoping for a boy.'

Five months later, Grace was pregnant again, and on 14 March 1958, blonde and blue-eyed Albert Alexandre Louis Pierre was born, weighing the same as his sister. Rainier made Grace regent, declaring that in the event of his death, she would assume the throne until Albert was twenty-one. Though Grace was taking more of an interest in Rainier's affairs of state, she was happiest caring for the children and decorating their new country place, Roc Agel, a converted farmhouse in the mountains above Monaco.

A good friend of the Kelly family, Bill Hegner, told journalist Arthur Lewis that Grace and Rainier started out having problems. 'She cried a lot and called her friends cross-Atlantic and said Rainier was terrible; difficult to get along with . . . They did not communicate that well physically.'

Madge ('Tiv') Tivey-Faucon, Grace's former lady-in-waiting, wrote an article for *Cosmopolitan* in 1964. Tiv had been hired as Rainier's secretary on the recommendation of Gisele Pascal and had been asked to stay on after his marriage. The article, tame by today's standards, related the Prince's criticism of Grace's wardrobe, which consisted mainly of old clothes. He told her she looked like a 'real emigrant' and 'a prison wardress'. Jack Kelly, the master of thrift, took a swipe at his daughter, too: 'Gracie, I think you must buy your clothes at the Salvation Army!' According to Tiv, when the Princess was expecting Albert, she wore the same maternity clothes she had worn for Caroline.

In January 1960, Grace's beloved poodle, Oliver, was attacked and killed by another dog. Rainier bought her another poodle but Grace was inconsolable for a long time. Tragedy struck again in June of that year when Jack Kelly died of stomach cancer shortly before his seventy-first birthday. His handwritten will was such a masterpiece that copies were selling for seven dollars each from Boston to Bombay.

> I don't want to give the impression that I am against sons-in-law,' he wrote, 'if they are the right type, they will provide for themselves and their families. As for me, just shed a respectful tear . . . I had more than my share of success . . . my wife and children have not given me any heartaches, but . . . have given me much happiness and pardonable pride, and I want them to know I appreciate that . . . if I had the choice to give you worldly goods or character, I would give you character . . . When I shove off for greener pastures or whatever it is on the other side of the curtain, I do it unafraid and, if you must know, a little curious.

Jack's bond of love with Grace on his deathbed made it all the more painful for her. At the end, his deepest affection was for Grace, who somehow managed to be strong enough for both of them. Grief-stricken, she returned to Monaco and faced another crisis. A 'well-meaning' friend thought Grace should know about Rainier's indiscretions during her absence. The story goes that the Prince had been seen dancing at a nightclub with Zénaide Quiñones de Léon, Grace's new, young, attractive lady-in-waiting. Madge Tivey-Faucon had been on hand to celebrate Rainier's thirty-seventh birthday, also. Zénaide was fired. There would be many tales about the Prince with other women, but none that compared to partying and dancing while his wife sat by her dying father's bedside.

In 1962, Alfred Hitchcock sent Grace the screenplay of *Marnie*, the story of a frigid compulsive thief who is given a choice of marrying a rich man or going to jail. Rainier had second thoughts about Grace's returning to films. She had suffered two miscarriages since Albert's birth and had been melancholic. Rainier thought it would be fun for the family to spend their autumn vacation in New England during the filming. He made the formal announcement on 18 March, making it perfectly clear that Her Serene Highness was not returning to films permanently. But the Monegasques did not want their Princess kissing other men on the screen. They protested to the press and in writing to the prince. MGM got into the act and threatened to take legal action if Grace violated her contract. Pope John XXIII sent a letter of objection to the palace, but Rainier did not change his mind. It was Grace who yielded to the people of Monaco and gave up all hope of acting again.

On 1 February 1965, Grace had another daughter, Stephanie Marie Elisabeth. The fear of not being able to have more children vanished with other doubts she had about her capabilities as a princess. Grace was able to identify, at last, with the people of Monaco, who adored her. She had given them a male heir, chosen them over the acting profession, and proven herself a political asset to the Prince, who gradually walked in her shadow.

After ten years of marriage, she accepted Rainier's stubbornness, moodiness and bouts of temper. Grace said their belief in Catholicism brought them together in difficult times. What was not generally known is that she had signed away all rights to her children if her marriage failed; the Prince's heirs to the throne belonged to Monaco.

In July 1967, while visiting the World's Fair, Expo '67 in Montreal, Grace suffered another miscarriage, her sixth pregnancy in eleven years. The baby, a boy, had been dead for more than a month inside. Doctors told the princess there would be no more pregnancies. She had planned on a big family but it was not to be.

Grace turned forty on 12 November 1969. 'I'm an absolute basket case,' she said in an interview for *Look* magazine. 'I can't stand it. It comes as a great jolt . . . For a woman, forty is torture, the end.'

She sent birthday party invitations with the heading 'Scorpio' to a dinner-dance, with a swimming pool brunch the following day: 'Hotel de Paris wholly converted for Scorpian occupancy. Your private nest awaits you. Courtesy of the High Scorpia. Other signs married to Scorpians tolerated.'

Elizabeth Taylor chose the occasion to debut her fabulous Krupp diamond, a gift from Scorpian husband Richard Burton. A horde of security guards accompanied the famous couple, causing more commotion on this already hectic event. The Burtons escorted Grace to social gatherings that Rainier chose not to attend. European society considered the Princess too pompous and stiff with Rainier in attendance. The Duchess of Windsor referred to Grace as a 'boring snob'. But in the company of the Burtons, Her Royal Highness let her hair down. At Elizabeth's fortieth birthday party in Budapest, Grace did wild Hungarian dances and kicked her heels up in a conga line.

Leslie Bennetts, a reporter for the *Philadelphia Bulletin*, claimed that Grace had less warmth and less spontaneity than anyone she had ever interviewed. 'She's an awful stick. Her life revolves around the rituals of her position.' Bennetts described Grace's accent as 'stilted bastardised French in this incredibly affected voice'. It appeared that Grace was puritanical in her role of princess, but let loose with the Hollywood crowd. Ava Gardner remarked that Grace was just another gal dishing the dirt after a few dry martinis.

Rock Hudson's friend, Tom Clark, said, 'Whenever Grace visited Hollywood, Rupert Allen always gave a party for her. Rock and Grace would wind up in a corner, laughing it up over who knows what silliness. They would collapse in a puddle of laughter.'

Grace needed these diversions. Life with Rainier was taking its toll of her. 'He's not interested in me, any more,' she told a friend. The decision to take an apartment in Paris was Grace's means of separating herself from Rainier though she claimed it was to be near a rebellious Caroline, who was attending school in France.

Grace's futile attempts to restrain Caroline were minor compared to Margaret's brutal control over 49-year-old Kell, who was seeking the Democratic nomination for mayor of Philadelphia. Separated from his wife and six children, Kell was linked in the gossip columns with a beautiful transexual, Rachel Harlow. Knowing that the opposing party would use this against him, Margaret threatened to go on television and tell the people why they should *not* vote for Kell. Mother and son were never the same again. A few months after Margaret ruined Kell's chances in politics, she was felled by a stroke that crippled her mind and body. Kell had a fatal heart attack in 1984 at the age of 57 and, in January 1990, Margaret died of pneumonia.

'Caroline wants to fly with her own wings, live for herself,' Grace said in

1976. Handsome Philippe Junot, a well-educated European playboy, proposed to Caroline. Grace had no choice but to make plans for the wedding that took place on 29 June 1978. 'Perhaps it's for the better,' Grace told Rainier. 'This way she'll have a successful second marriage.'

Grace was right. Caroline and Junot were divorced two years later, but she would find happiness with Italian businessman Stefano Casiraghi whom she married in 1983. Seven years later he was killed in a powerboat accident.

Robert Dornhelm, a young Hungarian director, convinced Grace to narrate *The Children of Theatre Street* (1977), a film documentary about the Kirov Ballet School in Leningrad. In 1979, he also worked with her on a short film promoting Monaco and its Flower Festival. *Rearranged* had a comical plot about an astronomer who ends up by mistake in the bouquet contest. On behalf of her Garden Club, Grace produced, financed, and acted in the film. Whether it was Dornhelm's inspiration or her own awakening after the *Marnie* disappointment, Grace could no longer restrain her creative energies. Though many suspected she was involved with Dornhelm, he denies it. Grace was, however, very fond of 29-year-old business executive Jeffery Martin Fitzgerald whom she met on a Concorde flight in 1980. By her own admission they were intimately involved. There were other young men who flattered and flirted with Grace. They made her laugh. They were attentive. They made her feel alive and wanted – all the little things that Rainier was not providing.

Grace eased her frustrations by drinking and overeating. She had put on considerable weight but said, 'I'm fifty-two and the mother of three children. Why should I care?'

In August 1982, Rainier, Grace, Caroline and Albert cruised to Scandinavia on the *SS Mermoz*. Stephanie stayed behind with her boyfriend Paul Belmondo, the eighteen-year-old son of the famous French actor Jean-Paul. Mother and daughter were at odds during the summer and quarrelled bitterly. Grace had consented to Stephanie's studying dress design but the young Princess resented the idea of being chaperoned in Paris. Then Stephanie decided she wanted to attend racing-car driving school with Belmondo. Grace put her foot down and the angry discussions with her 'wild child', as she referred to Stephanie, heated up.

Grace was going through a difficult menopause and she had high blood pressure that went untreated. After the cruise, a lingering head cold and bronchitis made her irritable, listless and depressed.

On Monday morning, 13 September 1982, Grace's chauffeur parked her car, a Rover 3500, in front of the house at Roc Angel. Before leaving for Paris with Stephanie, she had an appointment with her seamstress and hurriedly laid out on the back seat dresses that needed altering. Grace dismissed the chauffeur because Stephanie was going along and the car was packed with their belongings. Grace got behind the wheel and waved goodbye at about 9:30 a.m. She had a terrible fear of dying in an airplane or car. When she drove, which was seldom, it was erratic and at a snail's pace. She never wore seat belts because they were too confining or, as a friend said, 'Grace felt trapped . . . locked in.' She was accustomed to the five-mile ride between Roc Angel and the palace, despite the winding roads. On this sunny September morning, she complained to Stephanie about a headache.

The driver of the truck behind them noticed the Rover swerving back and forth. Assuming the driver was sleepy, he blew his horn and the car was back on course. Doctors theorised later that Grace had had a minor stroke and was bewildered. If so, it could not have happened at a worse time.

The Rover was on a decline headed for the sharpest turn on the Moyenne Corniche. The truck driver said, 'The corner came up. I did not see the car slow down . . . the brake lights didn't come on . . . she did not even try to turn and I had the impression that she was going faster and faster . . .'

The Rover shot straight ahead over the edge of the hillside and into the air. It turned over and fell 120 feet into a garden patch. Stephanie lost consciousness briefly and came to crouched underneath the glove compartment, the only section of the Rover intact. Stephanie managed to crawl out but Grace was pinned in the back seat. Ambulance attendants had to break the back window to get her out. She had a wide gash on the forehead and her right leg was twisted. Although Grace's eyes were open, she did not respond. Her CAT scan revealed two brain lesions. Doctors suggested that the minor stroke that Grace had suffered in the car would not have killed her. The other lesion was a massive haemorrhage caused by the accident. The deadly stroke in conjunction with Grace's other injuries proved to be fatal. She was put on a life-support system, but on Tuesday morning the encephalogram indicated Grace was braindead. At noon, Rainier gave permission for his wife to be taken off the life-support system, and at 10:35 p.m. on Tuesday, 14 September, Princess Grace was dead.

Her body lay in state for two days. A cheap wig had been pulled down below her hairline to cover the forehead wound. It appeared as if the beautiful Grace had been hastily prepared for burial. A close friend remarked, 'She was gussied up.'

On Saturday 18 September 1982, family and friends gathered in the Cathedral of St Nicholas, where the royal wedding had taken place twenty-six years earlier. At 10:15 a.m., the eerie silence was broken by trumpets and the funeral procession began from the palace chapel to the cathedral. No one was more pathetic than Rainier. A broken and shattered man, his bowed head sank into his chest. He looked at no one – his eyelids drooped in despair. Prince Rainier's only gesture was reaching out for Caroline's hand during the service. No one can forget his inconsolable torment, and sadly, we ask ourselves, 'Did he really love Grace that much?'

The Films of Grace Kelly

Fourteen Hours (20th Century-Fox, 1951)
High Noon (United Artists, 1952)
Mogambo (MGM, 1953)
Diam M For Murder (Warner Brothers, 1954)
Rear Window (Paramount, 1954)
The Country Girl (Paramount, 1954)
Green Fire (MGM, 1954)
The Bridges at Toko-Ri (Paramount, 1955)
To Catch a Thief (Paramount, 1955)
The Swan (MGM, 1956)
High Society (MGM, 1956)
The Children of Theatre Street (Peppercorn-Wormser, 1977)

10

Elizabeth

She was married three times in five years, divorced at eighteen and a widow at twenty-five. By the time she was thirty, she had stolen her second husband from gorgeous legend Marlene Dietrich and her fourth husband from America's Sweetheart, Debbie Reynolds. She was banished from Hollywood at twenty-seven, welcomed back with an Oscar two years later and was the first Hollywood star offered one million dollars to make a film. Women envied her and men idolised this spoiled, self-absorbed goddess whose scandalous behaviour was condemned by the Vatican. She got heated criticism for taking what and whom she wanted, hurting innocent people and making it clear that she couldn't have cared less what the public thought of her. 'I don't owe them a damn thing,' she said. 'If they want to see my movies, fine. If they don't, that's fine too.'

But we bought every magazine with her picture on the cover and stood in line to watch her films because she was a magnificent specimen of womanhood, naughty or nice.

As a teenager Elizabeth Taylor's rare and remarkable beauty carried her through mediocre films. With her black hair, violet eyes, tiny waist and volupous breasts, she needed only to appear on screen to maintain her star status. Liz and the camera had a mutual love for each other – the only lasting love affair in her lifetime.

Elizabeth Rosemond Taylor was born in London on 27 February 1932, the daughter of an American art dealer, Francis, whose wife Sara had given up her acting career for marriage. With the threat of World War Two looming, the Taylors settled in Los Angeles where Francis's wealthy uncle owned an art gallery. In a town of beautiful people it would seem unlikely that seven-year-old Elizabeth could command attention but she did and it didn't take much encouragement for Sara to have her daughter take a screen test. Unfortunately MGM was looking for a little girl to replace singer Deanna Durbin and Elizabeth couldn't carry a tune. It's a mystery why she wasn't tested for the part of Rhett Butler's daughter, Bonnie, in *Gone With the Wind* because of Elizabeth's resemblance to Vivien Leigh's Scarlett.

Sara, ever the social butterfly, managed another screen test at Universal Studios and Elizabeth was signed to a short term contract that was cancelled after one forgettable film because, '. . . she can't sing, she can't dance, she can't act and her mother is an overbearing bitch'.

Meanwhile, Sam Marx, an MGM producer, was involved in casting *Lassie Come Home* and was looking for a little girl with a British accent. 'I knew Francis Taylor,' Marx said, 'and heard his daughter was exceptionally adorable so I asked him to send her over for a screen test. Had I known MGM had turned her down previously I would never have called Francis. When Elizabeth came into my office I couldn't believe my eyes. She was the prettiest child I had ever seen.'

Metro-Goldwyn-Mayer offered Sara's daughter the usual seven-year contract at a salary of $100 a week. (Lassie was making $250.) Sara signed the agreement on 15 October 1942, and was alloted $100 a week as her daughter's coach and chaperone. Elizabeth followed the very successful and sentimental *Lassie Come Home* with small parts in *The White Cliffs of Dover* and *Jane Eyre*.

In 1939 Elizabeth told Sara she had finished reading the book *National*

Velvet and loved the story about a girl, Velvet Brown, who rides her horse Pi to victory in the Grand National. 'MGM's going to make the movie,' she added, 'and I want to play Velvet Brown more than I've wanted anything else in the world, Mummie.' The film would eventually be released in 1944 but in 1943 eleven-year-old Elizabeth was told she wasn't old enough to portray Velvet. Rumour had it she willed herself to grow three inches taller for the part but that was not the problem. Elizabeth lacked physical maturity. On the brink of womanhood she made up her mind to help nature along by doing exercises to develop her chest.

Producer Sam Marx said,

> I never knew a child who was so determined. She learned to ride a horse and in her spare time begged and pleaded for the part of Velvet. She literally pestered everyone connected with the production of *National Velvet*. What amazed me was how she came across in her screen test for the film. The camera seemed to caress her beautiful young face and she responded with a quality rarely seen. I can't say she was a good actress. In fact she always had a shrill voice that no amount of training could change. But even at that tender age she had that special something every Hollywood producer hopes he's found until the camera proves otherwise.

Elizabeth was not a skilled rider, however, and it was a stuntman who did the steeplechase jumps in the film and took the fall that has been so well publicised as the mishap responsible for Elizabeth's persistent back problems.

When Francis Taylor heard his daughter's hair was going to be cut off to disguise her as a male jockey, he stepped in for the first and only time during her career, and a wig was custom-made and clipped in the scene. Though Elizabeth said in later years that Velvet Brown was an extension of herself, much credit for her praised performance must be given to her co-star Mickey Rooney who took the time to coach Elizabeth. He taught her some tricks of the trade and most importantly, to listen carefully to the dialogue and react rather than recite her lines.

As a result of the enormous success of *National Velvet* MGM gave Elizabeth a $15,000 bonus and raised her weekly salary to $200. Now an established member of L.B. Mayer's family, she was attending MGM's Little Red Schoolhouse. Graduate Lana Turner recalled,

> Our life revolved around MGM from early morning until we finished filming late in the afternoon. We attended Mr Mayer's birthday parties on the lot and were expected to show up at his house on Sunday for his pool parties and picnic lunches. We lived and breathed MGM. The studio did everything for us. A limousine was at our disposal. They made first class reservations for us on trains and planes and we got the best suites in hotels. If we made a public appearance, they arranged for a hairdresser, make-up man and selected our clothes. They manufactured our backgrounds if our real childhoods did not live up to their standards. They changed our names, our hair colour and our diction. We were constantly scrutinized on the lot. If we didn't walk or stand correctly, we heard about it. Our manners had to be perfect. At the time it was a bore and a burden but looking back I felt like Cinderella.

For many young contract players, MGM was home. Elizabeth accepted this with mixed emotions. She needed a haven apart from the studio but did not find it with the domineering Sara and saw very little of her father who was living at a hotel with her brother, Howard, whom she idolised. He was two years older than Elizabeth and very handsome, but he fought Sara by shaving his head for a screen test. It's not clear if either of the children knew their father was a homosexual but Hollywood insiders were aware that Francis was having an affair with MGM fashion designer Adrian, married to actress Janet Gaynor. At best, the Taylor marriage was rocky. Sara was the stronger of the two and now that Elizabeth was the breadwinner in the family with Sara a close second, Francis felt useless, but not too proud to accept his daughter's support. Sara would soon begin an affair with director Michael Curtiz.

Press agent Jim Merrick felt that Elizabeth was rightfully confused. 'She had a love-hate relationship with MGM,' he said.

> She needed the pampering and feeling of importance that most teens get from their parents. MGM offered her protection from the outside world but she knew very little about what went on in that world. She was chaperoned every minute of her young life and though she complained about this confinement, she would find out how cruel life could be outside MGM's golden gates.
>
> I have always defended Elizabeth. Yes, she was spoiled. Yes, she was a man-eater. This was a form of rebelling. Once she had her

freedom she was going to grab whatever happiness came her way. In her heart, she deserved it after years of what she considered servitude not only from MGM but her mother's control, as well.

Elizabeth fell in love with older men to substitute for the father she loved but rarely saw. I think her second husband, Michael Wilding, was the spitting image of Francis and just as weak. Mike Todd was much older but he was strong and she did what Mike told her to do. I think Richard Burton was both lover and father, most likely the love of her life which threw her for a loop. I'm not a psychiatrist but looking back on her relationship with her father and romantic involvements, the puzzle fits.

After the success of *National Velvet*, Mayer planned for Elizabeth to make *Sally in Her Alley*, a film that Sara felt was beneath her daughter. She expressed her displeasure to Mayer, who made it very clear to Sara that it was he who made decisions at MGM and his stars did what they were told. Knowing Francis could barely support his family when they settled in Los Angeles, Mayer said it was he who took her out of the gutter. It was a bad choice of words but he was furious if anyone defied his choice of assigned pictures. Sara, who was in love with Mayer, sat quietly and listened but Elizabeth stood up to her boss. 'Don't you ever talk to my mother like that!' she cried. 'You and your studio can go to hell!' She ran out of Mayer's office and never set foot in it again during her eighteen years at MGM. Sara remained calm and chose to stay behind with the little man for whom she would gladly have left her gay husband.

MGM press agent George Nichols said there were rumours that Mayer and Sara had a brief affair. 'I doubt it very much,' Nichols explained. 'Sara was a stunning woman but she was also the mother of one of MGM's most promising stars. Becoming intimate with Sara would have given her power and that was something he surely didn't want. Elizabeth's hatred of Mayer stemmed from the fact that her mother was in love with him. She was too young at the time to understand the nature of her parents' separation so she blamed Mayer.'

Elizabeth did not make *Sally in Her Alley*, of course. Instead she did *Courage of Lassie* and received top billing over America's favourite collie. Her first role as a blossoming teenager was *Cynthia* in 1947. If Elizabeth worried about her flat chest as Velvet Brown she now had to tone down her ample breasts for the censors. At fifteen she was showing all the signs of becoming a voluptuous woman, according to Orson Welles, who noticed her entering the MGM canteen. 'I am not a man who stares at little girls,' he explained, 'but when I saw Elizabeth Taylor I lusted for her. I felt like a dirty old man.'

Life With Father was a delightful film with Irene Dunne and William Powell. Elizabeth was loaned to Warner Brothers in 1946 to make the picture, directed by Michael Curtiz, a 58-year-old Hungarian with whom Sara became involved. His wife's love affair gave Francis more time to spend with his great love Adrian. Though Elizabeth was not exposed to the truth, she felt the tension when her parents were together for social events. And she undoubtedly noticed the warmth between her mother and Curtiz. Irene Dunne thought Elizabeth was very tense while filming *Life With Father* and suffered from colds and nasal infections. 'She had crying spells and was frequently absent with colds and sinus ailments,' Dunne remembered. 'This was the beginning of Elizabeth's many bouts with every imaginable illness for the rest of her life. If she was nervous or unhappy, she got sick.'

Elizabeth was also tired of making movies. She might have retired at the tender age of fifteen if she hadn't been her family's sole means of support. If she was in the dark about Sara's sexual affair with Curtiz and her father's gay relationship with Adrian, Elizabeth was very aware of her obligation as the breadwinner in the family.

She was also becoming aware of boys. She got her first screen kiss from Jimmy Lydon in *Cynthia* and her first off-screen kiss from actor Marshall Thompson on her first date that was well publicised by MGM. She said in an interview, 'I prefer older men.' Thompson was four years older than Elizabeth but she developed a painful crush on actor Peter Lawford who made the mistake of taking her to the beach. 'She has ugly legs,' he told a friend. 'They turn me off.' Peter was too much the gentleman to say anything to Elizabeth but he told her to exercise and firm up her calves if she wanted to look like the slim models in their bathing suits that caught his eye. Sara intervened and telephoned Peter about taking her daughter out. He responded, 'I'm sorry, Mrs Taylor, but she's not my type.' Elizabeth groaned, 'Why is it the men I like don't like me?'

Following the delightful *A Date With Judy* costarring Jane Powell and Robert Stack, Elizabeth swooned with delight that she would be filming *Julia Misbehaves* with Peter Lawford. In the movie she is engaged to be married but falls in love with Lawford's character. After a romantic kiss, Elizabeth blew her line. Instead of saying, 'Oh, Richie, what are we going to do?' she sighed, 'Oh, Richie, what am I going to do?' The other cast members were aware of the situation and applauded.

Lawford was dating Lana Turner whom Elizabeth envied for her perfect figure and sophisticated aura. But it was only a matter of time before she would find a young man of her very own to love. West Point football hero Glenn Davis was every young girl's dream of the perfect man in 1948. He and Elizabeth met at a dinner party and they dated a few times. 'There was nothing to it,' Davis said. 'I gave her a gold football to wear on a chain around her neck and she told everyone we were to be engaged. That's not true.' But Elizabeth wanted it to be the real thing and MGM press agents did the rest.

Shortly after completing *Little Women*, Elizabeth bid a tearful farewell to Glenn who was shipped to Korea. Howard Hughes took this opportunity to offer Francis a million dollars for Elizabeth's hand in marriage. She cringed at the idea and turned her nose up when Hughes handed her a box of priceless gems. Though shocked at the thought of 'selling' his daughter, Francis was tempted by the million-dollar offer and regretted not following up on the idea.

In the autumn of 1948, Elizabeth sailed to England to make *Conspirator*. Her handsome leading man was 37-year-old Robert Taylor. 'This is my first adult role,' she exclaimed.

Despite rumours that Bob Taylor kissed Elizabeth too passionately, it was quite the opposite. He was upset when the press went overboard regarding Elizabeth's first adult kiss on the screen and phoned MGM to protest. 'Give the kid a break,' he said. But Bob was not immune to his beautiful leading lady in a bedroom scene. 'I was forced to tell the cameraman to shoot me from the waist up because I had an erection,' he said. 'Go figure it. I had played opposite Lana Turner, Ava Gardner, Greta Garbo and almost every other MGM beauty so I should have been immune to a sweet teenager, for God's sake.'

Elizabeth retired to her dressing room where her tutor announced, 'Time for your algebra lesson.'

'Who can think about algebra at a time like this,' she swooned on a chaise lounge. 'I've just been kissed by Robert Taylor!'

Before returning home with Sara, Elizabeth paid a visit to her uncle in Miami Beach and celebrated her seventeenth birthday. At the party she met handsome William Pawley Jr, a wealthy 28-year-old businessman, who followed her to Los Angeles with a 3.5 carat diamond engagement ring. Shortly after Sara made the announcement of her daughter's impending marriage, the Pawley family became disenchanted with Elizabeth. Her clothes were too tight and too low cut. Bill had a solution to that. He asked Elizabeth to give up her career. She refused and the engagement was off. Poor Elizabeth was still an old maid at seventeen . . .

But she wasn't a *poor* maiden. MGM was paying her $2000 a week, with an added $250 for Sara. Yes, she was satisfied with the money, but let it be known she wanted better roles after making *The Big Hangover*, a tacky film with little to offer. Director George Stevens thought Elizabeth would be perfect as the spoiled debutante in *A Place in the Sun*, based on a true story about a young man who drowns his dowdy pregnant girlfriend to marry a rich and beautiful young socialite. Elizabeth fell deeply in love with her 29-year-old leading man, Montgomery Clift. She was aware of his gay friends but didn't let it bother her, writing love letters to him and making up excuses to be with him after hours. Monty took her advances in his stride and concentrated on making her a better actress. He took the time to coach Elizabeth, who responded with all her being.

Wanting desperately to please Clift, she proved herself a fine actress in *A Place in the Sun*. The first love scene, a classic today, is a close-up of Elizabeth seducing Monty with a kiss and whispering, '. . . tell mama. Tell mama all . . .' When she viewed the rushes she squirmed in her seat. Was it possible she could portray such passion for the camera? When the picture came out the buzz in Hollywood was, 'Who taught Elizabeth Taylor to make love like that?'

Though Clift leaned toward men, he was bisexual. For a long time he'd had an on-and-off affair with torch singer (of love songs mostly) Libby Holman and now he was embarking on one with Elizabeth or so she hoped, luring him to go over their script while she soaked in the bathtub. According to Monty he tried intimacy with Elizabeth but failed to perform. She proposed marriage to him several times and he made light of it, referring to her playfully as 'Bessie Mae'.

Monty was a confused young man who was hooked on pills and liquor to ease the pain of reality. He understood Elizabeth better than he understood himself and though he knew marriage to her was impossible he had to be part of her life. Their friendship was like no other – a complicated relationship of frustration, guilt and devotion until his untimely death.

Nicky Hilton Jr, 23-year-old son of Conrad, chairman of the Hilton Hotel corporation, caught a glimpse of Elizabeth at a party and called his pal Peter Lawford to arrange an introduction in the autumn of 1949. Nicky was the man who had everything – good looks, charm and money – the latter most appealing to Sara who was in awe of Conrad's 47-room mansion in Bel-Air. When she asked for a tour of the sprawling manicured grounds, tennis courts and pool Conrad replied, 'Oh, my dear, that would take at least two hours.' Sara smiled sweetly and said, 'The highlights will do.'

Elizabeth was on the rebound after completing *A Place in the Sun* and Monty's rejection of her. She was ripe for romance and Nicky provided that with flowers sent to her daily followed by gifts of expensive jewellery. After a brief courtship, Sara announced her daughter's engagement to the heir of Hilton's $125,000,000 fortune. Nicky gave Elizabeth a square-cut diamond engagement ring that covered both knuckles. MGM was ecstatic and arranged for her latest film *Father of the Bride* with Spencer Tracy to coincide with the May wedding. (Paramount did not release *A Place in the Sun* until 1951.)

The studio also arranged for Elizabeth to graduate from the Little Red Schoolhouse earlier than her classmates. At University High in January 1950 wearing the traditional white cap and gown, she receivevd her diploma.

MGM paid for Elizabeth's magnificent $3500 wedding gown created by Helen Rose and they took charge of the event, claiming exclusive rights to the wedding photos. One might say that Metro-Goldwyn-Mayer had a copyright to the Taylor–Hilton nuptial.

There were those who had their doubts about Nicky Hilton as a candidate for marriage. Like Elizabeth, he was spoiled and self-indulgent. He was an alcoholic, a dope addict and compulsive gambler. He also preferred a variety of girls and had his pick of gorgeous women including his stepmother Zsa Zsa Gabor with whom he had an affair. She confirmed his staying power in bed and how well-endowed he was.

On 6 May 1950, Francis Taylor walked a radiant Elizabeth down the aisle of the Church of the Good Shepherd in Beverly Hills. When the monsignor pronounced the couple man and wife, Nicky embraced his bride with a long and passionate kiss that was the last touch of ardour for three days into their honeymoon. While Elizabeth was waiting in the bridal suite at the Carmel Country Club on her wedding night the groom was seen in the bar downstairs getting drunk and flirting with several women. The second night he did the same. It wasn't until the third night that observers assumed the marriage was finally consummated. A depressed and disillusioned Elizabeth was not looking forward to their sailing for Europe on 23 May aboard the *Queen Mary*. Her fears became reality when Nicky ignored and abused her with such remarks as 'I'm tired of your face', and 'You're a fucking bore'. After losing $100,000 at the gambling tables, Nicky returned to their stateroom and punched her in the stomach while she was taking a shower. According to author Ellis Amburn, Nicky continued his abuse during their nine-month marriage, kicking her in the stomach and causing a miscarriage. At the time she was not aware of her pregnancy until '. . . I saw the baby in the toilet', she reportedly said.

On 26 January 1951, Elizabeth testified in court that she had been mentally and physically abused by her husband. She did not ask for alimony but kept her one hundred shares of Hilton stock. When Nicky died of a heart attack in 1969 at the age of 42, she had no comment.

Estranged from her parents, Elizabeth tried in vain to get out of making *Ivanhoe* in England, claiming she was recovering from a nervous breakdown, but MGM was steadfast. On her way to Europe she stayed in New York with Montgomery Clift, who had warned her about Nicky and was not in touch during her marriage. Elizabeth hoped he had been jealous enough of Hilton to accept another proposal but Monty responded by introducing her to his boyfriends in seedy gay bars. Those close to the situation felt only sadness for Clift who, by his own admission, loved Elizabeth but did not know how to deal with it. He drank heavily and she kept up with him to drown her own sorrows. This was the beginning of many years of alcoholism for Elizabeth who could absorb more liquor than most without showing the effects.

Elizabeth gave a wooden performance in *Ivanhoe* with Joan Fontaine and Robert Taylor. Her dialogue was inaudible and had to be redubbed, much to her chagrin. But she soon changed her attitude when 39-year old British actor Michael Wilding called to invite her for lunch. Elizabeth had met him briefly when she was making *Conspirator* but this time around she appreciated his gentle nature and wry British humour. Michael was in the process of divorcing his wife but was deeply involved with sultry Marlene Dietrich, who was no match for Elizabeth. 'What does she have that I don't have?' Marlene asked a friend. The answer was simple. What Elizabeth wants, Elizabeth gets, and she chased after Michael who was too meek and overcome to resist. He did not, however, agree to marry her. 'If I were older, you would,' she said. When Elizabeth kissed him at the airport before boarding a plane for New York, she did so with fervour and whispered, 'Goodbye, Mr Shilly-Shally. Forget we ever met.'

Though Michael was a respected actor in British films he had never experienced the fame that Elizabeth afforded him, but it was love that prompted him to follow her to Los Angeles. A few days later she called him to meet her at Cartier at Rodeo Drive to help her pick out a very expensive sapphire ring. Poor Michael was close to bankruptcy after his divorce and was in a sweat on his way to meet Elizabeth. She paid for the ring, however, asked him to put it on her engagement finger and announced her betrothal to Wilding on 1 February 1952. Sara said her daughter needed an older man and gave her blessing. Marlene referred to Elizabeth as 'that British tart with big tits'.

Three weeks later, on 21 February Elizabeth and Michael were married in a civil ceremony in the registry of London's Caxton Hall. Following a brief honeymoon they returned to Los Angeles and Elizabeth wasted no time in approaching MGM about putting her husband under contract. He signed a three-year agreement for $3000 a week. This was barely a living to Elizabeth who agreed to another seven-year deal with MGM for $5500 a week. In addition she asked MGM to loan her $50,000 to buy a house. Sara, who was entitled to a salary as long as her daughter was under contract to MGM, received $300 a week.

Michael sued columnist Hedda Hopper for writing about his wartime homosexual affair with actor Stewart Granger. She retracted her insinuation and Wilding eventually received $500,000. The fact that Michael was bisexual did not bother Elizabeth and she seemed oblivious to his epilepsy that put a damper on his Hollywood career due to occasional slurred speech. Stewart Granger felt that Marlene was better for Michael because she was very concerned about his health, making sure he took his medication and got enough rest. If he didn't eat properly Marlene prepared his meals.

'Liz can't boil an egg,' Granger said.

In June 1952 the Wildings moved into their new house. Elizabeth, having survived her traumatic marriage to Hilton, was overjoyed with her new life. She announced her pregnancy that summer and MGM reduced her salary to $2000 a week as opposed to taking her off the payroll, which was customary. She sat around getting fat while Michael cleaned up after her and cooked. This domestisity amused Montgomery Clift who was an occasional visitor. He told friends the marriage would never last because Michael was too tame for Elizabeth who didn't care what Monty thought as long as they could be together.

Michael Howard Wilding, named after his father and uncle, was born by caesarean section on 6 January 1953. Elizabeth had been disappointed at having to turn down *Elephant Walk* because she was pregnant. Vivien Leigh got the part and filmed the long-distance shots before having a nervous breakdown. Elizabeth replaced Vivien with co-stars Peter Finch and Dana Andrews. It was a mediocre movie but Elizabeth was relieved to be back on full salary. Michael foolishly turned down *Latin Lover* at MGM and was suspended without pay so the Wildings needed money badly.

In 1953 Elizabeth made four films – *Elephant Walk, Rhapsody, Beau Brummell* and *The Last Time I Saw Paris* (all released in 1954). She was not in a position to argue with MGM and did movies she hated. Critics said she did little else but gaze into the camera with nothing to offer other than her beauty. The exception was *The Last Time I Saw Paris* with Van Johnson. 'I was proud of that one,' she said. 'When I saw it I realised I could act.' The film was a tragic story of a spoiled young woman who comes into money during her marriage to a penniless writer. Their life of drinking and parties leads to his locking her out in the rain by mistake and she dies of pneumonia. Elizabeth was right about her acting maturity. She had been given a good script and she ran with it.

When she became pregnant with Christopher Wilding, Elizabeth negotiated with MGM. She could not afford a reduction in salary and opted for an extra year tacked on to her contract. She was becoming bored with Michael, who did little to contribute to their dire financial situation by turning down Rex Harrison's role in *My Fair Lady*. In later years Michael admitted, 'I was just too damn lazy.' He was not too lazy, however, to take his wife shopping for jewellery that Elizabeth usually charged to her own account.

Sara visited her grandchildren once a week and was appalled not only by the cats and dogs running around but their droppings on the floor and the smell of urine on the rugs. Elizabeth's clothes were scattered on top of or under this mess. Sara asked Michael about it. 'I can't keep up with the animal menagerie,' he said.

'Doesn't she hang up her clothes?' Sara asked.

'Yes,' Michael replied. 'She hangs them on the floor.'

Elizabeth was perfectly content, despite Sara's concern that the children might crawl over the animal droppings. 'Cats and dogs are clean, mother,' was the casual reply. 'Their saliva heals, you know.'

After being turned down for *The Barefoot Contessa*, the lead going to Ava Gardner, Elizabeth decided to fight for the part of Leslie Benedict in *Giant*, to be filmed by Warner Brothers. Despite the fact that Grace Kelly turned it down, Elizabeth exclaimed, 'I don't care if I am second choice.' This time MGM agreed with Elizabeth, and so did co-star Rock Hudson, much to her delight. Filming in Marfa, Texas, meant leaving her husband and children in L.A. , but Edna Ferber's *Giant* was worth it.

James Dean was the other major player in *Giant*. It would be his third and last film. Though he and Hudson were both bisexual, they did not get along well. Dean claimed Rock made a pass at him but the problem was Jimmy's scene-stealing obsession. The other actors had to know their lines and keep an eye on Dean as well. Elizabeth considered this very unprofessional and sided with Rock, whose wife Phyllis said she was sure her husband and Elizabeth were intimately involved. Wilding got the same impression during a brief visit to Texas when he was ignored by his wife in favour of Hudson. Elizabeth told Michael, 'I always fall in love with my leading men.'

Rock said, 'Elizabeth needed someone. Her marriage was a shambles and she worried about bringing up two kids alone. Then there was the embarrassing story in *Confidential* magazine about Michael bringing home two strippers. You can ignore these things but they still hurt.'

As she got to know James Dean, Elizabeth began spending more time alone with him. Years later she said Jimmy was unhappy and poured out his heart to her. 'We just talked,' she said.

Shortly after completing *Giant*, James Dean was killed in a car accident on 30 September 1955.

Elizabeth returned to a broken home. She and Michael no longer shared the same bedroom. He was drinking and running around. Elizabeth had flings with other men, including Victor Mature and Frank Sinatra who, according to Eddie Fisher, impregnated her. 'She wanted to divorce Wilding and marry Frank,' Fisher wrote in his memoirs, 'but Sinatra's manager put her in a limousine and drove her to a dirty place in Mexico for an abortion.'

Elizabeth's next scheduled film was *Raintree County* with Montgomery Clift, who moved temporarily to Los Angeles. On 12 May 1956 he attended a party at the Wilding house, lost control of his car on the winding canyon road and was seriously hurt. Elizabeth cradled his bloody head in her lap until the ambulance arrived. MGM suspended filming of *Raintree County* for nine weeks until Monty recovered.

On 30 June the Wildings accepted an invitation from producer Mike Todd to join his friends on a weekend cruise to Santa Barbara. The jaunt was well timed by the flamboyant Todd who had been waiting for the opportunity to meet Elizabeth. While others fawned over her, Todd made a point of fawning over his girlfriend, Evelyn Keyes. He gave the same performance at subsequent get-togethers he hosted. When MGM announced that the Wildings had separated, the 49-year-old Todd made his move and called Elizabeth to meet him at MGM about a business matter. Chomping on a huge Havana cigar, Mike confessed his love and said he was going to marry her. Elizabeth said she had a plane to catch but Todd knew that and when she arrived in Danville, Kentucky, to film *Raintree County*, she was greeted with an emerald bracelet and a card from Mike that read, 'I love you'. He called her every night and asked Monty to present her with a magnificent $30,000 black pearl ring and two hundred long-stemmed roses. 'Mike wants you to know your engagement ring is almost ready,' Monty said, shaking his head as if to say, 'Here we go again'.

Though Elizabeth and Monty were sleeping together during the filming of *Raintree County*, they fought over her increasing fondness for Todd. 'He's using you, Bessie Mae.' Elizabeth insisted Todd was the only man who didn't need her. In October Mike gave Elizabeth a 29.4-carat diamond ring that he had previously given to Evelyn Keyes but asked for it back 'because it doesn't quite fit'. She never saw the $100,000 diamond again. When Todd was asked why 29.4 carats, he replied, 'Because thirty carats would be gaudy.'

In late 1956 Elizabeth took a bad fall aboard a yacht that crushed three spinal discs. During her two-month stay at Columbia Presbyterian Hospital, she found out she was pregnant. In January 1957, she flew with Mike to Acapulco for a quickie divorce from Wilding, and on 2 February, she and Todd were married. Eddie Fisher was Mike's best man and his wife, Debbie Reynolds, was Elizabeth's matron of honour. It was the beginning of a glorious year for the newlyweds. Todd's film *Around the World in Eighty Days* won an Oscar for Best Picture and baby Lisa was born 'prematurely' on 6 August. Mike gave his wife priceless paintings, fur coats, emeralds, rubies and a magnificent diamond tiara.

Eddie Fisher and his wife Debbie witnessed a shocking episode during dinner at the Todds'. During an argument, Mike slapped Elizabeth and dragged her by the hair into the bedroom. Debbie dashed to the rescue only to find the couple about to make love. 'She liked to be roughed up,' Fisher said.

MGM approached Todd about his wife doing *Cat on a Hot Tin Roof*. If he approved, she would go along with it. Press agent George Nichols said, 'If you wanted Liz to do something you had to go through Todd. She'd do anything if he said so. Mike was first and foremost a promoter and he liked the idea of his wife being a movie star. In his opinion, she'd win an Oscar portraying Maggie the Cat. Though he made millions from *Around the World* he spent millions on Elizabeth and he always needed cash. I think Mike used her but he was also madly in love. They were one and the same to Todd.'

In March 1958, not long into the filming of *Cat on a Hot Tin Roof*, Elizabeth came down with a head cold complicated by a bronchial infection but she was determined to accompany Todd to New York for the Friars Club roast. He was very proud to be chosen Showman of the Year and she wanted to be with him at the Waldorf Astoria Hotel for this gala event. Doctors forbade her to go with a temperature of 102 so Mike boarded his plane 'The Lucky Liz' with friend Art Cohn on the night of 21 March.

The following morning Elizabeth awoke to the tragic news that Mike had been killed when his plane crashed in New Mexico. Though many friends rallied to her side, she leaned on Todd's closest friend, Eddie Fisher, while wife Debbie took charge of the Wilding children. Three weeks after Mike's tragic death, Elizabeth resumed filming *Cat on a Hot Tin Roof* and started seeing Fisher on the sly. When she flew to New York, he followed and their affair began. Hedda Hopper called Elizabeth and wanted to know how she could break up Fisher's marriage.

'You can't break a happy marriage,' was the reply.

'What do you think Mike would say to all this?' Hedda asked.

'Well, Mike is dead and I'm alive. What do you expect me to do? Sleep alone?'

Banished by friends in Hollywood, Elizabeth and Eddie patiently waited in seclusion for his divorce. They were married in Las Vegas on 12 May 1959. Unfortunately it was Fisher who suffered most from the scandal. Divorcing Debbie drained him of whatever money he had and N.B.C. cancelled his television show. Eddie drew crowds at his Las Vegas performances, but he had an added attraction to these shows – the appearance of his famous wife in the audience. Though Fisher had a splendid voice, he was now professionally redundant as many people walked out if Elizabeth failed to show up.

When 20th Century-Fox offered Elizabeth a million dollars to do *Cleopatra*, she became the highest paid actor in the world. MGM, however, reminded her she owed them one more film under her contract before she could do *Cleopatra*. Elizabeth was furious and went into a rage when she found out they expected her to play a prostitute in *Butterfield 8*. She told producer Pandro Berman, 'If you think I've been trouble in the past, you just wait. You'll regret the day you forced me to make that awful film.'

MGM agreed to give Eddie a part in the movie, hoping Elizabeth would behave herself but she refused to co-operate with anyone connected with *Butterfield 8*. She feigned illness and was rushed to hospital on one occasion, supposedly in a coma, but as the ambulance was about to pull up at the emergency entrance she asked Eddie, 'Where's my lip gloss?'

Finally the ordeal was over and Elizabeth signed a contract to do *Cleopatra* for a million dollars and ten per cent of the gross. Eddie was paid $1,500 a week to get his wife to the set on time and keep her sober. He became butler, baby sitter, porter, nurse and general flunky. Fisher was, however, the greatest lover Elizabeth ever had, by her own admission.

20th Century Fox planned to film *Cleopatra* in England until Elizabeth almost died from double pneumonia. One news service reported her death in a London clinic. Her survival was considered a miracle and the world was at her feet once again. Fisher, who was by her side throughout the ordeal, said the real cause of his wife's illness was booze and pills.

Elizabeth, weak, thin and beautiful, limped on stage at the 1961 Academy Awards and accepted an Oscar for her performance in *Butterfield 8*. She considered it a sympathy award, but many of her peers said the Oscar was compensation for Elizabeth being blackballed due to the Eddie Fisher scandal at the time when she'd been nominated for *Suddenly Last Summer*, *Raintree County*, and *Cat on a Hot Tin Roof*.

Concerned that the damp weather in England would be bad for Elizabeth's health, Fox decided to film *Cleopatra* in Rome. She did her first scenes with Rex Harrison as Caesar, and then faced 37-year-old Richard Burton's Mark Antony. His hands were shaking from a hangover and she helped him hold his coffee cup steady. 'My heart went out to him,' she said.

The pompous Burton predicted he would seduce his leading lady and in January 1962 he announced not so gallantly to his male chums, 'I just fucked Elizabeth Taylor in the back seat of my Cadillac.'

For Burton, a notorious womaniser, this was not unusual. Being married to his Welsh wife, Sybil, for twelve years did not prevent him from having affairs with many women, including such leading ladies as Susan Strasberg, Claire Bloom and Jean Simmons. Blatantly, he invited Pat Tunder, a 21-year-old blonde chorus girl, to Rome with the promise of a part in *Cleopatra*. Elizabeth told producer Walter Wanger, 'Either she goes or I go'. Miss Tunder was on the next plane out of Rome.

Within a few short weeks, rumours of Elizabeth's romance with Burton had reaching the public. 'I've had affairs before,' he said, 'but how did I know the woman was so fucking famous? She knocks Khrushchev off the bloody front page.' Sybil apparently felt the same way. By mid-February she threatened to leave Rome, and Richard panicked. He told Elizabeth he would not risk losing his wife. The romance was over. Elizabeth took an overdose of sleeping pills and was rushed to Salvator Mundi Hospital. Walter Wanger told the press she had food poisoning. Eddie Fisher went to Bulgari and bought his wife a $250,000 emerald necklace. 'One thing I learned about Elizabeth was the value of gifts,' he said. 'Just a little fifty-thousand-dollar diamond would make everything wonderful for up to four days.'

Roaring drunk, Burton showed up at the Fishers' villa demanding to see Elizabeth, pointed to her and said, 'She's my girl. You are my girl, aren't you?'

'Yes,' she replied in front of Eddie.

'If you're my girl come over here and stick your tongue down my throat.'

Elizabeth responded passionately and Eddie retreated to his room. Before leaving for New York he told Sybil everything that had been going on between their spouses. In a few days, she left Italy also, leaving Burton and Taylor alone in Rome. She bought him a Rolls-Royce. He gave her a $150,000 emerald brooch from Bulgari.

Eddie Fisher, pursued by the press in New York, told reporters that rumours of an affair between his wife and Burton were not true. To prove it he got Elizabeth on the phone.

'Tell them it's nonsense,' Fisher said.

'I just can't do that,' she replied, 'because there is some truth to the story. I just can't do that.'

The following day, 'Le Scandale', as Burton now referred to his affair with Taylor, made headlines around the world.

Richard Burton was born Richard Walter Jenkins Jr on 10 November 1925 in Pontrhydfen, South Wales. His father was a hard-drinking coal miner. His mother died giving birth to her thirteenth child when Richard was four years old. In 1943 he moved in with his mentor Philip Burton, a drama coach and Shakespearean authority. Richard took Burton's name because it was more prestigious in England than the Welsh name Jenkins. He appeared in stage plays and at the Old Vic Company in *Hamlet*, *Henry V*, and *Othello*, to name a few. Among his films were *My Cousin Rachel*, *The Robe*, *Alexander the Great*, and *The Longest Day*.

Burton married nineteen-year-old Sybil Williams, a prematurely silver-haired Welsh actress, in 1949. Their first child, Kate, was born in 1957. Two years later Sybil gave birth to a mentally retarded daughter, Jessica, who was later institutionalised.

Richard's guilt over Jessica haunted him during his lifetime and was one reason he vowed never to dissolve his marriage. Though he was devoted to Sybil, the consensus was that Richard was highly sexual and craved affairs with other women, all of whom were passing fancies. Until Elizabeth Taylor, that is. There were many people who insisted Burton chose her over Sybil because marriage to Elizabeth offered him wealth and worldwide fame, but it soon became obvious that he had fallen deeply in love with her. Sybil may have suspected this was the real thing when she attempted suicide by slashing her wrists. Not to be outdone, Elizabeth told Richard she would die for him. At a secret hideaway for the weekend, he ignored what she said until she gulped down a handful of sleeping pills. Somehow he managed to get her to a Rome hospital in time.

When *Cleopatra* was finished in the summer of 1962, Elizabeth had a change of heart. She felt Burton's devotion to the autistic Jessica might destroy him if he divorced Sybil so she broke off her affair with him. They both retreated to their homes in Switzerland, she to Gstaad and her children, he to Celigny and his family. Elizabeth contacted Eddie Fisher about a reconciliation and offered to send him a plane ticket from New York. Then came a call from Burton. Could they get together for lunch? She agreed and the affair was on again. When Richard was offered $500,000 to do *The VIPs* with Sophia Loren in London, Elizabeth said she'd do it for $1,000,000. Looking around the movie set in London, Elizabeth said sarcastically, 'Will I never be finished with MGM?'

Burton's divorce from Sybil would eventually cost him over $1,000,000 and an undisclosed annual income. Eddie Fisher, however, was not about to give in without a financial fight. In time he would receive close to $1,000,000 after dividing up his business ventures with Elizabeth. Waiting for her final divorce decree, she accompanied Richard to Puerto Vallarto, Mexico, where he made *The Night of the Iguana* with Ava Gardner, Deborah Kerr and seventeen-year-old Sue Lyon of *Lolita* fame. Eddie Fisher wrote in his memoirs that Burton had a fling with Sue. It wasn't easy with the ever present and possessive Elizabeth watching his every move. She and Richard drank from sunrise after sunset. When he tried to cut down on his alcoholic intake, she discouraged him. 'When you're sober, you're a bore,' she told him.

They liked Puerto Vallarto so much they bought their rented house, Casa Kimberley, with six bedrooms and six baths that was expanded into a compound with ten bedrooms, eleven baths, three kitchens and a huge swimming pool.

On 6 March 1964, Elizabeth was free to marry the man she loved. Since Burton was doing *Hamlet* in Toronto, the lovers flew secretly to Montreal for the wedding. Burton drank himself into oblivion on the flight. 'I don't know what you're so nervous about,' Elizabeth said. 'We've been sleeping together for two years.'

Drunk but able to stand, Burton waited for his bride in the eighth-floor bridal suite of the Ritz-Carlton Hotel on 15 March 1964. 'Where is that fat little tart?' he harped. Finally she arrived – a vision in a low-cut bright yellow chiffon gown complemented by recent gifts from Richard – an emerald and diamond necklace with matching earrings. After the brief ceremony Elizabeth exclaimed, 'This marriage will last forever.' Richard, a drink in his hand, said, 'I'm relieved'. At his next performance of *Hamlet*, Burton took several curtain calls and told the audience, 'There will be no more marriages!'

In *The Sandpiper*, filmed in Big Sur, California and Paris, Elizabeth played a Bohemian painter who falls in love with a married Episcopal minister (Burton). She received her usual million dollars, ten per cent of the gross and $4,000 a week living expenses. Burton, who was aiming for $2,000,000 in the future, got $500,000 for *The Sandpiper*. Elizabeth demanded top billing above and the same size as the title. Her hours were from ten to six with Saturdays, Sundays and evenings off. For tax purposes, she became a British subject and, in private, renounced her American citizenship. The Burtons banked in Switzerland, their legal residence, and were not subjected to U.S. income tax.

Warner Brothers wanted Elizabeth for the role of Martha in *Who's Afraid of Virginia Woolf?*, the story of a middle-aged couple whose bickering bordered on brutality and which many people thought mirrored the Burtons' life. Elizabeth offered to do it for $1,100,000 and ten per cent of the gross. The problem was casting the part of Martha's meek husband, George. Many well known actors had turned the role down because the movie was too risqué. Elizabeth urged Richard to play the part. Elizabeth, who put on twenty-five pounds for the role, was made up to look like a bloated middle-aged floozy. Richard took this opportunity to talk about his wife who was considered the most beautiful woman in the world. 'She's pretty enough,' he said, 'but she has an insipid double chin, big feet, stumpy legs, a potbelly, and she's as pouty-breasted as a pigeon.'

Elizabeth and Richard were nominated for Oscars, both for the fifth time, but it was she who won. In Paris she was so infuriated that Burton lost that she refused to accept the usual congratulatory call or give a statement to the press. Elizabeth was sure her husband had been snubbed because of 'le scandale'.

Who's Afraid of Virginia Woolf? was the best of their ten co-starring vehicles . . .

On 22 July 1966, while the Burtons were filming *The Taming of the Shrew*, Elizabeth received a phone call to say that Montgomery Clift had died of a heart attack brought on by alcohol abuse. He was 45-years old. Ironically, he was preparing to fly to Rome for *Reflections in a Golden Eye* with Elizabeth. Unable to attend Monty's funeral, she sent flowers and a card that read, 'Rest, perturbed spirit'.

One critic referred to the Burtons as 'the worst act in show business'. Their films *The Taming of the Shrew*, *Doctor Faustus*, *The Comedians*, and *Boom!* were a waste of time except for the millions of dollars that they deposited in their Swiss bank account. Elizabeth was well aware that her popularity at the box office was slipping. Though she made fun of the studio system she was, nonetheless, a graduate of Metro-Goldwyn-Mayer whose motto was 'Art for Art's Sake'. With fervour she told Richard she wanted to play Anne Boleyn to his Henry VIII in *Anne of the Thousand Days*. Burton looked her in the eye and said, 'Sorry, luv. You're too long in the tooth.' Elizabeth went berserk when youthful Genevieve Bujold was cast as Anne. Richard referred to his leading lady as 'Gin', a sign that he was embarking on an affair. Bujold requested that Elizabeth should not be present on the set of *Anne*, but the Burtons' contract stated that both were permitted. Bujold was a beginner but she got even with Elizabeth for her jealous passion during filming. When she accepted the Golden Globe Award for Best Actress, Bujold said, 'I owe my performance all to Richard Burton. He was generous, kind, helpful, and witty. And generosity was the one great quality.'

Though it's doubtful that Richard and 'Gin' were intimate, he showed all the signs of wanting it to happen. Burton the womaniser was re-emerging and Elizabeth knew it. Not that she wasn't a satisfying bed partner –

according to Richard's diary 'Elizabeth is an eternal one night stand. She is my private and personal bought mistress. And lascivious with it. It is impossible to tell you what is consisted in the act of love.'

But, as so many friends noted, it was shortly after the Bujold incident that Richard bought his wife the famous 33.19-carat Krupp diamond for $305,000 in 1969, followed by the $37,000 La Pereginia pearl suspended from a $100,000 diamond, ruby and pearl necklace, and the magnificent 69.42-carat diamond, one inch wide and one inch thick, worth $1,100,000. *Look* magazine referred to Elizabeth as 'a fading movie queen who has much and wants more'. Sheila Graham wrote in her column that Elizabeth 'looked like a woman who has made it rich and was wearing all her possessions on her ample back'.

Richard proudly announced that he had spent $192,000 on a yacht that was refurbished for another $240,000 and a twin-jet with kitchen, lounge, bar and movie screen, for $1,000,000. Elizabeth told stunned reporters how cosy it was to relax at home with the likes of Picasso, Renoir, Monet and Van Gogh hanging on the wall.

On 20 November 1968, Francis Taylor died at the age of seventy. He had been in ill health for several years following a stroke. Elizabeth attended his funeral and made peace with Sara. 'Despite her protestations about her mother,' Richard said, 'Elizabeth only wants to protect and cherish her now.'

The Burtons continued their globe-trotting and mingling with the elite. They often dined with the Duke and Duchess of Windsor, the Rothschilds, Princess Margaret, Princess Grace of Monaco, and, as Burton put it, '. . . Count what's his name and the Earl of whatever'.

Elizabeth's precarious health problems, however, put a strain on Richard, who was terrified of losing her and, at the same time, terrified of illness and death. He blamed her heavy drinking and painkillers for many of her health-related problems. Thus far she had had 27 operations with more to follow. During her marriage to Burton, she was hospitalised with gynaecological and recurring back problems, anaemia, haemorrhoids and drug addiction. In 1970 Richard attempted to change their life, which was a web of drunken binges and hangovers. He went on the wagon, but Elizabeth continued her heavy drinking. In a sober state, he found her behaviour less than desirable. She wanted sex and he did not, due, Richard said, to his body's adjustment to total abstinence. If life was unbearable when both were drunk, it was worse now that Elizabeth was drinking alone. Richard was no longer his charming self, she said. He was dull and listless. No fun in and out of bed. After ninety days he gave in to her and had a drink.

In 1972 the Burtons sent out invitations to Elizabeth's fortieth birthday party: 'We would love you to come to Budapest as our guest for the weekend of 26 and 27 February to celebrate my big 40 birthday . . . hotel is very Hilton . . . dress slacks for Saturday night . . . something gay and pretty for Sunday night . . . dark glasses for hangovers in between . . . lots of love Elizabeth and Richard.'

Burton told reporters he was giving his wife a $50,000 heart-shaped diamond inscribed with his everlasting love. 'I would have liked to buy the Taj Mahal for Elizabeth,' he said, 'but it would have cost too much to transport it.'

Richard managed to get through the gala weekend without a drink but shortly after the birthday party his brother Ifor died and Burton returned to the bottle with a vengeance. He had to be carried to the set of *Bluebeard* in the morning. Friends agree that Ifor's death sent Burton into states of depression, nastiness and drunkenness that would end his marriage to Elizabeth.

During night filming of *Bluebeard*, Richard was shooting a scene with Nathalie Delon, walking with her down the street and around the corner. He didn't return for twenty-four hours. Richard said, 'Once I started being attracted to other women, I knew – the game was up.'

Elizabeth phoned Aristotle Onassis and met him in Rome for a dinner that was interrupted by a mob of paparazzi who so enraged Onassis that the police were called. The incident made headlines. Where were Jackie Kennedy Onassis and Richard Burton?

At five in the morning Elizabeth called Richard. When he answered, she screamed, 'Get that woman out of my bed!' Burton asked a friend, 'How did she know?'

In September, 1972, the Burtons did a made-for-television movie *Divorce;His/Divorce;Hers*, their last film together. *Variety* wrote, 'Holds all the joy of standing by at an autopsy'.

The press labelled them 'The Battling Burtons' because their ugly fighting became public. They berated and hit each other, to the embarrassment of others. Richard said all it would take to patch up the marriage would be another expensive bauble, but he did not give in this time. In July 1973 Elizabeth sought solace with old friends in California. Peter Lawford was so upset that she was seeing his eighteen-year-old son,

Christopher, that he introduced her to used-car salesman, Henry Wynberg, whom Peter described as 'a great cocksman with the type of equipment that appealed to Elizabeth'.

Richard was playing the field and enjoying it. When Elizabeth found out he was in New York, she wanted to see him. He told her not to come, but she did. He told her to leave and, in tears, she checked into the Regency Hotel where she issued a statement in July 1973 –

> I am convinced it would be a good and constructive idea if Richard and I were separated for a while. Maybe we loved each other too much – I never believed such a thing was possible. But we have been together constantly, never being apart but for matters of life and death, and I believe it has caused a temporary breakdown of communication. I believe with all my heart that the separation will ultimately bring us back to where we should be – and that's together . . . wish us well during this difficult time. Pray for us.

Drinking from a bottle of vodka Burton's reply was,

> It was jolly well bound to happen. You know, when two very volatile people keep hacking constantly at each other with fierce oratory and then, occasionally, engage in a go of it with physical force . . . well, it's like I said, it's bound to happen. You can't keep clapping a couple of sticks together without expecting them to blow up. Perhaps my indifference to Elizabeth's personal problems triggered this situation. I have only twenty-four hours a day . . . she worries about her figure, about her family, about the colour of her teeth. She expects that I drop everything to devote myself to these problems. I cannot . . . The frightful thing is I'm amused by all this. I find the situation wildly fascinating.

To get himself in shape for filming *The Voyage* with Sophia Loren in Rome, Burton went on the wagon once again, and once again Elizabeth followed him. Wearing a T-shirt, jeans and her 69.42-carat diamond ring, she rushed into Richard's arms in the back seat of his Rolls-Royce. The reconciliation lasted for nine days. Suspecting that he and Sophia Loren were involved, Elizabeth moved to another hotel and asked Henry Wynberg to join her in Rome. Richard was amused, and used the press to punish Elizabeth. 'I don't approve of divorce as a blank thing,' he said, 'but if two people are absolutely sick of each other or the sight of one another bores them, then they should get divorced or separated as soon as possible. That is certain. Otherwise life becomes intolerable – sort of waking morning after morning and having to have breakfast with the same miserable face.'

Dejected and hurt, Elizabeth returned to California and faced another crisis – an operation to remove an ovarian tumour. Fearing death she begged Richard, 'Please. Can I come back home?' He flew from Rome to Los Angeles, walked into Elizabeth's hospital room and said, 'Hello, Lumpy.' She smiled, 'Hello, Pockface.' With the good news that the tumour was benign, the Burtons headed to Puerto Vallarta for the holidays and then to Oroville, California, where Richard was to film *The Klansman*. The fighting and drinking resumed, of course. Burton started his day with vodka martinis and ended his day seducing cocktail waitresses. Shortly after Elizabeth left, Burton collapsed and was rushed to St John's Hospital in Los Angeles. Diagnosed with diseased kidneys, influenza and bronchitis, he was given blood transfusions and put into detoxification. Six weeks later he was released from the hospital looking pale and old.

On 26 June 1974 Elizabeth filed for divorce in Switzerland on the ground of irreconcilable differences. She returned to California and moved in with Henry Wynberg. 'He fucks me beautifully,' she told a friend. In October, Richard announced his engagement to Princess Elizabeth of Yugoslavia. She changed her mind when Richard was making news with Jeanne Bell, a black *Playboy* model.

Reading about Burton's romances took its toll on Elizabeth who eventually called him. They talked on the phone every day until she convinced him they should try again. A sober Burton reunited with his ex-wife in Geneva, Switzerland. It was a repeat performance – Elizabeth nestling into his neck, both in tears. On an African riverbank in Botswana they were married by the District Commissioner on 10 October 1975. By the time the 'newlyweds' celebrated the holidays in Gstaad, they were in separate beds. Burton left for New York to do a Broadway play, *Equus*, shortly after Christmas. With him was a stunning tall blonde model, Suzy Hunt, whom he'd met on the ski slopes.

In February 1976 Richard asked Elizabeth to meet him in New York. She was shocked when he asked for a divorce so he could marry Suzy Hunt. 'Why the hell did you have me come all this way to tell me that?' she bellowed. Before he had a chance to explain this was not something he wanted to do on the phone, Elizabeth had stormed out of his hotel suite.

This time it *was* over. Richard told his lawyer to give her everything and they were divorced. He married Suzy Hunt and Elizabeth returned to Henry Wynberg, who had been living in her rented house and transporting young girls there in her Rolls-Royce. Furious that Elizabeth was having flings with other men and returning to him in between romances, Wynberg packed up Elizabeth's clothes, put her dogs on leashes and tied them to the suitcases before calling a cab to 'take her to the Beverly Hills Hotel'.

On 8 July 1976 Elizabeth was in Washington D.C. for a dinner at the British Embassy that Queen Elizabeth was giving for President Gerald Ford to celebrate the American Bicentennial. British Ambassador Ramsbotham arranged to have John Warner, the 49-year old former Secretary of the Navy, to be her escort. The tall, handsome silver-haired Warner was a man about town after his 1973 divorce from multimillionaire Paul Mellon's daughter, Catherine.

After a night of drinking and dancing until five in the morning, Warner dropped Elizabeth off at her hotel. A few hours later he picked her up for a look at Atoka, his 2,700-acre farm in Middleburg, Virginia, that his father-in-law had given him as part of his divorce settlement. Elizabeth spent the weekend with John who called in sick for two days – a first for the workaholic Warner, who confided in her about his ambitions to run for the U.S. Senate. When he proposed marriage, John said frankly, 'Those days of expensive jewellery and stuff are over.' Elizabeth said she would devote herself to his way of life. They were married on a hilltop at Warner's farm on 4 December 1976. He gave her a blue corn silo with a heart saying 'John Loves Elizabeth'. She gave him two cows and a bull. In January the newlyweds set off on the campaign trail. Elizabeth glanced at the Greyhound bus and commented, 'Why not? I've never been on one before.'

In March they did a television interview with Barbara Walters. Sitting in the kitchen at the Virgina farm, Warner referred to his wife as 'Chicken Fat' and 'My Little Heifer'. Though Elizabeth attributed her weight gain to cortisone injections for her back pain, John suggested she give up potatoes for breakfast. 'I *am* fat,' she admitted. 'God, yeah. I can hardly get into any of my clothes, but I eat out of enjoyment. I think eating is one of the great pleasures in life.' During the interview Elizabeth took charge, making Warner appear henpecked. When he tried to get a word in she exclaimed, 'Will you please let me talk?'

Her weight ballooned to 180 pounds, prompting some women to comment, 'We always wanted to look like Elizabeth Taylor and now we do.' Joan Rivers joked, 'Liz has more chins than a Chinese phone book.'

The consensus was that Elizabeth was taking a sabbatical – enjoying life with a husband who was not an actor and meeting a public who were a blur to her in the past. Though she worked very hard on her husband's campaign, it was difficult to place her shaking hands, choking on chicken bones and waving from a Greyhound bus. John Warner had a sense of humour, but he was laid-back and very particular about his wife's wardrobe, urging her not to wear her expensive jewellery or drink too much liquor or swear in front of potential voters. She went along as the staid wife of a politician and was responsible for the huge turnout at his rallies. On 7 November 1979, John Warner was elected to the U.S. Senate, the beginning of the end of Elizabeth's sixth marriage. Working long hours, he rarely came home for dinner. She suggested they move into his town house in nearby Georgetown and spend weekends at the farm, but this arrangement did not rectify the situation. Frustrated and alone on her forty-seventh birthday, Elizabeth called her favourite restaurant and ordered dinner. Owner Dominique D'Ermo delivered it to Georgetown and dined with her.

Facing the possibility of another divorce, Elizabeth wanted to resume her acting career. In a phone conversation with Richard Burton, he told her his marriage to Suzy Hunt was over, and he was returning to Broadway in a revival of *Camelot*. Hoping to win him back, Elizabeth jumped at the chance to do a stage play when producer Zev Bufman suggested Lillian Hellman's *The Little Foxes*. She shed fifty pounds and on 7 May 1981, Elizabeth Taylor made her entrance as the shrewish Regina Giddens at the Martin Beck Theater in New York to thunderous applause. Though John Warner was there to present her with flowers, the marriage was over. In December they announced their formal separation.

Elizabeth arrived in London on 23 February 1982, to prepare for the opening of *The Little Foxes* in March. She had been on the phone daily with Burton, who was planning to be in London for a benefit performance of *Under Milk Wood*. Elizabeth grabbed this opportunity to ask him to be her escort at her fiftieth birthday celebration at London's trendy Legends disco. An observer said,

> Elizabeth was overweight and bloated from too much booze and too many painkillers. She was bulging from the seams. Burton came to the party rather late and very drunk. He was terribly thin and his skin was pasty. I couldn't help but remember what a beautiful couple they used to be and yet it was very romantic listening to him put on a show

for everyone, talking about how much he loved Elizabeth. She came from his loins, he said. They were linked. It was a bit much but he had tears in his eyes and that made it very real indeed. They danced together and then he took her home. I can only say that she was still very much in love with Richard, but despite all his bravado about Elizabeth, I think he was turned off by her. Yet he had to brag to the press that he made love to her that night and that she begged him to marry her. I think he was peeved that she was appearing in a play on the West End. Richard never made it that far, so he had to put her down just as he did when they were doing *Cleopatra*. Richard couldn't compete with her fame and that bugged him because he was a far superior actor. She drew crowds because she was Elizabeth Taylor, and now she had invaded his sacred territory – the theatre. He was blunt about her not being a good stage actress.

Continuing to cash in on his relationship with his famous ex-wife, Burton told the press he took her home after the party and threw out her worshippers, 'homos and hangers on'. He described how he took her in his arms and pulled her down on the couch 'for old times' sake'. She laughed his remarks off by saying, 'He was too drunk to make it to my bedroom.'

Burton told a reporter, 'The best way for Elizabeth and myself to keep each other together is to be apart.'

In March 1982 *The Little Foxes* opened in London and received scathing reviews. One critic said Elizabeth had made 'an entrance worthy of Miss Piggy, trailing mauve lingerie'. Another wrote that her voice was like 'a needle screeching across an old 78 record'. A third critic thought it amusing that *Foxes* was playing at a theatre once known for vaudeville.

Richard Burton had not seen the play as yet. He was busy courting a 34-year-old TV production assistant, Sally Hay, who bore a striking resemblance to his former wife, Sybil. 'She can do everything,' he said. 'She can cook, type, do shorthand – there's nothing she can't do. She looks after me so well. Thank God I found her.'

Sally was terrified of meeting Elizabeth and tried to avoid seeing *The Little Foxes* with Burton, knowing that Elizabeth was trying her best to get him back. In her dressing room after the play she said to Richard, 'What do you say to having some fun and making a pile of money on Broadway?' She was referring to Noël Coward's *Private Lives* about a divorced couple with an obsession for each other. Perfect casting, to say the least.

Sally said, 'It all seemed accidental but now I'm inclined to think it was very clever on Elizabeth's part, unconsciously perhaps. The original idea was to tape it. Then it was decided to stage it first. Then it was suggested that it be a lead play in Elizabeth's new theatre company. The taping was put back and back. It never was finally taped. Had it been: "Do you want seven months on tour with *Private Lives*?" Richard would have fled. But it only came to that when he was too far in.'

Rehearsals for *Private Lives* began in New York in March 1983. Richard wrote in his private diary that Elizabeth was 'OK but figure splop! Also drinking. Also has not yet read the play. That's my girl!' Though she was 'engaged' to Mexican attorney, Victor Luna, Elizabeth told Richard how lonely she was. He wrote that she was as exciting as a flounder, reeked of garlic, came to rehearsals late and drunk and couldn't read her lines.

Private Lives opened at the Lunt-Fontanne Theater in New York on 8 May 1983, to disastrous reviews, but played to packed houses every night and made millions. During one of Elizabeth's frequent health emergencies in July, Richard and Sally eloped to Las Vegas. Elizabeth said that she was 'thrilled and delighted' for them but it was very depressing for her to work with Burton after that. She relied on liquor and pills to get her through the run of the play that eventually went on tour and closed in Los Angeles in November 1983. A month later Elizabeth collapsed mentally and physically. Friends and family intervened to get her into the Betty Ford Clinic to recover from drug and alcohol abuse. Feeling very alone, Elizabeth Taylor began one of the most frightening experiences of her life. Her days began promptly at 6:30 a.m. After a brisk walk each day, she had to clean up her room, take out the garbage and hose down the patio. Group therapy was a major part of recovery, as was Alcoholics Anonymous meetings or Narcotics Anonymous meetings.

Elizabeth emerged from the Betty Ford Clinic sober, thinner and radiant. She settled into her new $2,800,000 Bel-Air home with enthusiasm and a bright outlook on life. She and Victor Luna met Sally and Richard for dinner in London. This would be the last time Elizabeth would see Burton whose last impression of her would be a beautiful and healthy one. Friends said he spoke of her often, sometimes going on and on about their life together. Frequently he referred to Sally as Elizabeth without correcting himself. It seemed so natural to him.

On 4 August 1984, Burton suffered a cerebral haemorrhage at his home in Celigny. He died the next day in the hospital. Elizabeth, at her home in Bel-Air, fainted when she heard the news. Sally asked her not to attend Richard's funeral, claiming her presence would cause a media circus. On 14 August

Elizabeth paid a visit to Richard's grave in Celigny, and on 30 August she attended a memorial service in London. Wearing a black dress and turban, she sat with Burton's family at the Church of St Martin's in the Fields. The *Daily Mail* said Elizabeth was the last to arrive 'so she could make the best entry – oh, it was wonderful!' Sally said that Elizabeth couldn't face the fact that when you've lost someone twice, you really have lost them . . .

Lost, maybe, but not forgotten because Richard and Elizabeth had talked on the telephone almost every day.

Elizabeth broke off her engagement to Victor Luna, who could no longer keep up with her financially. She was dating entrepreneur Dennis Stein who gave her jewellery and furs. But who could match what Mike Todd and Richard Burton had given her? Then there was journalist Carl Bernstein who nearly got into a fist fight with Dennis Stein over Elizabeth. Her problem these days was finding a man who didn't drink or take dope – an independently wealthy man who had the time and money to be with her on a steady basis.

On 2 October 1985, Rock Hudson died of AIDS. Elizabeth was one of the very few friends who dared visit him in the hospital, holding him in her arms and kissing him on the cheek. She was instrumental in convincing Rock to 'come out of the closet' for the benefit of others. Made aware of her AIDS foundation, Hudson bequeathed $250,000 to the organisation, and Elizabeth was off and running to raise money. Said a friend, 'Taking up this cause was the greatest thing that could have happened to Elizabeth. She had always been for the underdog and the more people who tried to talk her out of it the harder she worked.'

In March 1986, Elizabeth began dating the handsome 48-year-old actor, George Hamilton. He gave her expensive gifts, and was not only a gracious escort but a great lover, as well. A health-addict, George was good for Elizabeth though he failed to get her to stop smoking. Their fling lasted six months but they remained the best of friends. Also in 1986, Elizabeth had cosmetic surgery principally in the 'double-chin' area. Looking stunning and slim in January 1987, she introduced her perfume 'Passion' that was such a success that she followed up with 'White Diamonds'.

In 1987 billionaire publisher Malcolm Forbes offered to donate $1,000,000 to AmFAR, the American Foundation for AIDS Research, if Elizabeth would attend the seventieth anniversary of his magazine *Forbes*. The 67-year-old distinguished-looking Forbes was a divorced grandfather, who enjoyed the adventurous life of ballooning, motorcycling, yachting, and globetrotting. Though he was rumoured to be gay – his preference being young boys – Malcolm was the ideal escort for Elizabeth. Both enjoyed the limelight and together they were the media's delight. She was attracted to rich and powerful men who gave her expensive gifts, took her to the finest restaurants and gave lavish parties in exotic corners of the earth. It was a platonic relationship that benefited Elizabeth's new perfume venture and her AIDS crusade. Malcolm was enjoying the twilight years with the most celebrated woman in the world. In August 1989 Elizabeth was hostess at his seventieth birthday party at the Forbes castle in Tangier, Morocco. Columnist Liz Smith, who was a guest at this posh celebration, said many of the guests felt used in yet another publicity blast for Malcolm, his magazine and Elizabeth's perfume. Smith said Elizabeth tired of greeting the 700 guests and hid in an anteroom, swearing, 'I don't believe he made me do this.' When asked if she had ever been to a party like this before, she replied, 'No, I never have. And I never will again!'

Malcolm Forbes died suddenly in Febuary 1990. Though Elizabeth hadn't been seeing him as frequently, she attended his funeral. In the previous two years she'd suffered from back problems and she turned, once again, to painkillers. In October 1988, Elizabeth returned to the Betty Ford Clinic. 'I had the arrogance to think I could be a social drinker,' she said. 'And I was addicted to painkillers.' In group therapy she met 36-year-old Larry Fortensky, a hunky construction worker. Though counsellors at the clinic advised patients not to get romantically involved with anyone for a year, the defiant Elizabeth abided by her own rules. A month after her release, Larry moved in with her. Divorced twice, he had a daughter from his first marriage. His second wife said Larry was an alcoholic who smoked pot and popped pills all day long. She said he was an abusive husband – 'a total nightmare'.

In the beginning Larry got up early every morning and set off with his lunch box to the construction site. 'When he came home from work,' Elizabeth said it was wonderful. He was sweaty, he had dirty hands, he was beautiful.' Malcolm Forbes was 'turned off' by Larry and advised Elizabeth against marriage. He gave her a pair of magnificent diamond earrings, hoping to dissuade her. When she attended Malcolm's fabulous party in Tangier, Larry was told to stay put at her home in Gstaad. He'd never been on a jet before nor had he been to Europe. While Elizabeth wined and dined him, Larry yearned for a McDonalds and a cold beer. It was she who suggested they become engaged in July 1991, and on 5 October they were married at Jackson's Neverland estate. Former U.S. Presidents Reagan and Ford attended with their wives as did many celebrities, Eva Gabor and

Gregory Peck among them. A deeply tanned Elizabeth, looking magnificent in a bright yellow Valentino gown, was escorted down the aisle by Michael Jackson whose $1,500,000 paid for the wedding. While helicopters hovered above and one man with a camera parachuted down not more than ten feet from the bride and groom, they exchanged inaudible vows. After a honeymoon in Europe, Elizabeth began moulding Larry to suit her lifestyle. Though he was sincere about working at his trade, Larry was too busy travelling with his wife to raise money for her AIDS crusade and to promote her perfumes. Elizabeth had his hair styled, his speech refined and his wardrobe custom-made. Larry remained in the background, saying very little or nothing. Elizabeth became too possessive of him, wanting his undivided attention when they were alone. It was just a matter of time before he got bored with watching television and waiting for her to call for him on the intercom. In 1994 Elizabeth had her left hip-replacement operation that left her with one leg shorter than the other. After the second hip operation, Larry grew tired of playing nursemaid, and slept in another room. He went out with his construction buddies for a few beers, and when, in 1995, Elizabeth went to the hospital to be checked for an irregular heartbeat, he entertained his friends at wild parties in her home. In August, Larry stayed out all night and Elizabeth told him to leave. She filed for divorce and eventually Larry would receive a $2,000,000 settlement.

Elizabeth Taylor's last film for the big screen was *The Flintstones* in 1994. She played a small part as Fred Flintstone's nagging mother-in-law. John Goodman, as Fred, said he found it difficult to call her 'a dried up old fossil' in the film. Her last major TV movie role was as Tennessee Williams' ageing star in *Sweet Bird of Youth* in 1989. Though Elizabeth was worth over $120,000,000, she wanted to work in films. 'But there are no roles for older women,' she said, To promote her perfumes Elizabeth appeared on *The Nanny* and *Murphy Brown* as herself.

When her dear friend and former co-star in *Lassie, Come Home*, Roddy McDowall, was dying of cancer in 1998, Elizabeth sat by his bedside with Sybil Burton whom she had not seen since *Cleopatra*. Roddy was caught in the middle of 'Le Scandale' in Rome, soothing Sybil and trying to help Elizabeth. He had proved his devoted friendship to both women.

Though Elizabeth and Debbie Reynolds had buried the hatchet years ago, their TV movie *These Old Broads* was big news when they agreed to appear with Joan Collins and Shirley MacLaine. Debbie's daughter Carrie

Fisher penned the story with her mother and 'stepmother' in mind. At the time Elizabeth refused to utter Eddie Fisher's name. She and Debbie referred to him as 'Harry Hunter'. To this day she keeps in touch with Senator John Warner, who had a homemade Southern-fried-chicken dinner flown to Los Angeles and delivered to her home when she was released from the hospital after a near-fatal bout of pneumonia in 1990.

In 1997, Elizabeth was diagnosed with a brain tumour the size of a golf ball. She came through the operation with flying colours and a bald head that didn't seem to bother her since she permitted photographs to be taken. Not allowed to dye her platinum-white hair when it grew back, Elizabeth looked stunning as a blonde – a symbol, perhaps, of what she had endured. But she stayed at home by herself after the operation, rarely leaving home until actor Rod Steiger (who starred in *On the Waterfront* and *In the Heat of the Night*) called her about a movie and stopped by for a talk. When Elizabeth told him she hadn't been out socially for almost two years, he insisted they go out for dinner. They began seeing a great deal of one another but both denied a romance. Steiger remained by her side when she broke her back in 1998. 'I've had seventeen falls,' she explained. 'I broke my ribs, my ankle and then my back.'

Elizabeth credits Steiger for getting her out of her bed and out of a depressed state. 'He saved my life,' she said. 'I love him but in a platonic way. Thanks to him, I haven't felt this good in years.'

Steiger joked, 'I was after her diamonds but I didn't get anywhere.'

On 10 October 2000, he married actress Joan Benedict. Elizabeth said she was very happy for Steiger but would miss their weekly dinners together.

Elizabeth Taylor lives alone now with her ever-present white Maltese dog, Sugar, a gift from Fortensky. Sara Taylor had died in September 1994 at the age of ninety-nine. She was buried next to Francis at Westwood Memorial Park. Sara lived a very good life. Supported in grand style by her daughter, she lived in a Rancho Mirage condo at the Sunrise Country Club, playing bridge with retired film people and talking about the old days at MGM.

On 16 May 2000, Elizabeth Taylor stood before the Queen who conferred the title Dame Commander of the Order of the British Empire on her. There were tears in her eyes when she said, 'I wish that Richard had been here to share this with me . . .'

The Films of Elizabeth Taylor

There's One Born Every Minute (Universal, 1942)
Lassie Come Home (MGM, 1943)
Jane Eyre (20th Century-Fox, 1944)
The White Cliffs of Dover (MGM, 1944)
National Velvet (MGM, 1944)
Courage of Lassie (MGM, 1946)
Cynthia (MGM, 1947)
Life With Father (Warner Brothers, 1947)
A Date With Judy (MGM, 1948)
Julia Misbehaves (MGM, 1948)
Little Women (MGM, 1949)
Conspirator (MGM, 1950)
The Big Hangover (MGM, 1950)
Father of the Bride (MGM, 1950)
Father's Little Dividend (MGM, 1951)
A Place in the Sun (Paramount, 1951)
Callaway Went Thataway (MGM, 1951)
Love is Better Than Ever (MGM, 1952)
Ivanhoe (MGM, 1952)
The Girl Who Had Everything (MGM, 1953)
Rhapsody (MGM, 1954)
Elephant Walk (Paramount, 1954)
Beau Brummell (MGM, 1954)
The Last Time I Saw Paris (MGM, 1954)
Giant (Warner Brothers, 1956)
Raintree County (MGM, 1957)
Cat On a Hot Tin Roof (MGM, 1958)

Suddenly, Last Summer (Columbia Pictures, 1959)
Scent of Mystery (A Michael Todd Jr Release, 1960)
Butterfield 8 (MGM, 1960)
Cleopatra (20th Century-Fox, 1963)
The VIPs (MHM, 1963)
The Sandpiper (MGM, 1965)
Who's Afraid of Virginia Woolf? (Warner Brothers, 1966)
The Taming of the Shrew (Columbia Pictures, 1967)
Doctor Faustus (Columbia Pictures, 1967)
Reflections in a Golden Eye (Warner Brothers-Seven Arts, 1967)
The Comedians (MGM, 1967)
Boom! (Universal Pictures, 1968)
Secret Ceremony (Universal Pictures, 1968)
The Only Game in Town (20th Century-Fox, 1970)
Under Milk Wood (The Rank Organization, 1971)
Zee & Co. (Columbia Pictures, 1972)
Hammersmith is Out (Cinerama Releasing Corp., 1972)
Night Watch (Avco Embassy, 1973)
Ash Wednesday (Paramount Pictures, 1973)
That's Entertainment (MGM/United Artists, 1974)
Identikit (Avco Embassy, 1974)
The Blue Bird (20th Century-Fox, 1976)
A Little Night Music (New World Pictures, 1977)
Winter Kills (Embassy Pictures, 1979)
The Mirror Crack'd (EMI/Associated Film, 1980)
Genocide (A Simon Wiesenthal Center Release, 1981)
Il Giovane Toscanini (Carthago Films/Canal Plus/Italian International, 1988)
The Flintstones (Hanna-Barbera/Amblin Entertainment/Universal, 1994)

11

Famous But Not So Naughty

Hedy Lamarr

HEDY LAMARR had a beautiful face, but MGM photographer George Hurrell said she didn't project anything. She was stunning but stagnant. How do you make Hedy Lamarr sexy? She has nothing to give. She thought if she just sat there posing, that was enough. It wasn't. She looked as if someone should wake her up and no one did.

Hedy appeared to have nothing but a pretty face so we were stunned to find out that she invented 'spread spectrum', the basis for the cellular phone and other wireless communications, including the internet. Hedy wasn't recognised until late in life, but she died a very wealthy woman after many years of barely making ends meet. Remember her arrests for shoplifting? Was it true our gorgeous Hedy stuffed make-up and Ex-Lax in her handbag at Eckerd Drug Store? Yes, but the public was so outraged that Hedy had been arrested, the charges were dropped. In Los Angeles she took a pair of gold slippers in the May Company. Reportedly Hedy was carrying $14,000 in uncashed cheques in her purse when she was arrested. It's been said she might have been a kleptomaniac. If that was Hedy's worst fault, she was a better person than most of the Hollywood crowd.

Hedy Lamarr is known for her great beauty, her autobiography *Ecstasy and Me*, and, at long last, her inventiveness. Her mind was obviously on the 'spread spectrum' when she turned down *Laura*, *Gaslight*, and *Casablanca*. As for her beauty, she said, 'My face has been my misfortune. It has attracted six unsuccessful marriage partners. It has attracted all the wrong people into my boudoir. My face is a mask I can't remove. I must live with it. I curse it.'

By her own account she was a tiger in bed and something of a nymphomaniac. Occasionally she had a woman or romped with a threesome. She was vain but a committed parent. Nobody cared that she was a mediocre actress because she was so amazingly beautiful. Who can forget Hedy in *Ziegfeld Girl*? We were in awe watching her walk down a flight of stairs in a flowing white gown and a halo of stars framing her dark hair. She stole the spotlight from Lana Turner and nobody ever invented a way to do that.

Then there was her 'I am Tondelayo' in *White Cargo*. This bit of dialogue became part of motion-picture history.

Hedy Lamarr died at the age of 86 on 19 January 2000. Her ashes were scattered over the Vienna Woods where she was born Hedwig Eva Marie Kiesler on 9 November 1914. Her father was a director of the Bank of Vienna and she was brought up in luxurious surroundings with servants and a tutor. As the only child she was showered with love by her mother and father. She had it all but she wanted more. She wanted to be an actress. Her parents gave their permission so she would get it out of her system. But Hedy surprised them. She made several movies that led to the controversial *Ecstasy*, filmed in Germany. She was eighteen years old when she took off her clothes for the camera. Hedy is seen swimming in the nude and running through the woods without any clothes. In another scene there is a close-up of her in the throes of orgasmic bliss.

Hedy went back to Vienna and was appearing in a play *Cissy* about Queen Elizabeth of Austria when she was royally courted by wealthy industrialist Fritz Mandl. They were married on 10 August 1933. Shortly after the wedding *Ecstasy* was released and Mandl set out to buy every print of the film. When word got out that he was paying a high price for these prints, more were made and dubbed in every language.

As Madame Mandl, Hedy lived in several mansions and a castle, and entertained Hitler and Mussolini. But she was kept a virtual prisoner by Fritz. One night she managed to escape and he chased after her into a peep-hole sex club. She snuck into a room and had delightful sex with a strange man.

In 1937 Hedy impersonated her maid and escaped with her jewels to Paris where she obtained a divorce. Her one regret was not being able to return for her father's funeral in Vienna, but she would eventually send for her mother to America. Using her jewels for money, Hedy got to London where she met talent agent Bob Ritchie who was sent to Europe by Louis B. Mayer to separate him from the woman he loved, Jeanette MacDonald. Ritchie arranged for Hedy to meet Mayer, who said, 'I saw *Ecstasy*. We don't make that kind of motion picture. Our ladies take off their clothes only for their husbands.'

'Mr Mayer, I had no idea the cameras would zoom in on me that way. It was quite unexpected,' Hedy explained.

'But you were nude.'

'I'm an actress.'

'Miss Kiesler, we make family pictures. Clean and wholesome. My stars don't take off their clothes in front of the camera. If they want to screw around in their dressing room, I can't stop them.'

'You think I'm vulgar.'

Mayer smiled. 'I'll give you a six-month contract at $125 a week. You pay your own expenses to America and I'll make you a big star.'

'No, thank you,' Hedy said and walked out of Mayer's hotel suite. Bob Ritchie followed and tried to change her mind. Over coffee she realised her mistake but it was too late. Mayer had gone out for dinner and was sailing home the following day. Hedy's only chance was to take that boat, too, and on 30 September 1937, Hedy boarded the *Normandie* for New York. Despite her bad manners in walking out on him, Mayer said his offer was still open. Hedy said she'd think it over and proceeded to parade around in elegant gowns with any handsome man on board. Mayer watched her intently and came up with a better offer. 'Seven years at $500 a week with escalators of $250. You'll have to learn English and change your name. Is it a deal?'

'For now,' Hedy said.

In New York she was swamped by reporters who wanted toknow about *Ecstasy*. Hedy said there was nothing wrong with nudity. 'I don't know why the censors banned it. Men look at women all the time and undress them with their eyes.'

The MGM publicist quickly led her to a waiting limousine. 'I don't know what Mr Mayer is going to say when he reads the newspapers tomorrow,' he told her.

Hedy took a train to Hollywood and expected Mayer to have a change of heart but he was businesslike and gracious. 'I thought up a wonderful name for you,' he said. 'Hedy Lamarr after "the woman who was too beautiful" – Barbara La Marr. She was our biggest star but overdosed on pills. Very sad. Very sad. At MGM we try very hard to maintain our stars' images. Be sure to read the morals clause in your contract. Don't talk to reporters or allow pictures taken unless you're with an MGM publicist. If you have any problems come to me.'

Hedy concentrated on perfecting her English and taking diction lessons. With no picture assignment, she went to the usual Hollywood parties with the debonair actor Reginald Gardiner. He introduced her to Charles Boyer who thought she'd be perfect for his leading lady in *Algiers*. Mayer loaned her out in return for Boyer, who co-starred with Greta Garbo in *Conquest*.

Though 'Come with me to the Casbah' wasn't in the dialogue, it sprang from *Algiers*, which fared very well. Mayer put Hedy in *Lady of the Tropics* with Robert Taylor. One critic said, 'Hedy Lamarr is more beautiful than Robert Taylor, if you can believe that . . .'

I Take This Woman with Spencer Tracy was another flop but, Hedy forgot about it temporarily when she met writer Gene Markey, who was divorced from actress Joan Bennett. He and Hedy were married in Mexico on 4 March 1939, the day after they met at a party. The marriage lasted long enough for them to adopt a baby boy, James.

Hedy spoke to Clark Gable about his next film, *Boom Town*, and begged him to talk to Mayer about her playing his mistress in the film. Gable tried in vain so Hedy approached everyone connected with the picture and finally found someone who 'had something' on Mayer and the role was hers. *Boom Town* with Spencer Tracy, Claudette Colbert and Clark Gable was a smash hit, and Hedy was a star. She divorced Markey and retained custody of James. Six years later Markey married actress Myrna Loy.

After *Come Live with Me* with Jimmy Stewart, Hedy went to Mayer again. She wanted to do *Ziegfeld Girl*. He picked up the phone, and Hedy was cast opposite Lana Turner, Judy Garland and Jimmy Stewart. As usual, Hedy had little to do other than look beautiful and she never had a problem doing that. She had meatier roles in *H.M. Pulham, Esq.* with Robert Young, and *Tortilla Flat* with Spencer Tracy and John Garfield.

Hedy was very good as a Russian streetcar conductor in *Comrade X* with Clark Gable. Making $25,000 a picture, she was on a roll, but there was a war going on. She sold war bonds and volunteered to work at the Hollywood Canteen twice a week. She danced with servicemen, made sandwiches and, on Christmas Eve 1942, washed dishes. Bette Davis, a founder of the Canteen, introduced her to John Loder in the kitchen. 'If you wash, John will dry,' Davis told her. Though Hedy was practically engaged to the handsome actor George Montgomery, she was attracted to Loder, who was under contract to Warner Brothers. Of English descent, he had been knighted by the Queen and had a family crest. Twice divorced, he was seventeen years older than Hedy, and not impressed by her screen status.

In her memoirs Hedy said Loder was amused with her Tondelayo in *White Cargo*. But then, she added, he was so proper he wore shorts under his pyjamas during their courtship.

They were married on 27 May 1943, and settled down in a house in Benedict Canyon. While making *The Conspirators* with Paul Henreid, Hedy found out she was pregnant. She gave birth to a girl, Denise, on 29 May 1944.

After a series of bad films – *The Heavenly Body* with William Powell, *Experiment Perilous* with Paul Lukas, and *Her Highness and the Bellboy* with Robert Walker and June Allyson, Hedy asked to be released from her contract. Mayer agreed on the condition she make three more films for MGM over the next five years. She formed her own production company and made *Strange Woman* with George Sanders, *Dishonored Lady* with Loder, and *Let's Live a Little* with Robert Cummings, all of them flops. 'My lack of judgment was to blame,' Hedy confessed. The same could be said for her marriage to Loder that was falling apart. She did, however, want another child, and 'seduced' Loder to get her wish. Hedy told him, 'I'm pregnant and I want a divorce.'

On 1 March 1947, she gave birth to a boy, Anthony John. Three months later Hedy divorced Loder, alleging 'mental cruelty'. Boredom was another word for it. Apparently John fell asleep at the dinner table, at parties and even dozed off during testimony in court!

Hedy claimed to have had affairs with a hundred men in Hollywood, among them Howard Hughes and Stewart Granger, who said she talked too much during sex.

One of her most memorable films was Cecil B. DeMille's *Samson and Delilah* with Victor Mature. But she made the mistake of turning down DeMille's next flick, *The Greatest Show on Earth*, essentially ending her movie career. But for a little while, anyway, Hedy was every man's Delilah and riding high. L.B. Mayer offered her $90,000 to do *Lady Without a Passport* with John Hodiak, but the film died at the box office. *Copper Canyon* with Ray Milland and *My Favorite Spy* with Bob Hope followed. Even though her films were second rate, Hedy might have had a chance in Hollywood if she hadn't balked at going on promotion tours.

While vacationing in Acapulco, she met restaurateur, Ted Stauffer. They were married in June 1951. Nine months later they were divorced. She claimed Mexico was bad for her children's health and that her husband was more interested in his business ventures than in her.

Hedy married rich oilman Howard Lee on 22 December 1953, and settled down in his Houston mansion. They were divorced in 1960. Lee agreed to a $500,000 settlement but Hedy said she never saw a penny of it. Lawyer Lew Boies became husband number six in 1963. Two years later they divorced. Her 1966 autobiography *Ecstasy and Me* was so shocking, it ruined any chances of a film comeback for Hedy. Those who liked her candour were disappointed to find out that the book was ghostwritten when she sued the publisher, denying its veracity. She was arrested for shop lifting twice and she sued Mel Brooks for making fun of her in *Blazing Saddles*.

Hedy moved to Florida and faded out of the news until she sued Corel Corp, a software manufacturer, which had been using her image without permission. She settled out of court for a rumoured $3,000,000 in 1999.

But the most outstanding disclosure was an acknowledgment of her 1941 invention of spread spectrum. She and composer George Antheil used paper rolls from a Pianola to devise a method for frequency hopping during wartime. Torpedoes were guided toward their targets by radio frequencies that could be jammed. The Lamarr-Antheil patent foiled jamming by rapidly switching radio guidance among a set of frequencies. They called it The Secret Communication System and it was utilised during the Cuban Missile Crisis. By the mid-eighties the spread spectrum was used for wireless communications such as cellular phones and Internet communications.

In 1998 Lamarr and Antheil received many belated awards for their contribution. Hedy said, 'It's about time!' Wi-Lan, a company that provides wireless communications, acquired 49 per cent of the original patent rights. In return Hedy allowed Wi-Lan to promote her as a pioneer in spread spectrum and received an undisclosed amount of shares in the company.

After years of near-poverty, Hedy was back on her feet at the age of eighty-five. She moved from a one-bedroom condo in Altamonte, Florida, to a three-bedroom, $130,000 house in Casselberry in October, 1999. Three months later, on 19 January 2000, Hedy died in her sleep. Police Lieutenant Chuck Stansel, who checked on Hedy several times a week, found her body. He was such a loyal friend, Hedy had included him in her will, made out in November 1999. The bulk of her estate was left to her son Anthony and daughter Denise. Hedy's adopted son James, who was not mentioned in Hedy's will, said he would challenge it so he could be included in her $3,000,000 estate.

After a private funeral in Casselberry, Hedy's children opened a bottle of Dom Perignon champagne from her refrigerator and lifted their glasses in a toast to 'Mrs Hedelweiss'. It was a nickname she had given herself – a hybrid of her name and the edelweiss flower. Anthony Lodor said he would scatter his mother's ashes over the Viennese woods . . .

The Films of Hedy Lamarr

Sturme Ein Vaser Glase (Sascha, 1929)
Mein Braucht Kein Geld (Sascha, 1930)
Das Geld Liegt auf der Strasse (Sascha, 1930)
Die Blumenfrau Von Lindenau (Sascha, 1931)
Die Koffer der Herr I.F. Herne (Allianz Film, 1931)
Symphonie Der Liebe (*Ecstasy*) (Elecktra, 1933)
Algiers (United Artists, 1938)
Lady of the Tropics (MGM, 1939)
I Take this Woman (MGM, 1940)
Boom Town (MGM, 1940)
Comrade X (MGM, 1940)
Come Live With Me (MGM, 1941)
Ziegfeld Girl (MGM, 1941)
H.M. Pulham, Esq. (MGM, 1941)
Tortilla Flat (MGM, 1942)
Crossroads (MGM, 1942)
White Cargo (MGM, 1942)
The Heavenly Body (MGM, 1943)
The Conspirators (Warner Brothers, 1944)
Experiment Perilous (RKO, 1944)
Her Highness and the Bellboy (MGM, 1945)
The Strange Woman (United Artists, 1946)
Dishonored Lady (United Artists, 1947)
Let's Live a Little (Eagle-Lion, 1948)
Samson and Delilah (Paramount, 1949)
A Lady Without a Passport (MGM, 1950)
Copper Canyon (Paramount, 1950)

My Favorite Spy (Paramount, 1951)
The Loves of Three Women (Italian, 1954)
Femmina (Italian, 1954)
The Story of Mankind (Warner Brothers, 1957)
The Female Animal (Universal, 1957)

Katharine Hepburn

KATHARINE HEPBURN was nominated for an Academy Award twelve times and walked off with four Oscars. Though her friend Greta Garbo is considered the finest actress to ever grace the screen, Hepburn conquered diverse roles, an accomplishment that Garbo never attained. In contrast, Hepburn was not considered beautiful, but she had a quality that transcended beauty – class. In *Alice Adams* she plays a girl from a poor family who invites a wealthy young man home for dinner. Everything, so properly planned, goes wrong but Hepburn gives her Alice Adams a heart filled with love and a face glowing with optimism.

Hepburn was, of course, more the Tracy Lord type in *The Philadelphia Story*, well-bred, spunky and audacious. And she was perfect as the career-minded and fiercely independent Tess Harding in *Woman of the Year*. Tess falls in love with a sports writer, played by Spencer Tracy. This was their first movie together and before filming was over they began a twenty-six-year love affair. The press knew about it but never reported the truth. Tracy had a wife and two children but Hepburn didn't care. She never wanted marriage and never regretted a minute of her eternal romance with Tracy.

Kate's marriage to Luddy would not officially end until 1934, but two weeks after the wedding she returned to the theater. Her fiery temper held her back until she was acclaimed for *The Warrior's Husband* in 1932. RKO studios offered Kate a contract for $1500 a week and she boarded a train for Hollywood. Director George Cukor was shocked when he met the skinny freckled girl in a gray silk suit with her hair swept primly under a pancake hat.

Cukor showed Kate some sketches of dresses she would be wearing in her first film *Bill of Divorcement*.

'What do you think of these?' he asked.

'I don't think a well-bred English girl would wear anything like that,' she replied.

'What do you think of what you have on?'

'I think it's very smart,' she spoke up.

'Well, I think it stinks,' Cukor said.

Kate's screen test was no better than her outfit. Cukor said she looked like a gargoyle and barked through her nose. But he noticed something the others overlooked. With the camera to her back she picked up a highball glass, moving with enormous feeling, described by Cukor as a 'sad lyric moment.'

In *Bill of Divorcement* Kate plays the daughter of a mentally unstable man (John Barrymore) who returns home on the day his ex-wife is to marry. His daughter is torn between her mother's finances and her father. Barrymore thught Kate was a 'nut' but changed his mind when they began working together.

Bill of Divorcement was a success, and critics said of Katharine Hepburn, '. . . a new star is born . . .' But off the screen Kate hardly acted like one. She was insulting to the press, never wore makeup and dressed in men's trousers and sloppy sweaters.

Kate's next film, *Christopher Strong*, was a flop but, as an aspiring actress in *Morning Glory*, she won her first Oscar for Best Actress in 1933. Luddy hoped Kate would come back to him now that she had achieved her goal, but she was having an affair with her agent Leland Hayward. In 1934 Kate divorced Luddy in Mexico, but she was not ready to marry again. Hayward shocked and hurt Kate when he married actress Maureen Sullivan in November 1936. As she tried to mend her broken heart, millionaire Howard Hughes literally swooped into her life, landing his plane on the fairway of the Bel Air Country Club where Kate was playing golf. Hughes grabbed his clubs and joined in. They began living together in early 1937. Though they talked about marriage, Kate knew she would have no privacy as Mrs Howard Hughes, not to mention his infidelities.

Nor did Hepburn regret her association with Louis B. Mayer. When he was squeezed out of Metro-Goldwyn-Mayer, she left the studio out of respect for her friend. Mayer, on his death bed, asked to see Kate and she was there for him.

Katharine Houghton Hepburn was born on 12 May 1907 in Hartord, Connecticut. Her father was a doctor, and her mother the president of the Connecticut Women's Suffrage Association. The Hepburns were not prudish about nudity, and they discussed sex as openly as politics. Kate adored her older brother Tom who hung himself in 1921. She was only thirteen when she found his body in the attic. Kate concluded her brother was trying to reenact the hanging scene in *A Connecticut Yankee in King Court*. Tom had tried this trick once before. She refused to believe he committed suicide, but his death was a terrible blow and she grieved for a long time.

In 1928 Kate graduated from Bryn Mawr and set her sights on the theater. After several failed attempts on the stage she married Ludlow Ogden Smith on 12 December 1928. 'Luddy,' who came from a wealthy prominent family, was prepared to give Kate whatever she wanted, but all she asked for was that he change his name to Ludlow Ogden so she would not be known as Kate Smith, the popular singer

Hepburn was nominated for another Oscar for *Alice Adams* with Fred MacMurray, and she was lauded for *Little Women* and *Stage Door*. Cary Grant was her leading man in the hilarious *Bringing Up Baby* and *Holiday*.

In 1938, the Independent Theater Owners of America released their list of stars who were 'Box Office Poison.' Hepburn headed the list that included Joan Crawford, Mae West and Greta Garbo. Kate was deeply hurt that her films were not doing well at the box office. She had been branded publically and though she was not one to let such things bother her, she felt betrayed.

So Hepburn returned to Broadway in *The Philadelphia Story* with Van Heflin, Joseph Cotton and Shirley Booth. Though Kate had turned down another marriage proposal from Howard Hughes, he financed the play and bought the movie rights for her. But Kate continued to hound producer David Selznick to let her play Scarlett O'Hara in *Gone With the Wind*.

'The part was written for me,' she told him.

Selznick replied, 'I can't imagine Clark Gable chasing you for ten years.'

After that let-down, Kate concentrated on *The Philadelphia Story*, and sold it to Metro-Goldwyn-Mayer. When L.B. Mayer bought it for $175,000, Kate looked at houses to rent, trying out the showers in each one before deciding. Hepburn took up to eight showers a day and brushed her teeth just as often. She liked the shower in a house on Tudor Road that once belonged to John Gilbert and rented it.

In *Philadelphia Story*, Cary Grant plays Kate's ex-husband whom she would remarry when her stuffy fiancé is shocked by her drunken antics with writer Jimmy Stewart on the eve of her wedding. Kate received another Oscar nomination, but Stewart won an Academy Award.

Hepburn sold *Woman of the Year* to Mayer for $211,000 and signed on as a contract player with Metro-Goldwyn-Mayer in 1942.

She considered Mayer one of the most honest and trustworthy persons she had ever met.

Kate had made up her mind she wanted Spencer Tracy to play the part of her sportswriter husband. Though he was a brawling alcoholic, Tracy was considered the best actor in the business. Hepburn had never met him before and was nervous when producer-writer Joe Mankiewiecz arranged an introduction at the side entrance of the Thalberg Building at MGM. Kate was five-feet-seven inches tall and wearing high heels at the time. She realized her mistake when the five-foot-nine inch Tracy approached She apologized for the spike heels, but Mankiewiecz said, 'Don't worry, Kate, he'll cut you down to size.'

Tracy wasn't keen on working with Hepburn. She rehearsed and he didn't. She wanted retakes. He was bored doing a scene more than once. If there was a minor mistake, Tracy went right on with his lines and it worked. He learned his lines and let instinct take it from there.

In *Woman of the Year*, Tess Harding is a genius, but she can't cook. At the end of the film she makes a hilarious attempt at making breakfast, separting eggs with a strainer as Tracy watches the coffee boil over on the stove and the waffles erupt like lava. *Woman of the Year* was a smash and Kate got her fourth Academy Award nomination.

Hepburn said she fell in love with Spencer Tracy when they met. It might have been his resemblance to her father or his helplessness when she found him drunk in a bar and sobered him up for work. When he fell in love with Kate isn't known because he was too proud to admit it. And he enjoyed putting her down. When she called him 'Spenzuh' with her New England accent he bellowed, 'You sound like you've got a broomstick up your ass!'

Spencer Bonaventure Tracy was born on 5 April 1900 in Milwaukee, Wisconsin. His first ambition was to be a priest, but he didn't think he had the right temperament. After appearing in several college plays he was encouraged to try acting. He graduated from the American Academy of Dramatic Arts and joined the Wood Stock Company where he met Louise Treadwell. They were married in September 1923 and their first child John was born the following June. When Tracy found out that the baby was deaf, he went on his first drunken binge, blaming himself for the rest of his life, even though their second child Susie was normal. Legend has it that Tracy did not divorce Louise because they were Catholic, but the real reason was blaming himself for John's deafness.

After his success in *The Last Mile* on Broadway, 20th Century-Fox in Hollywood offered him a contract for $1000 a week in 1930. Three years later he was loaned out to Columbia for *A Man's Castle*. He and leading lady Loretta Young began a serious love affair. He left Louise, moved out of his Encino house and into a hotel. But Loretta, a devout Catholic, broke off their affair in 1934 and had a romance with Clark Gable. She became pregnant with his baby and secretly gave birth to a girl Judy whom she 'adopted' a year later.

Tracy would eventually sign with Metro-Goldwyn-Mayer. Thanks to Irving Thalberg, he was cast in *Captains Courageous* and won an Oscar for Best Actor in 1937. He picked up another Oscar for *Boys' Town* the following year. Tracy was also enjoying affairs with Myrna Loy of The Thin Man series, Joan Crawford, and Judy Garland. He was seeing Ingrid Bergman when he met Hepburn.

During their years together, Tracy and Hepburn used discretion at all times, out of respect for Louise, John and Susie. They were never seen in public together and though everyone knew about the affair, the press never reported it until 1962 when a rookie reporter innocently wrote an article about them in *Look* magazine.

Kate and Tracy teamed up in *Keeper of the Flame* in 1942, *Without Love* in 1945, *A Sea of Grass* in 1947, *State of the Union* in 1948, and the very funny *Adam's Rib* in 1949.

Kate went to the Congo in April 1951 to film *The African Queen* with Humphrey Bogart. The hardships they faced in the movie were nothing compared to working in the jungle infested with ants and snakes. Bogie and director John Huston survived on liquor and stayed healthy while Kate preached about the evils of booze, drank gallons of water and got very sick with dysentery, losing twenty pounds. Bogie's wife Lauren Bacall became a lifetime friend of Kate's after their three months together in the Congo.

Bogie was prepared to dislike Kate but, though she made him nervous with her constant chattering, he grew very fond of her. Hepburn was nominated for an Academy Award, but Bogart walked off with an Oscar for Best Actor.

Tracy, who got to London before Kate, tried to date actress Joan Fontaine. She tried to explain her friendship with Hepburn but he said, 'You don't understand. Kate and I are just good friends.' Fontaine was floored and used the excuse that he was a married man. Tracy said he could get a divorce anytime he wanted to, but everyone was happy with the arrangement. Fontaine was relieved to go on location with *Ivanhoe* to avoid an embarrassing situation.

Kate was still recuperating from dysentery when she arrived in London. She would not regain her strength for several months. *Pat and Mike*, with Tracy, was Hepburn's last picture under her MGM contract. She didn't have faith in Dore Schary's regime, but it was her loyalty to the departed Mayer that undoubtedly prompted her not to renew her contract.

Despite Tracy's pleading objections, Kate went ahead with her plans to appear on the London stage in *The Millionairess*. He made *The Plymouth Adventure* and plunged into an affair with Jean Tierney, his leading lady. It was only a matter of time before Kate found out, but she had all she could do to complete her stage run in *The Millionairess*. She had come down with the flu and suffered from laryngitis. She got through it because she loved the theater and because she was Katharine Hepburn.

Tracy had moved into George Cukor's guest house on St Ives Drive. When the forgettable *Plymouth Adventure* was finished so was his affair with Jean Tierney. Kate realised that it was their many separations that bothered Tracy. Without Kate he was prone to drunken binges and romantic interludes. In the summer of 1954 they vacationed in London, at separate hotels, of course. He was more than a little concerned when the manager of Claridge's asked to speak to him about something personal. Tracy was ready to tell them to go to hell when he found out it had to do with Kate's walking through their lobby in slacks. Would Miss Hepburn please wear a dress? Kate laughed it off and from then on entered Claridge's through the service entrance.

Kate made *Summertime* with Rossano Brazzi in Italy. Her performance as the spinster who falls in love with a handsome Italian while on vacation in Venice was a memorable one. It's a charming film that holds up today. She was nominated for Best Actress as she was for *The Rainmaker* with Burt Lancaster. While Hepburn was adding to her list of Academy Award nominations, Spencer was having a brief affair with Grace Kelly, who was slated to be his leading lady in *Tribute to a Bad Man*. Kelly backed out and was replaced by Irene Papas. On location in Colorado, Spence disappeared on drunken binges, and acted up on the set. When Dore Schary had had enough, he fired Tracy, who broke down in tears. This marked the end of his association with MGM.

Kate decided it was time for them to make another film together. Her choice was *Desk Set*. She plays Bunny Watson, the head of a television network's research department, and Tracy is Richard Sumner, inventer of a wall-size computer that threatens to replace Bunny and her staff. There are several classic scenes in *Desk Set* – Sumner taking Bunny to a picnic lunch on the roof of an office building in the dead of winter, was especially funny and possibly reflected their relationship off the screen.

On 29 October 1957 Louis B. Mayer died. It was the beginning of the end for Metro-Goldwyn-Mayer. Many of his followers felt he took Hollywood's Golden Era with him to the grave. Kate was one of them as she listened to Tracy give the eulogy:

'The merchandise he handled was completely intangible. He couldn't weigh it with a scale or measure it with a yardstick. For it was a magical merchandise of laughter and tears, of enlightenment and education. It was nothing more than a gossamer . . .'

For Kate and Spence, the next few years were painful as, one by one, their Hollywood friends passed on. Humphery Bogart's death was particularly sad since they visited him the day before he died on 23 January 1957. Spence had tears in his eyes when Clark Gable died of a heart attack on 16 November 1960. His widow gave birth to the son Gable always wanted in March 1961. The great leading men of Hollywood were dying in succession – Tyrone Power in 1958, Errol Flynn in 1959, Gary Cooper 1961, Dick Powell in 1963 and Alan Ladd in 1964.

Kate made *Suddenly Last Summer* in 1959 with Elizabeth Taylor and Montgomery Clift. She clashed with director Joe Mankiewicz, who had introduced her to Tracy. On the last day of filming she asked Joe if he was finished with her. He said he was.

'You're sure I won't be needed for retakes, dubbing or close-ups?'

'I've got it all, Kate.'

'You're absolutely certain?'

'Absolutely,' he said.

'Then I'd like to leave you with this,' she said, spitting in his face. Hepburn was nominated for another Oscar, but never saw *Suddenly Last Summer*. After *A Long Day's Journey Into Night*, in 1961, Kate did not make another film for five years. Tracy was not in good health, but she thought work was the best thing and she wanted to be nearby in case he needed her.

In an article in *Look* in January 1962, Spencer spoke too freely about his relationship with Hepburn and the young journalist did not edit out personal revelations. Spence referred to Hepburn as 'My Kate' and confessed he hadn't lived with his wife in years. Very few people were surprised or shocked by the article except Kate who perhaps had lived most of her life trying to cover up her relationship with Tracy. His health was failing after years of alcohol abuse. Rushed to the hospital several times, he always rallied. Louise was there for Spence, but she knew he was better off with Kate looking after him

In 1967 producer-director Stanley Kramer approached Kate and Spence about doing *Guess Who's Coming to Dinner?* Since Tracy was uninsurable, Kate and Kramer put their salaries in escrow in case Spence had to be replaced. On 26 May 1967 he finished filming, but two weeks later he was dead. Kate heard him fall in the kitchen and expected the worst. She called her good friend, Howard Strickling, publicity director at MGM, to take over, and then she slipped into the background. She did not attend Tracy's funeral.

Spence and Kate were nominated for Oscars in *Guess Who's Coming to Dinner?* She won, he lost. Holding the statuette, she said, 'I guess this is for both of us.' She won another Academy Award the following year for *The Lion in Winter*, and her fourth Oscar for *On Golden Pond* with Henry Fonda. In 1994 Kate played Warren Beatty's feisty aunt in *Love Affair*. Her last appearance was in a TV movie, *One Christmas*.

Katharine Hepburn is still feisty at the age of ninety-four. She sold her New York City townhouse in 1997 and retired to her home in Fenwick, Connecticut.

George Cukor said of her, 'From the beginning, Miss Hepburn chose a direct line and stuck to it. It can frankly be said that Hepburn has not grown up to Hollywood. Hollywood has grown up to her.'

When Hepburn decided to settle down with one studio, she chose Metro-Goldwyn-Mayer. Why Louis B. Mayer didn't court her isn't known because she hoped to be part of his family long before she approached Mayer with *The Philadelphia Story* and *Woman of the Year*. Even then it was her suggestion to sign a contract because MGM had class like the lady herself, and she didn't have to abide by the morals clause in her contract. Mayer knew all about Tracy's drunken binges and he was reluctant to sign him up. It was Irving Thalberg's influence that convinced Mayer, who was thankful that Hepburn came along to keep Tracy out of trouble.

Hepburn kept in touch with Greta Garbo in later years. They both lived in Manhattan and got together occasionally. A few days before Garbo died she visited Kate. Undoubtedly they were both wearing trousers and baggy sweaters . . .

The Films of Katharine Hepburn

Bill of Divorcement (RKO, 1932)
Christopher Strong (RKO, 1933)
Morning Glory (RKO, 1933)
Little Women (RKO, 1933)
Spitfire (RKO, 1934)
The Little Minister (RKO, 1934)
Break of Hearts (RKO, 19 35)
Alice Adams (RKO, 1935)
Sylvia Scarlett (RKO, 1935)
Mary of Scotland (RKO, 1936)
A Woman Rebels (RKO, 1936)
Quality Street (RKO, 1937)
Stage Door (RKO, 1937)
Bringing Up Baby (RKO, 1938)
Holiday (Columbia, 1938)
The Philadelphia Story (MGM, 1940)
Woman of the Year (MGM, 1942)
Keeper of the Flame (MGM, 1942)
Stage Door Canteen (UA, 1943)
Dragon Seed (MGM, 1944)
Without Love (MGM, 1945)
Undercurrent (MGM, 1946)
The Sea of Grass (MGM, 1947)
Song of Love (MGM, 1947)
State of the Union (MGM, 1948)
Adam's Rib (MGM, 1949)
The African Queen (UA, 1951)
Pat and Mike (MGM, 1952)
Summertime (US, 1955)

The Rainmaker (Paramount, 1956)
The Iron Petticoat (MGM, 1956)
Desk Set (20th Century-Fox, 1957)
Suddenly, Last Summer (Columbia, 1959)
Long Day's Journey Into Night (Embassy, 1962)
Guess Who's Coming to Dinner (Columbia, 1967)
The Lion in Winter (Embassy, 1968)
The Madwoman of Chaillot (WB-7Arts, 1968)
The Trojan Women (Cinerama, 1971)
The Glass Menagerie (TV Movie, 1973)
A Delicate Balance (American Film Theatre, 1973)
Love Among the Ruins (TV Movie, 1975)
Rooster Cogburn (Universal, 1975)
Olly Olly Oxen Free (Rico Lion, 1978)
The Corn is Green (TV Movie, 1979)
On Golden Pond (ITC/IPC, 1981)
The Ultimate Solution of Grace Quigley (Cannon/Northbrook, 1985)
Mrs. Delafield Wants to Marry (TV Movie, 1986)
Laura Lansing Slept Here (TV Movie, 1988)
The Man Upstairs (TV Movie, 1992)
This Can't Be Love (TV Movie, 1993)
Love Affair (WB, 1994)
One Christmas (TV Movie, 1994)

Esther Williams

ESTHER WILLIAMS was unparalleled in Hollywood history. She was one of a kind. MGM had the most talented entertainers in the world. If dancer Fred Astaire wasn't available, they had Gene Kelly, but there was only one mermaid on their roster. If soprano Jane Powell was busy, they used Kathryn Grayson. But there was only one Esther Williams. 'How on earth do we make movies in a swimming pool?' Louis B. Mayer wanted to know. The answer to that was – Esther Williams, who rarely used a double in her magnificent but often dangerous swimming feats. As lavish and as popular as they were, Esther thought every film she made would be her last, but she made 26 of them, earning her the title of Million Dollar Mermaid. Esther Williams was born on 8 August 1922 in Los Angeles. Her parents moved to California from Salt Lake City when their son Stanton was put under contract to Garson Studios. He died from a ruptured colon at the age of sixteen. When Esther was eight she attempted to swim for the first time in the ocean at Manhattan Beach. Her mother was campaigning to have a pool built in a playground near their home and promised her daughter would inaugurate it.

Esther got a job at the pool counting wet towels for the five cents a day it cost to swim. The lifeguards gave her lessons in their spare time, and before long Esther was competing in swimming events. She won several local championships and was signed for the 1940 Olympics in Finland. When World War Two erupted and the Olympics were cancelled, Billy Rose offered Esther a job in his San Francisco Aquacade. She swam with Johnny 'Tarzan' Weissmuller who, at the end of their performances, took delight in exposing himself to her underneath the stage as they made their exit. Esther managed to reach the stair before he caught her. Wanting to settle down, she decided to marry Leonard Kovner, a pre-med student she met in school. They eloped on 27 June 1940.

When the Aquacade closed in September, Esther was approached by

MGM. Would she like to be in the movies? 'I don't think so,' she replied. What Esther had in mind was to be a good wife and have children. With Leonard in school, she got a job at I. Magnin department store on Wilshire, hoping to work her way up to assistant buyer of women's sports clothes. Then one day agent Johnny Hyde came to the store and told her Louis B. Mayer wanted to see her. Esther borrowed an outfit from I. Magnin and met Mayer, who offered her a contract. She said she'd have to think about it. Leonard was opposed to Esther going into show business and refused to discuss it. Esther told him she had to pay his tuition fees and the rent so why not take the offer? When the argument turned nasty, Esther left Leonard and moved in with her parents. In October 1941, the Million Dollar Mermaid signed a contract with Metro-Goldwyn-Mayer for $350 a week. Esther referred to the studio as MGM University as she went through the rigours of diction, ballet, singing, dancing, and posture.

Esther did her screen test with none other than Clark Gable, who kissed her twice, unexpectedly. Mayer was hoping to co-star them together but it never happened. If he had, Esther was ready for a fight. She was a swimmer, not an actress. She made her screen debut in *Andy Hardy's Double Life* with Mickey Rooney, followed by *A Guy Named Joe* with Van Johnson, Spencer Tracy and Irene Dunne. Esther's first major picture was *Bathing Beauty* with Red Skelton. To her amazement Stage 30 had been converted into a ninety-by-ninety-feet swimming pool, twenty-five feet deep. Equipment was set up for underwater effects and a hydraulic lift. All this to the tune of $250,000.

Mayer knew all along he was going to make Esther a swimming sensation even though they clashed on the day they first met when she asked for some of his orange juice 'in a clean glass'. She also defied him when he insisted she replace Lana Turner in *Somewhere I'll Find You* with Clark Gable. Esther concluded he was punishing Lana for eloping with Artie Shaw. This proved to be true. Lana was forgiven and made the picture with Gable.

How do you keep an aquatic queen glamorously wet? It wasn't easy. The make-up department came up with a waterproof body make-up that would stay on Esther's body all day in the water. Then there were the hairdressers who were responsible for her hair staying in place underwater. They finally devised a preparation with baby oil and vaseline. She said, 'By the time I came out of hair and make-up I was as waterproof as a mallard.'

When Esther finished *Bathing Beauty*, she divorced Leonard Kovner, and began dating former radio announcer and singer Ben Gage who, she said, was the first man she met who was tall enough for her. Esther was five-foot-eight in her stocking feet.

Thrill of a Romance was Esther's first starring role. Her leading man was Van Johnson who also co-starred with her in *Easy to Wed.* Moviegoers flocked to see Esther's pictures because of the swimming extravaganzas. The plots were usually the same but no one cared.

Preparing to make *Fiesta* in Acapulco, Esther decided it would be a lovely place for a honeymoon so she married Ben Gage on 25 November 1945. During production, Gage, after having a few drinks, got into a tussle with a Mexican and spent the night in jail before being deported back to the United States.

Louis B. Mayer confronted Esther about the incident. He called Gage a clumsy cigar-smoking asshole. Esther said Ben was her husband and she intended to stay with him and have children.

'No babies until you get my permission,' Mayer exclaimed.

'I have no intention of asking you if I can start a family,' she said.

Esther said, in an interview, 'Mayer thought his stable of stars were one big happy family. First of all, he was the son of a push cart junk dealer and here he has all this power. What does he come up with so that he can get by with his lack of education and culture? Intimidation! That was his number-one tool. Such an actor. He was the biggest ham on the lot. He'd throw himself on the floor and foam at the mouth. I always wondered what he put in his mouth so he could do that.'

In the summer of 1948 Esther replaced Judy Garland in *Take Me Out to the Ballgame* with Gene Kelly and Frank Sinatra. Just prior to *Neptune's Daughter*, Esther found out she was pregnant and, on 6 August 1949, she gave birth to Benjamin Stanton Gage.

Esther got back in shape quickly for *Duchess of Idaho* with Van Johnson, and *Pagan Love Song* with Howard Keel. On 30 October 1950 she gave birth to Kimball Austin Gage. In early 1951 she began *Texas Carnival*. While Esther was working diligently and having babies, husband Ben was playing golf and investing her money.

Though Esther had her differences with Mayer, she was upset to hear he was leaving MGM. In her memoirs she said, 'He'd stopped being my "Daddy". I liked our mutual respect.' She and Ben were having dinner at Chasen's and saw Mayer approaching their table. 'They're kicking me out, Esther,' he said wearily. 'If I start up another studio would you come with me?'

'Thanks, Mr Mayer, but where are you going to find a pool like the one on Stage 30? How can I go with you if you don't have a pool?'

'I'll build one,' he said.

'No, you won't, but call me if you do.'

Esther felt terrible on 22 June 1951, the day Mayer left the studio that bore his name. 'He was the first to envision me as a star,' she said.

In *Million Dollar Mermaid,* Esther played swimmer Annette Kellerman. Her leading man was Victor Mature with whom she had an affair. Covered in gold sequins with a crown perched on her head Esther was lifted fifty feet in the air with water cascading all around her. She did a swan dive, hit the water and heard something pop in her neck. She had broken three vertebrae in the back of her neck and was in a cast for six months. She did not complain because she could have broken her spine and lived for the rest of her life as a paraplegic. Victor Mature came to visit Esther during her recuperation, but the affair was over . . . 'I don't regret a minute in his arms,' she said. 'Romances with beautiful leading men don't last forever, but don't knock it until you've had one.'

With such a hectic schedule, Esther had no time to find out how Ben was investing her money. When she came home from a long day at the studio, she was too tired to talk business. Looking back, she saw warning signs but ignored them. He was a heavy drinker too, but then everyone drank too much in Hollywood.

When Esther found out Fernando Lamas hesitated doing *Dangerous When Wet* with her she asked him why. 'Because,' he said, 'I don't want to be Nelson Eddy to your Jeanette MacDonald in a swimming pool.'

'Is it true you were a swimming champion in Buenos Aires?'

'My dear Esther, at one time I was one of the five fastest men in the world.'

'I know about that, but can you swim?' she joked.

Lamas and Lana Turner were having an affair at the time. Her dressing room was next to Esther's and the sounds of hot lovemaking were hard to ignore. During *Dangerous When Wet,* Lamas flirted with Esther and she loved it, but there was no affair. She wouldn't give him the satisfaction. Just as well. After he and Lana broke up, he began dating Arlene Dahl whom he would marry. Their son is Lorenzo Lamas, who is the spitting image of his father.

Esther and Ben separated in 1952 because his gambling and heavy drinking had become an embarrassment. When she was invited to Eisenhower's inauguration in January 1953 she asked Ben to take her. They had such a good time that Esther became pregnant again. This would be a problem in her next film *Easy to Love* to be shot in Cypress Gardens, Florida. Arrangements were made for her to do the waterskiing grand finale first, but she refused to dive from a helicopter. She called a friend who was a platform diver to do the eighty-foot fall.

On 1 October 1953 Susan Tenney Gage was born . . .

After her maternity leave, Esther returned to the studio to do *Athena*, but Schary had taken out all the swimming sequences and turned it into a musical with Jane Powell. The idea for *Athena* was Esther's so she confronted Schary. 'What's going on?' she asked.

'We have a studio to run here,' he barked.

Esther said Schary's actions were absolutely indefensible. Instead she did *Jupiter's Darling*, which was her first flop. Dore Schary had her in mind for *The Opposite Sex*, a remake of the stage play *The Women* by Clare Booth Luce. She told Schary she wanted no part of it. 'What do you know about plays?' he asked sarcastically.

Knowing she would be put on suspension, she refused to do it. Schary was not making the type of movies she wanted to be in. Rather than continue turning him down, she might as well break her contract and leave. But this meant giving up $3,000,000 under her deferred payment contract. In her opinion this was what Schary wanted, but she preferred this rather than destroy her image. So Esther Williams left MGM just as Clark Gable had done. No fanfare. Just a goodbye to the guard. The only two MGM stars who lived out their deferred contracts were Cyd Charisse and Robert Taylor.

Universal paid Esther $200,000 to play a threatened schoolteacher in *The Unguarded Moment*. Little did she know that this money would come in handy because Ben had squandered her millions. She was broke. In shock she boarded a plane for Italy to do *Raw Wind in Eden* with Jeff Chandler. The $250,000 Universal was paying her would help pay off her debts. In April 1959 she filed for divorce from Ben.

Esther was now seeing Jeff Chandler, who wanted to marry her. He was everything any woman would want – handsome, considerate and responsible. Jeff even offered to pay off her debts. Esther probably would have married Jeff if he hadn't exposed himself as a cross-dresser, but there he was in a red wig, a chiffon dress, high heels and make-up.

Depressed over her broken romance, Esther was glad to do a TV special 'Esther Williams at Cypress Gardens'. She chose Fernando Lamas to work with her because he could sing and swim like a fish. She was also very attracted to Fernando and they soon made up for lost time. In 1960 they co-starred in *The Big Show*, filmed in Germany, and *The Magic Fountain*, shot in Spain. After travelling together for several years they returned to Los Angeles and were married on 31 December 1969. In return for marriage Esther agreed to give Lamas the spotlight and forget about Esther Williams, the Million Dollar Mermaid. And he would not permit her children in their home. For a tough gal like Esther to give in to these demands, she had to be deeply in love. They were married for 22 years until Fernando died of pancreatic cancer in October 1982.

When Esther introduced synchronised swimming to the Olympics, she exclaimed, 'I'm godmother to a sport.' Thanks to businessman Edward Bell, whom she would marry, swimsuits and swimming pools bear her name. In 1999 her autobiography *The Million Dollar Mermaid* became a bestseller in the U.S. She writes about Jeff Chandler who died in 1961, and about those wonderful years with her 'beloved MGM'. Watching her films, it's hard to believe she risked her life making those swimming extravaganzas. But she was always there promptly on Stage 30, working long after the others had gone home even when she had pneumonia. That's why there is only one Esther Williams . . .

The Films of Esther Williams

Andy Hardy's Double Life (MGM, 1942)
A Guy Named Joe (MGM, 1943)
Bathing Beauty (MGM, 1944)
Thrill of a Romance (MGM, 1945)
The Hoodlum Saint (MGM, 1946)
Ziegfeld Follies (MGM, 1946)
Easy to Wed (MGM, 1946)
Till the Clouds Roll By (MGM, 1946)
Fiesta (MGM, 1947)
This Time for Keeps (MGM, 1947)
On An Island With You (MGM, 1948)
Take Me Out to the Ball Game (MGM, 1949)
Neptune's Daughter (MGM, 1949)
Duchess of Idaho (MGM, 1950)
Pagan Love Song (MGM, 1950)
Texas Carnival (MGM, 1951)
Callaway Went Thataway (MGM, 1951)
Skirts Ahoy (MGM, 1952)
Million Dollar Mermaid (MGM, 1952)
Dangerous When Wet (MGM, 1953)
Easy to Love (MGM, 1953)
Jupiter's Darling (MGM, 1955)
The Unguarded Moment (Universal, 1956)
Raw Wind in Eden (Universal, 1958)
The Big Show (20th Century-Fox, 1961)
The Magic Fountain (Spanish, 1961)

Debbie Reynolds

DEBBIE REYNOLDS is best remembered for *Singin' in the Rain* and her marriage to Eddie Fisher, who ran off with Elizabeth Taylor. During the scandalous affair when Eddie and Liz were sipping champagne, little Debbie was photographed in pig tails and diaper pins attached to her blouse. Women sided with Debbie, of course. Men kept their mouths shut because no red-blooded male could resist Elizabeth Taylor. Debbie believed Eddie would come back to her and their two kids. But he married Elizabeth and was then pushed aside to make room for Richard Burton. Fisher was a very popular singer, who had the world at his feet, but Elizabeth was his downfall and he never got back on track. As for Debbie, she was, and will always be a survivor, and was tested to the limit when her second husband Harry Karl left her heavily in debt. Later, she was forced to give up her Las Vegas casino. There were no easy solutions for Debbie, but her optimism and energy were valuable assets during these trying times.

Through it all, Debbie went on a crusade to preserve MGM's backlot of memories before they were demolished. She had a solution but was overruled by power and greed. While other stars, who owed their fame to MGM, did nothing, Debbie bought costumes and relics at the MGM auction in 1970, hoping to preserve them in a Hollywood museum.

Debbie was born Mary Frances Reynolds on 1 April 1932 in El Paso, Texas. Her parents moved to Burbank, California, when Debbie was six. She was an active Girl Scout and twirled the baton in school parades. When she was sixteen, Debbie entered a talent contest and was crowned Miss Burbank of 1948. Warner Brothers put her under contract for $65.00 a week and changed her name to Debbie. After two films, Warners dropped her, and MGM signed her up. In *Three Little Words* Debbie was the Boop-Boop-a-Boop Girl. She sang 'Aba Daba Honeymoon' with Carleton Carpenter in *Two Weeks With Love*. Her recording of 'Aba Daba' sold more than a million copies. But her big break came in 1952 when she co-starred with Gene Kelly and Donald O'Connor in what is considered the greatest musical ever made – *Singin' in the Rain*. Kelly, who didn't want Debbie in the film because she couldn't dance, worked her unmercifully through their dance routines. Tired and discouraged, Debbie hid under a piano in tears one day. Fred Astaire was passing by and took her by the hand. 'You have to practise until you get it right,' he told her. Since Astaire never allowed anyone to watch him rehearse, she was surprised when he invited her to observe his mis-steps behind locked doors. It never occurred to Debbie that a perfectionist like Astaire would spend endless hours rehearsing his numbers.

By 1954 Debbie was making $1250 a week at MGM, but she still wore clothes that her mother made and lived with her parents in an unpretentious house like all the others on the block. She was introduced to singing hearthrob Eddie Fisher on the set of *Hit the Deck*. He had been impressed with five-foot-one Debbie in *Singin' in the Rain* and found her as attractive in person as she was on the screen, so he invited her to his opening at the Coconut Grove. They became an item after that. Debbie, at twenty-two, was the 'All-American Girl', and Eddie, at twenty-six, was the 'Boy Next Door.' His TV show 'Coke Time' was a big hit and Debbie was wowing audiences in MGM musicals. Gossip columnists labeled them 'America's Sweethearts' and the courtship began. Eddie said years later that they were victims of their own publicity. By the time the wedding was planned at Grossinger's in the New York Catskills, Eddie was having second thoughts, but on 26 September 1955, he married Debbie. They spent their wedding night in a nearby farmhouse, and their honeymoon at the Coca-Cola bottlers convention in Atlanta, Georgia.

The newlyweds settled down in Los Angeles in the beach house once owned by Norma Shearer and her husband Irving Thalberg. Though it was a thrill to live in the home that the great Thalberg built, Debbie preferred the simple life. She saved her money. Eddie spent his. Sexually, they were not compatible, either. Though he wrote in his memoirs that Debbie was not tuned into sex, the truth is he lived for it. Eddie was very well endowed and involved with women of all ages, including Marlene Dietrich, Ann-Margaret, Merle Oberon, Hope Lange, and chorus girls from the New York Cocacabana and Las Vegas.

When Debbie made *The Tender Trap* with Frank Sinatra, he told her, 'Never marry a singer.'

RKO borrowed Debbie to co-star with Eddie in *Bundle of Joy* about a single girl who finds a baby and doesn't know how to explain it isn't hers. Coincidentally, Debbie was pregnant with her first child. *Bundle of Joy* was terrible but it did better than expected and Debbie gave birth to Carrie Frances on October 21, 1956.

A year later Eddie asked for a divorce. Debbie agreed to meet with their lawyers and then discovered she was pregnant again. On February 24, 1958, she gave birth to Todd Emannuel after Mike Todd, who was killed in a plane crash a month later. Eddie accompanied Elizabeth Taylor to her husband's funeral in Chicago while Debbie took care of of Elizabeth's children. Then they became a threesome – Eddie and Elizabeth and Debbie, who was unaware that her husband and the widow Todd were holding hands under the table. Eddie followed Elizabeth to New York where they became lovers at the Plaza hotel. Debbie got wind of it and, pretending to be Dean Martin, got Eddie on the phone. 'I'm in love with Elizabeth,' he told her.

'We'll talk about it when you get home,' Debbie said.

Eddie got back to Los Angeles and expected a violent argument but Debbie understood that Elizabeth was irresistible and accepted the brief affair as over and done with. But Eddie wanted a divorce and the day it was final he married Elizabeth in Las Vegas on 12 May 1959.

Some people believed that Debbie's hit record 'Tammy' from her movie *Tammy and the Bachelor* was a cause of friction between her and Eddie. It sold over a million copies and is her theme song to this day. Debbie went on to co-star with Glenn Ford in *It Started With a Kiss* and *The Gazebo*.

In 1959 Debbie and MGM parted company. As a result of the enormous publicity during her divorce from Fisher, she was now world famous and in great demand. She went to Paramount for *The Pleasure of His Company*, a delightful comedy with Fred Astaire. In *How the West Was Won*, Debbie dominated the cast of players that included a host of stars.

At a Thalian benefit she met multimillionaire Harry Karl, owner of a chain of shoe stores. A much older man, Karl had been previously married to actress Maria MacDonald and to Joan Perry Cohn, widow of Columbia Pictures' mogul Harry Cohn. Debbie and Harry were married on 25 November 1960. She suffered a miscarriage shortly before doing *The Unsinkable Molly Brown*. Released in 1964, it was one of Debbie's greatest achievements, and earned her an Academy Award nomination. In 1969 she said, 'I stopped making movies because I won't take off my clothes. Maybe it's realism but I think it's utter filth.'

Debbie and Karl lived in a million-dollar mansion with three swimming pools. It was a great life until she came home one day and found the house boarded up. Karl had gambled away $30 million, $8 million of which was Debbie's money. She got a divorce in 1973 and appeared in *Irene* on Broadway. It took Debbie ten years to pay off her debts.

Her marriage to real estate developer Richard Hamlett in 1984 ended in divorce ten years later. By then she was busy with Debbie's Hotel and Casino in Las Vegas. Her Hollywood Movie Museum is also housed there. In 1999 the casino went bankrupt and was auctioned off. Debbie's reaction? 'That's life!'

Over the years Elizabeth Taylor and Debbie have become good friends. They received a lot of publicity when they appeared together in *These Old Broads*, a movie made for TV in 2001. Co-written by Debbie's talented daughter, Carrie Fisher, the script contains a delicious scene in which both Liz and Debbie appear. 'Who cares?' Debbie said about her ex, who wrote a tell-all autobiography *Been There, Done That* in 1999. Carrie agreed. 'After the book he wrote, I don't think he's allowed to take exception to anything,' she said.

In the end, Fisher's two broads, who are vibrant in the movie, got the last laugh . . .

The Films of Debbie Reynolds

June Bride (WB, 1948)
The Daughter of Rosie O'Grady (WB, 1950)
Three Little Words (MGM, 1950)
Two Weeks With Love (MGM, 1950)
Mr Imperium (MGM, 1951)
Singin' in the Rain (MGM, 1952)
Skirts Ahoy (MGM, 1952)
I Love Melvin (MGM, 1953)
The Affairs of Dobie Gillis (MGM, 1953)
Give the Girl a Break (MGM, 1953)
Susan Slept Here (RKO, 1954)
Athena (MGM, 1954)
Hit the Deck (MGM, 1955)
The Tender Trap (MGM, 1955)
The Catered Affair (MGM, 1956)
Bundle of Joy (RKO, 1956)
Meet Me in Las Vegas (MGM, 1956)
Tammy and the Bachelor (Universal, 1957)
This Happy Feeling (Universal, 1958)
The Mating Game (MGM, 1959)
Say One for Me (20th Century-Fox, 1959)
It Started With a Kiss (MGM, 1959)
The Gazebo (MGM, 1959)
The Rat Race (Paramount, 1960)
Pepe (Columbia, 1960)
The Pleasure of His Company (Paramount, 1960)
The Second Time Around (20th Century-Fox, 1961)

How the West Was Won (MGM, 1963)
My Six Loves (Paramount, 1963)
Mary, Mary (WB, 1963)
The Unsinkable Molly Brown (MGM, 1964)
Goodbye Charlie (20th Century-Fox, 1964)
The Singing Nun (MGM, 1966)
Divorce American Style (Columbia, 1967)
How Sweet It Is (National General, 1968)
What's the Matter With Helen (US, 1971)
Charlotte's Web (Voice Only: Paramount, 1972)
The Bodyguard (Warner, 1992)
Battling for Baby (TV, 1993)
Heaven and Earth (Warner, 1993)
Mother (Paramount, 1996)
In and Out (Paramount, 1997)
Zack and Reba (1998)
Halloweentown (TV, 1998)
The Christmas Wish (TV, 1998)
A Gift of Love:The Daniel Huffman Story (TV, 1999)
Virtual Mom (TV, 2000)
These Old Broads (TV, 2001)

June Allyson

JUNE ALLYSON was the girl next door, petite, perky, blonde and pretty. Her husky voice, in contrast to her pixieish image, gave her an interesting quality. She could sing a little, dance a little and look virtuous. June was the perennial teenager. She never aged even when she graduated to playing the perfect little housewife on screen. Like many of her MGM sisters, June grew up without a father and leaned on L.B. Mayer whom she referred to as 'Pops.' He suspended her for marrying an older man, but agreed to give her away at the wedding.

June Allyson was born Ella Geisman on 7 October 1923 (records indicate the year was either 1917, 1921, 1923 or 1925) in the Bronx. Her father was a heavy drinker and left home when she was six months old. When she was eight a branch from a rotten tree fell on her, killing her dog and breaking half the bones in her body. After a long recuperation she went from a wheelchair to a brace and finally swimming lessons to rebuild her muscles. If she could walk, she could dance and that's what she did. Not able to afford dancing lessons, she watched Ginger Rogers and Fred Astaire movies. She saw *Gay Divorcee* seventeen times until she had the dance routines down pat. Still in Junior High she was hired for the chorus line in *Sing Out the News* on Broadway and her name was changed to June Allyson by the choreographer. She was Betty Hutton's understudy in *Panama Hattie* and got her big break when Hutton came down with the measles. As a result George Abbott signed her for his hit show *Best Foot Forward*, and sent her to Hollywood when MGM bought the film rights. In 1943 she made three films, including *Girl Crazy* with Mickey Rooney and Judy Garland, but after six months it appeared as if MGM would not sign her to the usual seven-year contract.

It was producer Joe Pasternak who told Mayer about June. 'You have a kid on the drop list. I think she's got something. Take a few minutes to view her screen test but do me a favour. Look at her eyes and listen to her voice. Don't pay any attention to the rest of her.'

Mayer viewed June's test and said, 'You know, you're right. I don't know what she's got either but it's something, so if you want to use her in a picture, go ahead.' Pasternak put June in *Two Girls and a Sailor* with Gloria DeHaven and Van Johnson.

June had met actor Dick Powell when he and his wife Joan Blondell invited some of the MGM newcomers to their house for a barbecue. He told them to call him if they needed help or advice. June, who was in awe of Powell, phoned him at home. Would he read a script and help her with it? A few days later Powell invited her to lunch and discussed *Two Girls and a Sailor*, but his suggestion shocked June. 'I want you to tell Mayer that you want the part of the plain sister. Nobody will believe you're prettier than Gloria DeHaven. For the test I want you to cut off your hair. Straight bangs, straight on the sides and no makeup.'

June was so mesmerised by Powell, she followed his directions and got the part. After *Best Foot Forward*, Allyson was a full fledged MGM star. When she began dating composer-musician David Rose, Mayer told June, 'Stop seeing Rose. He's married to Judy Garland.'

'But they're getting a divorce. Judy said it was okay.'

'You're not to see him anymore.'

'But he's teaching me a lot about music.'

'Buy a book.'

'Who should I date?' she asked.

'Van Johnson. I'll arrange it.'

June and Van went out a few times, always dutch treat. She was also seeing Peter Lawford and Jack Kennedy, but her dating days were over when Dick Powell filed for divorce. Mayer was livid. 'June, I don't want you seeing married men. Is that clear?'

'He's getting a divorce.'

'Powell is twenty years older than you. Being seen with him doesn't fit your image.' June and Dick continued dating, but not in public. Her innocence amused him as he proceeded to teach her the art of sophistication. One of her lessons was how to eat caviar daintily with chopped egg and onion. June developed such a passion for caviar she ate a whole bowl of it before dinner. Powell was patient and took June to Hollywood parties that terrified her. 'I was an introvert, learning to be an extrovert,' she said in her memoirs. June wanted to marry the twice-divorced Powell, but the subject never came up until she blurted out, 'What are your intentions?'

'I have no intention of getting married again,' he said.

'Then I don't think we should see each other again.'

She was in tears when he called her later that night, and he gave in. Louella Parsons announced their engagement in her gossip column. The inevitable happened, of course. L.B. Mayer told June she could not marry Powell. 'He's a divorced man and much too old for you,' he said. 'This will ruin your career.'

'I don't care,' she said. 'I love him.'

'Then I'll have to put you on suspension. You know the rules.'

'Yes, sir.'

June left Mayer's ofice, realised she'd forgotten something went back to see him. Mayer was all smiles, thinking she had changed her mind. 'I don't know where my father is,' she said, 'so I wondered if you'd give me away.'

Mayer's mouth dropped open. 'I'd be happy to,' he exclaimed. But he did not change his mind about the suspension that did not last very long.

On 19 August 1945 June and Dick were married at the home of a friend. Dick Powell was born on 14 November 1904 in Mountain View, Arkansas. He was a crooner, film star, director, producer and eventually TV executive. He was a popular leading man in the thirties, appearing in *42nd Street* with Ruby Keeler, followed by a series of routine but successful musicals. In 1925 he married his childhood sweetheart Mildred Maude. After his divorce, Powell wed actress Joan Blondell. They had two children before parting in 1945. Blondell married Mike Todd two years later.

Shortly after his marriage to Allyson, Powell played Chandler's private eye Philip Marlowe, and did other melodramas, but his greatest achievement was the formation of Four Star Productions, making him a pioneer in television. He was also in demand as a director-producer in such films as *The Conquerer* and *The Enemy Below*. His full potential would not be acknowledged until the fifties.

June plays an invalid in *Her Highness and the Bellboy* with Robert Walker and Hedy Lamarr, who said she hated her role as a princess 'because it was June Allyson's picture. In *Till the Clouds Roll By*, June did the popular 'Cleopatterer' number. *Good News*, in 1947, with Peter Lawford was a smash musical and one for which Allyson is best remembered. She played Jo in *Little Women*, but was compared to Katharine Hepburn's 1933 portrayal. June tried to convince Mayer she was not right for the part of Lady Constance in *The Three Musketeers*, but he thought otherwise and was right. June was more comfortable wearing Peter Pan colours and saddle shoes. When she was cast as Jimmy Stewert's wife in *The Stratton Story*, she balked, but Powell convinced her to go through with it. He felt she had far more competition in musical comedy. Allyson does a fine job as the wife of a baseball player who loses his leg in a hunting accident.

To make her happy marriage complete June tried to have a baby but doctors said, she might not conceive, because of her childhood accident. So in 1948 they adopted a baby girl Pamela. Two years later the Powells put in their application for a boy as June prepared to co-star with her idol Fred Astaire in *Royal Wedding*. But June had to bow out because she was pregnant. When she checked into the hospital, she forgot her name and signed in as June Dick Powell. Eighteen hours later, on Christmas Eve, she gave birth to a boy Richard (Ricky).

June's last film for MGM under her contract was *Remains to be Seen* in 1953. Dore Schary, who had replaced Mayer, was not renewing contracts of the great stars such as Lana Turner and Clark Gable. June was reluctant to leave MGM, which she explained, 'had been mother and father, mentor and guide, my all-powerful and benevolent crutch. When I left them it was like walking into space.' However, she went on to make the top-grossing *The Glenn Miller Story* with her screen husband, Jimmy Stewart. June became the all-American housewife in such movies as *Executive Suite* with William Holden, *Woman's World* with Cornel Wilde, and *Strategic Air Command* with Stewart.

Then, in 1954, she met Alan Ladd, her leading man, in *The McConnell Story*, and fell in love. According to Nick Tosches, author of *Dino*, June had a brief tryst with Dean Martin in 1948 not long after the Powells adopted Pammy. But the Alan Ladd affair was serious. He was married to his agent Sue Carol, who discovered and guided him. Ladd was not a contented man. He had watched his father drop dead of a heart attack when he was four, but the worst was fighting with his mother over a quarter she wanted for a drink. He gave her the money. She bought ant paste and suffered a horrible death.

Ladd, born in 1913, was a good actor but a short one at only five-feet-five. He was a genius with real estate and might have been happier if he had concentrated on that rather than winning an Oscar. His last heartbreak was June Allyson. Though they were never seen in public together, his wife Sue Carol was aware that Alan couldn't take his eyes off June at their son's wedding reception and was tempted to push her in the swimming pool. Sue told a friend, 'I'd like to drown her in a teaspoon of water.' Instead she called Powell. 'I suppose you know my husband is madly in love with your wife.'

'Isn't everyone?' Powell responded.

Alan was so angry with his wife that he packed his bags and left home, but they were soon reconciled. After *The McConnell Story*, the only contact between Alan and June was by phone late at night. If he was drinking, Powell would talk to him also.

In 1955 June did *The Shrike* with Jose Ferrer. As Powell predicted, it was a mistake and a dreadful flop. *The Opposite Sex* was a musical rendition of *The Women* with June in the Norma Shearer part. *My Man Godfrey* and other Allyson movies in the late fifties left a lot to be desired. So did her attempt on television in 1960. 'The June Allyson Show' lasted one season.

Powell was so deeply engrossed in business he had little or no time for June. Impatient, she filed for a divorce that was granted on 31 January 1961. When she got home from court Powell was waiting for her. 'The divorce won't be final for a year,' he said, 'but if you cohabit with your spouse it's null and void . . . which I believe is about to happen.'

Reconciled, the Powells took a long vacation to Mexico on Dick's boat.

In October, 1962, Powell was diagnosed with throat cancer. He wasn't told it was terminal . . .

On 1 November 1962, Ladd spoke to Powell on the phone and said he was alone at his ranch in Alsulana. Could Dick drive out there? The conversation went on for a long time, June said. In the morning Alan was found with a bullet near his heart. Apparently he had stumbled and the gun went off accidentally.

On 2 January 1963 Powell, who had been in a semi-coma, opened his eyes and said to June, 'I'm sorry. Oh, I'm so sorry.' Then he was gone. His estate was an estimated $2,000,000.

On 29 January 1964, Alan Ladd died as a result of alcohol and sedative poisoning. He was fifty-years old.

Ten months after Powell's death, June married his barber, Glenn Maxwell, owner of two barbershops. They divorced in 1965, remarried in 1966 and eventually divorced. The second divorce was prompted by Powell's will that allowed June $4000 a month if she were single, $700 if she was married. In her memoirs, Allyson said she suffered several nervous breakdowns and tried to drown her sorrows with wine. Somehow June managed to do *Forty Carats* on Broadway and toured in *No No Nanette*.

On 30 October 1976, June Allyson married Dr David Ashrow, a retired dentist. Her most recent TV appearance was an interview with Robert Osborne on Turner Classic Movies. She still looks as if she could do the Varsity Drag with Peter Lawford!

The Films of June Allyson

Best Foot Forward (MGM, 1943)
Girl Crazy (MGM, 1943)
Thousands Cheer (MGM, 1943)
Two Girls and a Sailor (MGM, 1944)
Meet the People (MGM, 1944)
Music for Millions (MGM, 1945)
Her Highness and the Bellboy (MGM, 1945)
The Sailor Takes a Wife (MGM, 1945)
Two Sisters from Boston (MGM, 1946)
Till the Clouds Roll By (MGM, 1946)
The Secret Heart (MGM, 1946)
High Barbaree (MGM, 1947)
Good News (MGM, 1947)
The Bride Goes Wild (MGM, 1948)
The Three Musketeers (MGM, 1948)
Words and Music (MGM, 1948)
Little Women (MGM, 1949)
The Stratton Story (MGM, 1949)
The Reformer and the Redhead (MGM, 1950)
Right Cross (MGM, 1950)
Too Young to Kiss (MGM, 1951)
The Girl in White (MGM, 1952)
Battle Circus (MGM, 1953)
Remains to Be Seen (MGM, 1953)
The Glenn Miller Story (Universal, 1954)
Executive Suite (MGM, 1954)
Woman's World (20th Century-Fox, 1954)

Strategic Air Command (Paramount, 1955)
The McConnell Story (WB, 1955)
The Shrike (Universal, 1955)
The Opposite Sex (MGM, 1956)
You Can't Run Away from It (Columbia, 1956)
Interlude (Universal, 1957)
My Man Godfrey (Universal, 1957)
Stranger in My Arms (Universal, 1959)
They Only Kill Their Masters (MGM, 1972)

Bibliography

Amburn, Ellis, *The Most Beautiful Woman in the World: The Obsessions, Passions and Courage of Elizabeth Taylor*, HarperCollins, New York, 2000.

Bacon, James, *Hollywood is a Four Letter Town*, Henry Regnery Co., Chicago, 1976.

Cassini, Oleg, *In My Fashion*, Simon & Schuster, New York, 1987.

Clarke, Gerald, *Get Happy: The Life of Judy Garland*, Random House, New York, 2000.

Crane, Cheryl, *Detour*, Arbor House/William Morrow & Co., New York, 1988.

Crawford, Joan, *Joan Crawford: My Way of Life*, Simon & Schuster, New York, 1971.

Englund, Steven, *Grace of Monaco. Garden City*, Doubleday & Co., New York, 1984.

Fisher, Eddie, *Been There, Done That*, St. Martin's Press, New York, 1999.

Flamini, Roland, *Thalberg*, Crown, New York, 1994.

Fountain, Leatrice Gilbert, *Dark Star*, St. Martin's Press, New York, 1985.

Gardner, Ava, *Ava, My Story*, Bantam, New York/London, 1990.

Graham, Sheila, *Confessions of a Hollywood Columnist*, William Morrow, New York, 1969.

— *Hollywood Revisited*, St. Martin's Press, New York, 1984.

Guilaroff, Sydney, *Crowning Glory*, General Publishing Group, 1996.

Hanna, David, *Ava*, GP Putnam & Sons, New York, 1960.

Hay, Peter, *MGM: When the Lion Roars*, Turner Publishing, Atlanta, Georgia, 1991.

Heymann, C. David, *Liz*, Coral Publishing, New York, 1995.

Higham, Charles, *Ava*, Delacorte, New York, 1974.

— *Merchant of Dreams: Louis B. Mayer, MGM and the Secret Hollywood*, David I. Fine, New York, 1993.

Huston, John, *An Open Book*, Alfred A. Knopf Inc., New York, 1980.

Hyams, Joe, *Misled in Hollywood*, Peter H. Wyden Inc., New York, 1973.

Kelley, Kitty, *His Way: The Unauthorized Biography of Frank Sinatra*, Bantam Books, New York, 1986.
Kobal, John, *People Will Talk*, Alfred A. Knopf, Inc., New York, 1986.
Lacey, Robert, *Grace*, GP Putnam & Sons, New York, 1994.
Lamarr, Hedy, *Ecstasy and Me*, Fawcett Crest, New York, 1966.
Lambert, Gavin, *Norma Shearer: A Life*, Alfred A. Knopf Inc., New York, 1990.
LaSalle, Mick, *Complicated Women*, Thomas Dunne Books/St. Martin's Press, New York, 2000.
Lewis, Judy, *Uncommon Knowledge*, Pocket Books, New York, 1994.
Loos, Anita, *Kiss Hollywood Goodbye*, Viking Press, New York, 1974.
Mann, William J., *Wisecracker: The Life and Times of William Haines, Hollywood's First Openly Gay Star*, Penquin Books, New York, 1998.
Marx, Samuel, *Mayer and Thalberg*, Samuel French Trade, Hollywood, California, 1986.
McLellan, Diana, *The Girls*, St. Martin's Press, New York, 2000.
Parish, James Robert and Ronald L. Bowers, *The MGM Stock Company: The Golden Era*, Arlington House, New York, 1974.
Pero, Taylor and Jeff Roven, *Always, Lana*, Bantam, New York, 1965.
Quirk, Lawrence J., *Norma: The Story of Norma Shearer*, St. Martin's Press, New York, 1988.
— *Fasten Your Seat Belts: The Passionate Life of Bette Davis*, William Morrow and Company, Inc., New York, 1990.
Reynolds, Debbie, *Debbie*, Morrow, New York, 1988.
Rich, Sharon, *Sweethearts*, Donald A. Fine, New York, 1994.
Rooney, Mickey, *Life is Too Short*, Villard Books, New York, 1991.
Server, Lee, *Robert Mitchum: "Baby, I don't Care."*, St. Martin's Press, New York, 2001.
Shipman, David, *The Great Movie Stars of the Golden Era*, Crown, New York, 1970.
— *Judy Garland: The Secret Life of an American Legend*, Hyperion, New York, 1992.
Spada, James, *Grace*, Dolphin Doubleday, New York, 1987.
Stenn, David, *Bombshell: The Life and Death of Jean Harlow*, Lightning Bug Press, Raleigh, North Carolina, 1993.
Thomas, Bob, *Joan Crawford*, Simon & Schuster, New York, 1978.
Tornabene, Lyn, *Long Live the King: A Biography of Clark Gable*, GP Putman & Sons, New York, 1976.
Turk, Baron Edward, *Hollywood Diva: A Biography of Jeanette MacDonald*,

University of California Press, Berkeley and Los Angeles, 1998.
Turner, Lana, *The Lady, the Legend and the Truth*, Dutton, New York, 1982.
Wayne, Jane Ellen, *Gable's Women*, Prentice Hall, New York, 1987.
— *Crawford's Men*, Prentice Hall, New York, 1988.
— *Ava's Men*, St. Martin's Press, New York, 1990.
— *Grace Kelly's Men*, St. Martin's Press, New York, 1991.
— *Lana*, St. Martin's Press, New York, 1995.
— *Robert Taylor: The Man With the Perfect Face*, St. Martin's Press, New York, 1989, Robson Books, London, 1987.
Wellman, William, *A Short Time for Insanity*, Hawthorne Books, Inc., New York, 1974.
Williams, Esther, *The Million Dollar Mermaid*, Simon & Schuster, New York, 1999.

Other Sources

Library of Performing Arts, Lincoln Center, New York City.
The E! Hollywood True Story on the Entertainment Network reveals invaluable and often shocking information about celebrities by celebrities.
Biography on the Arts and Entertainment Network offers insights into the lives of famous people.

The MGM Girls Get the Last Word:

'MGM was known as the studio that made the family pictures – the lovely pictures that people talk about today. Pops (Mayer) was a family man. We were his family.'

June Allyson

'We were taught to do as we were told. We're going to make that movie and we're going to be at the studio at 6 a.m.. And we're going to do the sittings and we're going on tour to promote the film for six weeks. We never refused an autograph. We never questioned anything because we were taught to say 'yes.' Mr Mayer said, 'Make it good, make it big, and give it class."

Debbie Reynolds

'MGM University – that' s what I called my apprenticeship on the studio lot, the college education my family couldn't afford to pay for. The studio was going to teach me how to look and sound like a lady – an MGM lady.

Esther Williams

'My God, if we so much as were photographed in a night club with a cigarette the studio would insist it be airbrushed out.'

AVA GARDNER

'If MGM had a fault, they overprotected us. Life was taken care of . . .'

MAUREEN O'SULLIVAN

'We were in awe of each other.'

JOAN CRAWFORD

MGM was the pot of gold 'Over the Rainbow.'

THE AUTHOR